Apache Mothers and Daughters

Narcissus, 1931, in mourning for her mother. The original charcoal drawing was done by Frank R. Southard, who was visiting Rev. Peter Van Es of the Dutch Reformed Church in Mescalero. Short hair indicates the state of mourning. *(Courtesy of Narcissus Duffy Gayton)*

Apache Mothers and Daughters

Four Generations of a Family

by
RUTH McDONALD BOYER
and
NARCISSUS DUFFY GAYTON

University of Oklahoma Press
Norman and London

On the jacket front, clockwise from upper left: Apache woman using grinding stone *(courtesy of the Arizona Pioneers' Historical Society, Tucson);* Christine Kozine and Gwendolyn Magooshboy *(courtesy of Narcissus Duffy Gayton);* Apache woman in front of wickiup *(courtesy of the Arizona Pioneers' Historical Society, Tucson);* Molly Gayton in her buckskin robes *(courtesy of L. Bryce Boyer);* Family portrait, Fort Sill, 1913 *(courtesy of Narcissus Duffy Gayton).*

Library of Congress Cataloging-in-Publication Data

Boyer, Ruth McDonald, 1918–
    Apache mothers and daughters : four generations
of a family / Ruth McDonald Boyer, Narcissus Duffy
Gayton.
        p.   cm.
    Includes bibliographical references and index.
    ISBN 0-8061-2447-4 (alk. paper)
    1. Apache Indians—Women—Biography.
    2. Apache Indians—Social life and customs.
    I. Gayton, Narcissus Duffy. II. Title.
E99.A6B85   1992
305.48'8972—dc20   92-54149
                                                          CIP

Decorative motifs dividing sections are from Apache
beadwork and/or basketry.

Permission to reprint the following material is gratefully acknowledged: "Not the Dance" by Daniel Dervin, which first appeared in *Hellas,* 1990, 1(1): 115; "Apache villages and cultivated fields, Fort Sill, 1897" (map), from *Geronimo,* by Angie Debo, copyright © 1976 by the University of Oklahoma Press.

The paper in this book meets the guidelines for permanence and durability of the Committee on Production Guidelines for Book Longevity of the Council on Library Resources, Inc. ∞

1   2   3   4   5   6   7   8   9   10

To Beshád-e
She was a "steadfast pole" to which
Narcissus and her kin could cling

Contents

Illustrations

Figures

Preface

Apaches acknowledge the stamina, the vigor and vitality, and the emotional strengths of their women. So it is today; so it was in large measure in the past. Among the people of the Chiricahua tribe, with whom this book is concerned, the divinity of White-Painted-Woman has been recognized since the very beginning of time.

According to their myths, Yusen, the Life Giver, existed. There was White-Painted-Woman as well. Created by the power of Yusen, she was sent to the world to live in a cave. He who is called Owl-Giant dwelt in the world, too. Children were born to White-Painted-Woman, but while they were very small and helpless, Owl-Giant feasted upon them. So White-Painted-Woman prayed. The rain fell. White-Painted-Woman lay face upward in a place where the rain made a little waterfall. The rain ran into her. Lightning struck her four times, and a boy child was born. White-Painted-Woman was happy. She named the boy Child-of-the-Water. With ingenious and calculated strategy, she protected him from Owl-Giant's cannibalism throughout the baby's childhood days.[1]

Ever since these origins, White-Painted-Woman lives again during the Feast that honors a maiden who has had her first menstruation. During that celebration, the girl is called "White-Painted-Woman," and the puberty rite itself is conducted precisely as the first woman taught.[2]

Just before mother and son ascended into heaven, White-Painted-Woman called the Apaches together. This took place near Warm Springs (Ojo Caliente), New Mexico, where four prairies converge, a location beloved by the chief Victorio. White-Painted-Woman told the Indians that during her Feast the maiden would possess the power to bless The People, and that the girl must keep herself pure, awaiting this special time.

There is a medicine man who presides at the Mescalero tribe's rite, and although Chiricahuas do not hire such a shaman, his actions and songs are appropriate to the spirit of the Feast. Standing before the Big Tipi, he holds high his right hand, which is painted with pollen, representing the rays of the sun, and he sings:

> . . . The sun has come down
> It has come down to the earth,
> It has come to her.
> He will paint her with red clay,

> Long life! Its power is good.
> He will paint her with white clay,
> Long life. Its power is good, . . .[3]

The maiden's buckskin dress, the white clay, the red clay, the pollen, and all her paraphernalia have supernatural significance.

The puberty rite, with its prayers and teachings, is the most important and ancient of all Apache rituals. Ceremonies honoring the hunter and the warrior have survived only in memory since the days of Chiricahua incarceration, but that which honors a girl's womanhood remains vital. It is a sacred symbol of esteem and worth today, just as it was yesterday. As such, its theme will be central to the story of each of the four generations.

Although the Apache warrior was acknowledged by friend and foe as an unparalleled master of strategy and cunning as he traversed the Southwest—from Pueblo settlements to the north, deep into the recesses of Sonora and Chihuahua of old Mexico to the south—the tribe's women were ultimately responsible for In-déh survival.

During the 1870s Gen. George Crook indicated that if the Indians were ever to be compatible with white society, they must be trained away from their ancient nomadic and raiding practices. He advised that this could be accomplished only through the efforts of their young women.

In 1891 Capt. John Bourke agreed, writing, "In all tribes the influence of the women, though silent, is most potent."[4] Apaches, too, would agree. They believed, and still do to large extent, that the foremost task of a woman, in addition to collecting and preparing food, was properly raising and educating her children. Above all else, she must be a good wife and an excellent mother.

John C. Cremony, who had extensive contact with warring Apaches in Arizona and New Mexico, gave due credit to their women:

> . . . when it is understood that the Apaches neither sow nor plant, that they do not cultivate the ground, that they manufacture nothing except their arms, that they depend altogether upon their wars for plunder as a means of livelihood with the exceptional occasions of hunting, that their women collect all the mescal for food and intoxicating drink, that they dig all the roots, gather all the seeds, and make them into food, there will be no difficulty in perceiving that the women are their real supporters.[5]

In short, Apache women were and are the mainstay of their culture. Yet we know so little about them. This book, an effort to begin to fill the void, consists of the life stories of four women, four generations of the same family—mothers and daughters. They were Tchi-héné.[5] Tchi-héné, meaning Red Paint People, is the name given one of the three major bands of the Chiricahua tribe, a band whose warriors wore a masklike stripe of red or sometimes white clay across their eyes when going to battle. Their women wore a yellow stripe during those warpath days.

According to linguists, the language of all the Apaches of the American Southwest is Athapascan, each tribe and band having its special dialect. Spanish, too, was known to certain members of the tribe, especially to the warriors who lived in, traded in, or made periodic raids on isolated ranches and small towns south of what is now the United States border. There were also a certain number of Apache women who had been captured by Mexicans and who later returned to their own people, bringing their newly learned vocabulary with them.

Three of the women whose accounts follow were once honored in the girls' puberty rite. Thus, for the period of that celebration, *they* had been called White-Painted-Woman and had felt the aura of that supernatural force. All four of these Chiricahuas were respected individuals and were a credit to their tribe. That each faced hardships peculiar to the years of her specific generation becomes clear in the contrasts among the four parts of the book.

The first of the women was Dilth-cleyhen.[7]

Dilth-cleyhen witnessed the most bitter of all warfare between the Apaches and the encroaching whites. There was brutality and ruthlessness on both sides. There were good and bad men, men with foresight, and men filled with blind hatred and deceit. Some were red; some were white. Among the Apaches there were mostly moral, resourceful women. A few, such as Victorio's sister, went to war with the men. There were even a few who delighted in being troublemakers.

Much of the time, beginning during Dilth-cleyhen's early childhood, her people were "on the run," eking out a poor subsistence when there was too little time to hunt or to gather the wild crops. Nonetheless, the Chiricahua clung to their traditional faith, to their belief in the powers that provided the life force of their environment, in the blessings they would receive if they paid those powers rigid respect, and in the dangers facing them if they erred in proffered prayer.

Many Apache leaders of this early period tried to placate the Anglo invaders: they tried to farm, to cooperate. They sought to keep a peace that was threatened continually by arbitrary and often conflicting decisions made by various white administrators and military men. Most land-hungry newcomers donned blinders; they denied even the humanity of the Indians.

Such was the world that Dilth-cleyhen faced.

Dilth-cleyhen was proud and stately. She was the daughter of Bi-duyé, who came to be known as Victorio. He was a man of wisdom, of great clarity of vision. His forefathers had been respected in Mimbreño as well as Warm Springs tribal affairs.[8] As Bi-duyé's eldest child, Dilth-cleyhen had special privileges. With her first husband, whose name is now lost because of the Apache custom of not uttering the name of the deceased, she had one daughter, Beshád-e. With her next mate, she bore Elsie Vance Chestuan. And with the last, Carl Mangas, who was one of the sons of the chief Mangas Coloradas, she had another, named Lillian. But it is her first daughter with whom we are concerned primarily.

Beshád-e is the main personality in our second generation. Born in approximately the year 1870, Beshád-e lived through the atrocities of the Victorio Wars. She suffered the constant threat of bounty hunters and despaired at the death of her famous grandfather. She underwent the twenty-seven years of Chiricahua incarceration beginning in 1886—as did Dilth-cleyhen. Every day Beshád-e and her kin were forced to face the unknown. She had to juggle the old and the new, which she rarely understood. But she tried. Even the later reservation life among the people of the Mescalero tribe was, in a sense, an imprisonment. She and her third husband, Abner Kozine, had two children, one of whom was named Christine.

Christine forms the basis of our third generation. She represents the beginning of "modern" Apaches, trained in Indian schools by white teachers. Her ways tended to be alien to those of the tradition-bound Dilth-cleyhen and of the equally old-fashioned Beshád-e. Christine was an Apache with an Anglo education; she wore her stylish skirts and blouses with flair. But she was caught by disease and died in her mid-twenties, leaving the care of her daughter Narcissus and her son Wendell to Beshád-e and other female kin.

Today Narcissus lives on the Mescalero Apache Reservation in south-central New Mexico. Christine's modern ways were a powerful influence, contributing to Narcissus's desire for advanced schooling and her will to benefit her tribe. At the same time, the traditions of her grandmother, her great-grandmother, and "Little Grandmother" Lillian were deeply engrained. Narcissus's training to become a registered nurse resulted solely from her own resourcefulness. Later she used her professional expertise and her Apache common sense to set up sorely needed health programs for the people of Mescalero. She married a Ponca Indian, Wheeler Gayton. As of 1991, when the manuscript for this book was completed, they had one daughter, Molly, who has given them two granddaughters whom they adopted and are rearing as their own. Since then, Molly has had yet another daughter.

Wheeler fell prey to the ravages of cancer during the final days of the writing of this book. He died in Mescalero on March 14, 1991. An ailing Narcissus depends now on the care of female kin.

It is important to note that *Apache Mothers and Daughters* is largely oral history. It consists of the memories related by living and recently deceased individuals, stories passed from generation to generation. When oral traditions and beliefs were missing, I turned to scholarly literature and my own fieldwork with other Chiricahuas; facts congruent with Narcissus's family recollections were used.

Narcissus is the coauthor of this publication. She is responsible for the personal anecdotes concerning her forebears. Often her versions of events conflict with what has been written elsewhere, or she gives them a different slant. When this occurs, it is because the Apache oral tradition varies from the whites' written record. Narcissus learned Apache oral history from Beshád-e, other relatives, and friends as they gossiped about old times and wartime happenings during long convivial evenings. Over and over again they retraced their past. Further, Beshád-e always preferred to do things in traditional ways. Never did she really enjoy white man's food. She spent hours, days, months, and years teaching Narcissus how to prepare wild plants for tasty consumption. She told amusing folktales as well as sacred myths, all of which were internalized by her receptive grandchildren. She pointed out the locations where Chiricahua life began and where the first Crown Dancers dwelt.

The written words of this book are mine. In the beginning parts of the book, the reader will discover some conversations dictated neither by Narcissus nor quoted in the literature. When I have included such, as in the case of Cradlemaker, I based my writing on the way in which today's informants had expressed themselves to me as they worked at constructing cradleboards. I then read their words to Narcissus, verifying *probable* authenticity. In searching the literature, the words attributed to leaders of the past may have a similar degree of accuracy.

Listing the names of all my Apache informants is not possible, inasmuch as my fieldwork continues and is of a strictly confidential nature. However, Evelyn Martine Gaines, Sam Kenoi, and Dan Nicholas gave permission to use their information and to name them in publications. Some notes made by my husband, L. Bryce Boyer, M.D., who is a psychoanalyst and who worked as such on the reservation, are included.

Narcissus has long desired that the lives and ways of Apache women be known. Her pride in them is well deserved. I, too, have recognized that the strength behind these Apaches is based largely on the endurance and abilities of their distaff side. Thus, our collaboration seemed inevitable. When Narcissus approached me some twenty years ago with the idea of such a record, I accepted gladly. I have learned much in the course of preparing the text. There is no doubt in my mind, however, that it is the "new truths" presented by Narcissus, based on the memories of her own womenfolk, that provide the major contributions of the work.

Acknowledgments

On behalf of Narcissus and myself, I wish to acknowledge the help of the following individuals: L. Bryce Boyer, M.D., who read and reread various versions of the manuscript of this book and took many photographs; Wheeler Gayton, Narcissus's husband, who likewise read and waxed enthusiastic when he was pleased; Professor Alan Dundes, of the University of California, who encouraged our writing from the beginning and who also read earlier renditions of the work; Beverly Munson, who contributed the Mexican song about Victorio and who offered suggestions all along the way; recently deceased Professor Harry Basehart, of the University of New Mexico, who gave us permission to adapt maps he used in his Chiricahua land claims studies and without whose help in the field my husband and I would never have been able to continue our research; Corinne and Stanley McNatt, who were postmaster and trader, and their sons, James and Terry; and Peggy Wilson Stone, who solved the computer problems of a novice. When Virginia Klinekole was president of the tribe, our research team was given access to invaluable information. We acknowledge also the help of Wendell Chino as president. My sons were also helpful: Kim attended Tularosa Junior High School with the Apaches and became a "blood brother" of a few; as a youngster, Dewey spent summers on the reservation and later, as a physician, served The People at the Mescalero Hospital.

This work was assisted by University of California Department of Design Faculty Grant 877, 1968–70, which facilitated the transcription of tapes in the collection of biographical data from Narcissus. The National Institute of Mental Health, Department of Health, Education and Welfare, Grants M–2013 and M–3088 partly supported my early research from 1957 through 1965.

This book is a tribute to Tchi-héné women. Many of them have continued to exhibit the underlying perseverence that Narcissus attributed to her grandmother Beshád-e: "She was a steadfast pole in all our lives."

RUTH McDONALD BOYER

Selected Dates Important in the Lives of the Four Generations

1820   Birth of Victorio, father of Dilth-cleyhen.

Beginning in the seventeenth century there had been conflict between Mexicans and hunting-and-gathering Apaches. A recognized pattern emerged involving trading, raiding, and warfare.

1835   Apache scalp bounty law established in Sonora.

1837   Scalp bounty law established in Chihuahua.

1846   The Mexican War began, terminating with the Treaty of Guadalupe Hidalgo in 1848. Except for the influx of soldiers, the war had little effect on the Apache way of life.

1848   Birth of Dilth-cleyhen.

1849   The beginning of the California Gold Rush. White men traversed Apachería in greater numbers; white settlements multiplied, and the Apache food supply began to diminish.

1851   Gold found near Santa Rita. Miners flooded the area.

Late 1860s   At the end of the Civil War, contradictory U. S. administrative policies were confusing to the Apaches. Their territory fell under two separate military commands, the Departments of California and Missouri, which were administrative units of different divisions.

1870   Birth of Beshád-e.

1871   Gen. George Crook inspects territory and organizes Apache Scouts to aid him in locating Indians "on the run."

1872   Victorio's followers sent to Tularosa.

1874   The group is returned to Ojo Caliente.

1875   Crook is transferred to the Department of the Platte to fight the Sioux.

1876   Chiricahuas are concentrated in San Carlos.

1877   Victorio's people are permitted to return to Warm Springs.

1879   Dilth-cleyhen's mother is killed, and Victorio begins a rampage throughout the land.

1880   Victorio is killed.

1881   Dilth-cleyhen and Beshád-e hear of Nakai-doklini, the Dreamer.

1882   Crook returns, only to be replaced by Nelson A. Miles in 1886.

1886   The Chiricahuas are incarcerated in Florida.

1887   Chiricahua prisoners of war are sent to Mount Vernon Barracks, Alabama.

1895   Chiricahuas are transferred to Fort Sill, Oklahoma.

1904   Birth of Christine Kozine.

1913   Chiricahuas are given the choice of staying in Oklahoma or moving to Mescalero, New Mexico. Dilth-cleyhen and family choose the latter.

1924   Birth of Narcissus Duffy.

1931   Death of Christine.

1941   Death of Beshád-e.

Part One

Warfare and Flight

The Early Life of Dilth-cleyhen

It was said of Dilth-cleyhen, even when she was in her seventies, that she was an active one, "one who really got around." This was a compliment.

Old people said, "It's because her cradle ceremony was just right. Cradlemaker said the right prayers; used all the proper materials."

Others added, "It's because she ran so well at her *da-i-dá*, her Feast at puberty, when she was White-Painted-Woman and had blessing power. That's why she has long life and vitality."

Birth: Family and Band Affiliation

Dilth-cleyhen was born in 1848. That is the date given in the tribal census, and we assume it to be approximately correct.[1] Today her living kin remember hearing that her birth occurred in the springtime.

Dilth-cleyhen was a proud Apache, of the Chiricahua tribe. She was one of The People, In-déh[2], as they call themselves.

Precisely where was she born? Somewhere within the confines of recognized Tchi-héně (Red Paint People) territory—roughly in the southwestern part of the present state of New Mexico, just west of the Rio Grande—and most probably in the area known as Warm Springs.

Slightly south and west of Tchi-héně lands, in what is now Arizona, were the Tchok'-anen,[3] an Apache band sometimes referred to as the "true Chiricahua." They were the "Mountain People," the "Rising Sun People," whose name was occasionally rendered to mean "chatterers" because of the calls and code sounds they made during their attacks. The Bedonkohe or "Bronze Apaches" were close allies of the Tchok'-anen. Their name, meaning "In Front At The End People," indicates their geographical location, for they dwelled farthest west toward the Pima raiding grounds. Frequently, the Bedonkohe and Tchok'-anen are classified together. And finally, there was the band known as the "Enemy People," the Net'na,[4] whose homeland was primarily in Old Mexico. Here its members incorporated certain aspects of Hispanic culture, and many mastered the Spanish language. Based upon this partial assimilation, they received the name "Net'na," which translated literally means "Indian-White Man." The camping sites they favored were within the recesses of the northern part of the states of Sonora and Chihuahua. All these bands composed one people, their customs differing somewhat from those of other Apaches, including their more easterly friends, the Mescaleros.

In prereservation days each Chiricahua band had a specific territory, the boundaries of which were respected by red men. Nonetheless, there was much fluidity of movement among The People, depending on historical and subsistence circumstances. All the bands pushed periodically into Old Mexico to raid for livestock, ammunition, or food; sometimes they united during forays against the Mexican and United States military. Male status depended on warlike prowess.

"All our young men must be strong. They must be able to endure hardship. They must be able to kill, to know when to advance and when to retreat. They must be skilled in stealing necessary supplies. They must kill during warfare, and if they so desire, they must take captives—particularly those Mexicans!" Such were words spoken around the campfires.

Nonetheless, the bands were firmly tied together. And if an Apache gave his word, whether to another Indian or to white military men, it was dependable. Responsibilities and friendships were not to be taken lightly.

The Tchi-héne visited the Tchok'-anen; even the Net'na sometimes spent as long as a year camping side by side with the Red Paint People. Intermarriage between members of the three bands, especially when it united the sons and daughters of acclaimed leaders, created a strong link, trustworthy during days of war.

Working behind the scenes, women provided the daily bulk of food; hunters brought in game only sporadically. Family migrations were suggested by the womenfolk and depended on the locations and ripening of crops. Women's words superseded the opinions of the warriors at such times—and, occasionally, it was wives or sisters who demanded warfare or a raid. After all, they were the mainstay of The People.

Warm Springs[5] (Ojo Caliente) was an area beloved by Dilth-cleyhen's family. It was near the Mexican town of Cañada Alamosa, now known simply as Alamosa or Monticello.

"This is our heartland," the old folks said.

It was in Warm Springs that Dilth-cleyhen's father, Victorio, a Mimbres Apache,[6] had come to woo her mother.

The Mimbres, or Mimbreños,[7] designate a group of the more easterly Tchi-héné. The Black Range, or Mimbres Mountains, were their most frequented haunts, but during winter months there were prolonged stays in northern Old Mexico. The group's name, and that of the mountains, was probably derived from the Mimbres River. This tributary heads high in the range and then disappears near what is now the city of Deming, just below the old Overland Stage crossing.[8] "Subgroups" within Apache bands were often designated by the name of their most usual geographical location. Victorio grew up in the Mimbres Mountains.

Near Deming is a cave situated between two high, pointed peaks where once the sacred Crown Dancers dwelt. "Listen, my child, listen carefully," Dilth-cleyhen's mother had said. "Listen, and maybe you can hear the songs, the drumming—but you must listen. It is very faint. It is the sound of our sacred ones, the Mountain Gods."

Near Deming, perhaps close to the Tres Hermanas and the sacred cave, Dilth-cleyhen was later given her Feast, the da-i-dá, to honor her upon becoming a woman.

The Indians called the handsome Mimbreño warrior "Bi-duyé." "Victorio" was the name given him by Spanish-speaking peoples; later, the Anglos who recognized his prowess, his strategy in battle, perpetuated the apt designation.

Bi-duyé first saw the Warm Springs maiden during her Feast. "A woman-girl worth running for," he thought. For a time he was more concerned with hunting and raiding matters, but then in some few years he was attracted once again. He sought her parents, bringing them horses as a token designating he wanted their daughter as his wife. The horses were accepted; the two were recognized as wed. "Let us boil water," they said, and thus coffee was made. A feast was held and guests invited.

In accordance with Apache custom, Victorio left the camp of his kin. Dilth-cleyhen's mother built the newlyweds a wickiup near her tipi. This was the beginning of what would become Victorio's first *ranchería*. For the rest of his life, his primary home was near that of his bride's parents, where he could best help and honor them. He would provide game; he would bring them bounty from his frequent raids. As a means of showing respect, Bi-duyé avoided looking at his mother-in-law. He did not speak directly to her. Even with her husband, utmost politeness was the rule in all communication.

Here in Ojo Caliente, and along the pools and streams flowing down from San Mateo Peak or within the canyon of the Alamosa River, the couple were most content. Had the young man been permitted to stay in the vicinity of this early ranchería, he might never have committed the horrors that marked the Victorio Wars.

Bi-duyé was a groom of considerable honor and wisdom, one who preferred and preached peace—but whose skill in battle intimidated his enemies.

Dilth-cleyhen was the first child of this union. As such, she was considered "special," and in coming years she enjoyed privileges denied her siblings.

Dilth-cleyhen had brothers and sisters, or at least half-siblings. After all, successful Apache hunters and warriors often had several wives, each bearing children. Such was the case with Bi-duyé. For example, when he visited in distant locations, such as Mescalero, there, too, he had a wife.

A census taken at Ojo Caliente in May of 1876[9] lists "Victorio and wife." Possibly, the latter was Dilth-cleyhen's mother. Dilth-cleyhen, then in her early thirties, would have been recorded with her two daughters and perhaps with her second husband, if he were yet alive. For Victorio, five children and four other dependents are mentioned. Was Dilth-cleyhen his dependent? We cannot tell. Today we know the names of only two youngsters identified with Bi-duyé. How many other children he had, we do not know—but there were probably more of whom we have no record. There were many deaths during childbirth; oftentimes infants and young children died in the course of everyday life or were killed by enemies. All Apaches were vulnerable to the hazards of flight and war.

The two children who belonged surely to Bi-duyé were Washington[10] and a much younger boy called Charlie Istee. Possibly, the mothers of Washington and Dilth-cleyhen were sisters; the sororate was the preferred form of polygynous marriage. To take a second wife it was necessary for the groom to seek permission of both his first mate and her parents. Marriage to a wife's sister was the least complicated solution. There was usually little or no friction between the women, the wife finding her sister good company in their husband's absence. Further, the groom had but one set of in-laws to watch over and show due respect.

But if he wished to marry a much younger and more beautiful woman, a girl unrelated to his first wife—this sometimes posed a problem! It might require more than a little persuasion if he were not to encounter extreme displeasure from his spouse. Eventually, it was common for the first wife to capitulate to her eye-straying husband, knowing full well that her man might beat her if she were too unpleasant. Some second matches were made as political alliances, and these could be understood.

"Well, I could use some help when gathering mesquite beans and digging roots," from a spouse might mean she gave approval to the match.

Warriors of lesser status, whose leadership was less pronounced, might marry only one woman, perhaps an elderly widow whose capabilities had long been proven, one who knew well how and where to gather the best fruit, the roots, the seeds, the medicines—how to prepare buckskin and fashion sturdy body coverings.

Then, too, there were often females available to warriors and raiders who followed the same paths more or less routinely. Although it was rare for a Chiricahua woman to be promiscuous (and the noses of such women were disfigured by slits to make clear their indiscretions), still they sometimes accompanied the warriors. Further, many raiders captured attractive young women in Old Mexico, and these "slaves" might accompany the men on dangerous treks too risky for a real wife with children. Usually these females were accepted as being "Apache" and joined the households of wives. Although the Indians now call them "slaves," ordinarily their status deserved a somewhat kinder term. Sometimes their presence caused domestic strife. And, while slaves might serve as bedmates, they bore the stigma of "non-spouse." So, how many names of children of *all* unions, "legal" and otherwise, have disappeared? We know not.

In any event, Washington was born in 1848 or 1849,[11] of a "legal" wife, probably within one year of the date of birth estimated for Dilth-cleyhen. If their mothers were related—and this is highly probable—these two youngsters may have grown up much as full brother and sister, as members of the same camp. At the time of the Ojo Caliente census, he was a married man without children but with three dependents.

Charlie Istee was born in 1872,[12] and thus was of the next generation. It is said that his mother was very young when she married Victorio. Again, we do not know if she was kin to Dilth-cleyhen's mother, but apparently the two wives shared much affection. Dilth-cleyhen was between twenty-two and twenty-four years old, married, and mother of a two-year-old daughter at the time of Charlie's birth. It is believed she was nearly the same age as his mother. All three of these wives of Victorio undoubtedly lived in the same cluster of tipis when at Warm Springs, or in adjacent wickiups when elsewhere, as did his "slave" girls, who were possibly paramours.

Early Childhood

The infant Dilth-cleyhen was loved, pampered, and indeed slightly spoiled, as befits the youngest child of any family among The People.

"Look how straight her back is—how black her hair."[13]

"She is alert, looking all around. She is smart!"

Every smile and coo were noted, every whimper heeded and hushed promptly by anyone within the ranchería. Her laughter or tears could be tolerated when no enemy was near, but the baby must learn silence as a precaution against the unknown.

The sturdy cradleboard or *tsoch*[14] provided the perfect solution in terms of the infant's comfort and safety. Dilth-cleyhen slept, was held, rocked and often breast-fed while within it, from the time she was four days old until she was just over two years of age. It protected her physically and supernaturally. It must be made in the proper Chiricahua way, with the correct materials, by a respected woman whose qualities would be imparted to the child. The effect of the prayers associated with the cradle and the cradling ceremony would be evident until death.

Immediately after Dilth-cleyhen's birth, her maternal grandmother pondered, "I think we should ask Cradlemaker. She is a good woman. She has lived a long time, and she is not close kin."

The acceptance of four gifts by Cradlemaker sealed the commission. Tobacco, buckskin, yellow pollen, and a white man's black-handled knife: these were the items requested for payment.

In early dawn of the day before the cradle was to be completed, Cradlemaker pushed aside her blanket and rose from her bed.

"I need to get some 'heavy wood,'" she muttered, half to herself.

Cradlemaker needed black locust. She looked for branches of proper size. One long limb would suffice, or two shorter ones that would measure one inch in diameter after being stripped of bark. "This wood is so nice and hard, close-grained." She needed enough to form an elongated oval of approximately one yard from top to bottom, with the width at the center based on a measurement of the mother's arm from the crook inside the elbow to her closed fist. This width made the cradle easy to carry, easy to hold when the mother gave her child the breast.

Cradlemaker prayed as she worked. When she cut branches, she lifted her prayers to heaven; she sang to the power of the locust tree, "May this coming year be without sickness. May the babe be as straight and strong as this limb—against all wrong."

She thought to herself, "Pine is so much easier to chop. But it attracts the lightning. It must not be used."

Cradlemaker returned to camp. She stirred the small fire burning in the pit at the center of her wickiup. Fortunately, it had not gone out; she would want to eat something warm later. She shaved the locust branches to make them smooth, saving every remnant of the bark and wood chips. She heated the limbs until they were sufficiently pliable. Then she bent them to the oval, binding them with sinew on what would be the right side of the cradle. Deftly, she drew the center of the oval to the proper width, keeping the measurement constant by means of two lengths of buckskin tied some twelve inches apart.

Cradlemaker viewed her work critically. It was fine. The top of the frame bowed slightly, so that it was an inch or so wider than was the bottom. Fifteen or more smooth slats of "heavy wood" were yet to be secured with sinew and buckskin in perpendicular direction across the central portion of the frame, leaving free a wide arch at the top and a narrower one at the bottom of the oval.

"I guess I could have used split yucca stalk, the yucca with blossoms, instead of 'heavy wood'—but this is really better."

All day as Cradlemaker sat on the earth, intent on her task, she sang the prescribed sacred melodies. The chorus was heard outside the wickiup: "There she comes, this little girl. She says 'Granny' to me. She says 'Granny' to me." Over and over again, she repeated the words. For the rest of their lives Cradlemaker and Dilth-cleyhen would be "special" to each other.

There were other refrains and melodies, each appropriate to the specific stage of the work. Cradlemaker sang of the creation.

"In the beginning He was the Creator." "He" referred to Yusen. "He made all the things upon this earth—the trees, the mountains, the stars that shine."

The frame was done. Now for the second major part, the canopy, the "rainbow" to cover Dilth-cleyhen's small head. For this Cradle-maker needed a series of strips of the "heavy wood," some forty or more inches long and about one-quarter inch in width. She laid these side by side on the ground until they measured eight or ten inches across, then held them in place by twining twelve pieces of locust, regularly spaced, at right angles, creating what looked like a long mat. This was heated slightly and bent. It was ready to fasten to the top of the framework, forming a protective arc, a kind of rainbow.

"Now, if the cradle tumbles while the baby is inside, no harm can touch her face and head."

Cradlemaker sewed a strong rod to each outer edge of the canopy. She kept the desired curvature by means of two strands of buckskin which she crossed diagonally from the top to the bottom of each opposing bar. Then she pulled the cords taut until the arch fit the top of the frame exactly. She sang prayers for the child's health, its continued well-being.

"Now where is that piece of red cedar?" Cradlemaker searched among her treasures for a rectangular piece of cedar that would pro-vide a footrest for the babe. Some time ago she had shaped one of suitable size into a slight curve. "There it is." She chopped out a small V at the back, so that air could circulate from below, and then fastened the cedar to the bottom of the frame.

"Fine," she thought. "It can be lowered as the baby grows."

She chose soft buckskin to use as padding, tying and sewing it in place and making it particularly thick on the sides to ensure comfort. Cradlemaker included precious amulets for the baby's welfare. She lined the inside of the canopy loosely with a length of buckskin. Between it and the locust slats she stuffed the bits of bark and shav-ings saved from earlier stages of construction. Then she pulled the buckskin taut with a zigzag of lacing in such a way that it extended for an inch or so beyond the top and bottom of the front of the canopy.

"Now to make it safe and pretty, both." She decorated the front overlaps with tiny bird bones. Beads were unavailable so long ago. Cradlemaker had made pockets on both the inner and outer sides of the canopy. Into the left pocket she placed a buckskin piece that had been folded four times. It enclosed pollen and special gray sagebrush.

"No lightning will strike the baby." Into the right pocket she put two precious items. The first was a small bag decorated to resemble a turtle, its motif sewn in a circle. The bag contained a piece of Dilth-cleyhen's umbilical cord and a bit of the root of the plant that prevents a person from taking cold. Further, the root had deodorant properties and prevented unpleasant odor from the cord. The second item enclosed was pollen, meant to deter illness. Pollen was sacred, the symbol of life and renewal.

Cradlemaker cut a circular piece of buckskin. It fit perfectly over the top of the canopy and was fastened to the upper slat at the back of the cradle with sinew stitches so fine that they were scarcely visible.

Cradlemaker surveyed the remaining buckskin on the ground at her side. She had used a good half of the skin of one female deer, but there was still enough to cut two rectangles that would extend down the sides of the cradle, covering the basic framework. They were wide enough to meet at the center of the child's body when it was inside.

"Do I have enough?" She contemplated. "Yes, I think so." The neck part of the deer must be at the top of the cradle. And so Cradlemaker sewed them on, using long running stitches with a strip of buckskin, neatly enclosing the oval framework on the sides. She decided reinforcement was needed and tied skin and frame with additional thongs.

"Now for the lacings and the slits to keep them place." Cradlemaker made four three-quarter-inch-long horizontal cuts along the edge of each of the rectangular extensions. Through them she threaded lengths of buckskin, dividing the flaps into two sections: one tie closed the top portion, the other the bottom. Thus, on warm days, one half of the cradle might be left unlaced, so that either the baby's arms or her legs could be left free.

"I'll put on some dangles—hang them up top, from the canopy. She'll like reaching for them."

The lacing would cross the baby's body in diagonal zigzags.

"Lightning," thought Cradlemaker. "For a little girl, I must start by attaching the laces on the right side. The left is for a boy."

There were other signs to designate Dilth-cleyhen was a girl-child. With her knife Cradlemaker cut a small half-moon in the center of the buckskin at the top of the canopy. Now everyone would know. This was a tsoch for a child who would one day be a good and faithful wife, a mother, who would provide continuity in the ways of Tchi-héně.

Finally, Cradlemaker attached a rawhide tumpline to the sides of the cradle so that the board could be carried on a woman's back. Tightly she secured it.

She began to pray: "I am putting on the strap. Then the baby will soon be ready to walk and run and play." She stood up, careful not to step over the cradle or any of the scraps left over from its making. To do so would shorten Dilth-cleyhen's life.

"It needs something more for her to play with," she thought. "But I am tired. It has been a good day's work."

That night as she lay on her bed of spring boughs, Cradlemaker's mind dwelt on the amulets she might add. Had the cradle been for a boy-child, she would have included a turkey wattle to protect him further from lightning and to free him from fear of that zigzag bolt accompanied by its deafening thunder.

But Dilth-cleyhen was a girl. Cradlemaker decided to tie a small gourd to the front of the canopy, come sunrise. "It will make a good pacifier . . . and I think I'll add long strips of one-half-inch buckskin. She'll like to pull on them."

Cradlemaker turned over, pulling the blanket close beneath her chin. "I'm glad I finished the tsoch before the dusk." She fell asleep.

The first rays of morning sun struck the wickiup. Cradlemaker stirred, threw off the bedding, and arose. Quickly she sought the meadow, gathering an armful of sweet-smelling grasses to make a kind of mattress. Back in her shelter, she lay them within a length of buckskin which she covered with a square of rawhide back and front, meant to retard the baby's wetness from the more precious skins. The disposable pad of grasses served as a diaper. She attached a tiny gourd and the buckskin strips as the final touch.

It was time to go. One last time she lifted the cradle, inspecting it with satisfaction. She left the wickiup.

Cradlemaker walked briskly. As she neared Victorio's camp, she sniffed the brisk air. How good was the odor of smoke. "They must be cooking."

"I could use something hot to drink," she thought. "I hope they have 'Apache coffee.'" She referred to a kind of tea made from coneflower.

When she entered the cooking shelter, everyone was assembled. Cradlemaker nodded, thus acknowledging the presence of Dilth-cleyhen's mother, grandmother, and grandmother's sister. There were others there, sipping their tea, but for Cradlemaker there was no time for indulgence. The cradling ceremony must begin. Already the sun was high in the heavens. The rite must be completed before noon.

Reverently, prayerfully, Cradlemaker held the tsoch to the cardinal directions, first toward the east—toward the sun—then clockwise, south, west, and north.

She took the solemn, wide-eyed, naked babe from its mother. The child was held to the four directions. Then, carrying the little one inside the shelter, Cradlemaker rubbed her feet with water. Three times the baby was held toward the cradle and then drawn back. The fourth time she made the gesture, Cradlemaker placed Dilth-cleyhen within the tsoch. The infant's grandmother tied the laces.

Cradlemaker continued to pray. With a pinch of sacred pollen she touched the top of Dilth-cleyhen's mother's head and then her lips. The yellow was beautiful. While it was still within her fingertips, she gestured four times toward the baby and completed this part of the ceremony by applying the blessed powder to the infant's lips.

It was time to partake of ritual food.

The grandmother handed Cradlemaker a bit of "wild banana," the fruit of the yucca. This was touched to Dilth-cleyhen's mouth. Her tiny tongue explored the taste. Then the guests ate. There was plenty for all.

Cradlemaker was proud of her handiwork. She was pleased that she had been asked to install the child. Sometimes the maker of the cradle was not so privileged, and another respected woman took charge during the cradling rite. She glanced at the tsoch. The baby's eyes were closed. Dilth-cleyhen slept, content within the cradle. Its support was soft yet firm; it would comfort the little one during most of every day and night until she was a walking child.

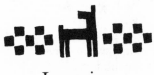

Learning

Springtime passed, and the summer months began. It was time for ear-piercing. Dilth-cleyhen's grandmother was equal to the task. She gathered a long leaf of the Spanish sword.

"Hold still, little one," she cautioned as she punctured both lobes. Dilth-cleyhen howled. She was not used to such treatment. Grandmother inserted a short stick of piñon wood in each hole. Then she sang and prayed just as she would in a future month when the child would try her first steps.

Dilth-cleyhen tried to crawl at a younger age than most infants. "No! No! It's too dirty! It's not safe!" her mother cautioned, snatching her from the earth. "There are bad things in the grass. I can't keep my eyes on you every single minute. There are ants and bugs and all those evil creeping things."

So Dilth-cleyhen was held on someone's lap until her legs were sturdy enough to walk. That was better. Walking was not discouraged. A mother was proud of a toddling child. Meantime, the cradle kept her safe for many hours a day.

Creeping things were not the major danger. There was the enemy: Mexicans, American soldiers—even the miners near Santa Rita. "There's a white man in that bush! *In-dáh!*" warned of a realistic bogey.

Victorio's camp was never without its lookouts. At a stranger's approach a signal was given and the quiet ranchería came alive. Suddenly everyone rushed about in seeming confusion—which was really part of The People's emergency plan. Such interruptions were frequent.

The first alert after Dilth-cleyhen's birth occurred in the deep autumn of the year. The family was camping near the Mogollons. Victorio and other men had left mates and children and headed their restless steeds toward higher ground, toward the haunts of many deer. The women planned to check the fruit of the datil, the broadleafed yucca, which grew in abundance quite near the shelters of the camp. The women wondered, "That fruit might be too ripe, or gone, by now. I hope not. It should be real pink by now, more than ready to dry."[15]

Suddenly a whistle sounded, like a slightly unfamiliar bird. The warning!

Dilth-cleyhen's mother grabbed the reins of her horse instantly. She was already mounted when Grandmother urged, "Quickly! Quickly! Quickly! To the mountain!"

The In-déh simply disappeared. For a time the old men remained, hidden in strategic locations. Only if necessary would they shoot their rifles; their function was to discourage enemy pursuit of the womenfolk. Then they, too, would be gone, blending imperceptibly with the environment.

The cradled Dilth-cleyhen had been slung across her mother's lap. When fairly sure they were unseen, her mother adjusted the tsoch so that it hung down the side of the horse, secured by means of the tumpline. Then, once again, off they flew. The cradle bumped, jostled, and swayed.

Finally mother, child, and mount slowed, wending their solitary way silently through underbrush.

"You were good, my child. You did not cry out. That is how you must always be."

For hours they maneuvered among bushes, hillocks, rocks, and trees that might protect horse and riders from view. From one corner of her eye little Dilth-cleyhen sensed, rather than saw, masked bobwhites—the "bandit quail" scuttling to safety. She strained to see, but her mother had no intention of slowing down. Not for some time—and not at all during this escape—could the baby focus leisurely on the softness of the birds' red-toned breasts, speckled backs, and distinctive black head-masks.

At last her mother pulled hard on the reins. The jouncing stopped. The two had reached the designated meeting place, secure behind great stone crags. A handful of Warm Springs people had arrived already. Her mother dismounted and unfastened the cradleboard.

The women were busy making lean-to brush shelters. Wickiups could come later if it were safe to stay.

"Who is lookout now?" was her mother's first query. Even here, security was a matter for caution. Were there plenty of guards? Would women have to take over?

For any prolonged stay an escape hideaway must be near water. Roots or berries or small game of some kind were hopefully available within the vicinity, and obtaining an immediate supply was an initial priority.

Confidently, for this retreat was an oft-used camp, a woman began to pull away branches until she came to a mud-covered spot among the crags. She chipped away the hardened earth, revealing a crevice filled with dried foods left previously. She found strips of venison, fruit from the prickly pear cactus, and a few kernels of corn; all were dried and well preserved. She continued to widen the opening until she found a mortar and pestle.

In another cache Dilth-cleyhen's mother located wide-mouthed twined burden baskets and a few large rawhide envelopes, or parflêches, some bearing painted designs. There was a water jug—a basket covered inside and out with piñon pitch. Equipped with these carrying containers and their always-present knives, several women set out to find water and plant life. They needed sufficient foodstuff to sustain the group for days, a week, or weeks, if that were necessary.

Dilth-cleyhen's mother left with them, handing Dilth-cleyhen to her grandmother, who was busy tending fire.

This was the preferred and natural thing to do—a child could stay with mother or sisters or even more distant distaff kin for a few hours, or perhaps days, while her mother gathered crops or kindling. But if local food supplies were totally diminished, or if harvesting of a special root or blossom or fruit of some kind required a woman to travel far and be gone for a very long period of time, it was expected that her child accompany her. A wet-nurse was not considered desirable. Unless a child was an orphan or part of an unusually large family, not even a mother or mother's sister should be expected to provide for the infant indefinitely.

"What is she doing, just running around, not taking care of her children?" was a question of condemnation. So, during long—and short—ventures, infants were often taken along, their cradles borne on a mother's or older sister's back, held firmly in place by a tumpline over the adult's forehead or shoulders. As the child neared the age of two, the cradleboard might be omitted, the youngster held close by means of a blanket or wide cloth.

Off they went, mothers, daughters, sisters and their children, an old man or two accompanying them to serve as guards. For the most part, full-fledged hunters went along only when the taking of large game was a simultaneous possibility.

Arriving at their destination, mothers propped their cradled babies against the trunk of a tree or a bush free of thorns. If the child were not too heavy, the cradleboard was suspended from a sturdy branch, or placed where the baby could watch the women at their tasks, and mothers could monitor.

In this way young Tchi-hénè learned patience, for mothers could not be interrupted. Little ones learned they must be silent, for there were many enemies; they saw the women glance about furtively, even while working. Children learned that they, too, must be watchful, that they must observe as chores were done but not ask questions.

Much of the daily conversation of womenfolk concerned wild produce, the best sites and camping spots, as well as favorite ways of food preparation. They spoke of roots, seeds, nuts, and all the various fruits.[16] One must always be prepared to accommodate guests.

"We must not let anyone go hungry. We must always have food in case of visitors." The moment a caller arrived, it was good manners to start boiling water for tea and then to prepare and offer food. "It is a matter of being polite—showing we are good providers for our family. We are generous. You don't ask if they are hungry! You just fix a meal for them."

Dilth-cleyhen's mother talked to her as she went about the daily business of tending fire and having food on hand. She spoke of things she hungered for. "Most of all, for special treats, I like the wild honey, the sweet wild honey, that we find in the stalks of the mescal, the sotol, and the narrow-leafed yucca—or sometimes there are nests in the ground—or in the trees.[17] You will like honey, Dilth-cleyhen."

And as the child matured, "You will learn, my child, that most of the things we eat grow in a special place and in a special season. So we move about, following the bountiful food supply. I love the migrations, seeing all the different places, eating those things that Yusen has provided." It was only natural that Dilth-cleyhen, just like her mother, grew to love the nomadic existence of The People and the nourishment that later was called "traditional."

Sometimes the In-déh went from Warm Springs to the flat lowlands where the mesquite was plentiful and the bean pods were eight inches long.

"Let's go east, closer to the Muddy River, the Rio Grande," the women counseled their husbands. "There's lots of mesquite all the way from east of the Magdalena Mountains south to where the river bends north. Let's camp somewhere there. I'm hungry for mesquite." And when the beans were gathered, some were stewed with deer or antelope meat or just boiled, forming a thick, sweet gruel. Any excess was ground on a metate and stored for future use.

During the late summer months, in the foothills below the rise of the Peloncillos and Animas Mountains, the red fruit of the three-leaved sumac ripened and provided succulent fare, especially when dried and mixed with mescal gathered late the next spring.

Mescal, from the agave or century plant, could be found quite near the sumac, or on the west side of the Mogollons, but the very best grew west of Tchi-hénè territory, at Mount Graham, south of present-day Safford, Arizona.

"The weather is getting warm. Already we've gathered the stalks of the narrow-leafed yucca and roasted the thick ones, sun-drying them for times when we are hungry. Now, we must think about a longer trip—one where we find the big mescal."

To get to Safford, the families left the home camp for several weeks. Dilth-cleyhen was a year old when first she made the journey.

The women packed those supplies they might not be able to find along the way. The men brought in sufficient horses.

"We must be there before the blossoms appear."

Once there, men did the most strenuous work, but an older woman supervised. A pit about seven or eight feet wide and about four feet deep was dug near the center of a stand of plants. It was lined with rocks, flat ones if The People could find them. Younger women collected wood and laid pieces crisscross in the hole and then covered this, too, with rocks, layer upon layer until the pit was full. Fire was touched to the kindling—four times in the four directions.

"Now we thank the Power," She-Who-Supervised prayed. The fire burned to ashes.

Dilth-cleyhen's mother and other women who had come along were busy parting the crown of the mescal from each of the many heavy stalks that had been cut. They did this by driving a sharpened oak or sturdy hardwood stick into the lower part of the stem. The mescal was put within the pit, each woman marking her own heads.

"Wet down the grass, and put it on now."

When this was completed, the whole was covered with dirt.

The mescal steamed all night, all the next day and night, and sometimes more. The families rested and visited, playing with Dilth-cleyhen and the other children. Mothers smiled at their young ones, gossiped, and watched over the precious food. When evening came, the gatherers and their helpers sat around the campfire, singing songs and recounting stories of brave deeds or amusing events, checking the pit from time to time. Occasionally they gambled, playing cards with decks obtained from Mexicans—cards made of cowhide, the symbols being painted designs and stick figures rather than numbers.[18]

After the crowns were fully baked and cooled, the women pounded them with rocks, forming great flat sheets. They laid them to dry in the full hot sun. In this form, the mescal was carried home. Sometimes the mescal was left in cakelike clumps, encased in parflêches or in burden baskets slung over the backs of the horses. All year it could be eaten after soaking in water.

"I like it best with piñon nuts." "I prefer it with walnuts, those nuts we get near Tres Hermanas." "That's good, too, but I find juniper berries give it even better flavor." Thus the talk went on. The gathering cycle became a part of Dilth-cleyhen's world, a life to savor.

In this way Dilth-cleyhen began her "schooling."

As a small baby Dilth-cleyhen stretched her hands toward the dangles from her canopy. As she matured, she observed more important things. She heard the women pray as they offered thanks and gave respect to the power of each food they put into their baskets. She saw them return to the earth a portion of whatever they gathered in order to insure renewal the following year. She saw them look about every few minutes, in a kind of reflex action. There was continual vigilance by everyone—but watching the distance was the major job of the elderly men and young boys who came along.

Dilth-cleyhen learned to fear creatures other than Mexicans and Anglos. There were bears. They were ferocious. Only a few men had encountered them in battle and remained alive. There were reptiles. Snakes liked the warmth of some locations.

"Don't ever say its name!" her mother cautioned even before Dilth-cleyhen was uttering words. The name of any thing that is dangerous would summon it. "It must be addressed in terms of respect, in the third person. It is a relative. Call it 'father's father.' Always be careful of Snake. He is dangerous. He crawls."

"No Chiricahua ever eats the meat of that wild turkey that runs around. That's because the turkey eats snakes. It's contaminated meat." [19]

It has been recorded that some Apaches say that snakes are fond of turquoise and pollen. Long ago, certain elderly women had the power to cure snake sickness in mortals. Rumor prevailed that they fed yellow powder, pollen from cattails, to the snakes. Old medicine men claimed that if you touched a snake, or even a lizard, your skin would become scaly, so you too would resemble the reptile. [20]

In the winter of 1848, or perhaps early in 1849, Dilth-cleyhen took her first steps. Haltingly, she stumbled between her mother and grandmother. She was now a toddler-child.

Victorio announced, "We will boil coffee for her. We will have a small feast to honor my firstborn, to celebrate her new ability."

Dilth-cleyhen's mother made moccasins to place upon the child's feet.

And the day of that feast came.

Dilth-cleyhen wore a simple buckskin dress made from the skin of a doe. Had she been a boy, her attire would have been more elaborate. Boys' shirts, on the occasion of first steps, bore fringe bedecking the seams. Those of girls were plain. But Dilth-cleyhen looked beautiful to her kin.

So did her mother. She donned her best buckskin blouse.

"I had some Apache perfume," she remembered. When she located it, she tucked the small sachet of mint inside the top edge of her skirt. Her long hair shone, having been scrubbed vigorously in suds of yucca root. It was drawn back and secured under a piece of buckskin shaped like a flat hourglass.

One of the women guests wore a blouse of calico taken by her husband during a recent raid on a wagon train traveling in Mexico. Another flaunted lace—rare loot indeed.

At this time the Tchi-héné had barely begun to observe white women's styles, let alone copy them. However, a few adventurous women had taken some purloined cloth to Mexican ladies in Monticello. Many of the families living there had long been friends of the Warm Springs people. The Indians trusted and visited them, giving their word that the pueblo would not be disturbed. These ladies had helped the Apache women cut proper lengths from the long bolts and had shown them how to sew the pieces together. Needles were of bone rather than steel.

Fashion in calico would not become common among the Chiricahua for another twenty years.[21] Dilth-cleyhen's mother was not sure she liked it; it made her uncomfortable. She clung to her buckskin robes, as did most others. That special day she wore moccasins that were almost new, their disc-like toes rising. They were the size of dollars. She felt elegant for this special celebration honoring her daughter.

The day was good. The sun shone. The rite signaled an important point in Dilth-cleyhen's physical development. Victorio stood tall and dignified, proud of his womenfolk, proud that he had ample provisions, food for as many guests as would arrive. "Yes, my girl-child is growing up."

Late that spring Dilth-cleyhen's baby hair was cut. Bangs were left over her forehead, and a small tuft remained at the base of her skull. Pollen was applied to her cheeks and head during the ceremony, remaining there until it wore away.

"May this child live long, through many seasons," the medicine man had prayed.

Within the year, Dilth-cleyhen was eating the same foods as her parents, only rarely demanding the breast.

She was walking, talking, and learning the names of many things. And she listened, even while she played.

It was during food gathering excursions, or times that families accompanied the hunters, that Dilth-cleyhen became acquainted with most of the creatures of the desert, the forest, and the mountain lands: the red hawks soaring overhead; the prairie dogs, erect, chirping; the speedy roadrunner—clown of the desert—half-running, half-flying, searching for insects, lizards, centipedes, mice, and snakes for his daily fare.

Dilth-cleyhen learned that within the land of The People, the Gran Apachería according to Mexicans, all animals and birds and insects, even the rocks and streams, and the stars, the moon, the sun, the winds, and the lightning as well—*everything* was endowed with supernatural power. Each of these "Powers" chose a human host to endow with certain abilities. The recipient then owned the associated songs, prayers, sacred paraphernalia and rituals. Some powers were stronger than others, but even the smallest among them demanded prayer and respect from man and if affronted would punish with illness, "bad luck," or even death.

"Be grateful for our land," her mother told her daughter long before the child could really comprehend. "It gives us all we have. In the flats there are the prairie dogs, rabbits, and antelope. In the mountains there are elk, deer, and mountain sheep. Only once in a great long time can we travel to the plains, where there are buffalo for our men to kill. It is closer for us to go down into Old Mexico. Besides, when we are very hungry, we Warm Springs, we can manage by living on fish. Unlike some other Apaches, we don't mind the taste, nor do we fear eating them." [22]

In autumn the Tchi-héně gathered and prepared the sacred pollen of the tule, or cattail; they took the bananalike fruit of the yucca and the succulent growth of the prickly pear; they dug roots for medicine and for food.

In high elevations The People collected the root from a kind of herb related to the carrot family. They called it *há-eechee-de*; Mexicans used it as well, for headaches and colds, but referred to it as osha. [23] "It smells so good," was always the comment. But the pungent odor was sufficiently strong that há-eechee-de must not be chewed before a man went hunting. The deer would detect his scent. For headache, a concoction of water and ground osha root was rubbed on the ailing forehead.

In some locations live oak trees yielded acorns; in others piñon pines provided delectable nuts. In some desert areas the ripened beans of the mesquite were harvested from the thorny bushes. In springtime Dilth-cleyhen watched the women pull young wild onions. This was a crop that lasted throughout the early summer.

The Indians searched for the narrow-leafed yucca, taking with them the stalks that were later roasted on a bed of embers or within a heated pit. When the yucca bloomed, its lovely white flowers were gathered and later were boiled with meat or bones. Late in May and June the plant for which the Mescalero tribe was named, mescal, was ready.

When summertime came, other foods were ready. Many varieties of onion were ripe. Indian spinach, or lamb's-quarter, was plentiful. There were wild potatoes as well as the seeds of various grasses. Delicious fruits were tempting: currants, strawberries, raspberries, gooseberries, mulberries, and cactus fruit.

Dilth-cleyhen's mother laughed as she was talking to her daughter: "See those black chokecherries. Those crazy Mescalero Apaches eat them! Why, they are nothing but bears' food—not fit for men!" Little did she know that many years later her granddaughter would bake them in pies and preserve them in jellies.

On those gathering excursions, after the women had filled the burden baskets, they were ready to go home. The load was hoisted to each woman's back and held in place with the tumpline. Only those women who carried cradleboards in similar fashion were exempted from such duty. It was good to have horses and mules on such trips. Then more produce could be taken back. Parflêches were piled high on the animals' backs.

How wonderful was the Tchi-hénè land! The band knew every spring of sparkling water, every waterhole. The Indians knew the most sequestered camps and the shortcuts to reach them. They knew the wide arroyos, the dangerous washes. They avoided foothills bearing tangled underbrush that impeded travel, yet the craggy recesses of certain mountains, those which spelled "peril" to whites, were considered to be safe retreats. Arriving there, The People simply disappeared among the poised boulders. The slip of a foot meant being impaled on jagged spires below.

They were cognizant of all the campsites of other Chiricahua peoples. Here they joined their tribesmen when there was something special to communicate, or just for friendship's sake, to have a tulapai party or to gamble. Everyone loved to wager.

Usually, the Tchi-hénè preferred to be in the mountains, but they were equally efficient in the desert land. All young Apaches were trained to endure hardships, severe cold, and intense heat without complaint. They were sturdy. They could travel even on foot as much as seventy-five miles a day should that be necessary.

Each day Dilth-cleyhen's vocabulary grew. She communicated more and more in words rather than coos and babbling. Like her elders, she spoke softly.

Education was gradual and was usually a matter of observation, then trial, and sometimes error.

Even as a child of three Dilth-cleyhen carried containers of water from the streams to the campsite. Sometimes she stumbled.

"Be careful! You must not spill water. It is precious!" she was chided.

She gathered twigs for the fire within the cooking shelter. She watched the women preparing buckskin. Discipline was usually gentle; no one ever spanked or slapped her. But when she was particularly naughty, there was a warning.

"Ja-jo will get you!" Ja-jo is the small nightbird, the whippoorwill who "bathes" in the dust of the road or the wayside of a trail. "You must not listen to Ja-jo," her mother said. "Listening brings misfortune—if not to you, to one of your relatives, someone very close to you. If you hear the sound of that bird, just go away. Go where it cannot be heard." The call of the whippoorwill resembles that of the Crown Dancers who live in the mountains—down in the Tres Hermanas—those sacred beings who descend from their home to aid Apaches in time of tribal need or when there is a great celebration and someone is to be blessed, such as the maidens at their Puberty Feast.

When Dilth-cleyhen asked to go to their dwelling place and see what was happening, her mother whispered, "No girl or woman is allowed to watch them when they are getting ready to bless us. If you hear the Mountain Gods singing over there or near a feast ground while they're preparing to dance, you must go away. You must not listen to their calls until they want you to. If you do, something bad will happen. You will die."

"You watch out for Ja-jo. That bird will pick you up and carry you away! You just better be good. You better mind!" Dilth-cleyhen learned that that bird, Ja-jo, was always around, ready to punish her for naughtiness.

There were further warnings about the four Crown Dancers and especially about the Clown or Clowns who perform with them. "That Clown, he must be treated with respect. He serves as intermediary between The People and supernatural power." "That Clown, the 'Gray One,' he will grab you and put you in a basket and he will take you off somewhere!" Gray One, the color of ashes, and Coyote—all are called by the same name among the Chiricahua.[24]

The darkness of the night, owls, and wild men were things to be feared. So was the eagle. "That is a sacred bird. It requires respect. If you don't behave, it, too, will take you away."

Later Childhood

Dilth-cleyhen grew to be a sensitive, intelligent girl. From the very beginning of her life she had learned to recognize the many moods of the people within Victorio's camps. She sensed tensions when hostile strangers were nearby. She was alert to the warnings of the lookouts and to her mother's admonitions and taboos.

Dilth-cleyhen shared the feeling of elation when men returned to the ranchería after a successful hunt, a victorious battle, or a raid that yielded lots of booty. She loved joining the adult women who joyfully sang and danced toward their warriors in order to greet and honor them. She felt discomfort and sadness when the women keened, when forays had led to Apache deaths, and not all the men returned.

An important part of Dilth-cleyhen's education was knowing precisely who was kin among the people she saw, among the many visitors to the camp. A stranger, even though obviously Apache, must identify himself by kin if he sought welcome at the camp. Dilth-cleyhen must know those callers who were good friends of the family and to be trusted. She must know which ones had reputations of speaking untruths.

At night, before she fell asleep, Dilth-cleyhen heard the conversations of adults who sat about the fire and related stories about raids and battles that had been won or lost, of locations yet to be raided. Men talked boldly on such occasions, but they listened closely when their women spoke, giving advice.

When Lozen, Victorio's younger sister, came, they were especially alert, giving complete attention to her words and prophecies. "What do you think, Little Sister?" "Lozen" was the name given by Mexicans; her kin and other Chiricahuas called her by a word meaning "little sister." She had special powers of knowing where the enemy would be; she was one of the few women invited to accompany the men on raids or war parties.

Many important warriors and their wives and children visited Biduyé. Leaders of other bands conferred with him, discussing policies and alternatives. As she grew older, Dilth-cleyhen sensed that respect for her father was increasing; many of his strategies had met with success. How proud she was of Victorio.

Mangas Coloradas was a good friend of Bi-duyé. He visited the latter's ranchería frequently.

Mangas was a giant of a man. He led many among the Tchi-héné. They called him Kan-da-zis-tlishi-en or Kan-da-zis-tlishishen. These Indian words, just like those in Spanish, mean "red (or pink) sleeves." He had acquired the name because of a shirt. The story told by Dilth-cleyhen's kin involved a raid on some trappers who were moving along a river in Chiricahua territory. The Apaches raided the camp, and part of the loot was a bright red flannel shirt that Mangas made his own and wore until it fell in shreds. A few whites said the translation of his name was "red hands," because his hands and arms were so often stained with human blood. But that was not true. He wanted peace, and fought only when driven to it, or when Apache custom was thwarted.

Dilth-cleyhen stared when first she saw him. Her father, Bi-duyé, was tall, but Mangas was taller still. Some said he measured six feet seven inches in height. His legs, paradoxically, were somewhat short and bowed, but his long straight back made up for them. His head was large, his chin heavy, and his mouth thin-lipped, but it looked broad even when he had no smile. His mantle of hair hung to his waist.

It was Mangas's eyes that Dilth-cleyhen liked best. They were not large, but above his slightly curved nose they shone brightly. When the great man lifted her toward the skies, Dilth-cleyhen was positive he could see right through her. They were kind eyes, laughing, but penetrating.

Nonetheless, those same eyes were sometimes fierce, flashing with anger. She remembered the day Red Sleeves and Victorio reminisced about the killing of Juan José, Mangas's predecessor as chief of all Mimbreños. That day the eyes of Kan-da-zis-tlishi-en had been black with hatred.

The event[25] had taken place in 1837 in the southwestern corner of New Mexico, at Santa Rita del Cobre, once a copper-mining town and Mexican penal colony some fifteen miles east of Silver City. Victorio had been seventeen or eighteen years of age at the time. A band of ruthless traders had arrived at Santa Rita. Knowing that the Mexican government offered a bounty for any Apache killed, they decided on a plan that included the unsuspecting miners. They would give a party, a banquet, and invite the Chiricahuas. Trade goods would be distributed; there would be some gambling. For every Apache man's scalp the bounty hunters would receive one hundred dollars, fifty for that of a woman, and twenty-five for a child. The Indians accepted the invitation; the traders were jubilant.

Juan José was guest of honor; he brought Mangas with him. The two men watched in stoic splendor, as befitted their rank. There were women and babies in cradleboards. Then came the moment of betrayal. Juan José was among the four hundred victims. He was a fat old man and had been plied with liquor. Others who were not shot were hacked to death with knives and sabers. Mangas escaped, but he did not forget. He swore revenge. As a Coppermine-Mimbres Apache, he would not tolerate the murders! News spread among all his people and the other bands. Victorio remembered hearing.

The ensuing slaughter lasted some fifty years. Trappers, hunters, those in charge of supply trains—all who ventured into Mangas's territory risked their lives. Everyone knew the land near Santa Rita[26] was favored above all others by Red Sleeves. He loved the greasewood flatlands, the patches of yucca and cacti, the low-lying creosote brush that provided sanctuary for mammals, birds, and especially important to Kan-da-zis-tlishi-en, the antelope. The arroyos that cut the earth, the humps of rolling mountains, gave the Indians ample cover for their attacks on Mexicans and Anglos.

"They shall no longer trespass," Mangas had declared. In the year of the atrocity Red Sleeves assumed leadership over The People.

Within a year[27] the miners and their families abandoned their small adobe homes, even their livestock, and left Santa Rita a ghost town until 1849 when the cavalry arrived to occupy the *torreón*, or three-cornered fort that had been built some fifty years before.[28]

Victorio and Mangas Coloradas reminisced.

"I'll never forgive the treachery—we cannot trust anyone with white eyes," Mangas said. Bi-duyé understood all too well, although he felt it wise for his people to keep the peace. That was not always possible. Forty-two years later, as Red Sleeves's successor, Victorio led attacks near Santa Rita.

Nonetheless, not all whites were enemies, nor were all Mexicans. And, of course, both Victorio and Mangas had slaves—and wives—from south of the border.

Dilth-cleyhen liked Red Sleeves's Mexican wife. All his other spouses—perhaps as many as four—were Apache women. Dilth-cleyhen's mother, on the other hand, found nothing attractive, and tolerated the Mexican woman only because of Mangas's prestige.

One time after a visit had terminated, Dilth-cleyhen's mother shook her head in disapproval. "By all rights, that Mexican is nothing but a slave!" As has been noted earlier in this history, most times when Apaches took a child or took a woman as a slave, the newcomer was not mistreated. Ideally, these women were like respected maids or helpers among the women of the extended household. They assisted with daily chores. In Indian, the word used for captives of this kind was not "slave"—this is a term applied first by whites and only later by Apaches. The Indian term, which has no equivalent in English, meant something like "they had to live with them."

"We all know Kan-da-zis-tlishi-en took her in a raid! There was lots of trouble over her. She puts on airs—she doesn't know her place. She's not like Victorio's 'slave.'"

But Victorio's "Slave-girl," as she was known, was a good worker, and the women of the ranchería liked and trusted her. She was part of the family; she served the various members well. She enjoyed belonging to a man of stature and carried herself with head held high. Dilth-cleyhen's mother helped her learn to speak Apache. They accomplished many tasks side by side.

Slave-girl sang as she gathered wood, sang as she scrubbed hides with brains to soften them. Dilth-cleyhen adored her, begging her over and over to sing the refrain:

> They are moving.
> They are on the move.
> But where they are going
> Is uncertain.

It was one of Slave-girl's own compositions,[29] describing the days of running, of flight days that were becoming more usual among her captors. She had other favorites, especially Chiricahua love songs.

The only trouble the family ever had concerning Slave-girl happened during a casual visit to Bi-duyé's camp by Loco. He came with his first two wives (he eventually had three[30]) and the children they cared for. His first wife's name was Chiz-pah-odles or "Burning Wood," the second was called Chish-odl-netln or "Wood Carrier."

Loco was Victorio's cousin, and was his elder by a few years. Both men were leaders during hunting and raiding trips, and each had a fair-sized following. There was rarely rivalry between them; their relationship was primarily one of cooperation. Often the families set up adjacent camps on gathering expeditions. Sometimes, as now, it was just a matter of companionship.

Loco was a gruff man. Although usually of an amiable nature [31] and desirous of peace with white intruders, Loco had a reputation for sudden bursts of temper. He walked with a slight limp; his face was disfigured. There was a scar over his left eye, affecting the eyelid. The child Dilth-cleyhen could not stop staring at him.

"Why does he look like that?" she asked her mother.

"He had a fight with a huge bear."

"Why do they call him 'Loco'? Slave-girl says that means 'crazy.'"

"It's all because of Bear. Bear is mean. Not many men can fight a bear and live to talk about it. But that man did. He killed Bear—but not before Bear clawed his face. Now, some say he has "Bear power." He is a medicine man. What it really means is that he has taken on the qualities of Bear. But Bear made him kind of crazy. That happens sometimes."

"Is that necklace he wears, the one with all the claws, are they bear claws?"

"Yes, my child. Because he won that battle, he is entitled to wear it. If he did not have protection from Bear, a necklace like that would be too dangerous. It might kill him."

"Well, he sure acts just like a bear," thought Dilth-cleyhen. When Loco was close within the camp, the child preferred being near her mother, clinging to her skirt. Nor did later events lessen her intimidation.

Victorio had left camp. On the day of his departure he donned his most elegant calico shirt and a necklace bearing a cross of abalone shell. His trousers were wide-legged, like those of Mexicans; he wore a breechcloth, a symbol of male Apache virility, buckskin leggings to the knees and moccasins with turned-up toes. His dagger-knife was inserted in the folds of the leggings. His bow and arrows, lance, and a rifle were taken along in case of assault along the way. The crowning touch to his apparel was a red band about his hair that hung to his shoulders and flowed with the passing breeze. [32] Victorio traveled north, to visit Navaho friends, perhaps to gamble. Loco and family remained in Warm Springs with their shelters near those of Bi-duyé's womenfolk.

For some reason, Loco was alone in his wickiup. [33] His fire was going out. He needed kindling wood.

"Slave-girl," he called. "Get me some wood."

The woman ignored him.

Again, "Get me some wood!"

"No. I don't have to serve you. I am not your captive. I belong to Victorio."

Loco was livid. He grabbed his spear, rushed to the girl, and stabbed her through the chest.

When Bi-duyé returned, his anger flared. He confronted his cousin, and the words he spoke were far from friendly. "*Shi-zooleh-na-ee-sheesh!*" Victorio cried. Literally translated, this means "You make me so angry, the blood goes to my throat."

As soon as Loco's women returned, the now-unwelcome guests packed their belongings and left, traveling east and setting up camp along the banks of a creek flowing into the Rio Grande. Victorio refused to speak to his relative for many, many months.

"I'm not surprised at that Loco," Dilth-cleyhen's mother said. "He even treats his *own* slaves like that. Remember the time we were all in that camp? It was a number of seasons back. We were all gathering nuts from the piñon."

Dilth-cleyhen had been too young to remember, so she questioned her mother further.

"Well, there was one particular day. Loco's family had brought along a slave to help the women pick the nuts from the ground. It's back-breaking work. Well, Loco gave that girl an order. She heard him, but she was stubborn. She did not jump right up and do what he told her. Loco became furious. That time he grabbed a whip. He whipped that slave, and he whipped her, and he whipped her."

"Did it take her long to get better?"

"She never recovered. She died from that beating." There was a pause and Dilth-cleyhen silently reconstructed the event. Then her mother began to talk once again.

"Your father was outraged by Loco's behavior. Just like now, he refused to speak to him for many, many moons. He would not help his cousin in any way. We quit camping together. We remained here in Warm Springs, and Loco was either in the Black Mountains or near Cuchillo Negro Creek. Your father and Loco never saw eye-to-eye concerning slaves."

The other visitor with whom there was friction was Geronimo.

Geronimo was Bedonkohe by birth, but Net'na during his youth and early manhood. His Indian name was Goyathlay or Goy-ah-kla, meaning "One Who Yawns,"[34] but a few elderly Fort Sill Apaches say that there is another Chiricahua word, sounding almost the same, which means "intelligent, shrewd, clever."[35] The Mexicans gave him the Spanish nickname by which he became known throughout the Southwest.

Dilth-cleyhen was a mere tyke when Geronimo, his first wife, and their three children[36] visited Bi-duyé's ranchería. He was a warrior of whom her mother said, "There is something about him. I think he does not tell the truth. He looks out only for his own interests." Dilth-cleyhen looked at him. "What does a man look like who speaks with double tongue?" she wondered.

He was not very tall, only five feet eight inches. But he had a sturdy body, one that revealed his strenuous boyhood training. "He's nothing very special," was the girl's evaluation. "I wonder. My mother has said he has lots of power, and he sings with a great, rich voice."

In just a few years, news of disaster spread to Victorio's camp.

"They've killed Geronimo's wife! They've killed his mother and the young ones."

The information proved to be true. In the summer of 1850 Geronimo started on a trading trip to Casas Grandes, Mexico, stopping en route at Janos. The Apaches had taken their spouses and children along, since it was to be a friendly encounter. Just outside the latter town they made camp. Each day the men left their dependents, horses, weapons, and supplies in the care of a few guards and went about their trading with the Janos villagers. Although the Mexicans had pledged friendship, the Indians were cautious and decided that should anything go awry, they would all meet in a certain thicket by the river that passed the town.

Late one afternoon the Apache traders returned to camp. They were met by a group of running women and crying youngsters.

"Those Mexican soldiers—troops from another town—they came and killed our guards. They took all the horses, the ponies, all the things we brought along. They started shooting at us!"

Immediately the Indians dispersed, merging one by one with the landscape and meeting eventually by the river as planned. When a headcount was made, Geronimo's mother, wife, and children were missing. Worried, he stole back to the village. "Maybe they were taken captive."

But no—he found all five dead, lying in a pool of blood.[37]

When the fifty-year-old Cochise[38] journeyed to Warm Springs, the attitude of Dilth-cleyhen's mother, and of all members of the ranchería, was one of respect. He was a great chief, a man of many powers, a leader of the stature of Mangas Coloradas. His followers were Tchok'-anen. His principal wife, Dos-teh-seh, was Red Sleeves's daughter, and the couple spent much time with her people, the Mimbreños. Their son, Taza, was five years older than Dilth-cleyhen and disdained paying her attention. Dilth-cleyhen was impressed by the boy's "maturity" and by his father's reputation.

"Cochise can be trusted. His word is true," people said.

The origin of the chief's name is uncertain. Some people say it was an Anglo corruption of the Apache word *chizh*, meaning "fire-wood."[39] At one time Cochise supplied wood for stage stations. It is possible that this task was responsible for the name by which he was known for the remainder of his life.

"Such a tall man—like my father," Dilth-cleyhen thought. Cochise measured about five feet nine inches tall, but he looked considerably more. His shoulders were broad; he was lithe and muscular. His hair was shoulder length, his forehead high; his face, the way she remembered him, was painted red across his large nose.[40]

"I guess he's been at war," she postulated. But now his face was genial; he was smiling, as were his friends.[41] Her father said that Cochise was one of the greatest of Apache warriors. Truly, The People were in need of men of wisdom, leaders who could reason with their followers and guide them in battle without losing novice warriors. More and more strangers were invading the homeland.

Even before Dilth-cleyhen was born, Mexican and American soldiers—white men and black—could be seen in the Southwest. The Americans were there to defend settlers—the ranchers and miners. Most mountain men, concerned with trapping, had been tolerated by the Indians; they understood each other. The military men were there to protect the boundary that separated the nations.

During the year of Dilth-cleyhen's birth, 1848, the Treaty of Guadalupe Hidalgo ended the war between Mexico and the United States. This was expected to bring a state of peace to the area. Unfortunately, the border that was established passed through the heart of Apachería.

"It means nothing," Victorio quieted the apprehensions of his wife.

The crucial part of the treaty, as it pertained to the Chiricahuas, was found in Article XI. This would stop Apache raiding in Mexico,[42] or so the intruders thought.

"The In-dáh is stupid! How can they imagine we will give up our entire way of life because they make a few marks on some paper! We need horses and mules and guns and ammunition, and we'll continue to take anything we want!" This was the talk among the younger, more aggressive men. "What is a 'border,' after all!"

"We'll do as always," Bi-duyé agreed.

In 1849 gold was discovered in California. Trails marked New Mexico and Arizona from east to west, the double lines left by wagon wheels becoming deeper and deeper as time passed. Some came in carts and buggies, too. All too often the vehicles carried the life-belongings of weary, money-hungry men who had no idea what the West was like but whose souls were filled with desperate hope. Laborers, farmers, preachers, gamblers, and prostitutes all headed west. Some of those who envisioned a permanent change of residence brought their wives and children. Others were out for sheer adventure. The Apaches watched them come, deliberating whether or not to attack and take the loot.

Aside from bounty hunters seeking Indian scalps,[43] unscrupulous traders caused most of the problems during these years of great migration. They bartered slaves, munitions, and whiskey with the Indians for stolen livestock. Many such unprincipled men stopped in the land near Santa Rita, near the miners, in the area beloved by Mangas Coloradas and later by his successor, Victorio.[44]

In 1851, when Dilth-cleyhen was three years old, gold was found at Piños Altos, northwest of the copper mines at Santa Rita. Miners flooded the area.

"Perhaps, if we let them have the gold, they'll be less troublesome. We have no use for it," Red Sleeves reasoned. "Perhaps then we can have some peace."

Mangas knew where the metal, so precious to the whites and Mexicans, was to be found in quantity. He went to the miners' camp. Unfortunately, the men who met him were drunk. When the Apache made his offer, they laughed at him. They decided to teach him a lesson for lying. "How can this old coot know where there is gold!"

Because of Mangas's huge size, it took a dozen men to wrestle him down. They cut his back to ribbons with a bullwhip. He made no outcry. He had been hardened from youth to show no cowardice, no matter how great the pain. Just as he was near collapse, the men freed him. He staggered to his horse, mounted with difficulty, and rode away.[45]

Later the wife of Mangas talked to Dilth-cleyhen's mother about the incident. "Those dirty miners just howled with glee."

There was little more to say. But the insult was grave and would not be forgotten.

"We will attack the miners' camp," was the unanimous decision of The People. "No matter how many soldiers there are in Fort Webster, we will have our revenge." And so they did. Mangas led his men on bloody raids for months.

In years to come, Dilth-cleyhen's mother and the other women related the atrocities, laughing over the terror the Tchi-héne had caused.

"We took the miners' horses and cattle. We destroyed all the supplies our men could not carry away. Those miners were terrified. They fled in all directions." That was not all.

For months, for a distance of hundreds of miles along every roadway, travelers saw the results of Apache anger. Dead Americans and Mexicans were suspended by their feet from tree limbs and wagons, their bursted heads eighteen inches above the ashes of what had been fires.

By July of the following year, the Indians tired of the slaughter. They agreed to a peace treaty with the Americans—but not with the Mexicans.[46]

"Those people—Yusen put them there for our convenience!" a friend of Dilth-cleyhen's mother laughed.

By the time this series of forays was over, Dilth-cleyhen was five, nearly six years old. She had listened to her elders. She had watched their reactions and felt similar stirrings within her heart. "When I grow up, I'm going to war, too. I'm going to be like father's Little Sister, Lozen." With great determination and purpose, she began to practice throwing rocks—and her knife. She increased her speed when racing.

On December 30, 1853, the Gadsden Treaty was signed. The United States acquired the lands it coveted in southern New Mexico and south of the Gila River. Again, what did it matter to Apaches? All it meant was that the United States was claiming land farther south. What was more pertinent was the fact that Fort Webster was closed, and that meant fewer soldiers.[47]

Dilth-cleyhen listened intently to all the talk. At night, she wrapped herself in a blanket and was very still, lest they send her to bed in another wickiup.

Mangas came to visit Victorio more frequently. They both wanted peace for their people. "We will show them the importance of our word. If we say we will keep peace, we will do so. We keep our agreements."

She noted, however, that the same was not true of the people with white eyes. They seemed continually to change their minds.

There were councils of the Indians. Even women attended. The talking, which included the opinions of all present, often resulted in a decision to take revenge. Then men began their preparations for battle, seeing first that their three-feathered arrows made of "hard wood" were in good order. Some points were dipped in a poison made of rotted deer's blood mixed with toxic plants. The arrows and bow were fitted into a quiver and a buckskin cover, respectively. Spears were readied, some with knives or bayonets attached to the ends. Dilth-cleyhen was warned not to step over them. "Do you have ammunition for your rifle?"

When all was done, a war dance took place, given to ensure Indian safety and success.

A great fire was built. Tulapai, the favored corn brew of the Chiricahua, was made by the women, and everyone drank, but not to excess. Victorio did not believe in drinking. A feast was prepared. For much of the night, those warriors who planned to participate in the coming foray were dancing.

Men of power covered their hair with decorated buckskin war bonnets held in place by a chin strap. At the top, on both sides of some of the skull caps, slight peaks rose as though antlers were about to bud. At proper times, these medicine men or shamans prayed to Yusen. They implored help from supernaturals; they followed scrupulously the ritual songs and chants taught them by their power.

Lozen, the seer, was present at the dances whenever possible. She told of the enemy locations, thus helping in whatever strategies would yield advantage. The People listened carefully to her and to the advice of Victorio, as well as to the complaints of those who had been wronged.

The shaman, a respected patriarch, sat on the side of a circle of seated warriors about the fire. He called on one man after the other to dance. No one so summoned ever refused. This was the period of "fierce dancing."[48] Dilth-cleyhen, seated in a circle of women about six yards beyond the warriors, watched with wide eyes. Her father was the first to be called. Then came three others known to be his followers.

Victorio rose. Naked from waist up, he wore his wide breechcloth, but no Anglo trousers. He reached back for the rear flap of the cloth, which hung nearly to his ankles. He drew it between his legs, then tucked it and the shorter front extension into his belt. Thus, he was "free." The upper parts of his legs were bare, but his moccasins with upturned toe protected his feet. One of the other men wore a cartridge belt as a bandolier. All four danced vigorously, following the cadence of drummers and singers. The men faced each other in two pairs. After dancing in place, they moved toward each other, changed sides, and then turned around, going back. Four times this was repeated. Then it was time for the others to dance. Some had spears; others had guns and, as they did their intricate footwork, they inserted cartridges. Gunshots rang out. A few men held bullets in their mouths.

During the dance the men refrained from shouting. Softly, under their breath, at appropriate times, they uttered what sounded like "wah, wah." It was not proper to make loud noises now, not preceding a battle. To do so would cause too many men to be killed. The only shouting during the war dance came from older males in the audience. Then there was the periodic high pitched cry of the women—the cry that is heard at the da-i-dá. And the warriors' women prayed silently.

For the period of the war dance, all women were called White-Painted-Woman, just as they had been during their Feasts. Except when men were called by name, each one was Child-of-the-Water.

Dilth-cleyhen followed the lead of her mother. She participated in the social round dancing that terminated the religious celebration. The men, in a circle, danced around the fire, the women forming a larger circle outside them. Then came partner dances. Dilth-cleyhen watched sleepily. The next morning the warriors (faces painted, and each man wearing his particular amulet and a small bag of sacred pollen) were gone before she awakened. All the adult women had seen them off, directing high cries to the heavens.

During the men's absence, their wives and children were circumspect. Their behavior was important to ensure the success of the males. The wood had to be stacked neatly.

"Dilth-cleyhen, don't let those little ones get on the woodpile. Don't let them scatter that kindling. If they do, like the pieces of wood, the warriors will disperse and your father will be lost!"

At the time of the warriors' return,[49] while they were yet approaching, the women of the camp were alerted by sentinels. They gathered together, forming a singing group that danced toward those arriving. Dilth-cleyhen soon learned the songs and joined in lustily to the beat of the drum. As the men neared, she searched their faces. "Was her father there?" She heard some women praying. And after all males were counted, if some were missing, there was the cry of women's keening.

If the battle had been largely victorious, then once again the women began to prepare for celebration. Food was prepared; tulapai was made. This time there would more widespread drinking and more social dancing.

"Did you bring back any spoils?" women asked.

Before the great central fire was lit, the shaman sounded a roll call of all who had gone to battle and come back. Each one, as he heard his name, responded by shooting his rifle. His loot was brought forward and presented to the women. Victorio brought his to his wife.

He turned and spoke to Dilth-cleyhen. "Very soon, when you are just a little older, you will be the one to whom the loot is given. You will have first choice of anything I bring back, whether it be a war or a raid. You will choose among the horses and saddles, among the blankets, among the bolts of yardage. You take what you want. Then it will be up to you, as my firstborn, to distribute all the rest. This must be done carefully and fairly so that all may prosper."

The feast and dance of victory began.

Again the men were called by name, this time to relate in fast steps the ways in which they had fought or looted. Each dance reenacted the warrior's behavior. The singers, who had been his co-fighters, transposed his steps into song. When all had received recognition, there was "fierce dancing" followed by the women approaching their men. All night, or several nights, they danced in celebration.

Between the times of battle the family traveled throughout Tchi-héné lands and beyond. Usually it was in quest of plant foods or game, but whatever their reason, the journeys provided Dilth-cley-hen's maternal kin time to inform the youngster more about the history and lore of The People.

There was the time shortly after the Gadsden Purchase that Victorio decided to travel south to be among the Mimbres near Santa Rita, to see Mangas Coloradas. The members of the family went along, including Dilth-cleyhen's maternal grandmother, who lagged behind her son-in-law in order to permit respect between them. All were riding horses. When they were some twenty-nine miles northeast of Silver City, in what is now the state of New Mexico, the old lady stopped. She spoke to her granddaughter.

"Look over there. See the water over there. That is a lake, a lake where Chiricahua life began. Life was raised from that lake.[50] That is where the Creator brought us forth—right over there. Do you see it?"

Dilth-cleyhen nodded in assent, straining to see the sacred place.

Her grandmother continued. "You must not forget this place. You must tell your grandchildren, and they will tell theirs. You must be sure you tell them the story of the creation."

"I can't remember it, Shi-choo, my grandmother."

The old woman looked at the child. "You have forgotten. I guess you were too young when I told the story to you before. Tonight, when you are going to sleep, I will repeat it once again. This time you will remember."

And so, as they lay wrapped in blankets on the earth, Dilth-cley-hen's grandmother began:

"In the very beginning, there was the Creator. There was also White-Painted-Woman. Later, Child-of-the-Water was born, and so was Killer-of-Enemies. Then there were four. Child-of-the-Water was the son of White-Painted-Woman, but Killer-of-Enemies came from evil people.

"There was another bad person, a giant, an Owl-Giant, who ate all the babies to which White-Painted-Woman gave birth. This had started even before she prayed and Child-of-the-Water was born. So when he came along, she was really worried. 'What shall I do?' she wondered. 'Every day that giant comes to me to find my babies because he is hungry.' She decided to dig a hole under her fire. She kept the infant there, nice and warm, taking him out only to feed and wash him.

"It wasn't long before Child-of-the-Water could walk. One day Owl-Giant came to her, and he could see little tiny footprints, little tracks. The giant was angry and wanted to know what made them. 'These are the tracks of something good to eat!'

"But White-Painted-Woman thought fast. She told him that she was so lonesome for a child that sometimes she herself made those little marks. Owl-Giant doubted her. He told her to make some then and there. So she marked the dirt and finally he believed her. Then, as he looked around, he saw baby blankets all smeared with excrement. Again, he wanted to know what they were all about. 'Here is the excrement of something good to eat,' he said to her. White-Painted-Woman countered again that she herself made the excrement, simply because she longed for a baby. He demanded that she make some. The wise woman picked up a blanket, turned from the giant, and smeared wild honey on the bedding. Owl-Giant looked. Again he believed. Thus it was that White-Painted-Woman always tricked that evil one, and Child-of-the-Water lived."[51]

For the next few nights the old woman continued to tell stories to Dilth-cleyhen. She told the way that Child-of-the-Water grew to be a valorous man, one who killed the evil creatures of the world, the ones who killed with power from their eyes. He killed the bull, the eagle, the prairie dogs. He even killed Owl-Giant.

She told of the way people were created.

"Child-of-the-Water took some mud and from it made two figures, just like men. Then he made two more, just like women. There were four. All of them could talk.

"Child-of-the-Water said to them, 'You—one man and one woman—you will be Indians. You other two will be whites with pale eyes.' Child-of-the-Water gave them earthly goods. There was a bow, an arrow, and then a gun. Child-of-the-Water said that he would choose what the Indians would have; Killer-of-Enemies would choose for the Whites. But even the great powerful ones could not agree. They argued over the choices for a long time. Finally, Child-of-the-Water took the bow and arrows, and Killer-of-Enemies was left with the gun.

"Then Child-of-the-Water made two mountains. One had trees and plants, heavy vegetation, all kinds of Indian food, nutritious things. There were deer and turkeys, too. The mountain he made for the whites was bare. But Killer-of-Enemies accepted it. It spread apart. From deep inside, animals emerged. There were horses, mules, cattle, sheep. Even chickens came out.

"This is the way it happened."

Dilth-cleyhen's grandmother continued to tell the child important facts as they rode the rest of the way to Santa Rita. "That Child-of-the-Water was the one who created all of life. He was the one who delegated the attributes of every living thing. The Indian would survive on the wild and growing things of the earth. The white man could cultivate what he ate."

Later she added, "Those four people, the two men and the two women, Child-of-the-Water told them that an ocean would divide them one from the other. That was a wise thing for him to do. Whenever white men meet red men, they fight. They don't trust each other."

Already during those tender years of her life, Dilth-cleyhen had come to realize this tendency.

Camping near the ranchería of Mangas was such pleasure.

Food was plentiful; there was lots of antelope meat. There was ample tulapai, the beer called *tizwin* among the Mescaleros, and everyone relaxed—visiting, gambling a bit, and competing at games.

To make tulapai, the "gray water," the women first dug a shallow trench. No boxes were available to them, such as would be used by Apaches in later days. Into the trench they poured layer after layer of dried corn, covering each tier with dampened gunny sacks or wet grass until sprouts emerged. When these had grown to a length of about one inch, it was time to go to work. While some ladies ground the kernels on their metates, others gathered wood and built a large, hot fire; they started boiling water in as many five-gallon cans as they could round up. The mashed corn was poured into the liquid. A few women suggested adding a little fermented juice from roasted mescal; others preferred liquid from the mesquite bean[52] or a bit of oak tree root. Dilth-cleyhen's mother always put in a handful of ground wheat. Whatever was added or omitted, prayers were necessary.

Tulapai-maker stirred in a sunwise direction and spoke to the Powers.

"This drink must be good. It is not for fighting. Everyone who drinks should be happy—not angry."

The mixture cooked all day long, becoming more and more concentrated. When it cooled, it was poured into special jugs—basketry jugs covered with pitch and called "something that is bubbly." Within the jugs fermentation began. When experts deemed the brew ready—perhaps as early as the next day—and the bubbles had subsided, the drink had a slightly bitter taste.

"Tulapai is good for you. It is food. Drink it wisely."

"Drink it tonight. It won't be good tomorrow."

While the tulapai was being prepared and meat was roasting or stewing, there was recreation. Boys and men held shooting contests with the bow and arrow. They wrestled. Women and children, as well as men, ran races on foot or competed with their horses. Endurance and speed were highly prized. The first time a boy ran in such a race, the bottoms of his feet were rubbed with mud. This would help him win. Another activity enjoyed by all was shinny—a rough, team game. This was played with a stick about three and one-half feet long and hooked at one end. The aim was to hit a wooden or buckskin ball, about half the size of today's baseball, between two upright objects—poles or trees. Those able to run well loved this game. Every time a goal was made, one point was scored.

The game men preferred above all others was hoop-and-pole. Women were not permitted to play it, nor could they approach the grounds, which consisted of an area some thirty feet long, aligned east and west, and carpeted with a smooth layer of grass or of pine needles. The hoops and the poles could be made only by a man owning special power, one who knew the proper ceremonies. The night before the game, specific songs were sung.

The hoops and poles bore special notches, each notch being named, and the worth of each, for the purpose of gambling, was decided in advance. Over a foot in diameter, the hoop had a knotted string across its center, the knots being called "beads." The aim was to roll the hoop down a kind of alley and then stop it with the thrown pole, which many men referred to as "the snake."

There were two contestants at a time. Each one slid his lance after the rolling hoop in such a way that the latter would fall on the butt end of the pole. The winner was decided on the basis of how many pole notches were within the hoop and how many knots on the hoop's crosspiece were over the pole. While the game was in progress, no one could walk around the field from the east. In this it resembles a similar restriction pertaining to the Feast Grounds during the sacred rituals of the maidens' Puberty Feast.

Because of their association with Coyote, no dogs were allowed in the vicinity. And any time you hear that Coyote lost in a wagering game, you can be sure he was playing hoop-and-pole. The rules and regulations were handed down long ago, as the myth relates, when animals were people. The game came from Snake and from dangerous four-footed beasts such as Bear. Sometimes the contest was accompanied by music. A bystander took up an ordinary hunting bow. He tightened the string. Then he put one end of the bow in his mouth and hit the string with an arrow. The resultant sound is like Chiricahua singing. The women heard it from the far distance. They became quiet and listened.

The Tchi-héně loved music. They had a fiddle, the "wood that sings." It was made from various kinds of wood, but the dried stalk of the century plant, four inches in diameter and about eighteen inches long, was generally preferred. Over the hollow cylinder, there was a single string of sinew. The bow was a length of sumac wood, with horsetail hair stretched its length.

The men may have had their hoop-and-pole, but the women had a counterpart. This was the stave game, called "gambling with sticks." It, too, was sacred, and once again, only a person endowed with proper power could make the various playing pieces. Action consisted of advancing a counter along a circle of stones, with the number of spaces being moved in each single turn determined by the throw of marked staves. These were thrown against a large flat rock in the center of the playing circle. The staves consisted of round sticks, six to eight inches long, split lengthwise so that one side was flat and the other round. The flat side was painted red or black; the round side was yellow or white. Rules of the game and the number of players varied considerably according to various family traditions. Women laughed when men begged to join in, and only rarely did the latter try their luck.

Then there was the moccasin game. It, too, was associated with tradition, myth, and song and could not be played in the summertime at Santa Rita.

"This game was played in the Mogollon Mountains during the very beginning of the world," Dilth-cleyhen's grandmother told her. "There was a contest between the birds and the four-footed monsters and all the other animals. They were gambling, trying to determine whether there should be perpetual daylight, or whether the earth should be forever shrouded in darkness. We can only play the game in winter and at night when there are no snakes around."

The players divided into two groups. One of the teams arranged four moccasins in the playing field, and hid a bone inside one of them. A blanket was hung to divide the two groups of players. As the game progressed, the contestants intoned the songs said to have been sung by the birds and animals who first played it. There was also dancing. The opposing team of players must guess which moccasin holds the bone. This was done by pointing it out with a stick. This game, too, has endless complications, countless variations.

There were activities other than games and cooking. A group of women from Mangas's kin and his followers, along with Dilth-cleyhen's grandmother, sat in a wickiup, and as they shared the latest news, their hands were busy. One was twining sumac into a burden basket that was now close to three feet tall. Another had finished a basket jug for tulapai or other liquid; the container was now ready to be smeared with warmed pitch from the piñon tree to make it watertight. Some were coiling bowls or traylike baskets using sumac stems for foundation and yucca leaves for decoration and binding. The women worked in a convivial group until each became hungry and went to her own wickiup to help prepare food for her family.

Sometimes several families shared their foodstuffs. They used spoons and dippers made of wood and broad yucca leaves. They sipped "coffee" or tea, made by steeping the coneflower (the "coffee weed" in Apache), or the bark of a certain tree, or pieces of dried "lip fern." Drinking vessels consisted of small gourds found in Old Mexico; sometimes larger ones held a gallon or more, making a good substitute for pitch-covered water jugs. Mostly, fingers served as utensils.

Then, once again, families joined together in the evening hours to sing and tell stories.

While they were in Mangas's favorite part of the homeland, Dilth-cleyhen saw from afar the ancient home of the Ja-ja-deh, the Mountain Gods. This was a cave some twenty miles from Tres Hermanas, at the top of a rocky slope covered with mesquite, yucca, small greasewood bushes, and tumbleweed. The family camped near the cave, and at night they heard the sacred beings as they beat their drums and sang.

"Shi-ma, my mother, I want to have my Feast down here, down here in the Tres Hermanas. I want my da-i-dá in this sacred homeland," Dilth-cleyhen requested.

The next morning she and her mother went to collect the ripe fruit of the prickly pear, the nopal, called *tuna* in Spanish. "It may be too early. They really aren't ready until the fall." But they found a few. Using two sticks as though they were chopsticks, they plucked the luscious red objects. They brushed away the fine stickers with stiff grass. Later, after arriving in camp, they would break the fruit in half and dry it for future use.

Not wanting to return home with such empty baskets, they decided to gather a few acorns. There were many oak trees within the general area. Then, tiring from their labors, they rode their horses by the sacred cave, so that Dilth-cleyhen could see it once more. Dismounting this time, they climbed the hill. Her mother whispered a prayer. They stood outside the entrance, looking over the landscape. In the distance they saw a mountain with a needle eye. "Look. The wind blew a hole in that rock," her mother informed her.

"All this land is sacred. This cave, all about, is a place to be approached with prayer. We must not go in. It is the home of the Mountain Gods."

Many years later, Dilth-cleyhen's granddaughter, Narcissus, with a party of present-day Tchi-héné, visited areas sacred to The People. They wanted to see the sacred cave. With difficulty they climbed the steep grade. The path was narrow and covered with loose rocks. "Be careful!"

No one mentioned that the area was infested with snakes. Everyone knew better than to mention the snake's name and thus summon him. A squirrel led them to the narrow entrance, which was partially hidden behind a slab of fallen rock. Once within the cave, the wall was slanted. There, a bit of the past came to life in pictographs. They saw paintings created by the Gods in charcoal black many, many years ago. There were depictions of the Crown Dancers gesticulating with their swords; there was a sacred Clown. There was a cowboy and some men on horses, the men apparently Spanish for they wore high hats with tasseled brims like those of early settlers. Indeed, the Apaches were filled with awe; it *felt* sacred within the cave.

When Dilth-cleyhen's kin were at home in Warm Springs, the girl's mother took time to check the family's clothing. The women still wore knee-length buckskin skirts and, usually, an untailored buckskin shirt. There was decorative fringe at the skirt's hemline, over the shoulders, and at the wrists. But a change in style was coming. The women loved the deep-hued calicos brought in by raiders. From this cotton cloth they fashioned full blouses with short pleated flanges instead of fringe at the shoulder line. All the pieces of cloth were squares or rectangles that could be torn easily from the yardage directly from the bolt. A leather belt over the blouse and a necklace of red beans and white seeds completed the outfit.[53] Dilth-cleyhen's mother was never without her necklace, and before she was a teenager, Dilth-cleyhen wore one as well. It was imbued with great protective power.

Styles for men included a buckskin shirt much like that of women, but with a wider opening at the neck. Nothing was worn above the waistline when men went to war or set out on a raid. More and more, when warriors wanted to be elegant, they wore shirts found in the loot of raided wagon trains. However, no matter what other kind of clothing was worn, a buckskin breechcloth, extending to ankles in back and to knees in front, was essential. This might be worn alone or over Anglo or Mexican trousers. In summer little children pranced about in nakedness; in winter they were clothed as though adult.

If there were ever such a being as an Apache dandy, it was the huge Mangas Coloradas. He delighted in sporting bright colors and loved the clothing he saw on military men. Early in 1851 a survey party under the direction of U.S. Commissioner J. R. Bartlett, with John C. Cremony as interpreter, was camped at Santa Rita. Mangas came one day to pay a visit. He was given a gift. Years later, Dilth-cleyhen's mother told her daughter:

"Well, that commissioner liked Mangas. He gave him a suit of blue broadcloth. The coat was lined with scarlet. It had gilt buttons down the front—and gold epaulettes. But Mangas was not entirely satisfied with the outfit. He asked them to slit the trousers of the suit, to slit them from the knee downward to accommodate his moccasins. He needed those moccasins.

"There was a broad strip of scarlet cloth, Mangas's favorite color as you know, on the outer side of the trousers from hip to ankle. The commissioner also gave him a white shirt and a red silk sash to wear."

"How come we never saw him wear it, Shi-ma?"

"Oh, Mangas gambled and lost all but the coat."[54] Then she began to laugh.

"You know, from then on, that old Mangas wore the jacket right over his breechcloth. He wore it so that the sleeve with its gold buttons hung like a tail behind him. It was a very fancy breechcloth, indeed!"

The high-topped buckskin moccasins were an essential part of Apache attire, not only for men, but for women and walking children. The footgear was so practical that even some white men such as Gen. George Crook adopted it. The turned-up toe designated the wearer as Chiricahua rather than Mescalero. The toe was a useful feature, permitting the foot to grow longer, serving to lessen tripping when walking on rough ground, and having greater lasting value in the rocky terrain. Although these "boots" could be worn full length, like leggings, they were usually shortened by making a horizontal fold or two along the length, the folds being held in place by wrapping the leg with a leather thong. Within these folds one could carry a knife or other useful objects. But the "moccasin with a nose" took long hours to make and required an entire buckskin. The sole was of heavy rawhide from the thick neck part of the skin.

With a sharp and sturdy knife Dilth-cleyhen's mother cut the sole to fit the wearer's foot. It included the extension of the circular half-dollar-size nosepiece. Then she cut the backs and sides of the footgear from well-tanned, thin, soft buckskin. She sewed the pieces together with an awl and sinew, taking care to stitch only midway into the sole, from the inside, so that the stitching was invisible. Before the white man brought steel, awls were made from a sharpened piece of the hard, brittle leg bone of the deer. Sinew from any large game would serve, but the best came from the loin of the deer. The seams of the moccasin were always inside. If there were time, and if beads were available, she completed the boots by adding designs.

Dilth-cleyhen's mother always helped Victorio with the making of certain of his war gear. No Apache male ever sewed, although he might make emergency repairs when alone and away from camp. When he needed a new quiver or bow cover, he asked his wife to prepare the buckskin. He then cut the pieces and gave them back to her for stitching and decoration, if any.

Dilth-cleyhen long remembered one incident concerning moccasins.

Victorio and his warriors had raided a very small wagon train, one with only two wagons. It was carrying groceries and dress material to Monticello. But it had not yet reached its destination and so was fair game.

He brought back one of the wagons to his ranchería.[55]

"This is your first booty to divide, my daughter," he said to Dilth-cleyhen. "You may take what you want, but be sure to divide it fairly."

It was wonderful. There were bolts and bolts of cloth, all kinds. The girl tore off lengths and passed them to all the women of the camp at Warm Springs.

One old lady was visiting. Dilth-cleyhen gave her a share. It was a beautiful bright red print. The woman was delighted.

"I'm going to tear me off pieces for a dress. I'll sew them together. I'm going to make me a beautiful red dress!" she said.

She paused, rubbing her hand over the cloth. Then, a broad grin on her face, she continued, "And I'm going to have me a new pair of moccasins. But that part" and again, she stopped for a moment as she pointed to the disc-like extension on the boots she wore, "that part, I'm going to cover it with this red material. And then I'm going to get my donkey, and I'm going to ride him down to Monticello. I'm going to ride to town! I'm going to see what the Mexicans and the white people think about my boots and my dress!"

The wickiup filled with laughter, everyone enjoying the thought. Cloth-toed boots, no less!

Although the first few years after the Gadsden Treaty was signed were ones largely of peace for Dilth-cleyhen's family, more and more "incidents" and atrocities began to rock The People, frightening and enraging them. They reacted in ways appropriate to their past, ways the military preferred to misunderstand. Only a few among the whites were sympathetic and helpful—men like Cochise's friend, Thomas Jonathon Jeffords, and later, Gen. George Crook, known to Chiricahuas as "Chief Gray Wolf." Every evening there was talk among the women—and sometimes their men—about what was happening, about raids, waylaid wagon trains, captives, cruelties on both Anglo and Indian sides.

It was 1860. Dilth-cleyhen was going to have her Feast. Indeed, it would be held in the Tres Hermanas Mountains. Already the maiden's mother had taken an eagle feather to the woman she sought as chaperone, the one who would instruct the girl in preparation for womanhood, who would make sure she was blessed by the Mountain Gods. All the traditional Chiricahua foods were being collected and dried. Buckskins for her robes were being tanned. All kin were enlisted to make the celebration memorable even though Victorio was involved with skirmishes with miners on the Mimbres River.

Then came a terrible event in Apache Pass. Apaches refer to it as the "Cut-through-the-tent"[56] or "1860 Tent Affair"; newspaper accounts refer to it under date of February 1861.[57]

Through the grace of Mangas Coloradas, and perhaps even more, of Cochise, the Apache bands adopted a policy of permitting the coaches of the Butterfield Stage Line and freight caravans to pass without attack along the Overland Trail within the Chiricahua Mountains. If at all possible, these Apache leaders wanted peace with Americans.

"We will continue raiding in Mexico for supplies we must have, but we can live here in the retreats that we love if we have a truce with the Anglos." Such was their plan, and Cochise did his best to make friends with drivers and operators at the stage relay station halfway up Apache Pass. The agent there, a man named Wallace, trusted him implicitly. There was no trouble when the leader and a number of families whose men constituted his followers camped near the station. On these occasions, Cochise made sure that Wallace had a steady supply of firewood.

In October of 1860 a group of Indians—not Chiricahuas—carried out a series of raids on settlers along Sonoita Creek. They carried away a boy of eleven, Felix, the adopted son of a squatter, John Ward. Attempts made by the military to recover the child, later known in the Southwest as Mickey Free, were unsuccessful.

Early the next year a young shavetail just out of West Point, 2d-Lt. George Nicholas Bascom, along with fifty-four troopers and an interpeter, arrived at the station with the assigned duty of finding the child. He would not listen to Wallace, who knew the Chiricahuas to be innocent. Instead, he demanded that the agent find Cochise, that the leader come to him.

Cochise appeared under a white flag. Bascom accused him of the raids, the abduction of the boy, and the theft of a number of cattle. Cochise, nearing sixty years of age, calmly denied knowledge of any of the charges.

"You are a liar!" Bascom shouted. He ordered the tent to be surrounded by soldiers, and Cochise was handcuffed.

Many years later, when Dilth-cleyhen described the incident, she told it as follows:

"Those soldiers went about their business. They were black men, buffalo soldiers. They had something to do. Two of Cochise's men crept down the mountainside. They were not going to leave their chief like that! Quietly, they sneaked toward the tent. They slit the tent down its back with a knife. Cochise was free! Off they went, running.

"Just as they reached the foot of the mountain, the soldiers discovered the escape. They went in pursuit, shooting. They shot one of Cochise's men, but the leader could do nothing about it. He had to leave the wounded man there. He ran, dodging in and out of the trees. He heard another gunshot. A black man, a soldier, had killed the disabled Indian.

"Cochise and the man who rescued him joined other Apaches up there in the mountains. They waited. They hid in the dark.

"The next morning, very early, they returned to the scene of the shooting. The same black man was on duty. Our men took him. They tied his wrists together and his ankles. They tied another rope between his hands and still another between his ankles.

"Then they hauled him to an ant hill. They laid him on top and gagged him.

"Oh, that day was *real* hot! The sun just beat down on the mound. Our men loosened the clothing of that soldier so the ants could have easy entry. And you know the way ants begin to sting when they can't get out. Well, the ants got inside his clothing and started stinging that black man. The gag prevented him from yelling. And they stung him, and stung him until he died."

When Dilth-cleyhen told the story, her audience laughed and laughed.[58] They laughed at the black soldiers. They laughed at the stupidity of Bascom. The story was repeated many times. Years later Dilth-cleyhen's daughter Beshád-e told it, and so did Arnold Kinzhuma, Beshád-e's husband. It always brought laughter—and disguised bitterness.

"Some of those white people, they blamed us for everything bad that happened to them. It didn't matter whether we had anything to do with it."

But, back then, peace was broken. The Indians attacked the mail coach; they confiscated supply trains; everywhere raids increased, as did deaths on both sides. Often Dilth-cleyhen's family was "on the run."

1861 was a year of relative tranquillity for the Tchi-héne. On the whole there were fewer soldiers in the Southwest. In many valleys white settlers had no military protection. Many of them departed, fearing for their lives, leaving stock and crops behind. Mines were

deserted. "There is war between the states." This announcement
puzzled the Apaches. "The whites are fighting one another!" No
matter, The People were free for a time to follow their traditional
ways.

The family gave Dilth-cleyhen her da-i-dá. They presented a long,
dark eagle feather with just a tip of white to the respected woman
who would be the maiden's sponsor, who would watch over her,
guide her steps, lecture her about the duties of becoming a good
wife and mother, who would massage her, feed her ritual foods, and
pray for future health and long life.

The family went to Basketmaker. They requested that a special
bowl-like basket be made, one that would hold sacred objects—
pollen, ocher, a deer-hoof rattle, a bundle of grama grass—all important for the girl's well-being. It would be placed on the ground
to mark the turning point of Dilth-cleyhen's four runs toward the
east and back to her attendant, one of whose names is "she who trots
them off." Another of the woman's names is "she who makes the
sound," for, whenever the name of a supernatural is pronounced
during the ceremony, the chaperone utters the high-pitched cry distinctive of the rite. It is the sound that was made by White-Painted-
Woman when Child-of-the-Water returned to her after defeating the
monsters.[59]

Dilth-cleyhen's grandmother made a long strand of "beads" consisting of four rows of bones, close together, each bone being five
inches long. This would be centered at the back of her granddaughter's neck, the two end panels pendant on her breast. At the end of
each wide strand was a piece of beaded buckskin and four tin jingles.

Grandmother fastened together two soft, white, fluffy eagle feathers and tied on a bit of white wampum. This would adorn her Dilth-
cleyhen's long, flowing hair, shiny from its washing in the suds of
yucca root. She made sure there was a proper drinking tube. The
maiden's lips must not touch water. Most important of all, the old
lady made Dilth-cleyhen's buckskin robe, with its long fringes and
design of beads. She fashioned the boots with the nose. She made
sure there was plenty of pollen.

Friends from all three bands were invited.

Dilth-cleyhen was solemn and impressive. Her head held high and
tilted in a manner characteristic of female kin-to-come, she followed
her chaperone's directions. At the bidding of their singer, the Mountain Gods blessed her; she in turn blessed The People who stood in
line, waiting their turn to be marked with pollen.

Songs were sung throughout the ceremony. One such is given
here:

In the east,
The White Painted Woman, when she is walking
    in accordance with the pollen of the dawn,
The White Painted Woman is happy over it,
She is thankful for it.
In the south,
She is walking in accordance with the sun's tassels;
Long life!
From this, there is good,
In the west,
When the pollen of the abalone shell moves
    with her, there is good;
Long life!
If she lives in accordance with it, there is good.
In the north,
She is the sister of the White-Painted-Woman;
When she is walking in accordance with this,
    there is good.
She is looking at her,
She is happy over it,
She is thankful for it.[60]

During her four runs around the basket of sacred objects, Dilth-cleyhen moved with fleetness rarely seen. Not once did she falter at the turn—not on the first morning of the Feast, not on the last.

Each night there was much dancing. The Mountain Gods and the Clown returned, lending supernatural sanction to the Feast.

Dilth-cleyhen *was* White-Painted-Woman, the mother of Child-of-the-Water. She was no longer a child.

In years to come, Dilth-cleyhen commented, "At the time of my Feast, it was then that our family first used white flour to make our bread. Before then, we used ground corn."

Trouble in Apachería

The decade following her Feast in 1861 was difficult for Dilth-cleyhen and The People. What they had hoped was a permanent return to the times in which they alone had ruled their home-land—and a response by Yusen to their prayers that the In-dáh would disappear—proved to be transitory illusion. Settlers and miners slowly filtered back, including military men under the command of the hated Gen. James H. Carleton. He was determined to annihilate all red men. Atrocities, acts of revenge and hatred, all kinds of tragedies began to occur in seemingly endless succession.

In order to provide better defense against the intruders, Mangas Coloradas and Cochise joined forces. Victorio, too, was often among their ranks; he learned from Mangas and served as second in command in raids or battles. His own following was growing.

Bi-duyé was rarely with his family, nor were other Chiricahua males. He visited his ranchería primarily to obtain supplies, to repair weapons, to make ready for the next foray—and to see to the horses.

Horses had been considered "wealth," part of the bride price, among Apaches for as long as The People could remember. They first saw the animals as early as the seventeenth century, perhaps earlier, and recognized their value to a nomadic hunting society.[61] Now horses were the cherished prize in most raids. Rapid escape from scalpers and soldiers was crucial; the mounts must be strong and swift. If they were lame or getting old, they and mules were slaughtered and eaten. Protein was becoming more and more scarce. There was no time for hunting deer and antelope; such game had fast diminished with the entry of the whites. Horses must be at the peak of performance. Their hooves must be hard. To make them so took work.

Victorio mixed the liver of a deer with ashes or with powdered limestone, stirring it into a paste and applying it to the hooves of horses, mules, and burros. After the first layer dried, others were added. Eventually a crust formed, rock hard. "It's almost as good as a white man's horseshoe," he noted. Sometimes animals needed even more protection.

"My wife," Bi-duyé inquired, "do you have some good rawhide?"

If her reply were positive, and she had skins of cow, horse, or deer, he cut them into circular pieces. These he fashioned into pouches that fit over the hooves of his steeds and were held tight by a rawhide drawstring.[62]

"We'll be going over hot sands and rocky boulders. Their feet must be protected. We have no time for a limping horse."

However, there was time for a ceremony before each raid in search of new mounts. There were prayers and songs supervised by a shaman with horse power.[63]

More and more often The People were hungry simply because the enemy was in the vicinity and they felt it wisest not make the usual treks for food and game. "They'll know exactly where we are. We've been camping there for years." Out of necessity, the raids then increased.

The Apaches began taking sheep from the Mexicans of Old Mexico. They herded the stolen animals into an oblong pattern, never wider than thirty feet, but as long as necessary. The sheep were kept in order by lashing the strongest together with yucca fiber, two by two. These formed a living fence on each long side of the flock; none of the animals could stray. Drivers strode or rode along each side and behind them. Two young men were at the head and set the pace. They drove night and day, sometimes moving as far as fifty miles before stopping. That was as much as even hardy sheep could stand. On particularly rewarding raids as many as several thousand animals were moved hundreds of miles in this way.[64] Sheep pelts were useful as seats, as padding for beds, and as saddle blankets. The meat of sheep was succulent.

Sometimes the Apaches took count of their booty, tying knots in lengths of yucca fiber or other string, each knot designating five or ten units—in this case, sheep. Occasionally there were many knots before the tally was complete. More than one Mexican hacienda was destroyed, its entire herd driven north.

The Apaches differentiated between their raids and their wars. Raids were crucial for Apache economy; war was to *kill* the enemy and escape unscathed. Retreat was no disgrace; it was necessary. The object was to destroy the enemy without death to a single Indian. Tchi-héně adult males were warriors, each having an individual strategy within a general plan suggested by a leader whose followers had a "say" in council. Each man could decide whether or not he wanted to join in an attack. How different was the role of Anglo soldiers, whose every move was dictated!

Women of every camp had a voice concerning the raids.

"My husband, we are nearly out of food. It's time you bring something in. I think you need to go down to Old Mexico. Those farmers down there have canned goods. Take some of that—and get some mules, some beef," Dilth-cleyhen heard her mother say.[65] The meat of mules was prized.

Newspapers of the 1860s and 1870s in Arizona Territory contained "how to's." One such article, written by the editor, described the best way to kill an Indian. It suggested that prospectors or ranchers "carry brown sugar, mixed with strychnine in quarter-pound cakes, wrapped up with crackers in a roll, on the cantle of the saddle."[66] When pursued by Indians, one was advised to cut loose the poisoned sugar and crackers. Then, one could return in an hour or so to collect a "crop of hair."

Thus the public press engendered hatred of Apaches, encouraging even more Anglo cruelty and deceit than the Indians had experienced before. The latter retaliated in kind, attacking ranches and slaying or making captive the occupants. More than one prospector was tortured slowly to death. Wagon trains and stage coaches were ambushed and burned. It was impossible for stockmen to maintain herds on Chiricahua land. The intrusive mines near Santa Rita were raided and all personnel slain.

A few towns, such as the Mexican Monticello, were fortunate. Victorio and the Warm Springs band had friends there, and these villagers were exempt from trouble.

Then in 1863 Mangas Coloradas was murdered.

There are various accounts of the event, but the one[67] believed by Dilth-cleyhen's parents was as follows. It was the story told to them late in January by a visiting brave from Mangas's camp, who had heard it from a man by the name of Daniel Conner, an eyewitness.

"Well, it seems that an old mountain man was prospecting near Piños Altos. He decided he needed an Apache hostage in order to get his party through our homeland. His group and some soldiers managed to capture our chief. It went like this. They carried a white flag, and Mangas trusted them. They tied him up. They took him at gunpoint to Fort McLane,[68] right there by Santa Rita. The soldier in charge demanded that Mangas be shot. He probably thought he would get a big promotion if he got rid of the leader.

"That night the guards tormented our chief by heating the end of a bayonet in the fire until it became white-hot, then they thrust it into Mangas's leg. He leaped up. Gunshots rang out. The other soldiers fired their revolvers into him.[69] They shot him then and there."

Victorio and his wife were silent as they listened, although Biduyés eyes grew deeper black.

"Conner said nobody did anything to the guards. And he said that the report from the military to the heads in Washington was that they had had to shoot Mangas—because he was escaping.

"But that is not the worst. The next morning, the soldiers cut off Mangas's head. They put it in boiling water. No one can find it now."

"Could it be that someone witched Mangas—someone jealous witched him so that this terrible thing would happen?" Such were the unspoken thoughts of Dilth-cleyhen. So many terrible things were occurring. "Could it be some powerful witch?"

That night, toward dusk, there was the sound of women's keening near the trees. The ranchería was in mourning. Choking rage seethed in Victorio's breast.

Distrust built up among the Apaches. Even a flag of truce meant nothing to the whites. Cochise sought immediate revenge.

Victorio, whose influence had been steadily increasing in these years, shared leadership of the Mimbres with his cousin Loco. Later, when the band was forced to remove from Warm Springs camp and go to the reservation at San Carlos, Nana shared with Victorio the honors of directing the actions of the group. Carl Mangas, the son of Chief Mangas Coloradas, was only twenty-three at the time of his father's death; the young man was neither ready for, nor inclined toward, such responsibility. He was too genial, too kindhearted, even though he was a highly courageous, lithe, and skillful man.

The Chiricahuas fought back fiercely after the heinous crime, filling the countryside with fear, leaving their capable wives to feed the children and keep the camps in order. There were many war dances and some victory celebrations. Considerable keening was heard at early dawn and dusk.

Sometimes women and youngsters accompanied their warriors part way on their ventures, but before the battle or raid took place, the men made sure their dependents were sequestered safely. If the fighters had business at one of the many forts that sprang up during the 1860s and 1870s—Fort Apache, Fort Bayard, Fort McLane, Fort Craig (just east of Camp Ojo Caliente), Fort Tularosa, Fort Webster, Fort West (north of Silver City), and still others [70]—they left their wives in a camp at a reasonable distance, guarded by vigilant elders, or even by some of the women, all of whom were skilled in defensive arts.

The Apaches were able and elusive but also apprehensive, alert, and fearful. They listened for the crackle within the underbrush; they scanned the trunk of every tree. They watched for smoke signals to learn their allies' whereabouts, to ascertain what to expect from the enemy.

The signal was made with a wet saddle blanket over a fire—a series of dots and dashes in smoke. High on the timbered slopes or from a bluff of any kind, slender columns of gray arose, silhouetted against the blue of the sky. First, the men burned a small handful of dry grass and twigs, then added wood. When the flames were sufficiently high, green grass or other plant life was thrown on the blaze until the thin line of smoke rose higher and higher. The wet saddle blanket was wielded so as to interrupt the ascent of the smoke and create the visual code that only the Indians could decipher.[71]

When battles or raids were about to begin, every adult prayed to the powers that each possessed. Everyone was careful not to offend the supernatural—or a human witch.

Lozen, Little Sister, sometimes came home with Victorio from his various forays. Dilth-cleyhen loved seeing her. More often now, the warriors needed the seer's powers of discernment. She went with them whenever she could, being as close to her brother, despite their respect relationship, as he was to Loco or Nana. Frequently she stayed in his camp where he could take full advantage of her extraordinary skills. Her importance increased with every success she predicted. She attended each war ceremony.

On such occasions Dilth-cleyhen and her mother sat in the circle, listening as each man's name was called. Every time now, they heard "Lozen!"

Dilth-cleyhen asked, "What exactly does she do?"

"She has power. It is very strong power, stronger than most. That power permits her to see the enemy. She can tell where the enemy is. Then Victorio can plan a suitable strategy."

Lozen was spiritual. She was magnificent on a horse. She could handle her rifle as well as any man, most of whom she could outrun on foot. She wielded her knife with utmost skill. Raiding males gave her a name, "Dextrous Horse Thief,"[72] others called her simply "Warrior Woman."[73]

Little Sister devoted her life to helping Victorio.

Between battles, when in camp, she did routine women's chores. Further, Warrior Woman was particularly mindful of the horses, their hooves, and their legs.

Lozen never married. There are unauthenticated stories[74] explaining why she remained a spinster in a society whose ideal woman is a wife and mother.

"It seems when she was very young, warriors reported seeing a man they called Gray Ghost. He rode alone and could not be approached. He was very large, very powerful. One time three warriors saw him pursued by enemy soldiers. They pointed out a secret hiding place, and he went there. When the soldiers gave up, he came to our camp here at Warm Springs. He visited. He told Victorio he was a chief from far toward the east, the rising sun.

"Then a wagon with a twelve-man guard came through our territory. There was a driver and an old woman and a very beautiful young woman as well. They were not Mexican, but they spoke Spanish or a Mexican Indian tongue. When they moved west, Gray Ghost followed.

"From that time forward, no other man interested Lozen. Although she was just a girl when she saw that stranger, he was the only one she fell in love with."

Dilth-cleyhen's mother laughed as she told the story. She added, "I think that Gray Ghost was Gray Wolf, that chief of the Seneca tribe who came here once from the east. He was looking for a place here in the west for his people, and he stayed with us. When he left, I know that Lozen was brokenhearted."

No one ever resented Lozen's going with the warriors. Her power was invaluable. Holding her arms high above her head, hands cupped, with her face directed toward the heavens, she prayed to Yusen, saying, "I search for the enemy."

"I see as one from a height sees in every direction." Then she moved in a circle until the palms of her hands felt a tingling sensation. They changed in color, becoming almost purple when she detected the enemy and calculated their distance from the braves.

When fighters were wounded, she used her powers of healing on the battlefield. When in camps, she visited the older shamans, the medicine men, to learn from them. She traveled into the mountains; she fasted and prayed to increase her power.

Although Lozen's place in Victorio's battle ranks was unique, there were other women, mostly widows, but some faithful married women, who might accompany their men to war. They fought ferociously when necessary. A few among them became messengers and emissaries between Apache warriors and Anglo military men; General Crook realized their abilities and used them efficiently. There were other females who more and more often served as sentinels. "Pretty Mouth" has been cited as having had the power to escape injury to herself. Was this Pretty Mouth the woman known also as Huera, the belligerent wife of Carl Mangas? We cannot now be sure. James Kawaykla reported that several of his female relatives had unusual powers of healing and escape.[75]

Among women there were shamans whose abilities were of a different kind, whose powers extended to skills involving obstetrics.

In the very near future, Victorio's daughter would join their ranks. Thus, she acquired her "permanent" name, Dilth-cleyhen, meaning "those ladies who place babies in the blanket." Many pregnant women would seek her services when about to deliver.

Some time during those troubled years that followed her Feast, Dilth-cleyhen married a warrior who supported Victorio. His name is now forgotten. He had presented many horses as a gift when he requested the hand of the leader's daughter.

The couple set up camp near her parents. Within a year or so, in 1870, their first child, Beshád-e, was born.

The baby was adored by the womenfolk, as well might be expected. She saw little of her father, who most times was engaged in preparations for departure or was gone on ambush or raid. It was not a period of plenty for the Tchi-héne. Often The People were hungry; game was scarce.

Beshád-e was still in her cradleboard when her father was killed.

He had raided a nearby ranch for livestock, trying to provide meat for his family. Somehow the rancher had suspected something wrong and had been prepared for the attack. There were gunshots, and the infant's father fell.

Others in the raiding party returned. They came to Dilth-cleyhen.

"Your man is gone. He died bravely, killing several before that fatal bullet struck."

"Aye-yaaa!" cried Dilth-cleyhen in mourning. She loved this man, her first husband, and they had but one child. She cut her hair; she keened to the heavens. The new widow called on the services of a medicine man. He blessed her and Beshád-e. He chased away the ghost.

Early in the 1870s, it became obvious that Carleton's extermination policy was a failure. On July 21, 1871, President Ulysses S. Grant appointed Vincent Colyer as his personal representative. He sent him to the Southwest with plenary powers to locate the various nomadic tribes on suitable territories. He wanted them brought under the control of proper officers of an Indian department.[76]

When informed of this, the Apaches held council in Warm Springs. Cochise came to visit Bi-duyé's ranchería. They talked.

"I hear there is a new general here in the Southwest. I've heard he is a good man, one we can trust. I hope so. His name is Crook, George Crook. He has been getting pack trains together, and he has come to us, seeking Apaches and Indians from other tribes to act as Scouts, to help rout us out of our mountain retreats," Cochise informed Victorio.

Victorio already knew. "Yes, I heard he asked some women to make him Chiricahua boots. He seems to have a better understanding of all humanity." Now, about this Vincent Colyer . . . shall we go along with him?"

Later that night Bi-duyé talked the matter over with his sister, Lozen. He talked it over with his wife. "I think we should listen to the peace commissioner who is supposed to come here."

Gen. Gordon Granger arrived at the Cañada Alamosa early in September. Cochise was also there, and other, minor leaders. The first offer to the Apaches was a reservation in the very valley in which the conference was held. This was acceptable. Actually, Camp Ojo Caliente, west of Fort Craig, had been in existence for a dozen years.[77]

Cochise spoke: "When I was young, I walked all over this country, east and west, and saw no other people than the Apaches. After many summers I walked again and found another race of people who had come to take it. How is it? Why is it that the Apaches want to die—that they carry their lives on their finger nails? They roam over the hills and plains and want the heavens to fall on them. The Apaches were once a great nation; they are now but a few. . . . Many have been killed in battle." And he turned to the commissioner, "Tell me, if the Virgin Mary has walked throughout all the land, why has she never entered the lodge of the Apache?"[78]

The Apaches accepted the direction of the military command at Warm Springs. Early the following year, they planted corn, squash, beans, and other crops, making a genuine effort to comply with the regulations and suggestions of the whites. The men performed the strenuous manual labor in the fields; simple weeding and planting of seeds were women's chores.

Victorio's ranchería went well for a brief period.

He had taken a third wife, one much younger than the others, and the full sister of his second.

Early in January 1872 a son was born to Wife Three. He became known as Charlie Istee. He was the half-brother of Dilth-cleyhen but was younger even than her daughter Beshád-e, who was as yet in her cradleboard. Unfortunately, Charlie's mother never fully recovered from his birth, and she died in a few weeks, even though Dilth-cleyhen had attended her and used all her powers.

As custom dictated, the motherless baby was cared for by Victorio's Wife Two who lived adjacent to her sister.

Shortly after the death, Victorio and some friends went hunting. All the women left behind in Ojo Caliente were pursuing their various daily tasks and visiting, unaware of danger. A few of them left the vicinity of the camp in order to find the succulent roots they hungered for. Suddenly, gunshots rang out. The women fell, Wife Two among them. Why! No one ever knew. Their scalps were untouched.

When Victorio returned, women and children were crying.

Dilth-cleyhen and her baby were safe, but she was inconsolable. Already she had shorn her locks in mourning. She had loved her co-wives, had depended on them for company and for help in gathering tasks.

An aunt, a distant relative of Wife Two, sent for little Charlie. "I'll care for him," she had told her husband, who came for the boy. He relayed the message.

Victorio's response to the tragedy was immediate. He resumed his rampages throughout the countryside.

It may be that this behavior, seen as savage, unruly rebellion by most Anglos, contributed to the acceleration of earlier decisions to put the Apaches under stricter supervision. "Concentration of the red men is what we need!" All reservations had long been under the jurisdiction of the Department of the Interior, whose Bureau of Indian Affairs put new policies to work,[79] and The People at Ojo Caliente were ordered to the newly established Fort Tularosa.

Early Reservations: Confinement and Flight

Fort Tularosa and the Tularosa Reservation were one place Cochise had sworn never to go. He kept his oath. When the order came, he rebelled and took to the Mogollon Mountains, continuing his war against the invaders of his homeland.

Victorio, too, refused at first. When he talked to the members of his family, including Dilth-cleyhen, he said, "They are threatening to cut off all our rations. Let them!"

His daughter was less sure; she had an infant to feed, and she told him so. Nonetheless, he put on a defiant front when facing the whites: "Take your rations! Feed them to the bears and wolves! We can get along without![80]

"We won't go to Tularosa. It is far too cold there to grow corn, and although we are a mountain people, we plant some crops—essential crops."

There were more Indian councils. Victorio mounted his horse and made a cursory survey of Tularosa. "It may be all right," he commented on his return.

The move began in late May 1872.

It was seventy miles from Cañada Alamosa to Tularosa the way the crow flies. It was perhaps one-third farther the way the Apaches went. About fifty or sixty aged, women, and children rode in some twenty wagons escorted by sixteen Eighth Cavalry troopers. Dilth-cleyhen and her baby were among them. Most of the remainder, an estimated three hundred followers of Victorio, Loco, and Gordo—Gordo was a Mogollon—accompanied by Thomas Jeffords, Cochise's friend, crossed the mountains on horseback or on foot. They crossed a spur of the San Mateos and the northern Mimbres Range, passed south of the Luera Mountains and the crest of the Elks, down into the forested valley of the Tularosa where the Agency was almost complete.[81]

Dilth-cleyhen knew that the move had been a difficult decision for her father. She was proud that he cared so much for the ultimate welfare of his people. She knew he would do most anything, aside from tarnishing his honor, to guide them wisely.[82]

Staying in Tularosa proved difficult. It was entirely remote from civilization of any kind. Nights were bitterly cold. The People demanded to return to the area of Warm Springs. There was general discontent for nearly two years. A number of Indians simply fled, or went on raids, traveling through the Chiricahua reserve down into Sonora, once again stealing livestock, women, and youngsters.[83]

While living in Tularosa, or perhaps shortly before, Dilth-cleyhen remarried. Her husband's name, once again, is unknown. It was not spoken after his death. Was he called Chestuan? That is the word associated with their baby, who was yet to come. Life was easier with a strong man around; all too soon her groom left with other raiders heading for Old Mexico. "We need so many things," he had consoled her. He did not return. "That man met with gunshot," survivors of the disaster told her.

"Aye-yaaa!" Dilth-cleyhen keened, as did other women who had lost kin.

She was several months pregnant when Victorio came to her. Her father did not know she was expecting a child. It is not the Apache way to talk about such things. Not even her husband had guessed. His death had come too soon.

In his arms Victorio held a naked, wide-eyed boy of about one year, his prolific hair standing in every direction.

"This is my little Charlie, Charlie Istee," her father said. "His aunt is ill, and he is homeless. Her husband brought him to me. Can you care for him?"

Without hesitation Dilth-cleyhen agreed, although she knew caring for another child might be difficult. She felt nauseated in the mornings.

"Of course I will take him. He will be as my own."

She rubbed the boy's back. He stared at her, not sure he wanted to smile. Dilth-cleyhen noted that the dark spot, the Mongolian spot, that appears in the sacro-lumbar region of Apache infants, had all but disappeared. "You are growing up, little Charlie," she said. Very shortly, when she held her arms to him, he entered willingly.

"We'll manage," she said aloud. Already, Beshád-e was tugging on her skirts, wanting to be held too. "Beshád-e, my three-year-old, you are going to have to grow up fast. I'll need lots of help." She patted the girl on the head.

She made a request, "My daughter, find a blanket of some kind. Little Charlie is going to live with us. He feels cold. I need to wrap him up."

And thus it came to be that her toddler—walking child lost the pampered status of babyhood and assumed responsibility. "Don't be jealous," the girl was told.

In about six months Dilth-cleyhen gave birth to Elsie Vance Chestuan. The year was 1873. The new mother sighed. Now she must stand in line to obtain enough rations for five. Fortunately, there was plenty of beef, plenty of coffee, plenty of issue corn. To this was added, eventually, some flour and sugar.

"I don't know about that corn. Too many of the women are using it to make tulapai," she reported to Victorio. "Too many people won't eat the food we get here and drink instead. Without food, the tulapai makes them disgusting. They fight and cause trouble." Victorio was all too aware of the problem, although most of the imbibers avoided him, knowing his attitude about drunkenness. Dilth-cleyhen continued.

"The only way they use that white man's coffee is in trade—and no one is making the slightest attempt to raise crops, either. It is a good thing there is a little mescal to gather and some nuts from the piñon tree."[84]

Life eased for Dilth-cleyhen when her father came to her and told her, "A great man has asked to marry you. He has brought me horses."

Dilth-cleyhen asked, "Yes, who is this man?" Within her heart she knew and was pleased. It was Carl Mangas, the son of the great chief, Mangas Coloradas.

Carl Mangas, two years Dilth-cleyhen's senior, was not huge like his father. He was a kind man with a broad smile and a general philosophy of peace. He would make a good husband and father. He hunted well. Dilth-cleyhen's memories took her back to the days of her Puberty Feast when she remembered the tall, gangly teenager who sometimes accompanied Red Sleeves.

"I agree to marry him," she told her father. Later, she expressed reservations, not enough to cancel the agreement, but one problem in particular that rankled. She would be Mangas's second wife. He was married to a woman by the name of Huera, a real troublemaker. She was always flaunting her independence and making tulapai. Mangas had tired of her tirades, and rarely were they together.

Huera was later called Francesca by the Mexicans who captured her. She insisted her name meant "White Face," but that her Chiricahua name was Tzé-gu-júni or "Pretty Mouth."[85] She wielded influence periodically on Mangas's and Geronimo's decisions throughout her lifetime, and she served as a trusted interpreter for John Gregory Bourke. She would not be an enjoyable co-wife, and it is doubtful that Mangas consulted her before marrying Dilth-cleyhen.

Shortly after Mangas and his new wife began living together, the two-year-old Asa (Ace) Daklugie was added to the household. He was the youngest son of Chief Juh, the Net'na, and needed parenting. Further, Dilth-cleyhen gave birth in rapid succession to Cora (1874), Faith and Flora (whose exact dates of birth are unknown), and Frank (1876).[86] Beshád-e's duties as a child-surrogate-mother increased accordingly.

At Tularosa the depredations of the Apaches against neighboring homesteaders continued, and many thefts were blamed on the Apaches for which they were not responsible. Even Victorio became defiant. From time to time he, too, escaped the reservation, coming back only when he was ready. The women, and certainly those with children, could not leave so easily, but on occasion even they packed and left, leaving only their wickiups. General unrest and unhappiness were the rule. Occasionally, Victorio took his gun, mounted his horse, and rode to confer with Cochise, still in a mountain retreat the whereabouts of which were unknown to the soldiers.

All during 1873 attempts were made by Maj. William Redwood Price to settle mutinies and to find a new location for the Mimbres Indians.[87] Further, Tularosa had proved to be incredibly expensive, with all its cargo freighted in from towns along the Rio Grande. It was decided to transfer The People back to Ojo Caliente. The move was accomplished in 1874, the year of Cora Mangas's birth; the fort at Tularosa was permanently closed, leaving an unpleasant memory for all concerned.

Barely had Dilth-cleyhen's family returned to the Warm Springs area when the sad news arrived of Cochise's death that June.[88] A friend from among his people brought them word.

"It was in our camp on top of a high butte. We could see the surrounding valley as far as the Chiricahua Mountains on the east, and the Dragoons on the west—and as far as eyesight would permit on south and north. The chief lay down where he could see all approaches to his camp, his face toward the east. He suffered intensely. Toward the end he was unconscious for several hours during the night.

"His friend Agent Thomas Jeffords came to see him. He was with Levi Edwin Dudley, superintendent of Indian Affairs for New Mexico. They came twice.

"The second time they came, Cochise was mounted on his horse in front of his wickiup. Some of us lifted him there. He told us, 'I want to get on my horse one last time before I die.'"

There was a long period of silence as Victorio, Mangas, Lozen, and Dilth-cleyhen thought about Cochise, his strength of character, his determination, his dignity.

"We are sure that our chief's illness was caused by a witch. Taza and a group of us—a twenty-seven-man war party—went to Dudley a few days after his visit to our ranchería, and we told him so. We told him we were going to find that witch and make him cure our leader. Dudley asked what we would do if he couldn't. We told him clearly just what we planned. If his medicines were not successful, we would hang him upside down from a tree and light a fire beneath his head. We would burn that witch to death."

Dilth-cleyhen nodded her approval.

"We found that witch all right. We tied him on his horse and took him back with us.

"The witch was not successful. Our chief died in just a few days. Now we plan to follow his eldest son, Taza. That is what Cochise wanted. Taza is a good man and gets along with whites. He will keep peace if it is possible."

There was keening at the end of the story; there was keening at night. Another great leader was gone. Anglos speculated that the illness was due to cancer, but who knows?

In fact, although a man of principle, Taza was not the dynamic chief The People needed. Leadership among all the Apaches shifted steadily in favor of Victorio. Fewer went with Loco now. Short stands were led by any number of men. Hostiles listened to Geronimo.

Again the stay at Ojo Caliente was a good one for Dilth-cleyhen. Mangas was often hunting; occasionally he went on a raid. She gathered native foods whenever she could.

"One time," Dilth-cleyhen related many, many years later to her great-granddaughter Narcissus, "we were out gathering mesquite beans. We were going to be there a week or so, so we built wickiups, a lot of us women. Suddenly there was a surprise attack, and soldiers began shooting at us. Somebody grabbed Cora, who was in her cradle. I grabbed Charlie Istee with one hand. With the other I pulled the canvas cover off our wickiup. We just started running. I dashed for a knoll nearby. We barely got away. We kept on running until we were on the other side of a hill. There was no more shooting. We made it to safety.

"It's a good thing I grabbed that covering. We really made use of it the next day. It rained."

There were other episodes and customs that Dilth-cleyhen was later to relate. Often when Victorio was going to visit the Mescalero Apaches to the east, he suggested that his daughter's family accompany him. The women did not go all the way, but stayed by the Rio Grande, where they had camped. All water is sacred, but the Rio Grande is especially so. When Dilth-cleyhen approached it, she prayed. She knew stories about supernaturals concerned with water. Four times she dipped her cupped hands into a place where the stream was still; she splashed the coolness on her face and prayed again.

If for any reason it was necessary to cross the turbulent, muddy tributary, prayers were more urgent. "May I cross safely. May the water be not too deep. May it flow around me, and not carry me away." Then she knelt and started digging in the earth with a stout stick. She removed her jewelry and buried it deep—silver rings made by the Navaho, earrings, beads of shell and turquoise. But not the red and white bean necklace that served as a safeguard. All else was buried in the earth where she might retrieve it on her return.

Sometimes there were excursions by the family into the homeland areas farther south. Dilth-cleyhen taught Beshád-e more about the Mountain Gods' home, about the lake, about the origins of all things around them. "You must teach your daughters too," she instructed.

Many years later, when Dilth-cleyhen was an elderly woman on the reservation in Mescalero, she and the friends who had been her companions during the uncertain days of the warpath got together. They reminisced. The following is a story they related in whispers, as though they still feared retribution.[89]

"At that particular time, Chatto and Carl and a lot of others, including that Tzoe, the one called 'Peaches' because of his pale cheeks, all went raiding all the time; they went all over the southern part of our homeland. One day they saw a little dust rising on the road between Clifton and Silver City, New Mexico. As they rode closer, they saw it was just one family, so they decided to go over and take it. They were just going to take the horses or supplies—whatever items they could find that the ladies in camp would like.

"Well, a skirmish developed. There was an exchange of shots. The man driving the buggy was later learned to be a federal judge, an H. C. McComas. He was killed. So was his wife. The warriors captured the boy and brought him back home to their wives.

"Well, it didn't take long for news of the killings to reach General Crook. He sent troops after us, but only Peaches was captured, and he blamed Old Man Chatto."

Sometimes Chatto was present when the old people were talking. So was Rogers To-clanny. Rogers spoke.

"I knew that boy. He became just like one of us. When he grew up, we called him 'Red Beard.'

"Well, we liked him when he was a boy, and we thought he might like to return to his own people. We took him down to a little town down there in Mexico and left him. But he came back. He walked all the way back to be with us Chiricahuas. We took him twice, and he came back twice.

"We really wished he would stay down there. We liked him, but when we found out his father was a federal judge, we were really scared. Crook wasn't going to like that! Crook was a good man and fair—but a *federal* judge! That boy's red hair was a real giveaway.

"Anyway, you remember how he grew up with us. He could fight and raid just like an Apache. When he was a man, his beard came in red.

"He began to like one of our Indian girls. But one of our warriors—one who is now gone—liked the same girl. The two men were jealous of each other. They had a fight, and the warrior stabbed Red Beard, who died.

"Well, during that fight, some soldiers arrived on the scene. Everybody in the camp began to run. Then, when things were quiet, and the military had left, the Indians went back and buried Red Beard."

Then Chatto continued.

"Those soldiers came back later. They arrested the girl that Red Beard liked. They took her to a jail down near El Paso. She was there for about a month and wouldn't eat or talk.

"So the soldiers came and got me. They wanted me to talk to her. So I did. She began to talk, and she began to eat. She took the soldiers back to the place the fight had taken place. They dug up the grave, and sure enough, there he was—that Red Beard."

Dilth-cleyhen laughed. "Well, you two are lucky they didn't take you to jail. You two—both of you—who were Scouts for General Crook. So was that Peaches."

Of all the white men with whom the Tchi-héné had contact, the universal favorite was General Crook. He had arrived in the area of the Apache homeland in June 1871. Although he knew little about the Chiricahua tribe at that time, he was humane and honorable. He began studying the Indians, trying to understand them. First, he made a systematic inspection of the military posts. He took un-marked trails, listening to civilians as well as army personnel. Each gave him but one side of the problems to be faced.

"Crook thought we were just vermin in those early days," laughed Lozen.

In time he developed the tactics that made him a successful Indian fighter—and champion of Indian rights.

"He got rid of all those clumsy supply wagons. He used mule pack trains, and he himself rode a mule. He even made the troopers walk when that was necessary instead of riding horses in a column that made an easy target for our bows and arrows," added Victorio. "And then he enlisted Indian Scouts—even some Apaches—for trailing us. They know how to find our retreats, how to follow our trail. They knew how to fight us. He grew smart, that Crook.

"And through the Apache Scouts, he learned that we are an honorable people, that we keep our word. He learned that we are loyal to our friends, not savages without morals.

"When he was trying to recruit Scouts, Crook said he wanted the wildest among us."[90]

Dilth-cleyhen thought aloud, "When I saw him, he was tall, over six feet, and broad-shouldered. His face was stern. He had narrow, blue-gray eyes set deep within his face, a sharp nose, and bushy burn-sides. Do you remember, my father?

"He didn't look like a soldier. He was wearing Chiricahua boots with a nose, corduroy trousers, and a heavy wool shirt—an old army blouse of some kind. His head was covered with a brown felt hat.

Oh, yes, my father, do you remember? He had an old army overcoat with a red lining and a wolf-skin collar."[91]

There were various names for General Crook, the common one among the Indians being Nantan Lupan or "Tan Wolf," based on the color tan of most of his clothing.[92]

Eventually Crook became completely in accord with the ideas, views, and opinions of the Indians whom he was sent to fight, round up, and put on reservations. He realized the inevitability of change for the Apaches and conferred with them honestly, telling they must not raid, that they must learn the arts of agriculture and be self-sustaining. But he understood their frustrations, and although he punished their infractions of regulations, he was honest in his dealings. Sometimes his promises were not kept, but that was due to his superiors' interventions, and the Indians tried to understand. They came to trust him, even though they they knew he would track them down and haul them into jail if necessary. He had the tenacity and shrewdness to go into mountainous retreats no other general had penetrated. Leaders such as Victorio sought and listened to his advice.

Because of Crook's efforts to alleviate Tchi-héne hardships on reservations such as San Carlos, he lost credibility within the military (except for most of those who served immediately under him) and was transferred to other duties. Long after the Apaches were imprisoned and beyond his supervision, Crook kept his eye on their welfare and fought diplomatic battles in their behalf. To this day, the descendants of Victorio and Mangas Coloradas speak of Gen. George Crook with respect.

The year 1875 was difficult at Ojo Caliente. White profiteers were prevalent, and rations were low. There was talk that the Mimbres and Tchi-héne and any other Apaches located there should be transplanted once again—this time to the reserve at San Carlos. Col. Edward Hatch of the black Ninth Cavalry headed for Warm Springs. When he got there, he found the Apaches defiant. The warriors were armed with Springfield, Winchester, or Sharps rifles and carbines, Colts, and Smith & Wesson revolvers. The women and boys carried muzzle-loading arms, and they had lots of ammunition.[93]

Victorio spoke, "Your government has acted in bad faith. We have had no meat for four weeks. Our young men have left. They will bring us horses and mules. I think we should all go. It would be better to go than remain here in this confinement and starve." Hatch noted their ponies had been shod with rawhide.

In later years it was said by kin that Bi-duyé continued, "It would be best if we all headed for Sonora. We can make peace with the people there. Then we will do our raiding up here. It would be better than a peace here and war with Mexico."

By the following year there was trouble on other reserves. Taza was persuaded that his followers, many of whom were living near the Mexican border on the Chiricahua Reservation, should go to San Carlos. The Indians dispersed; some headed for Ojo Caliente, others went to Sonora. Shortly after their departure the reservation was closed.

In May 1876 a census was taken at Ojo Caliente, and Victorio's and Mangas's families were counted. So were those of Nana and Loco, along with twenty other rancherías.[94] For a time there was continual disruption among The People. Dilth-cleyhen grew weary of fearing an ambush whenever she left her camp. It was so difficult with the little ones. Geronimo was stirring up trouble along the Mexican border.

Victorio had never approved the ways of Geronimo. His way of warfare cost the lives of too many of the younger, less experienced warriors. He fought for his own glory, not for the welfare of the Indéh. The unrest and raiding in the Southwest reached the ears of authorities in Washington, D.C., and in the spring of 1877 an order came to confine all Chiricahuas within San Carlos.

Shortly after the command was issued, Victorio walked into the Agency. He was appalled. There was the chief Geronimo in chains, in ankle shackles. "What happened?" he cried.

Geronimo and a few of his people had needed supplies the previous afternoon and had decided to simply take them from Ojo Caliente. John Clum, the Agent at San Carlos, had surprised them in looting the commissary. He disarmed them, and since there was no guard house, he put some of the men, including Geronimo, in chains.

Clum offered clemency to all of the captives if both the renegade and Victorio, as well as the Warm Springs and Mimbres followers, would go to San Carlos without trouble. Victorio conferred with Geronimo, and they decided it would be best to comply.

Victorio returned to his camp. "We must leave. We must go to San Carlos. Crook has told us we must comply with Washington."

And then he added, "But before we go, we must cache most of our arms. One day we will return."[95]

The transfer to San Carlos began immediately. The little fields of half-ripened crops were left behind.

The men in shackles were taken in wagons. Victorio, Mangas, and

Dilth-cleyhen were among the majority who trudged over the desert and mountain trails on foot. Beshád-e, now seven, helped with the little ones. Elsie Vance Chestuan was four and able to walk on her own, as was three-year-old Cora, at least most of the time. Sometimes Dilth-cleyhen carried baby Frank, sometimes Beshád-e took a turn. The children did not cry, but their tiny faces reflected strain and hunger. Dilth-cleyhen held her head high.

"We must show the Anglos we can endure."

It took three weeks before the bedraggled troup of 453 individuals arrived at their destination.[96] Many of the elderly died en route. Now, many people were ill from exposure, some from the dread smallpox. Not all the brave men who started the trek completed it. They simply disappeared into the landscape. Over two hundred others had avoided the march entirely by fleeing south from Ojo Caliente and escaping into the mountains.

"They were better off," thought Dilth-cleyhen when she saw the part of San Carlos where she would live.

The site assigned Victorio's people[97] was old Camp Goodwin, the flats, six miles of the present Fort Thomas. It was barren: no trees, no mountains, no canyons. Flies, gnats, and other insects swarmed in the swirling dust. Soon there was malaria to contend with.

"What will become of my children?" a despondent Dilth-cleyhen asked Carl Mangas. "The tents and wickiups will be so close together. We have no freedom to move around."

San Carlos was a hellhole that summer. The Tchi-héne were mixed with the Net'-na and the Tchok'-anen, with White Mountain, Coyotero, and other Apache groups with whom there was little compatibility. Quarrels became fights, and there were more than a few homicides. Batches of tulapai made by such as Huera—for she was there too—exacerbated the problems.

"That wife of yours," Dilth-cleyhen complained to Mangas, "she is nothing but a troublemaker! I don't even like you to talk to her. Everytime you do, she disconcerts you. You start drinking, and then you get into trouble. I think you should avoid her."

John Clum did all that he could to help his wards. An honest man at heart, he did his best to cope with an impossible situation on the reservation. He organized a system whereby much of the policing was done by Indians. Victorio was one of those offered a position on the Council of Apache Judges, a post he accepted. Some of the Indians tried to cooperate; others stole guns and ammunition and went looting.

Sometime during that summer Clum had had more than he could bear, and he resigned. The new representative from the Agency was far from satisfactory. Trouble increased. There was insufficient rationing of supplies to the Indians. Finally, early in September 1877 even Mangas, Loco, and Victorio broke away and left the reservation.[98] They stole horses from the White Mountain Apaches to mount their people. They swept away from old Fort Goodwin.

For a time most of them rode north, on the run, heading toward Navaho country. The military gave chase, and there were various confrontations, with deaths on both sides. For a time Victorio went among the Mescalero people, on the east side of the Rio Grande. It was a time of confusion and fear, particularly for the women and children, who were often sequestered in some well-hidden camp while their men rode away.

After many conferences among Anglo military authorities, it was decided to give in to Victorio's demands that his people be permitted to return to Ojo Caliente. By November most of the Tchi-héné were back in their homeland. During the next months there were rumors that they would even yet be returned to San Carlos. Nonetheless, The People planted gardens when springtime arrived; they attempted to put their lives in order. Raiding resumed in Old Mexico.

In 1879 Victorio insisted, "Let us stay here. That is all we ask. We would rather die than go to San Carlos."[99]

That same year, word came that Bi-duyé and his people were being transferred to the Mescalero Reservation. For a short time, the group simply disappeared once again until their leader reconsidered. He left his womenfolk and Mangas in Ojo Caliente. He crossed the Muddy River and talked with his friends of the easterly tribe. Perhaps if all the women and children who had not left San Carlos were brought to Mescalero. . .

Then he was warned. The citizens of New Mexico were enraged at the thought of more Apaches in Mescalero. They schemed against Victorio. In Silver City a grand jury was assembled and indicted the leader and his followers for murder and for stealing livestock. In August a judge and the prosecuting attorney of Grant County passed through the reservation. Victorio thought they were after him. He successfully avoided them, canceled all his previous negotiations, and was gone, taking a number of Mescalero Apaches with him.[100]

He headed for Mexico; he swept through the Black and Mogollon ranges. And then he returned home. The crops in the gardens were ready for harvest.

Something was wrong. All he could hear was keening, and the crying of children. Horses were neighing.

"Bi-duyé, the soldiers came! They began shooting, shooting everyone in sight. Women and playing children fell before their bullets.

Everyone ran. The soldiers shot at them, too. There was no warning. They just appeared!"

The camp was in chaos. Tipis and tents were ripped apart, their contents scattered.

"Your mother is gone. Your wife, the mother of Dilth-cleyhen, she is gone, too."

"Why? Why?" Victorio raged. There was no answer. No one knew. No one knew even who the soldiers were.

The great chief was inconsolable. He cried to the heavens, "There can be no peace. You Anglos, you're not going to take over my lands or my people until you kill *me!*"

With more fervent zeal than ever before, the great leader, Dilth-cleyhen's father, went on the rampage. The Victorio Wars began in greater earnest.

Victorio's Death

The next months were horrible. The men were usually gone, and the women and children were left in one reservation or another. Occasionally they accompanied the men on the warpath and simply hid in well-known retreats during battles; but that became rarer and rarer. "It is too dangerous," the men warned.

There was fighting all across the border. Sometimes Mescaleros joined the ranks of warriors. Lozen was in demand everywhere. Anyone who passed the path of the Apaches might suffer fatal consequences. Only a few Mexican friends, shepherds, and small ranchers who gave Victorio supplies were spared. Even the presence of General Crook was no deterrent to the many massacres.

War and raids, raids and war—the pattern continued.

In September of 1880 Victorio was traced to a remote area about a hundred miles north of Chihuahua City. The Mexican government revoked its policy of international cooperation, and American troops were ordered back to the United States. Gen. Joaquin Terrazas's men surrounded Victorio's group at Tres Castillos, far east of the Sierra Madre, where three rugged peaks rise above the plain. A battle ensued on October 14. Somehow, when it ended, Victorio was dead. Many contradictory stories are related concerning the tragic event. We will never know the facts.

Lozen was not with her brother during this battle; she was with other warriors, as was Carl Mangas. Huera was there.[101] She was captured by the Mexicans and shipped to Mexico City where she was purchased by the owner of a large hacienda. There she worked in the fields for three years, before she made her escape. She walked back to her people on foot, living off the land with one blanket and her knife.

Word of Bi-duyé's death finally reached Dilth-cleyhen within a few weeks of the tragedy.

That great man, the one many Apaches referred to as their "boss," he was gone. "He was something big."

Many Anglo military men acknowledged that Victorio was one of the finest wartime strategists who had ever lived.

The Mexicans, who feared and hated him, nonetheless held him in respect. They claim he composed a song, one that is still sung in Sonora:

> Yo soy el Indio Victorio.
> Es mi delirio pelear.
> Yo he de llegar a la gloria,
> Y haré al mundo temblar.
>> Yo quiero vivir,
>> Yo quiero morir.
> Quiero vivir, para pelear.
> A Mexico he de ir,
> He de ir a pelear,
> Y gritar Guerra! Guerra!
>> Hasta morir![102]

I am the Indian Victorio.
It is my passion to fight.
I must attain glory.
And I will make the world tremble.
  I want to live,
  I want to die.
I want to live, so I can fight.
To Mexico I'll go,
I will go to fight,
And shout War! War!
  Until I die.

Between the years of Victorio's death and the time the Chiricahua were rounded up, the Tchi-héne were always on the run, always attempting to elude the enemy. The military, even General Crook, who returned to the territory in 1882, stepped up plans to confine them.

Old Nana, whose Apache name was Kas-tziden, meaning "Broken Foot" or "Broken Ankle," was in his eighties.[103] He was troubled with rheumatism. Nonetheless, immediately after the Tres Castillos slaughter, he rallied the spirits of those who survived and called on other Apaches to fight. Mescaleros once again joined the Warm Springs people. Nana was intent on revenge.

For a while Mangas fought among them. He was rarely with Dilth-cleyhen and his children, but he managed somehow to meet them near Warm Springs when Beshád-e was about to become a woman.

"I want a Feast for her," announced Dilth-cleyhen. "Maybe that is what we need to change our fortune. We need the blessings of White-Painted-Woman and the Mountain Gods more than ever now."

The da-i-dá had fewer guests than would have been the case in other times. Beshád-e's buckskin robes were simple but elegant. She held her head high. She was of fine heritage! She ran with the fleetness and sureness expected by her mother. There was ritual food for everyone.

After this event, Mangas left the womenfolk once again. He felt unsure about the leadership of Nana. Maybe he should listen to Geronimo, who was raiding successfully down in Old Mexico. And so he did, although in his heart he realized that Victorio would not approve. He sensed that Dilth-cleyhen was reluctant to comply.

In 1881 Beshád-e and her mother had reason to go into Fort Apache seeking food. A Scout told them about a mystic, called the Dreamer. He was a White Mountain Apache, a medicine man.

"That man, Nakai-doklini (or Noch-ay-del-klinne), is preaching near here. He is teaching wonderful things. All Anglos are going to die; there will be a resurrection of all Apaches."

"Shi-ma, my mother, let us go hear that man," Beshád-e begged.

"Well, it is some eighteen miles away, the Scout said," replied her mother.

Later, rumors spread that Mangas Coloradas, Cochise, and even Victorio had been seen to rise in the misty light after the prophet's prayers. That was enough to convince Beshád-e that she must hear the preaching. She kept coaxing to go. Whether or not she and

Dilth-cleyhen actually went is an open question. Throughout her life, Beshád-e was intrigued by the promises of prophets. Perhaps this was the budding of such interest.

By 1886 Gen. Nelson A. Miles had replaced George Crook.

Shortly before, Mangas had persuaded Dilth-cleyhen to come with him to live in Old Mexico. He was disenchanted with Geronimo. They would stay away from the man everyone classified as renegade and liar. They would move farther and farther into the recesses of mountains known only to the Tchi-héné and eke out a living by themselves.

"All right," his wife said. "But I want nothing to do with Geronimo. Look at all the young men he has killed because of his arrogance! Why doesn't he surrender? He's the one responsible for all our recent troubles."

"He's determined. He'll never surrender," Mangas replied. "He'll kill all of us first."

The family disappeared from forts and reservations, taking up a way of life that had been familiar before the white man came.

Dilth-cleyhen's opinions about Geronimo were shared by many of The People, most of whom were ready for peace.[104] Many men joined the Anglo military forces, becoming Scouts. Old Man Martine, George Martine's father, volunteered to go into the mountains and help find Geronimo. Many years later, he talked about his adventures:

"All of us Scouts assembled down there in El Paso, at Fort Bliss. We were divided in three groups. One group came here, toward Mescalero. Another went west into Arizona, and the third went into Old Mexico.

"I was in the third group, and so was Kayitah and Jolsanny. That white man, George Wratten, came with us. He was a good man, that Wratten. When it was all over, and we got Geronimo, he went to Florida to prison with us, to help us."

While the search was going on for the missing hostiles, many of the Chiricahua were living at Fort Apache. Some had planted gardens and had accumulated livestock, believing it would be a long time before Geronimo would be brought in and they would be assigned a suitable reservation of their own.

In July 1886 General Miles went to Fort Apache to confer with some of the leaders there. He persuaded a delegation to go to Washington, D.C., to talk about a permanent site. Old Man Chatto headed the group of representatives who met with President Grover Cleveland. After the meeting, during which many promises were made, the Apaches left, believing they were headed for Fort Apache. They had seen the sights of Washington and New York City. Not so; instead, they were imprisoned and sent to Florida.

Miles was busy in the Southwest. He had set up an elaborate heliograph system[105] with thirteen stations in Arizona and fourteen in New Mexico. This system, one of the general's pet projects, permitted messages to be sent in Morse code at ten to twelve words per minute over distances up to one hundred miles. He was convinced that this type of communication was necessary in order to bring in all the renegade Apaches. The instrument combined a mirror in an adjustable mounting together with a means of keying beams of reflected sunlight in the necessary dots and dashes.

When Mangas and Dilth-cleyhen had seen the flashing lights, Carl grinned, saying, "I wonder if it's better than our smoke signals. Neither one works when it rains."

He continued, "I guess that old general is sick of our cutting his telegraph lines and putting them back with "Apache splices." These were false splices insulated with a bit of rawhide that put the line out of commission and were difficult to locate. "He has to do something better to warn his soldiers of our movements."

Undoubtedly, the heliographs helped the troopers. Geronimo was located. He and Naiche agreed to surrender to Miles. On August 25, 1886, they and their families set out on the march to captivity. Early in September Geronimo and the others were marched to Bowie Station and put on a train for Florida. Those living in Fort Apache had been counted already and were on their way. Their captive slaves had all been freed.

It took more than five thousand U.S. troops stationed in the Southwest to defeat the Chiricahua warriors. Further, an appreciable number of Mexican soldiers were involved.[106] All were intent, from time to time, on eradicating Apaches from their territory. Not all the troops chased Geronimo simultaneously, but the score of Indians who had retreated with him into Old Mexico gave American and Mexican strategists much to consider.

The troopers and Scouts *never* found Dilth-cleyhen and Carl Mangas. They and a handful of their kin remained in Old Mexico until, weary and disillusioned, they surrendered the following month.

Here we leave the life of Dilth-cleyhen.

The years to come—and she lived to be very elderly—form a tapestry of events shared with her daughter, granddaughter and great granddaughter. They will be described in the parts of the book devoted to those women. Some factual information is repeated, as necessary to present events as each woman viewed them.

Dilth-cleyhen had great strength of character. She endured to the end.

She was not swayed by the intrusive ideas of her captors or of the Indian prophets. The daughter of Victorio did not waiver in her belief in the powers that made up her world.

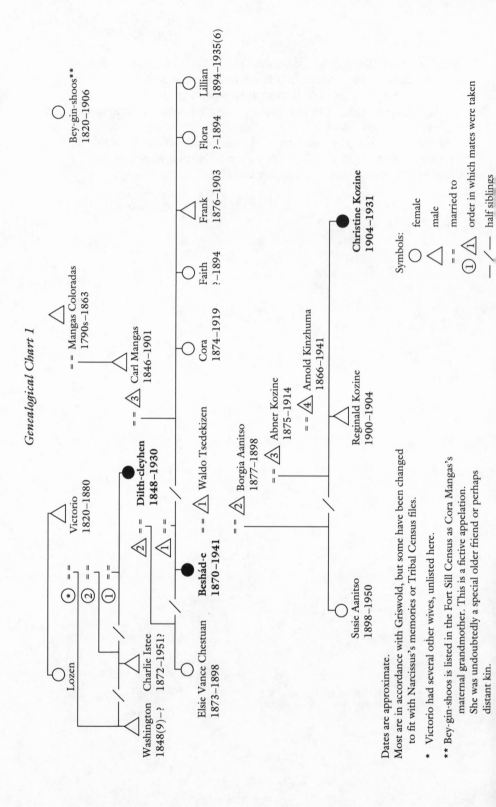

Genealogical Chart 1

Dates are approximate.

Most are in accordance with Griswold, but some have been changed to fit with Narcissus's memories or Tribal Census files.

*   Victorio had several other wives, unlisted here.

** Bey-gin-shoos is listed in the Fort Sill Census as Cora Mangas's maternal grandmother. This is a fictive appelation. She was undoubtedly a special older friend or perhaps distant kin.

Symbols:

◯   female
△   male
= =   married to
①△   order in which mates were taken
—/—   half siblings

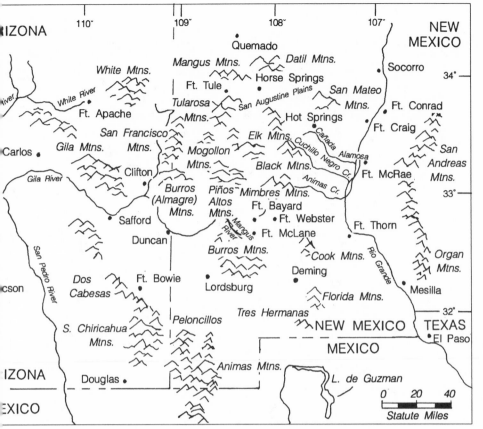

Chiricahua band territories, with major game and vegetation. (*Adapted from Basehart 1959, maps 2 and 4*)

Early forts and place-names. Fort Tule indicates area of Tularosa Reservation. *(Adapted from Basehart 1959, map 1)*

Chiricahua hunting territory. Note the strips of venison drying on a line. *(Courtesy of the Arizona Pioneers' Historical Society, Tucson)*

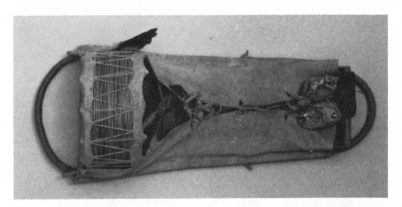

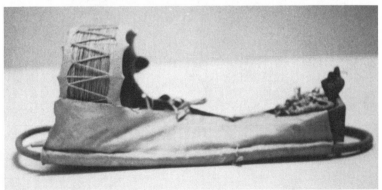

Two views of a cradleboard used by Molly Gayton. *(Courtesy of L. Bryce Boyer)*

Night dance of the Crown Dancers (Mountain Gods) and Clown, July 1962. Two dance teams are shown. The Clown is at the far right and wears no "crown" headdress. *(Courtesy of Barbara Funkhauser)*

Cochise's territory: Chiricahua National Monument. Sentinels or warriors concealed themselves in the mountain crags. *(Courtesy of L. Bryce Boyer)*

Apache woman using grinding stone. *(Photo 4570, courtesy of the Arizona Pioneers' Historical Society, Tucson)*

Apache woman carrying pitch-covered jug on her back. Note the absence of flanges on shoulder of blouse. *(Photo 21390, courtesy of Arizona Pioneers' Historical Society, Tucson)*

Apache woman in front of wickiup, 1880, with pitch-covered baskets—water jug and tray. *(Photo 30411, courtesy of the Arizona Pioneers' Historical Society, Tucson)*

Aged woman carrying firewood by means of tumpline over her forehead. Note tiers on skirt. *(Photo 21391, courtesy of the Arizona Pioneers' Historical Society, Tucson)*

Woman with mutilated nose making twined burden basket. *(Photo 4567, courtesy of the Arizona Pioneers' Historical Society, Tucson)*

Apache woman; nose cut because of infidelity. *(Photo 3237, courtesy of the Arizona Pioneers' Historical Society, Tucson)*

Victorio, 1877; from a photograph taken at Ojo Caliente. *(Courtesy of the Arizona Pioneers' Historical Society, Tucson)*

Plaza at Monticello. On a recent visit, Narcissus Gayton was told by a resident, who was teasing, that this was the Apache prison and the hangman's bar. *(Courtesy of L. Bryce Boyer)*

General George Crook, 1886. Note his Chiricahua boots, "with a nose." *(Courtesy of the National Archives)*

On horseback at left, Geronimo; *on horseback at right,* Naiche; *standing at right,* Geronimo's Son, 1886. Figure at left and child are unidentified. *(Courtesy of the Arizona Pioneers' Historical Society, Tucson)*

Above. Loco, Warm Springs. *(Courtesy of the Arizona Pioneers' Historical Society, Tucson)*

Left. Nana, successor of Victorio, 1884. *(Courtesy of the Arizona Pioneers' Historical Society, Tucson)*

Left. Carl Mangas, husband of Dilth-cleyhen. *(Courtesy of the Arizona Pioneers' Historical Society, Tucson)*
Above. Chatto, first sergeant, Company B of the Apache Scouts. *(Courtesy of the Arizona Pioneers' Historical Society, Tucson)*

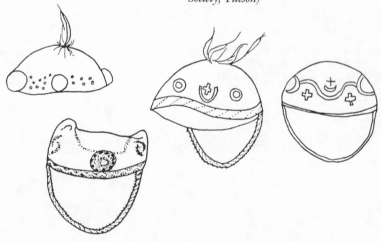

War bonnets, worn by medicine men during war dances. The bonnets are made of buckskin and most have chin straps, which are beaded. Two bonnets are adorned with eagle feathers, and there are metallic disks on the bonnet at the far left. Other bonnets have beaded decoration. *(Drawings by Ruth Boyer, from specimens at the Apache Museum, Mescalero, and from photographs)*

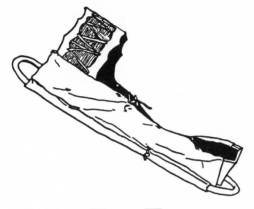

Part Two

Beshád-e

Turmoil and Imprisonment

1870—1886

The sixteen years from the time of Beshád-e's birth in 1870 to that of 1886, when the In-déh became prisoners of war, were filled with intense frustration, doubt, and fear. The People had always been nomads, warring and raiding, accustomed to periodic disruptions of camp and ensuing flight; but now the enemies were everywhere. There were ever-increasing numbers of intruding Anglos: military men, miners, gold-seekers, as well as entire families moving to California and, finally, homesteaders. There were Spanish-speaking peoples; those ranchers who lived in Old Mexico, those who worked the mines from time to time at Santa Rita, and of course the Mexican army personnel. To a lesser degree there was conflict with members of other Indian tribes. The Apaches were surrounded by hostile forces. Obviously, under such conditions Beshád-e's early childhood was far from ideal.

The most frequent emotion seen in Dilth-cleyhen's eyes was that of uncertainty, tainted with fear. All too often when war parties straggled in from forays, some men never returned. The sound of keening was a familiar refrain. That was not the way it should be. Brave men *should* return. An Apache leader should protect his followers. Always, his instructions to them were to retreat, to disappear into the underbrush if victory was not sure. Now that advice was proving useless.

Even when the In-déh complied with military demands and stayed within the boundaries of land set aside for them, there were atrocities. As related previously, when Beshád-e was a cradled infant at Warm Springs, some Anglos—perhaps prospectors, perhaps bounty hunters—came upon an isolated group of Apache women foraging for roots. Victorio was away from his ranchería, hunting game. On his return, he was greeted with the sound of keening. Learning that his beloved Wife Two had been murdered, his rage knew no bounds. Only recently he had lost his youngest wife.

Victorio was inconsolable. "How can this go on! We cannot live in our homeland in peace. They kill us wherever we are. They hunt us down."

For a while, the widower and his followers were intent on rampage, until reason finally returned to the doubly bereaved man. Once again, he tried promoting peace among his people. Peace, but constant vigilance.

Almost from birth, youngsters were cautioned repeatedly. "You must not cry!" Dilth-cleyhen had told Beshád-e, simultaneously offering her the breast. "Hush! The white man will hear you! He'll take his knife and scalp you!"

A child learned quickly to fend for itself. Almost before she was able to walk, Beshád-e clung to the mane of a racing horse, and shortly thereafter she carried a knife tucked in her belt or hidden within the tresses of her hair.

"Learn to use that knife. Defend yourself. Run, but fight if you have to. Don't let a white man get you! Disguise yourself. Cover your face with earth." These were messages to the growing girl.

Of all the sites in which her people lived, that of Ojo Caliente became Beshád-e's favorite, as it was for her mother and her mother's father, Victorio, near whom the family stayed whenever it was feasible. This Warm Springs area, even after it had reservation status and the Apaches were subjected to rationing and shortages,[1] was most desirable.

Here, too, however, all during her early years the child was well aware of the uncertainties that gnawed at most adults. Somewhere deep inside, perhaps below the conscious level, lurked the fright of that early atrocity.

Rumors were rampant in camp. Every night around a low-flamed fire the men and women talked, discussing various policies, the advice of leaders, what agents and military men were apt to do. Their backs were against trees and rocks so that no shadows revealed them to the bullets or arrows of marauders.

Victorio, the brave and intelligent warrior, the orator, was the one who calmed down those who were too impulsive.

"We are outnumbered. We must make plans. We must cooperate, just as Gray Fox, that General Crook, advocates. That is what is best for The People now. We must make the best of things. We will raid only when we are hungry, when there are insufficient rations. And not against the Americans. There are lots of horses and cattle and sheep down in Chihuahua and Sonora. We are hunters. We are warriors. But maybe we should replant some crops," he reasoned. Dilth-cleyhen, holding Beshád-e in her cradleboard, nodded compliance.

As she grew older, ever wiser and more experienced, Beshád-e had increasing respect for the words of her grandfather. She, for one, would follow him, no matter what Dilth-cleyhen and her stepfather Carl Mangas did. Murders should stop! Her own father had been killed in a skirmish with white civilians just outside the Ojo Caliente Reservation.

It had happened during a time when the family was starving. Dilth-cleyhen was big with child, and her husband resolved to find food. Weeks had passed since the Indians on the reserve had had protein. Hunting was useless: there was no game. Animals thereabouts had been slaughtered by the ever-increasing Anglo population. Government allotments were all but non-existent. And so, in the Apache way, he decided to raid a homesteader's ranch for livestock. Somehow, the venture became a catastrophe. The rancher had been alerted, and the confrontation that ensued proved fatal.

Thus, Beshád-e never knew her father—nor did she know for long her first stepfather. The latter was killed during a different raid when she was some two or three years old. Victorio's followers had been transferred to Fort Tularosa, a dreadful and isolated place of high altitude, east of present-day Aragon in the valley of the Tularosa River in northwestern New Mexico—a site where discontent reigned among the Tchi-hénè.[2] The warriors began riding south into Sonora, Mexico, in search of food, cloth, ammunition, horses, and whatever was in short supply. Even Victorio sometimes rode, despite his usual cooperative attitude with the military, who had a reserved trust in him and who once invited him to be part of a delegation of Apaches to Washington, D.C. But the train journey did not materialize, and Bi-duyé grew restless. He could not resist raiding.

On his return from one such trip he told Dilth-cleyhen, "We went right by Cañada Alamosa, by Ojo Caliente. It was beautiful. We must negotiate. We must get back there."

Beshád-e later heard that sometimes entire families, including her own, crept from the fort, women and children accompanying their raiding men. Tularosa was simply intolerable. What could the Apaches do? Even yet, Victorio sought compromise with whites. Unfortunately, his control of certain rash young warriors was not absolute.[3] Among Apaches group leadership was a tenuous matter, depending on mood and circumstance.[4]

As Beshád-e listened repeatedly to arguments for peace and others for war, she considered what she heard and strengthened her earlier resolves. "Don't trust *any* white eyes!" said one. Another countered, "Well, one or two of them are all right. They tell us the truth as they see it, and when they promise us something, they try to live up to their words. That is the way of Tan Wolf, Nantan Lupan, whom some call Gray Fox. He is an honest man—as honest as any Apache. He understands the chiefs in Washington. He can talk to that Ulysses S. Grant—that man the Anglos call a president—on our behalf. We must counsel with Tan Wolf. With him, we can compromise."

By no means did everyone agree that raiding should stop. "The lines for getting rations are too long. And then when we get the food, it tastes bad. It is not good like the meat we hunt for or that we take from wagon trains or ranches. And there is never enough. Our women and children go hungry."

"What is wrong with our killing! They take *our* scalps; they murder *us*—even our children. And Mexicans steal away our women and infants for slaves. We do no wrong when we kill and take what we need. That is the custom of the In-déh." And so the contradictory philosophies continued into the stillness of many nights, men and women giving vent to independent opinion.

When Victorio spoke, the Tchi-hénè listened most attentively; they weighed his words. When morning came, those who had agreed with his philosophy remained; those who did not, had disappeared, moving from the reservation to find guidance with which they were in greater accord, or simply to strike out on their own for a time. Beshád-e was glad Dilth-cleyhen and her mate were loyal to Victorio. They remained in camp.

Beshád-e was proud of her handsome grandfather. Nonetheless, when she was merely six or seven years old, she heard Dilth-cleyhen comment on his appearance. How tired he looked. Lines had deepened at the sides of his mouth. His smiles were rare and fleeting. A few strands of gray hair streaked the black. The strains of responsibility were obvious. He was always trying to negotiate, several times traveling across the Rio Grande to confer with the people of the Mescalero tribe. When he finally gave up on peace, when atrocities were too much to bear and the Victorio Wars began, the women and children of his extended family rarely saw him or his sister Lozen. The warriors left periodically, but their dependents were held by the Anglos in various forts—San Carlos, Fort Apache, occasionally at the Chiricahua reserve—all bad, as was the immediate situation at Tularosa.

At that latter location The People faced isolation, bitter cold, and the hostilities of the encroaching Anglos. Among themselves, there was discontent and wrangling.

Beshád-e had additional encumbrances to contend with. One new child after another had become part of the family. How it rankled to see *them* receive Dilth-cleyhen's attention—attention to which

Beshád-e was rightfully entitled! *She* deserved the cuddling, the nourishment, the spoiling traditionally due the youngest child.

It had started when she was about three years of age, after the family had gone that long, long way to Tularosa. It was then the black-mopped Charlie Istee had come to live with them.

That was bad enough, but almost immediately, there was that Elsie Vance Chestuan! A half-sister! "Why does my mother spend all her time with her!" Then came Asa (Ace) Daklugie.[5] Daklugie means "Forced His Way Through" or "One Who Grabs," phrases which describe the difficulties encountered during his birth. He was barely younger than Charlie.

Three babies! Three rivals for attention—as Beshád-e soon realized. This last one was the youngest son of the Net'na Chief Juh and of Ish-keh, the first cousin of Geronimo. Almost nothing is known of Ish-keh, except that she gave birth to Asa when they were high in the Chiricahua Mountains near Fort Bowie in Arizona Territory.

Records differ as to how long Asa was with Dilth-cleyhen. Evidence suggests that he was in her camp during most of his early childhood. During that period, Carl Mangas, who (for unknown reasons) replaced Dilth-cleyhen's previous husband, assumed responsibility for instructing the lad—and his own son, Frank Mangas[6]—in the male arts required for a boy's initiation as a warrior. Juh, a chief in his own right, undoubtedly began training his son when the latter was old enough to raid. But Juh drowned in 1883 when Asa was eleven or so.

It is reported that Asa and his brother witnessed their father's fall from a horse into the shallow waters of the river near Casas Grandes. There the old man, now in his sixties, lay stunned. The boys could not lift him. Asa held his head above water while the other son went for aid. Unfortunately, help came too late.[7]

Beshád-e tried to love the tiny newcomers and, to some extent, she succeeded. But they were indeed a nuisance. Dilth-cleyhen told her to watch out for them. She must fetch for them, secure them from mischief, and above all, keep them quiet.

"They are just babies," reminded Dilth-cleyhen. "You must love them and see that they have food. Just make sure they do not cry. Let them have their way." Or, "Make a little doll for Elsie." "Give Charlie some of your berries. He likes them." It was always, "You are bigger. Take care of them," despite the fact that the years between the ages of the children were minimal. "Give them!" "Give them!" "Give them!" But the task was not beyond the very small Beshád-e, who endured the exacting years.

Beshád-e grew to be a strong-willed, highly intelligent, sensitive girl, physically able. She was proud. She was no infant! Her head held high, she knew she could baby-sit for Charlie, Elsie, Asa or any other waif that came along!

The girl learned the arts of self-protection.[8] "You need to know how to shoot an arrow straight. Hold the bow like this," she was told. "There might be a time you need to know how to protect yourself or kill some game." Her knife was part of her everyday costume, and she threw it accurately; she knew where to thrust it with deadly surety. As soon as she could hold a rifle steady, she was permitted to shoot. "Don't waste ammunition," she was cautioned. "You must aim carefully, and always hit your target."

Beshád-e was reminded daily that preparation for rapid getaways was essential.[9] Every morning Dilth-cleyhen checked the two buckskin ration bags that she wore suspended from her belt by a thong. In one there was a supply of dried venison. The other held mesquite beans, or sometimes mescal. "Don't eat this now. It is for an emergency," her mother cautioned, as she examined the contents of the bags of all the youngsters.

Beshád-e's horsemanship was enviable. She rode bareback at breakneck speeds, just as boys of her age did. In foot races she rivaled their strides. "When I grow up, maybe I can run and ride with Lozen!"

When a mere girl, Beshád-e worked alongside the women of the camp. She helped tan hides and gradually learned to fashion the buckskin into articles of clothing. She could build a wickiup with dispatch and help with the poles of the tipis and tents. She was clever at camouflage, disguising even the most temporary shelter with the branches of nearby trees, bushes, or underbrush. She remembered to cover her face and arms with soil so as to escape enemy detection. She tracked; she snared; she hauled water and helped gather produce. She lugged cradleboards and their infants until her back ached with misery and the tumpline grew tight against her head. The cradle was so long that sometimes her hurrying heels made contact with the bottom arc.

She helped Dilth-cleyhen stow dried foodstuffs in caches at many a mountain retreat to which the family had escaped. Sometimes guns and ammunition as well as knives were stored. Grinding stones, baskets, and water jugs were left in larger cavelike holes, the access opening being plastered with mud and covered with brush or branches to make it all but invisible.

"Hide them deep. They'll be needed later—later when we come back."

The skills of survival were not learned overnight, but to Beshád-e it seemed, even by the time she was four years old, that she had always known them, just as demands from Dilth-cleyhen would never cease.

From the time of Beshád-e's birth in 1870 the family was constantly on the move. Ojo Caliente was their favorite location, but even from there, they made frequent excursions south, often hundreds of miles into Old Mexico.

In 1872 there was the terrible assignment at Fort Tularosa—until Victorio and the other heads of Mimbres and Warm Springs families demanded a return to the vicinity of Cañada Alamosa. They went to Gen. Oliver Otis Howard, who had come to the fort in hopes of negotiating with Cochise.

"We will not stay here," the Apaches told him. "You give us blankets that fall apart as soon as it rains. These conditions are intolerable. You must permit us to go back near Warm Springs if we are to maintain peace. And we all want peace."[10] Victorio played an important role.[11]

Howard compromised, and rations were increased; other promises were made but often not kept: Accusations and counteraccusations, as well as skirmishes, resulted. Even General Crook put in a few words. Nonetheless, it was two more years before Victorio's followers were once again—but all too briefly—in their homeland.

For a while there was peace, and the tenor of life was quiet. Men hunted; they farmed and irrigated the crops. Women prepared food, tanned hides, made clothing, and advised husbands and brothers. The rhythm of daily chores proceeded, although disturbing rumors caused some distress: "We're being sent to San Carlos. They are deceiving us again. We cannot stay here where we want to be."

The dreaded move did not occur until Beshád-e was about seven years old. By then she had other half-siblings: Faith and Flora and then the boy, Frank, who was born in 1876.[12]

Family diversions consisted of trips to locations where the women gathered foods. Sometimes they rode to nearby areas; other times the group ventured into Old Mexico. There were other excursions with Victorio, who had friends among the Mescaleros, and once they traveled in the land of the Navahos, where Beshád-e's grandfather loved to gamble.

The little girl liked it best when they journeyed to the heartland of the old Chiricahua territory. Then Dilth-cleyen took more time, slowing her horse as she taught Beshád-e the history of The People.

When they were some thirty miles northeast of Silver City, in what is now the state of New Mexico, Dilth-cleyhen pursed her lips toward a body of water.

"Over that way is where Chiricahua life started. Life itself raised out of that lake," she began.[13]

Impulsively, Beshád-e lifted her arm in that direction. Just as quickly, Dilth-cleyhen guided it back to the child's lap.

"Never use a finger to show direction. You know better. Only witches and white eye soldiers do that. Use only your lips." Beshád-e was shame-faced, this warning being one of the first things she had learned.

When they neared the area of the copper mines of Santa Rita, Dilth-cleyhen said, "This is where Mangas Coloradas liked to be. This is where your stepfather Mangas spent many childhood hours."

And when they rode south and east, near Deming, she spoke in hushed tones, "Over there. Tres Hermanas." But she did not use the Spanish name. She said the Apache words meaning "Home of the Mountain Gods."[14] During the course of future years, Beshád-e would learn more about their sacred qualities, information she would pass along to her daughters and their daughters in years to come.

Dilth-cleyhen broke the silence after her pronouncement, commenting, "Next time we come south, we'll go on to Chihuahua City in Old Mexico." The Apache designation for the site means "Town with Many Burros." "I have many Mexican friends there whom I would like to see."

When times eventually came for such visits, there was drinking and camaraderie among the adults; the children played games of tag or ran races—competitions that required no bilingual skills. If Victorio were present, imbibing of intoxicating drinks was minimal. He disapproved of inebriation.

It was another time, when they rode even farther and penetrated an Apache stronghold in a remote mountain escarpment, that Beshád-e took lessons in sighting the enemy from afar.

"You must always be alert. Both Mexicans and Anglos are taking our scalps and getting money for them," she was told. Ordinarily, when a group of women was in such a place, elderly men whose eyesight was still keen or youths nearly ready for battle served as sentinels. Only rarely did women volunteer, but Dilth-cleyhen took the opportunity, and Beshád-e was told to accompany her mother.

The two sat for hours behind the crags. They scanned the plains below for signs of rising dust.

Then Dilth-cleyhen pursed her lips, designating a line of cavalrymen in the far distance, long before Beshád-e could see the black skins and kinky hair beneath the men's caps. "In-dáh, the enemy, buffalo soldiers," she whispered.

She handed field glasses to her daughter, glasses taken recently by Mangas when he raided a wagon train. Beshád-e marveled and shivered at the closeness the lenses brought. What would such strange hair feel like!

"You must always pray when you come across an enemy," Dilthcleyhen continued, interrupting her daughter's musing. "You must show respect to the Powers. Then they will be there to protect you. Pray to them. You must carry your pollen, all your protections. Use them when you must." She showed Beshád-e once again the ever-present strand of beads beneath her cotton blouse, the red beans and white seeds obtained in Old Mexico.[15]

"It is powerful, this necklace. It has saved my life."

Not long after, Beshád-e witnessed its strength.

Somehow, while several families were camping, the buffalo soldiers surprised them. The warriors were gone. The aged lookout must have dozed. The military men shot even before they knew who was present. Women and children scattered in all directions. Dilthcleyhen grabbed the baby Elsie in her cradle and headed for the shelter of high mesquite.

"Run, Beshád-e, run!" she called in a voice louder than usual. The child followed her, scrambling for a place in the underbrush. Beshád-e heard her mother whispering, praying. She glanced at her and saw her mother swing the necklace over her shoulder, over her shoulder to the right, so that the strand hung down her back.

Immediately the shooting stopped.

Dilth-cleyhen and Beshád-e remained all but motionless where they were. Elsie made no sound. Finally, the soldiers rode away. They quit the chase. The queue of horsemen took off over the desert. The power of the beads, the power of Dilth-cleyhen's prayer, was evident.

Beshád-e and her family were subjected to dreadful experiences. At camps and agencies and forts they were made to feel less than human. Often they were cheated of rations and forced to go hungry. Their clothes deteriorated; they had access neither to calico nor to hides. Yet this was as nothing when compared with the panic of being shot at or the eventual confinement at San Carlos Reservation in 1877. Here the heat was abominable. Flies swarmed even in the swirling dust. There were no nearby trees, no mountains, no canyons.

John Philip Clum had been appointed Indian agent at that location in 1874 on the recommendation of the Dutch Reformed Church, of which he was a member. He was honest and served well, maintaining that the Apaches were intelligent and quite capable of self-government. He kept careful accounts, and no one was cheated. He involved the Indians in farming and in an extensive building program. His wards responded positively and labored long hours, for which work they received fifty cents per day.

In May 1876 the Bureau of Indian Affairs telegraphed Clum that The People of the Chiricahua and Warm Springs Reservations were now assigned to him. This meant trouble, for there were many in those locations who did not want to move. The first roundup and transfer involved about one-third of the Indians, the remainder escaping into Old Mexico.

"There are too many Indians there now. It will be too crowded." "The Indians there are hostile to us." "The Anglos are sending us there only because there are a few renegades among us." These were the comments made by the Tchi-héné.

But the orders stood.

In April 1877 Clum and a few Indian police from San Carlos went to Warm Springs. Almost by accident there was a confrontation with a defiant and probably thieving Geronimo, resulting in the latter and sixteen other men being put in chains, where they were seen by a furious Bi-duyé. Clum talked to Victorio, who agreed reluctantly to the transfer, knowing full well that to resist was useless. Nearly five hundred Apaches assembled at the Warm Springs Agency.

On May 1 the shackled men were put in wagons and headed north. The rest of The People walked the desert and mountain trail. It took three weeks. Four hundred and fifty-three limped into the reservation at San Carlos, many among them ailing. All were hungry and forlorn.[16]

The Warm Springs Indians were the last to arrive in the assigned location and were given the least suitable campsites. Their tents and wickiups were so close that they could hear the conversations of neighbors. Within a short time there were many deaths. The climate was hot, up to one hundred forty degrees; dust blew constantly. There were too few crops—instead, thorny underbrush, scorpions, and rattle snakes abounded. Women made illegal tulapai, and there was considerable imbibing and unruly behavior, quarrels, even killing.

"We had such good food back home," Beshád-e murmured. "Here there is nothing. All the people do is fight."

For a time Clum tried desperately to right the government's wrong. He appointed Indian police and judges. Victorio was among them. But Clum's efforts were insufficient, and in July he resigned.[17]

Victorio, Mangas, and other leaders, including Loco, broke out before the year ended, taking with them more than three hundred men, women, and children.[18] The harried group, with Indian police in pursuit, escaped briefly into Navaho country. They pillaged, killed, and then once again surrendered. They were not returned to the hated reservation because more and more prisoners were escaping. Once again, Victorio's followers were permitted to stay at Warm Springs. Here they developed farms, built wickiups and more permanent structures, and once again, until August of 1879, were more content with life.

In that month, rumors became more frightening.

"I hear Victorio is being sent across the Rio Grande, the Muddy River, across to the Mescalero lands—to that reservation."

Hearing this news, the leader and some of his loyal men once again disappeared, only to emerge, without wives and youngsters, within the heart of New Mexico.[19] He first appeared to be peaceful; it was only when he heard the indictments against him from Silver City that Bi-duyé began to rage. He fled, recruiting some 150 Mescalero warriors who went with him. Periodically he checked the ranchería to make sure his family had supplies.

On one such routine return he was greeted with the final disaster in Warm Springs, the one he could not tolerate: the murder of his mother and the mother of Dilth-cleyhen, his first wife, and the destruction of the entire camp and all the crops by soldiers.

The Victorio Wars began. They did not end until 1880 when the great man met his death at Tres Castillos.

There is no record of the whereabouts of Dilth-cleyhen and Beshád-e in the next few harrowing years of mourning, doubt, and fear.

Perhaps they were in or near Fort Apache for a while.

In 1881 a scout in that location reported to his superiors the presence of a mystic called The Dreamer, whose Indian name was Nakai-doklini or Noch-ay-del-klinne.[20] He was a White Mountain medicine man who preached of a resurrection and the death of all Anglos. Chief Nana, who heard his prayers in the misty light of one morning, later claimed to have seen Mangas Coloradas, Cochise, and Victorio rise slowly from the earth.[21] The Dreamer was now nearby, and his teachings were attracting crowds of Indians who whispered about him around their campfires. Droves of them, including some

Chiricahuas, flocked to the mountain valley some eighteen miles away, listening to the prophet's message and participating in the Wheel Dance, which he taught as an integral part of his new faith. He brought hope to a defrauded and malnourished people. It is quite possible Dilth-cleyhen and Beshád-e heard him. Certainly, the Apache grapevine conveyed his teachings to them.

Later, the women went briefly to Warm Springs.

According to recollections of her descendants, here Beshád-e came of age. Here Dilth-cleyhen gave a Feast for her daughter, to celebrate her womanhood in a sacred way. During that ritual Beshád-e was White-Painted-Woman, bestowing blessings on those who came to honor her. Crown Dancers descended from the mountains, their presence lending credence to a hope that *all* was not ill.

Shortly thereafter other rumors emerged.

"Did you hear? We are going to be permanent prisoners."

"Did you hear? They are going to take our children away from us. They are going to send them to a white man's school where they will become like Anglos. They call it Carlisle."

"Did you hear? They won't send girls if they are married."

It did not take long for Dilth-cleyhen to decide Beshád-e must have a husband, someone to protect her if need be.

Within the year it was decided that she should wed Tsedekizen, who was about ten years her elder. He was willing to oblige. She would be his fourth wife. His first spouse was much older than he; his second had died at San Carlos shortly after they were married, and his third had been captured in Old Mexico. His marriage to Beshád-e was not consummated, but her status as a wife proved to be politically strategic in future years when it became known that she was a married woman, "Mrs. Waldo Sundayman," the wife of Crooked Head.[22]

After Victorio's death the turmoil and bloody warfare raged for the next six years; Carl Mangas listened more and more to the counsel of Geronimo.

When that renegade sought refuge in the mountainous terrain of Old Mexico, Mangas, Dilth-cleyhen, Beshád-e, and other family members accompanied him for a short time. There was some reluctance on the part of the womenfolk who remembered Victorio's distrust of the hostile Indian. They finally reasoned that Old Mexico had always provided the Tchi-héné their summer camping sites. They would find safety in the rugged country that Anglos found difficult to navigate. That land would give Dilth-cleyhen and kin some breathing space.

Shortly, however, Mangas realized Geronimo was not to be trusted. "He speaks with a double tongue," Dilth-cleyhen agreed.

Altogether, thirteen stayed with Mangas, including six warriors.[23] They departed Geronimo's company, moving ever farther into remote southern areas. The men avoided conflict with the Mexicans, doing no raiding or killing of livestock except when absolutely necessary—or unless young men acted impulsively. The group communicated with no one, and no one found them, not even at the time of Geronimo's surrender. They lived largely on the meat of deer shot by means of bow and arrow. It was a lonely life. Early in October 1886 Dilth-cleyhen and Mangas conferred.

"Maybe we would be better off to surrender." And so they started north for New Mexico.

En route, Frank Mangas and Asa Daklugie, contrary to Mangas's orders, drove off a mule herd from a ranch and mining enterprise being managed by Britton Davis, formerly with the army. He sent word to Fort Apache, and General Miles sent Capt. Charles L. Cooper to find the last of the "hostiles," who were by now in the mountains east of the fort. Mangas discovered the army camp and made overtures of surrender.

On October 30 Dilth-cleyhen, Mangas, Beshád-e, five youngsters (including Frank and Asa) plus two adult males, Fit-A-Hat and Goso, were taken by wagon from Fort Apache to Holbrook. Blankets were given them, inasmuch as theirs had been confiscated. Mangas perched by the driver; the others sat flat in the bed, huddled together, wrapped in the bedding. Dilth-cleyhen, fearing future starvation, clutched a small pouch of dried corn until it, too, was taken from her. Guards on horseback rode in front, in back, and at the sides of the wagon. When the captives came to steep grades, they were ordered to walk. No talking was permitted, but the bedraggled group did not mind. There was nothing to say.[24] At Holbrook the prisoners were put on a train bound for Florida.

Mangas was despondent.

"What kind of Apache am I! I cannot even care for my family. I cannot defend them any more. I am worthless," he berated himself.

Dilth-cleyhen started to console him, but it was ineffective. Impulsively, he threw open the window and jumped from the moving train in an attempt to kill himself.

The train was stopped. An examination of the stunned Mangas revealed no serious injury.[25]

In Florida

At 2 A.M. on November 6, 1886, the brakes of the train from Holbrook screeched, and the cars lurched to a halt. The small party of Indian prisoners scanned the dimly lit platform. There were only two warriors now, for the aged and sickly Fit-A-Hat had died as they crossed New Mexico and had been buried at Fort Union.

The group heard someone say the word "Florida." Mangas and young Ira Goso, totally bewildered, continued to sit, staring.

"You two, get off the train. You're at the end of your trip," a guard said. The Indians looked blank. The message was repeated.

Finally, with the aid of pushes and shoves, Mangas and Ira disembarked. They were given further instructions.

"You wait right here. In about six hours a steamer will arrive here at the railroad wharf. It will take you from Pensacola, where you are now, across this narrow bay and over to Fort Pickens on Santa Rosa Island."

After the men got off, Dilth-cleyhen and Beshád-e huddled together, their arms hugging the two smallest children, while Elsie, now twelve years of age, sat close alongside. The third woman, perhaps an elderly aunt of Mangas, stared out the window. The teenagers, Asa Daklugie and Frank Mangas, nervously attempted nonchalance. For three hundred miles more the train lumbered on, finally reaching St. Augustine.[26]

It was almost 11 P.M. when they were forced to trudge up Orange Street toward Fort Marion. On arrival the women and boys were herded onto the drawbridge that extended over the moat, through the great wooden door that led to the guard room, across a wide courtyard, and into a cell with a high arched ceiling and barred windows. Even in November the air felt hot, moist, and clammy, a sensation that the musty-smelling stone walls did nothing to dissipate. They could hear the sound of sea waves lapping nearby. The guard indicated that they were to bed down on narrow wooden platforms that lined the walls. "We'll get you into tents on top of the fort as soon as we can. It'll be cooler there," he muttered as he left them. It was a long night.

The Castillo de San Marcos, later named Fort Marion, was built by the Spanish in 1672. It was constructed of natural shell rock called coquina, which was quarried on a nearby island. The edifice was surrounded by a shallow tidal moat containing a few mullet, blue crabs, and occasionally a sting ray that gained access from the bay.

The shape of the fort was basically a big square with diamond-shaped extensions or bastions at each corner. The center of the square on the ground floor consisted of the courtyard surrounded by cell-like rooms. In one corner a stairway led up to the gun deck above the cells. A few cannon were still located there, but the sight that most depressed Dilth-cleyhen and Beshád-e was the stand of some one hundred Sibley tents, closely aligned, outlining the outer edge of the terreplein. All around the fort, behind the tents, was a four-foot wall, and at each of the four corners of the bastion stood a lookout tower. These temporary canvas and wood structures, without beds of any kind, housed 497 Chiricahuas for the ensuing months.[27]

Sixteen year old Beshád-e and her mother stood, dismayed, at the top of the stairwell.

"Oh, Shi-ma, is it for this we gave up our homeland?" Beshád-e's lament was barely audible.

Ideal living conditions for the Tchi-héne were such a contrast. Family camps should be set up within calling distance of each other, but at least a quarter mile should separate them.

A soldier urged The People forward, pushing rudely.

A familiar figure then approached them. It was Chatto, their old and dear friend who had been a Scout, who had done all he could to keep Geronimo in line. The women embraced him, tears of sadness and joy intermingling.

"*Yada-chindi? Yada-chindi?*"[28] they asked, inquiring "What's the news?" but no response was really expected.

He walked them to their assigned tent, saying, "There's an oven down below in one of the dungeons. We all cook there. And there's a well out front where you can pull up drinking water. But take care and don't drink much. The water is real salty. Sea water gets into it." He paused, looking at the women in their ragged clothing, the children barefoot. "If you wait your turn, you can bathe. They have a couple of tin tubs for all of us to use, but sometimes the wait is so long that the women wash up when they go down to the beach."

The group moved to a spot where the hot breeze circulated more freely. Then Chatto shared more personal news.

"You remember, last summer, it was July according to the Anglo calendar, that man, General Miles, who took Crook's place, arranged for a delegation of us Indians to visit Washington, D.C. He said we were to discuss a suitable place for the Chiricahua to stay permanently, a reservation, but one better than San Carlos and Fort Apache and the others. He told me to head the delegation.

"Well, we got on the train, and we arrived in the capitol. We met with President Cleveland and the members of his cabinet. They treated us as though we were special. And after we talked for a long time, the President of the United States presented me with this medal." Chatto reached into his shirt pocket and brought out a large medal attached to a blue ribbon. Dilth-cleyhen and Beshád-e admired it.

"I wear it when we are doing things of real importance," the man said with an air of modesty. Beshád-e noted the shining pride in his eyes as he tucked the token back again.

"After all you have done to help the military, why are you here, in this prison?" Dilth-cleyhen queried. Old Man Chatto's face froze stoically. He shrugged.

"Who knows the mind of Anglos?"

Chatto urged Dilth-cleyhen and Beshád-e to move toward the tent allotted them. Then he shared a second confidence.

"I'm going to marry again. You know, my first wife has gone to Mescalero. She left with Dexter, the son of Loco. And my second wife is gone now. This girl, Be-gis-cley-aihn, is real young.[29] She needs someone to look after her. She does not want to be sent away to school, and they'll send her to Carlisle if I don't."

Fort Marion provided scant solace to women and children, aside from reuniting them with old friends. There was no full-time work or creative activity. The Chiricahuas benefitted when some Catholic sisters taught the children to speak English and to be clean. Perhaps the sisters were responsible for getting more toilets. There had been only two. Another benefit came when some compassionate white women bought calico and taught the Indian women to cut and sew new dresses.[30]

Even though she had her daughters, Dilth-cleyhen missed Mangas. Beshád-e did not want to be with Old Crooked Head, Tsedekizen, the man she had married at Fort Apache in order to avoid being shipped to Carlisle. He now lived with Rose (Ken-i-es-nidlth), a granddaughter of Chief Loco. He paid scant attention to Beshád-e, his fourth wife. They had little interest in each other but were not as yet "divorced."

Less than a month after arriving at the fort, Dilth-cleyhen was told to bring her youngsters before Lt. Stephen C. Mills, who had been placed in direct charge of the prisoners. He said, "You older children, those over twelve, are to go to Carlisle Indian Industrial School. The littler ones will be taught here for an hour each day by two sisters of the Convent of St. Joseph. I want you all to line up for physical examinations by the post surgeon."[31]

It was the same old story. Families were not going to be permitted to stay together. Many young people had already been sent to Carlisle, in the Cumberland Valley of Pennsylvania.[32] Children from San Carlos had been shipped there as early as 1883, sometimes under the directive of General Crook, who felt it would contribute to their betterment in terms of acculturation. The school was the military site of Carlisle Barracks, which from 1879 to 1918 was converted into a school for Indians of many tribes. The curriculum of the elementary grades at that time included boys' training in carpentry, farming, elementary care of farm equipment, animal husbandry and blacksmithing, and girls' training in general housekeeping, sewing, and kitchen gardening. During the summer months the students were placed in the homes of nearby Dutch farmers,[33] from whom they received a small compensation for their labor. Athletics were stressed: football, baseball, and various competitions in track events, including marathon races. But at the moment Beshád-e neither knew nor cared about the advantages of attending school.

Elsie, Frank, and Asa were among the first group selected to go. Departure was almost immediate.[34] Beshád-e protested, and her departure was delayed. She kept asking for the interpreter, George Wratten, who had accompanied Geronimo's family to the fort.[35] The lieutenant ignored her requests. She was given her physical examination and was issued new clothing for the journey. On December eighth she reached Carlisle in the second shipment of youngsters.

Beshád-e was desolate. She looked for Elsie. She looked for Asa and Frank.[36] All the boys looked strange to her. Their hair had been shorn, and they wore no breechcloths. This item of apparel, the last vestige of Apache male identity, was not permitted. The names of almost all had been Anglicized: Frank, the son of Mangas. Both boys and girls wore uniforms.

Beshád-e raised her shoulders and lifted her head, tilting it in proud posture.

"At least I'll know Asa and Frank and Elsie," she thought, her inner emotions belying her confident stance. "But I *must* find someone who will understand my status. I'm not supposed to be here. I'm a married woman!"

Finally someone listened. Beshád-e was returned to Florida where she remained imprisoned in St. Augustine for a dismal year.

Though Carlisle was the school to which most of the Apache

young people were sent, two orphans and a son of Naiche were registered at the Hampton Normal and Agricultural Institute of Virginia. This school was well known for training blacks, but in 1886 it accepted Indians as well.[37] No matter where students were enrolled, they mourned for their families, and their families grieved for them.

In later years Beshád-e was to recall the horrors of Florida: the crowded conditions, the inability to move freely, the salty water, the clammy heat, the damp clothing, the whimpering children, the mosquitoes, the sickness of The People, the deaths. Food had a strange flavor. Even fish did not taste like those caught in the cold mountain streams of home. Apathy, despondency, depression, and inability to understand Anglo ways pervaded waking and dreaming hours.

By 1887 twenty-three children had died. It was deemed necessary to have the Crown Dancers intervene, to act as intermediaries with the Powers. The sacred ceremony took place on the terreplein of the northwest bastion.[38]

Zah-mon,[39] the medicine man, presided, beating the drum he had made by drawing a soaped rag tightly over the mouth of an iron kettle holding a little water. There were three black-masked dancers wearing kilts and moccasins. They thrust their lathlike swords to the four directions as they moved in prescribed cadence. Each dancer bore a different yellow design on back and chest—the bear and the lightning among them. Zigzag snakes were painted on their arms. How impressive it was. How long it had been since Beshád-e had witnessed the sacred movements.

> So alive in lightning they dance without trying
> Their dance of the slumbering earth; perspiring
> Without tiring, around a spark-spun blaze
> They pace with slow purpose inside the slow-pulsing
> Drums of earth space, . . .[40]

At the proper time the troupe blessed ailing children. By the end of the dance some of the all-enveloping evil was gone.

How lucky were those Chiricahuas who missed General Miles's headcount on that September Sunday in Arizona when, with the assistance of the cavalry, he had announced that the In-déh must leave their homeland! After the count an additional few Indians had slipped away unnoticed, leaving their belongings unpacked. The unfortunate were those who surrendered. Four days later they had had to assemble on the parade ground at Fort Bowie, forced to listen while a band blasted the sounds of "Auld Lang Syne." The People were taken to Bowie Station and told to board the train for Florida.[41] How fortunate were those who were in Old Mexico at the time, and who remained hidden in the natural fortress, the Sierra Madre. Here their descendants continue living, largely undetected.[42]

With so many Indians housed in tents on the stark rooftops of the fort, there was little opportunity for privacy. Groups of women were herded to the sea, where they washed their clothing in pools safe from the breakers. They soaked the garments, then beat them with sticks, wrung them out, and spread them on bushes to dry. To smooth the dried cloth, they rubbed it round and round in their hands much the same way that they had previously worked hides to make them soft.

Later, Beshád-e described an incident to her grandchildren. "One day, I remember it so well, we were out there washing. We couldn't go to the sea too often to wash the clothes, and we didn't have many outfits, so we used to take off almost everything—right off our backs. We were out there that day, washing. We were all but naked. Suddenly, those soldiers appeared. They yelled at us, 'You women get back inside. Get back inside the fort!' That was a terrible time. Those soldiers shamed us. We had no clothing on. We were just animals to them. No privacy. They acted as if we had no right to bathe and wash privately."

By far the majority of prisoners at the Castillo were women and children; only some eighty-two were adult males. Of these, sixty-five had served the government of the United States as Scouts while Geronimo was causing trouble, from 1885 until late in 1886.[43]

At night the forlorn women sat outside their tents. They composed songs, and then they sang. They sang with lusty voices, hoping beyond all hope that the sound would carry across the many miles to Fort Pickens. The message was thus: "Escape, our warriors! Go back to the Southwest. Leave this bad land. Go home!"

Those men among the prisoners who possessed the strongest sacred powers told The People not to give up hope, and they never forgot to pray. They sketched likenesses of the Crown Dancers upon the gray stone walls of a dungeon room on the ground floor.[44] "We must have faith."

Perhaps placing Geronimo in Fort Pickens was useful after all. He became a celebrity, selling his photograph and even buttons (supposedly from his coat jacket) to gullible tourists. He complained bitterly about the dreadful conditions at both forts, and perhaps his words carried more weight than than those of any other individual save a few Anglos whose sympathies for the Indians were sincere.

In any event, the government finally agreed to transfer the Chiricahua prisoners. In April of 1887 family members were reunited—men and women and children. They were going by train to a new home, Mount Vernon Barracks near Mobile, Alabama.

In Alabama

On the evening of April 27, the train, filled with prisoners-of-war, stopped at Pensacola. Twenty women and eleven children, comprising the families of some of the men incarcerated at Fort Pickens, were removed from the railroad car and taken by launch to the island. The other passengers continued the journey to Alabama, arriving there the following day.

Dilth-cleyhen and Beshád-e were among those who disembarked. So was Huera, Mangas's other wife, but he did not welcome her. His genial and loving smile was bestowed on Dilth-cleyhen.[45]

The officer in charge housed the families in casements formerly used by the fort's officers. The structures were now in a sad state of disrepair, but this meant little to Dilth-cleyhen. Huera was in another room, and Mangas, keeping peace, did nothing to antagonize her. He simply left the woman (whom he soon divorced) alone. Bachelors, as well as men whose kin had chosen to go on, slept in the company quarters at the opposite end of the fort.

The women cooked in the open fireplaces of their rooms, laundered and mended clothes, watched their men pridefully, and visited. The former warrior-raiders worked industriously outdoors, clearing a ditch of its growth of wild indigo, planting the newly cleared parade ground with Bermuda grass, and cleaning wells.

"It's hard work but worthwhile now that you are here," Mangas said softly to his wife.

The couple began to plan.

"We should get hold of George Wratten, the interpreter. I'll bet he can write a letter for us, telling those army men we want to go somewhere permanently, where we can have a good home together—where we can plant crops, live in peace, and have our family."

Mangas, Naiche, and Geronimo conferred and then contacted Wratten, who wrote to Gen. D. S. Stanley, of San Antonio, with their request. But it was not yet to be.

On May 13, 1888, the prisoners were told to board the launch that took them across the bay to the train bound for Alabama.

The following day, they arrived at Mount Vernon Barracks. The fort was on the west side of the Mobile River, about twenty-five miles from the Gulf of Mexico. Built on a ridge, it consisted of brick buildings surrounded by a massive wall.

Before arriving the Chiricahuas had been in an optimistic mood. Spirits dampened when the hot, humid air enveloped and smothered them as they stepped from the railroad car; they sagged even more when, trudging up the hill, they realized they would be living in a swampland. They were yet to learn of the abundant downpours from ever-cloudy skies.

Desolately, the group sat on their belongings in front of a gate in the barracks wall. They looked down on the prisoners' village of log dwellings built by the Indians during the past year. The men had felled trees (the women helping dig out the stumps) and had sawed timber. Logs were chinked with clay. The homes, many still under construction, replaced former shacks. Eventually there were eighty houses surrounding a plaza.[46]

"At least there is more room for us here than in Fort Marion," Dilth-cleyhen thought. "I wonder why no one comes to greet us. Our friends are ignoring us."

She soon learned why. Sam Kenoi told her.

"There was a meeting, a council. Many of the people are lumping Mangas with Geronimo and the other hostile Indians of Fort Pickens. They feel Geronimo's holdout caused all the trouble, caused the government to be harsh on all the Chiricahuas. They don't blame you folks so much now. They know you deserted that old renegade long, long ago."[47]

Indeed, the rejection of Mangas's family did not last long.

Mangas inquired about the fort. It encompassed some three square miles surrounded by pine forests and swamps. The earth was rich bottomland, but heavy farming was out of the question. Here and there in the outlying country one could see a few log cabins, the homes of poor whites and blacks.[48]

Dilth-cleyhen and Mangas were assigned a house with two separate rooms joined by a roofed, open walkway. There were dirt floors, but these felt good beneath the feet—unlike the concrete of Fort Marion. There was no furniture of any kind, but Apaches had always slept on the ground, covered with a blanket.

"You are fortunate," Dilth-cleyhen was told by those who had arrived earlier. "We had army tents just outside the wall when they found we couldn't live in those hovels where the rain came through constantly, making muddy puddles for us to sleep in. This is much better."

There were distinct disadvantages, however. The housing site was in a hollow surrounded by trees that eliminated both air circulation and sunlight. It proved to be hot and close in summer, cold and damp in the winter. The circular open hearth over which Beshád-e and Dilth-cleyhen cooked was insufficient for warmth, nor did the addition of a Sibley stove supply adequate heat.

Many of the men spent their long leisure hours making bows and arrows. Women did beadwork. All such handiwork was sold to tourists at trainside. Otherwise, the chief occupation was gambling and trying to forget the misery of the oppressive wet heat.

A few energetic women, including Dilth-cleyhen and Beshád-e, planted and weeded a large garden that provided a greater supply of fresh vegetables. Despite its poor soil, the garden produced enough to eat and some to sell. The profits went into a special fund: for "salaries" for various services the Indians performed throughout the barracks, and for treats for the eighty or so children attending school in a one-room building furnished by the post. The youngsters were taught by two Catholic missionary teachers sent by the Massachusetts Indian Association of Boston in 1889. These women not only instructed the youngsters in English but also explained concepts of Christianity, which had been introduced in Florida and were now further amplified by a post chaplain. Teenagers were still sent to Carlisle for more intense acculturation.

Some Apache men enlisted in the army, Carl Mangas among them. He was handsome in uniform. In addition to helping construct even better housing, these former warriors drilled, assisted in building bridges, and practiced scouting, trailing, and skirmishing.

Unfortunately the prevailing attitude, brought on largely by the climate, was lassitude.

There was nothing the prisoners could do to eliminate the swarming mosquitoes or to meliorate the steamy environment. They were still intimidated by the presence of soldiers. Although George Wratten, the interpreter, was now superintendent of a work crew, many Indians had difficulty understanding the policies of the white man. The situation was so desperate that at least two Apache men took their own lives after killing or wounding their wives. One of these was Yiy-gholl, known among the Anglos as Larry Fun, a second cousin of Geronimo. He had surrendered with Geronimo and Naiche in 1886. Here at Mount Vernon Barracks he enlisted in Company I of the Twelfth Infantry and was eventually promoted to the rank of corporal. But this recognition was not enough to dispel Fun's frustration and feeling of worthlessness. On March 8, 1892, he attacked one of his two wives,[49] accusing her of infidelity. Thinking her dead, he killed himself, knowing that the white authorities would not understand his action, though it was perfectly consistent with Apache logic.[50]

Illnesses among The People increased; many died of malaria, dysentery, and tuberculosis. Some had arrived in a semistarved condition, and these began to pawn their meagre belongings for food. Victorio's sister Lozen, the erstwhile seer and woman warrior, also succumbed to sickness.[51] By the time the Chiricahua left Mount Vernon, at least fifty individuals had passed away. The situation was so bad that concerned Anglos intervened in their behalf.[52]

Among others, members of the Massachusetts Indian Society of Boston made an investigation, and once again Gen. George Crook tried to help. He visited the Chiricahua to see for himself.[53] In early 1890 he wrote to President Benjamin Harrison recommending that the prisoners of war in Alabama be transferred to Fort Sill, Oklahoma. After pressure from still more individuals, the president approved, turning the matter over to Congress. Four and one-half years passed while statesmen dallied under the guise of deliberation.

Finally, in August 1894 the move was approved. In 1895 the transfer took place.

Just prior to the official departure some thirty Apaches avoided the clutches of the military and made their way back to New Mexico where they joined the Mescalero Indians. A few entire families were among the Alabama escapees, but mostly only men made the break. A partial list follows:

There were the Choneskas. His Indian name was Chu-gan-essan.
There were the Seconds. Old Man Second's name was Itsán-itsán.
There was Old Lady Peso, Old Lady Magoosh, and Hattie Gonzales's mother, Be-ha-gust-huzn. Hattie's mother's name means "a

person getting whipped with it." It seems she married a Mescalero man, Poxmark. He became angry with her and whipped her with a rattlesnake.

Among the men were Old Man Ecludi, Elmer Wilson, Charlie Smith, and Jim Miller, known as "Chiricahua Jim."

1894: That was the year Lillian was born to Dilth-cleyhen and Mangas. Although her half-sister was twenty-four years her junior, Beshád-e and Lillian shared a relationship of beauty, one of ideal emotional closeness between female siblings. Their bonds with Cora (Lillian's full sister) and with Elsie Vance (half-sister to both Lillian and Beshád-e) were less intense.

1895: That was probably the year of Beshád-e's second marriage. This husband was a man by the name of Aanitso (or Ah-nit-sa), Borgia Aanitso, seven years her elder, who had been discharged from Carlisle on August 10, 1892. After enlisting in the United States Army, he had come to Alabama.[54] Beshád-e liked him; he was attracted to her, a woman of bearing and pride. Their life together started in Alabama but developed more richly in Oklahoma, a place of good climate, where they were allowed even more freedom. At Fort Sill they were to regain a greater sense of self-sufficiency, despite continuing status as prisoners of war.

In early October The People were put on a special train. They traveled to New Orleans and Fort Worth and on to Rush Springs, Oklahoma. From Rush Springs wagons conveyed them to Fort Sill. They arrived with nothing except a few boxes and trunks. Most of their belongings had been destroyed by fire in a railroad freight shed in New Orleans.[55]

In Fort Sill

The day of their arrival, October 4, the Chiricahua were a sorry spectacle. Bewildered from travel, they were not sure what they were expected to do. George Wratten was there to help interpret what officials told them, but even that was confusing.

For some years the Kiowas and the Comanches had lived at Fort Sill. When they first heard the army's plans for bringing more Indians to the area, they protested bitterly. But now that the day of arrival had come, they put aside whatever ill feelings they harbored and came to greet the unkempt Apaches. The Comanche leader, Quanah Parker, was especially responsive.[56]

The tribes tried to communicate with each other in sign language, but the Chiricahuas were mountain people and did not understand. Lt. Hugh Lenox Scott (soon to be a captain, and brigadier general by 1913), who was in charge of the prisoners, was expert in sign language, but since signs were ineffective, he found it necessary to try other means. He recruited a few Kiowa-Apaches, thinking their Athapascan tongue would be similar to that of the newcomers. It was not. The Kiowa-Apache dialect had changed too much; this tribe now belonged to the Plains.

Dilth-cleyhen whispered to Beshád-e, "After all, *those* Indians are only 'half-Apaches.'" It was not until teenage Comanche, Kiowa, and Chiricahua males were brought from Carlisle that the Indians were able to communicate—and then by means of the students' mutual knowledge of English.[57]

Even in the confusion of arrival, Dilth-cleyhen and Beshád-e took time to look about them, to breathe deeply the air that reminded them of their homeland.

Beshád-e sighed. "No moat, no parapet, no cannons. There aren't even fences here."

The Comanches, Kiowas, and some Kiowa-Apaches hauled the Chiricahuas to Cache Creek, where the latter set to work making private brush shelters for each family. There were many saplings along the banks. Where young trees stood adjacent to each other, their tops were tied together; those in the way were cut down. The framework of each wickiup was completed within an hour or two, and leafy branches were intertwined at the base. The army supplied old canvas to use as rooftop covering.[58] Beshád-e and Borgia's shelter was very near that of Dilth-cleyhen and Mangas.

When daylight dimmed, the weary newlyweds stood in their doorway, scanning the horizon.

"See. There are mountains, beautiful mountains. Maybe not as high as those in our homeland, but mountains."

"Listen to the water. It is a bubbling stream, not the roar of the ocean. I drank from it earlier. The water is clear and sparkling."

"Smell the sage."

"I heard quail crying a little while ago."

That night they heard a coyote howl in the far, far distance.

"It is good to be here."

The People continued to be under army command, but the control proved less oppressive than it had been in Florida and Alabama. Lieutenant Scott promised to give the Apaches food and blankets, and he lived up to his word. He also managed to find clothing to replace many tattered garments.

"Your children must be educated," Scott said further. When George Wratten translated this message, the Indians were totally silent but were concerned. "What can we do about it? We don't like this, but we have learned to accept the inevitable." In four days the youngsters were rounded up and hauled in wagons over the thirty-odd miles to Anadarko, where they were enrolled in a Catholic grammar school.

"We will get some schools for you here as soon as we can," authorities promised. Being separated from sons and daughters was one of the early hardships at Fort Sill. Some parents walked the entire distance to visit their little ones. They carried small treats, such as candy, hoping to appease the children's—and their own—loneliness.[59]

There was another frustration. The Apaches were continually in the dark concerning their fate, both daily and for the long term. George Wratten, whose present wife was a white woman (the first having been Apache), was given housing some distance from the Chiricahua camp, south of fort headquarters. He translated and explained policies to the best of his ability. Even so, there was confusion. Fortunately, Scott was a compassionate man, and, despite the linguistic and cultural differences between him and his wards, he practiced leniency whenever possible.

The Apache women heard that mesquite grew in southwestern Oklahoma and that there was a thicket of the shrubs some forty-five miles outside the fort. When they asked Scott if they could go there, he replied, "Yes, if you leave after noon on Saturday and get back here ready to work by 7:00 A.M. on Monday." He supplied them with a few horses to carry tents and supplies and the beans they would gather. In fact, the women—and this included Dilth-cleyhen and Beshád-e—picked some three hundred bushels of beans and jogged the entire ninety-mile trip. They returned on time to the fort.[60] It was an auspicious beginning.

The United States Congress had enacted legislation on August 6,

1894, which allotted $15,000 for the erection of buildings and for the purchase of stock and seeds, farm tools, and whatever else might be needed to give the Chiricahua a start in Oklahoma.[61] However, it was too late in the fall to start on permanent housing.

The winter proved harsh. The damp, cold wind penetrated the wickiups easily. Early the next spring Apaches began building according to government specifications that involved picket construction consisting of upright posts set in a frame.[62]

Although there were a few one- and three-room houses, most consisted of two chambers separated by an open-ended but roofed "dog-trot," slightly wider than a wagon—much like the housing in Alabama.[63] This breezeway provided circulation and shade during the coming hot summer. Further ventilation was available through the one or two windows in each room. Eventually, seventy-one units were ready for occupancy. A post-and-wire fence was built around each village.

Scott understood much about Indians. He knew that these Apaches were matrilocal and that extended families preferred living in spacious clusters, fairly near their friends but separated from those they disliked. With this in mind he arranged for some of their settlements to be along Medicine Bluff Creek and others a fair distance away, farther west on Cache Creek than the present wickiups.

After the completion of housing plans and assignments, he appointed a headman over each "Village." These were former Scouts or men with acknowledged leadership ability.[64] They were expected to maintain order and high living standards and to supervise the cultivation of the fields.

Carl Mangas was named head of Dilth-cleyhen's extended family.

Each headman was enlisted for three years as a soldier. Mangas served in Troop L, Seventh U.S. Cavalry Regiment. He was entitled to wear an army uniform and draw the pay of a private. Borgia Aanitso enlisted in the same unit, as did Frank Mangas when he returned from Carlisle. In earlier days of imprisonment Borgia had been attached to the army with Company I, Twelfth U.S. Infantry. It was not until 1897 that a Scout detachment of sixteen men was activated. These men were entrusted with special details such as supervising cattle and, later, of making sure that children attended school.

Mangas's Village, along with those of Kaahteney and To-clanny, would be centrally located, near northerly bends of Cache Creek; Loco's dwellings and farmland were located slightly farther south. To the far east of Mangas, by Cache Creek, would live the leaders

Geronimo, Perico, Chihuahua, and Kayitah, with Noche along the road to Anadarko. Chiricahua Tom, Chatto, and Naiche would have houses and fields to the west of Mangas, near Four Mile Crossing. Plural wives were given separate dwellings within each family cluster.

"I'm thankful Huera is not with us, and that Mangas discarded her," thought Dilth-cleyhen.

Mangas's Village consisted of three dwellings. Mangas, Dilth-cleyhen, and baby Lillian lived in one, along with whomever else they were looking after at the moment. Elsie Vance, who had been enrolled for three years in Carlisle before returning to Alabama, was now in her twenties, but she was unwell and stayed much of the time with her mother. Cora and Arnold Kinzhuma were newlyweds with a place of their own. The same was true of Beshád-e and Borgia.

There were a very few individuals who chose not to belong to any village but to live in a house somewhat isolated from their fellows. James Kaywaykla was one, Eugene Chihuahua another. When Ramona Chihuahua returned from Carlisle in 1895, she married Asa Daklugie and they lived near the fort itself.[65]

Even while building was progressing—in fact, while the Apaches were still in the Cache Creek camp—Scott began to train the men as cowboys. Mangas was pleased with the prospect as outlined by the lieutenant.

"It will be good to be around animals. I thought we'd get horses, but somebody said we will have to do our roundups on foot. Seems Scott thinks we're going to make a run for it."[66] He grinned. "Anyway, the cattle will be a reminder of old times, times when we raided in Old Mexico."

Congress had appropriated other funds sufficient to start a herd of range animals. Since the money would revert to the treasury if not used promptly, Scott arranged to buy the livestock at once even though there was no time to fence the military post or to plant feed.

"The cattle must be herded on the grassland, and you must keep careful watch that they do not stray onto the Kiowa and Comanche land," the Apaches were told. "We'll fence the reservation shortly, but for now there must be a constant patrol." Scott and 2d Lt. Allyn K. Capron felt it was necessary for them to camp with the cowboys in order to supervise the management of the herd.

Mangas smiled. He confided to Dilth-cleyhen, "Those officers are afraid of us. I guess they think we are going to scalp them!"

In fact, Scott was fearful that some Apaches might get drunk, commit some crime, and then attempt an escape. He had prepared for any such contingency but nothing perverse occurred.[67] The men proved to be good cowboys—learning to rope, brand, and treat the animals for heel-fly, screwworms, and anthrax; the women refrained from making tulapai. It was not long before cattle became the chief means of support for The People.

Hog raising was a less successful venture. As soon as they had a place to put them, each family had been given a sow; the whole tribe received two boars. The Indians hated hogs, and the whole enterprise was soon deemed a failure.[68] Turkeys and chickens were more acceptable.

As soon as fields could be tilled, the Chiricahua revealed their farming skills. Each male head of a household had a ten-acre plot, part of which was used for garden produce and part for animal feed. That first year more than 250,000 melons were raised. Those that the Indians did not eat were sold, usually just outside the post store. Scott had a nine-year-old daughter who stood beside the Indians' wagons, helping them bargain and make the proper change.[69]

Scott gave other advice. The sweet corn that Kiowas and Comanches had planted on a large scale had not done well; the wind and sun had been too fierce. He suggested the Apaches plant kafir corn, a grain sorghum. It grew successfully. The plants furnished fodder for the Indians' livestock, and again, surplus was sold to the government. Hay was also grown as a cash crop.[70]

Men worked the big fields; women helped with the weeding there, and, in addition, cared almost entirely for personal vegetable plots. "It is good to have variety," was the general consensus. Vegetables grown for home consumption included sugar corn, sweet potatoes, onions, peas, beans, and pumpkins.

"This sweet corn is so good. It tastes like that we grew at Ojo Caliente," commented Dilth-cleyhen to her daughter as they wielded hoes. "It's worth all the effort."

Gradually, as cattle raising became successful and animals were sold, Apache funds grew. From this money the army purchased farm machinery and mules, which were held in common.[71] Even earlier, Scott had acquired a few mules from army surplus when Fort Supply in Oklahoma was abandoned.[72] These made field tasks far less physically taxing. Eventually families were provided with horses, harnesses, and more wagons.

When evening came, many families, kin and non-kin, visited with each other, sharing information about crops, and, of course, gossiping. Who was ill? Who had been recently cured? Often the talk turned to Geronimo.

"That old rascal is up to his old tricks. He's such a tourist attraction, it is disgusting. That old liar. He sells his picture, his buttons, anything—even a feather—and he lies about every item."

"All the people in his village are busy making bows and arrows. Then Geronimo sells them to the tourists, saying, 'I made these with my own two hands.' Those white people are just taken in. They buy them immediately. They think they have some kind of treasure. It's pathetic that that old man gets more privileges than any one else."

"Even so, that Geronimo, his pumpkins are the best of all. I wonder if he uses his power to make them like that. He must make a good profit."

"Let's not talk about that old man. Where are the cards? Let's play a little. I lost a blanket last time, and nights are pretty cold!"

On the whole, this period of incarceration was a busy, productive time for the Chiricahua. Learning efficient ways of farming and caring for livestock occupied the village men. Some had military duties. Others helped build new roads and new reservoirs to catch summer rain. The women were far from idle; they did household chores and raised their youngsters. They made much of the family's clothing (although adult men wore Anglo shirts and trousers); they tanned hides from deer supplied occasionally by hunters. They fashioned the buckskin into moccasins. They cut venison or beef into strips, drying it for jerky. In "spare" moments, they tended the vegetable garden, several women working side by side whenever possible—chatting or complaining, as they mopped their brows, of the heat, or the lack of rain, the never-ending wind.

The major concern of The People was illness. Illness and death continued to take a high toll. Many Chiricahua refused to see a white doctor and were certainly fearful of the fort hospital. They preferred to rely on the powers of the medicine man, despite a growing concern that even he could not cope with the new crop of sicknesses. Further, there was continuing word that many students at Carlisle were dying. The sounds of mourning rent the skies at dawn and evening.

Then, too, although many of these years were prosperous ones, the In-déh were ever aware of their prisoner status. Even the acquisition of more land, due to the generosity of Quanah Parker, the Comanche leader, did little to allay this knowledge.

"Every morning of every day, I must line up at the fort to get rations for my family."

These handouts consisted of flour, sugar, and coffee plus a pound of beef for adults and one-half pound for children. Infrequently there were potatoes and onions.[73]

Further, no one could go for mesquite beans, no one could go hunting, no one could leave the Fort without permission.

Scott remained at Fort Sill until 1897. During the four years he was there, he noted, the Apaches had not broken a single promise they had made him.[74]

The following year, 1898, Beshád-e and Borgia had a girl-child. They gave her an Indian name; in English they called her "Susie."

On the day of the baby's delivery, Beshád-e sent her husband out of the house, telling him to summon her mother, who was a skilled midwife—as her very name, Dilth-cleyhen, revealed. Cora and Elsie came to assist. Borgia went to visit the To-clannys, for to remain near his mother-in-law, particularly at such a time as this, would have shown disrespect.

All went well. The prayers were beneficial.

Beshád-e knelt with legs apart, silent throughout, holding on to the doorpost. Her mother massaged her abdomen downward and as the infant emerged, Dilth-cleyhen caught her. The baby breathed promptly, but did not cry.

"That is good," Dilth-cleyhen murmured. "A child who does not cry grows to be strong."[75]

The infant was bathed in tepid water.

The afterbirth and umbilical cord were wrapped in a soft piece of the blanket on which Beshád-e had knelt. It was placed in a carton, safe for the time being. Later it would be placed in the branches of a sturdy tree that would be blessed by Dilth-cleyhen.

Beshád-e's mother strapped a buckskin band around the new mother's waist. "You must wear this until you feel totally strong once again. It will prevent your stomach from sagging."

To the women the infant was beautiful. Borgia was summoned in due time; he, too, admired his daughter.

For the remainder of the day Beshád-e rested, but the next morning she was up bright and early. When Dilth-cleyhen came to check on her, she was trying to nurse her babe.

Dilth-cleyhen returned home, saying to Mangas, "I must start the cradleboard." The cradle ceremony was held four days later, and the little one found security within the buckskin wrappings.

Susie was a sweet baby, but even as an infant, she seldom smiled. Toward the end of the year, Beshád-e seemed preoccupied, her time with the little girl was less comforting.

Borgia Aanitza was ailing. That year, the very year his daughter was born, he died. He was only twenty-one; his widow twenty-eight.

"Aye-yaaa. Aye-yaaa. Aye-yaaa." The high pitched wail of mourning rent the heavens near Mangas's Village.

Beshád-e could not remain in her assigned house. It might be taken over by the ghost. Most often she stayed with Dilth-cleyhen and Carl. Her dwelling was fumigated but left empty for a year, at which time it was blessed and fumigated again. Only then could she return.

That very year, Elsie Vance Chestuan was put to rest and mourned.

And years later, in 1901, the sound of keening again rose along Cache Creek, from the complex assigned to Dilth-cleyhen, her daughters, and their men.

This time the death was that of Mangas, Carl Mangas, a warpath leader and the son of the great chief, Mangas Coloradas. Mangas, so dear to Dilth-cleyhen and to her daughter, was buried in the Post Cemetery.

"Will it never end!" sobbed Beshád-e. "Aye-yaaa!"

Young Frank Mangas lived only two more years, succumbing to pulmonary tuberculosis. His sister Faith had died just before arrival at the fort; Flora was gone immediately after. Of the eight children born to Cora at Fort Sill, five would die before the tribe was offered land in New Mexico. By then she would have only Nathan, Prince, and Winifred.

Mourning was the commonplace, rather than the exception, in Fort Sill.

On their arrival at Fort Sill, the Apaches were again in contact with Christian doctrine. As early as 1895 the Dutch Reformed Church, the Reformed Church in America, had sent a missionary, a Choctaw minister by the name of Frank Hall Wright. Army officials suggested he not preach to the Chiricahua. "They've just arrived. Give them breathing time—time to settle in." In about a year the ban was lifted, and the church people called The People to a council. The Choctaw and a Dr. Walter C. Roe presided.

The headman of each Village had a say as to whether or not they wanted to hear Christian doctrine. Naiche spoke first, slowly, and at length, talking about the church's role in their past. Then Geronimo stood.

"I am Geronimo. I and these others are too old now to follow your Jesus road. But our children are young. They should know about the white man's God."[76]

Chatto spoke, and so did Rogers To-clanny. Even the usually quiet Carl Mangas had taken his turn.

"I think it is good for our children to know as much about the white man and his God as possible. I think you should preach to our young people about your beliefs." Dilth-cleyhen nodded her agreement. Beshád-e was of the same mind when later the family members pondered the points brought up at the meeting.

The War Department gave permission for the construction of mission buildings on the reservation. The site chosen was just east of Kaahteney's land, in a sheltered hollow about halfway between the most easterly and most westerly Villages. It was called the Punch Bowl. Because the primary interest of the Apaches was the education of their children, the first "church" building was a small frame schoolhouse with an added room to serve as living quarters for a teacher. In August 1899 Miss Maud Adkisson arrived. She served as teacher, nurse, and home visitor.

Her work pleased The People. Their younger children need no longer go to Anadarko. On Sundays the school was used for religious services. The Indians learned about Jesus and Christian ethics from ministers Wright and Roe. A Christian Endeavor Society was organized.

The Scout Noche was among the first converts, as were Chihuahua and Naiche, who took the name Christian Naiche. Chatto decided he should belong. Asa Daklugie was a holdout. He preferred the native ways, but he listened, and when his wife became a devotee, he accompanied her. Dilth-cleyhen and Beshád-e attended services a few times, and they tried to understand, although they were puzzled.

"Who is this Messiah they are talking about? Is it the same one that Nakai-doklini preached about when we were in San Carlos? I thought that in *his* religion all the white men would be killed!"

"And what is that thing they call a 'spirit'? "

But they continued to go from time to time, partly as entertainment, and partly because they recognized that the church was trying earnestly to better them.

"All the children of our family should be taught by these Dutch Reform people."

"I'm glad Susie will be able to go to school close by and not have to go off the fort grounds."

"Maybe we should be baptized."

"I think so. It can't hurt."

Especially welcome was the church's annual summer camp meeting. A large tent was set up for the services. The Indians erected their smaller tents nearby so that they would miss nothing. At first church leaders chose the Punch Bowl as the site for the camp but later moved to other locations. In July 1903 the meeting was held in an oak grove on Medicine Bluff Creek. It was then that an injured and contrite-appearing Geronimo, who had recently fallen from a horse, declared himself willing to find Jesus. Within a week he was baptized.[77]

The mission eventually constructed five buildings, including an enlarged schoolhouse. The mission staff increased to a superintendent, two teachers, two dormitory matrons, and several laborers. The pastor lived near the Comanches.

"When we can't get to Wratten, I bet those teachers will help us." suggested Beshád-e.

"But they don't speak much Apache," her mother noted.

When Susie was just over a year old, Beshád-e took notice of a handsome young Apache who was one of the few blacksmiths in Fort Sill. His name was Abner Kozine. Dilth-cleyhen teased her daughter.

"How come you always want to go to the trader's store? Is it because it's real near the smithy?"

Beshád-e's answer was a smile at the corner of her mouth and a toss of her proud head.

Abner's forebears were Tchok'-anen, the Mountain People or Rising Sun People. He was a full brother of Anice Simmons. Both had attended Carlisle, having been sent there directly from Fort Bowie. After completing her studies Anice had worked among whites in Concordville, Pennsylvania. She was now married to a white soldier at the fort, and they had decided to live outside its boundaries, in either Enid or El Reno.[78] She bore him two sons, Edmond and Morton, who came to be important influences in the life of Beshád-e's granddaughter.

Abner had enrolled at Carlisle on November 4, 1886, and remained there until the Chiricahua were settled at Fort Sill. He had missed the horrors of Florida and Alabama. Instead, he received training as a blacksmith. He and John Loco worked now with Jason Betzinez in the prisoner-of-war smithy. The young man served also as a Fort Sill Scout.

Abner Kozine was well aware of the pretty woman in her early thirties who sauntered so frequently past the blacksmith shop. He liked the way she walked, her modesty, the tilt of her head with its shiny hair. Very shortly he spoke to her kin, and he and Beshád-e were wed.

The next year a son was born to them, a boy whom they named Reginald.

Again Dilth-cleyhen assisted her daughter at the birth, and yet again she made the cradle. Unfortunately, Reginald was never a healthy child, and in 1904, he died of tuberculosis—as did so many of the In-déh.

Beshád-e keened, "Aye-yaaa."

Anice had been unhappy with her soldier husband, and now she came to Fort Sill, wanting to be near her people. While she sought employment, or was otherwise engaged, her small sons, Edmond and Morton, often stayed with Abner and Beshád-e, at least until Anice married Sam Kenoi.

The presence of the children comforted Beshád-e. She nonetheless continued to mourn—until she felt new life stirring within her.

That very year, 1904, she gave birth to a daughter, Christine Louise, a child who was Beshád-e's joy throughout the girl's life.

As 1912 neared many of the Chiricahua had become self-supporting, some having sufficient income to make them pleasantly comfortable. Most of them spoke some English; many were fluent as well as literate. Knowledge of white culture increased steadily as students returned from Carlisle.[79]

Beshád-e's daughters had outgrown the school at Fort Sill and had been sent to Chilocco, in northern Oklahoma. How she missed them! She awaited their letters, which had to be translated for her because she had not mastered the speaking of English, let alone reading and writing. All too often, she returned no letter. There was no one to turn to, no one who would take the time to act as scribe.

There were rumors that the Apaches were about to be moved once again. "How can they keep doing this to us! And yet they keep us prisoners!"

Two years earlier Fort Sill had been chosen as the site of an artillery school, but more land was needed. The prisoners would have to go. But what would the army do with them? The plight of the Chiricahua had become public information; there was mounting pressure that they be released. In August of 1912 Congress authorized such action and appropriated $200,000 for the resettlement. The next year another $100,000 was added to this. Now, where should they be placed? Several locations were possible.

A delegation of Chiricahua men was chosen to help make the ultimate decision. They visited Mescalero, where they had had many friends, where many tribesmen had once been sympathetic to Victorio's cause. Among those chosen to go was Rogers To-clanny.

"Im glad Old Man To-clanny will be there to represent the Tchihénè." Beshád-e remarked.

The delegates went to Ojo Caliente but found that much of their arable land had been sold to Spanish Americans and was not available. They went to the Mescalero Reservation and talked at length to certain leaders. One of the latter, Magoosh, consulted with his people, suggesting that perhaps additional Apache numbers would prevent further diminution of their homeland, as was being threatened.

"There are a lot of miners, a lot of ranchers, who would like to cut us down to their size," he argued. "These Chiricahua are our friends, and they could come join us. That would make the whites think again about reducing our land."

The transfer of the Fort Sill Chiricahua was thus possible. Councils were held, with officials trying to explain alternatives. Older Apaches, who still knew little English, missed the help of George Wratten. He had been ill for a long time; he died on June 23, 1912.

Just over one-fourth of the families chose to remain in Oklahoma. It was decided to purchase individual farms for them, largely from the heirs of deceased Comanches, Kiowas, and Kiowa-Apaches. Most settled finally in a rich agricultural area near the town that bears their name, Apache. There they began to support themselves by farming and trading in a predominantly white society.

By far the majority wanted to leave Oklahoma as soon as possible. They wanted to spend their remaining days in freedom—in New Mexico. Hopefully, they could resume and retain at least some of their traditional ways!

"Victorio liked Mescalero. He had lots of friends there. That is the best place for us," Dilth-cleyhen reasoned. Cora and Beshád-e agreed. A similar decision was made by Charlie Istee, and by Chatto, Martine, and To-clanny—kin and friends from earlier days of war.

"You must get your personal goods together—all your household things. We will sell your cattle. We will compensate you for the fence you have built around the reservation. We will give you credit for all of this," officials told The People. "We can freight your horses and mules, your wagons, all your wheeled vehicles. They can go with you to Mescalero."

The proceeds from the cattle amounted to between $165,000 and $170,000. The herd was said to be one of the finest in Oklahoma.[80] A list was made of the sum due each Apache owner.

Boarding a special train with passenger and freight accommodations, the Chiricahua left under escort of an army officer.

Two missionaries from the Dutch Reformed Church went also, ready to help in any way they could. Although their Mission at Fort Sill was closed, their dedication continued.

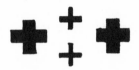

Early Days in Mescalero

On April 2, 1913, their trip westward began, not with fear as when The People had left Holbrook some twenty-seven years before, but with quiet anticipation, with hope.

In the very early morning hours of April 4, the Rock Island Railway train neared the small town of Tularosa, New Mexico, heading south toward the Sacramento Mountains.[81]

Just before their arrival, Dilth-cleyhen turned to Beshád-e. Her lips pursed to the west.

"Do you remember all that lava, that place of black jagged rock just before we got to the Mescalero land? I think it is right out there. We must be near." Beshád-e looked, but saw nothing. Dilth-cleyhen was lost in her memories, peering out the window into the semi-darkness until the train slowed and jolted to a stop.

Slowly the passengers stepped down and onto the platform. A few dogs (which they had been forbidden to take) darted out, barking excitedly, dashing among legs and skirts, glad to be free to move at last.

A number of Mescaleros had come to greet them. There was also a crowd of townspeople, some smiling and friendly, others curious about the "savages" and their cargo.

Although Anglos in the vicinity of Tularosa and the Mescalero Reservation were largely in favor of the transfer of the Chiricahua, some bitterly fought against the newcomers. In particular Senators Albert B. Fall and Thomas B. Catron [82] would continue to work against the Indians.

The Mescaleros had come in wagons and had prepared food for the Chiricahua. The two tribes made themselves acquainted. The hosts were genial to their permanent "guests." After sharing the meal, gear was loaded, and off they traveled, moving north. It was slightly over twenty miles to the Mescalero Reservation and its higher altitude.

Beshád-e and Abner sat close together. Dilth-cleyhen rode in the wagon following, in order not to embarrass her son-in-law. When they were on the outskirts of town, Beshád-e grasped Abner's arm. Her voice was higher than usual, more excited.

"Look, look, my husband, there is yucca. And look, mesquite bushes, too!" The desert land was just what she remembered from childhood.

The wagons and their precious cargo swayed along the rough road, later to be improved and known as U.S. Highway 70. It lumbered through the small white community of Bent, with its Catholic Church.

"We're almost there," the passengers were informed.

In just a few miles they reached the border of the Mescalero Reservation. The driver turned to his passengers. "Well, you are here. You are free."

The horses lumbered on.

"We'll soon reach Agency."

The Mescalero Apache Reservation,[83] established in 1872, is located in Otero County in the south-central part of the State of New Mexico. It consists of some 460,563 acres.

Dominating the northwestern corner of the reserve, at a height of over 12,000 feet above sea level, is Sierra Blanca, a landmark peak and part of the range of the same name. Only twelve miles southwest the terrain drops to 5,400 feet, the lowest altitude of Apache ownership.

The crests of the Sacramento and White mountains extend through the western portion of the reservation in a general north-south direction. The eastern slopes of the ranges drain into the distant Pecos River, whereas streams on the western laterals drain into the Tularosa Basin, ultimately sinking into the bleakness of White Sands. The steep western face of the mountain is cut by numerous short canyons covered with pine, fir, piñon, and juniper trees. The more gentle eastern side is riddled by deep and winding drainages.

Some 250,000 acres of the land, generally between altitudes of 6,600 and 11,000 feet, are classified as forest or timberland. The remaining expanse consists of rocky but rolling grassland. This is broken to the northeast by a small cluster of mountains, the tallest of which is Pajarito, reaching an elevation of 8,041 feet. The savannah is ideal for the grazing of cattle. Desert plants, supplying traditional Apache foods, can be found just outside the reservation.

The generally mild climate varies according to altitude. Summer days are relatively cool. Only in the heart of November and somewhat later does freezing temperature occur. Rains fall mostly between the months of June and September, but even then most days are filled with sunshine.

Wild game consists primarily of deer, turkey, and in some areas, quail. There are a limited number of bear, mountain lion, and antelope. In 1913 large herds of wild horses raced and romped in northern fields.

The eyes of the Chiricahuas were wide as they neared their destination. Finally, Abner could contain himself no longer, and even though it is impolite to ask questions, he enquired, "I see no tipis, no houses. Where do you Mescalero live now?"

"Well, we are all over, in scattered communities. We don't like being crowded together. Some live at Agency. That's what we call 'Mescalero.' That's where the Bureau of Indian Affairs and the Tribal Offices are. It's where Christian churches meet, and just east of the administration buildings, a little farther on, nearer East Mountain, is the ceremonial place called Feast Ground. Lots of camping there." He paused.

"Most of us are out, way out, nearer Ruidoso, in the place called Carrizo and in the canyon and meadows beyond, in Rinconada, or, on the east side of this road, way out in Elk Silver and beyond. Some live in Head Springs, too. A few like the lower altitudes—back where you came from on the train—before you get to Tularosa. That's Three Rivers. Some of us are there. But you have to go back the way we came and up another main road to reach it—off the reservation. Those people, like the Shantas, really like their privacy."

In a few minutes Beshád-e leaned toward Dilth-cleyhen. "Listen to that man. He talks Apache, but lots of the words are wrong!" she pointed out.

"It's the way all Mescaleros talk. Their dialect is much different—

different even than that of the Tchok'-anen and Net'na," reminded her mother.

Finally, the wagons reached their destination, the Feast Ground near Agency.

A number of heavy canvas tents had been set up on a level expanse. There was wood, good grass, and a small stream of mountain water nearby.

"You are to stay here temporarily," the Fort Sills were told.

The term "Fort Sills" was one that clung to the newcomers throughout the years. Their speech was distinctive; they had assumed more white ways than had the Mescaleros. They had a special style of bearing. Some Mescaleros termed them "uppity," whereas, more aptly, they should have been designated as "reserved," or "proud of heritage." Certainly, despite their demeanor, they were apprehensive, not knowing their future.

For the next months, that future involved remaining at the Feast Grounds in tents.

"*Why* did we come here?"

"We made a mistake. We should have stayed in Fort Sill. There's no freedom here. They've stuck us here—all in a bunch!"

Shortly after the Chiricahua had been a month in Mescalero, Maj. George W. Goode, the officer in charge at the time of their discharge from Fort Sill, came to see how his former wards were faring. Goode had turned their jurisdiction over to the Department of Interior, thus proclaiming the Indians' freedom. Clarence R. Jefferis had been named their agent and accompanied them from Oklahoma. Goode spent six days on the reservation, after which he suggested that the Fort Sills be encouraged to stand on their own. Agent Jefferis should have a free hand.

"Locate them in their own homes as soon as possible," the major advised. "Get them cattle. There is a fine range here, and these people proved in Fort Sill that they are excellent cattlemen."[84]

Nothing happened immediately.

In order to while away the days, some of the Fort Sill men began to practice their skills at playing baseball. In the middle of May they were challenged to a game in Cloudcroft, a resort town to the east of the reservation. The Apaches won easily, 22 to 2. The sports columnist for the *Weekly Cloudcrofter* stated the defeat was due to numerous errors on the part of the Cloudcroft team.[85] Although many

Anglos and Spanish Americans in the vicinity of Mescalero had feared aggression from the newly arrived tribe, this event proved to be the only battle. A return match was scheduled for July.

Summer arrived. The Fort Sills were still in tents.

Beshád-e spoke to Abner. "Christine and Susie want to come home from school. I got a letter."

"Don't you think they better wait until we're settled? Until I feel better?" was his reply. "There is so much sickness—death."

Lillian's boy, Edward, had died shortly after the Chiricahuas had transferred from Oklahoma, and many others at Feast Ground were coughing and congested. Diarrhea was prevalent.

September came, and Christine remained in the boarding school at Chilocco. So did Susie.

Somewhat earlier, thirty Fort Sill families had been assigned locations in the area known as White Tail. This district is some twenty-three miles northeast of Agency. Between seven and eight thousand feet in elevation, it consists of a narrow eight-mile-long valley covered with grama grass and intersected with streams from melting snows. Here, summers are short, sometimes subject to drought, and winters are severe and cold, with heavy snowfall. The growing season is short.

"You'll be able to grow some grains and some vegetables anyway. You should take up that kind of farming. And you can hunt. There is an abundance of small game here and, of course, as the region's name implies, there are lots of white-tailed deer, and a few elk, too."

Jefferis had chosen the spot primarily because it was unoccupied. Wells had to be dug for drinking water, stock tanks set up, and roads created. Construction must begin on houses. The agent made plans for twenty-five units. They would be four-room houses with porches. Each family would have a barn and chicken coop.

"Maybe we should start with barns," Jefferis speculated. "And I'd like them to start raising sheep; then we'll see about cattle."

Later, some of the families chose to own sheep, but at first they resented being deprived of the livestock they had expected.

"The Mescaleros may like those bleating animals, but we don't," was the consensus.

Long before any White Tail construction was completed, long before most of it was even started, the Mescaleros had helped move the Fort Sills to their canyon sites. To the left of the road, really little more than a trail, was Beshád-e's allotment; to the right of the lane, was that of Dilth-cleyhen. Lillian and George Martine's land was six miles beyond, down the canyon. Along the roadway there was a pipe with faucets at locations where houses were expected. Fifteen thousand dollars of the Fort Sill cattle money was spent on this domestic water system. When the Chiricahua learned this, there was an outcry.

"The government should have paid for our water! They promised us land and houses and water and a way to make a good living—one like we had at Fort Sill!"

Nonetheless, The People set to work.

Dilth-cleyhen and Beshád-e helped each other. Lillian lent a hand, and George did as much as he could. He rounded up other men to assist in constructing the bases of tents for the three families. Abner felt too feeble to do much of anything.

The doors of the temporary housing faced east. Beshád-e cut wood and stacked it along the north side of the entry. Later, she would extend the pile toward the east as a protection against snowdrifts.

"Abner, I'll try to get us an iron stove, but in the meantime we can use the fire hole in the center of the tent. I like that better for cooking anyway. Will you be warm enough? It will be chilly."

The next day she banked the tent with earth. During the night, she had felt a strong, cold draft.

These were troublesome, frightening times for Beshád-e.

By now Abner was very ill. He was too sick to intercede with government officials concerning his family's rights.

Beshád-e did not understand English well enough to comprehend the various business dealings. The well-meaning but somewhat inefficient Jefferis usually ignored her. She was a woman. Even tribal officials seemed to prefer dealing with men. "They would have listened in the old days, when I was young." When signatures were required, Beshád-e made an X with considerable foreboding. What if something should happen to Abner? How could she buy food and take care of her girls without his pension?

"What will we do, *Shi-ma*? How will I buy them clothing?"

The Chiricahua had many complaints during that first year.

They learned that although they had been promised 160 acres per family, they had received only 80. The water system had eaten some of their hard-earned funds, money which they now needed for food, more wagons, and tools. Further, some of the cost of the houses they were supposed to be "given" was deducted from part of what was left.[86] The remainder would come from money that was due the Fort Sills from the tribal lumber enterprise.[87]

Little did Dilth-cleyhen and Beshád-e know that it would be some four years before the promised housing would materialize. Many families had barns first, and so they moved into them, leaving animals outside.

Nor was the building construction adequate. Homes had no insulation. Wood was green when installed, and it shrank within a few months, leaving cracks through which wind whistled eerily.

Abner died that year of 1914. He never saw his home in White Tail.

Indeed, Beshád-e was alone. How grateful she was for Lillian and for Dilth-cleyhen.

The sad keening was heard in the early hours of dawn and sunset: "Aye-yaaa! Aye-yaaa!"

Abner's tent was abandoned, later to be fumigated. The wickiups in which he had spent much time were burned.

"Christine and Susie must be told. But I cannot afford to bring them home for the funeral," was Beshád-e's decision.

Cora Mangas Kinzhuma was also very ill. She and Arnold felt they should not leave the Feast Grounds. They wanted to be near transportation and medical help should they need it. White Tail was just too remote.

The summer after Abner died, Christine and Susie came home for vacation. Beshád-e and Dilth-cleyhen met them in Agency. The excitement of the girls was contagious. They wanted to know about everything they saw on the arduous all-day trip by wagon up to White Tail.

"Why aren't our houses started?" the girls had asked when finally they reached the family plots of land. Beshád-e had set up two wickiups for the summer season.

"What's planted in the fields? Are we still farmers like at Fort Sill?"

"We planted oats. That's what they advised."

"You mean *you* plowed up the fields, Shi-ma?"

"No. Lillian's husband supervised and worked a lot of the time, and the neighbors helped. Our fields are for me and for your grandmother. And then Hosteen Arnold came up from Feast Ground to plow and sow and weed whenever he could—whenever he could leave Cora."

Actually, the summer passed in pleasant fashion, with backbreaking work for adults, but time also for companionship, for enjoying the beauties of the meadows, the flowers, the coolness of the pines.

Beshád-e walked oftentimes with Christine, sometimes down the road, other times into the forest.

"All we lack are oak trees. Sometimes I get so hungry for their acorns."

She told her daughter stories of the days of the warpath, of the changes she had seen. "You must not forget you are Tchi-héne. You must not forget the valor of our warriors and the strength of their women. You must not forget your heritage. We have endured much that it might last."

In evenings, Lillian and nearby neighbors came with their families. They sat on the ground of the shelter, and there they talked and sang old songs. The air was clear and balmy, the shroud of nearby trees dark and mysterious, and finally when night surrounded them, the stars were so close that Beshád-e wanted to reach out and touch them.

As September approached, Beshád-e consulted with her mother.

"I think it best for Christine to go somewhere else to school. Maybe Albuquerque would be good for her. I want her to know all the white ways, all the things I don't know. There are lots of our Indian children there. Susie can stay here. She'll soon get married. But Christine can't stay here. We're in tents, and the winter months will be too harsh."

She told Christine. The girl pretended she understood in order to please her troubled mother.

"It's all right," she said.

Until she was eighteen years old, Christine remained off the reservation during the school terms, returning to be with Beshád-e only for vacations.

In mid-October Beshád-e looked out over her fields. She looked at Dilth-cleyhen's section. Both were black. A fire had consumed most of the crop. There had been weeks of drought.

The next day snow fell heavily, covering the trees and meadows with whiteness. It was far too early! There would be no threshing, even of what grain was left.

"No income," she thought. "How will we live? And the Indian Office has stopped all our rations.[88] Maybe I should get rid of the sheep. It's too hard to care for them."

Already Jefferis had admitted to The People that agricultural pursuits would be insufficient to sustain them. He had made some arrangements to better their condition. In June of 1914 a "tribal" herd was purchased with funds from a reimbursable government loan.[89]

Now he suggested, "I'll see what I can do about getting you some cattle. We may have to take out a loan."

He investigated. There was an Apache Fund that had been "laid aside" for the purchase of cattle for both Mescaleros and Chiricahuas. It never became available.

There was other trouble. Senators Fall and Catron were still enraged that the Indians had been permitted to remain in central New Mexico. Fall renewed his earlier attempt to turn the Mescalero Reservation into a national park. He had covert reasons. He wanted the rights and royalties on minerals extracted there, and he was adamant in protecting friends' and relatives' grazing leases. Through the efforts of the opposition, his plans came to naught, but the controversy lasted well over a year and caused great anxiety among the Apaches. Jefferis knew that they must be calmed and helped, and finally he enlisted the aid of Ted J. Sutherland.

Sutherland, a graduate of New Mexico Military Institute and an excellent judge of cattle, bought two thousand grade heifers from various ranches near the reservation. He also selected registered bulls, four to each one hundred cows. He branded them and turned them loose at Elk Canyon.

The purchase proved advantageous and alleviated considerable Apache tension. Nonetheless, it was a difficult winter.

The next year there was a cattle roundup in the flat at Cow Camp No. 1, near Pajarito Spring, for the branding of the first crop of calves! There were 1,984 young animals, an incredible increase. Each was marked "USID" (United States Indian Department) along with a bow and arrow. Sutherland was assisted by non-Indian cattlemen friends living in the vicinity and by a group of Mescalero cowboys whose mounts had been roped out of the wild herd of horses near Elk Silver. Asa Daklugie joined them. He had been in charge of the cattle herd at Fort Sill and was an expert at handling livestock. He worked without compensation.[90]

"I decided somebody should keep an eye on those Anglos. I still don't trust them," Asa confided to Beshád-e.

The cattle continued to be profitable, but Jefferis had had enough. He resigned November 15, 1915.

During the summer of 1917 Dilth-cleyhen and Beshád-e decided it was time to prepare for Christine's Puberty Feast, her da-i-dá.

"It will take well over a year to prepare, to gather the foods. But with the cattle doing better, I think we can manage. Lillian will help."

It was decided that Dilth-cleyhen should inform her granddaughter.

"My child, it is time that we celebrate your womanhood. It is time that you be White-Painted-Woman." It was a solemn pronouncement, met with joy.

Preparations began almost immediately. They needed buckskin for the robe, the collection of sacred foods would have to wait for the appropriate seasons. They would hire someone to take them to the other side of Mayhill, around the town of Hope. There they would find plenty of mescal to bake. Piñons, mesquite beans, yucca fruit, pollen from the cattail, all the sacred paraphernalia—everything must be collected and in readiness. Gifts must be purchased for the maiden's chaperone, for the workers who would do the cooking in the arbor, for those who would cut tipi poles and gather the wood for the great bonfire. Honorable helpers and supervisors must be selected. There was so much hard work in store, so many decisions ("how many beef must we slaughter?"), so much happy anticipation.

"We will be fully ready by the summer of 1919. That gives us plenty of time to save money and get things in order."

This was the year in which more Hereford cattle were added to the tribal herd, purchased from joint Chiricahua funds. Some of the Fort Sills were urged by the Agency superintendent to buy additional cattle of their own.

"You can use some of the money from the sale of the Oklahoma herd. There is still some left." Many did as advised. Owners had individual brand marks, but the cattle were run with the tribal herd.[91]

For a time after Christine returned to school that fall, Beshád-e was optimistic.

Then, once again her spirits were crushed.

In the spring of 1918 there was again severe drought. The oat crop withered to nothingness.

"What are we going to do, Shi-ma?" Beshád-e worried. "No oats means no money for our coffee and sugar, even for cornmeal. If we can't even find enough cash for clothing and utensils at home, how will we get a buckskin dress and all the big pots and pans needed for the Feast?"

"We've already used the funds from selling the sheep."

"I'll go talk to the trader next time we are in Agency. Maybe he will give us credit."

The trader was sympathetic, but credit was limited. All the Fort Sills suffered during this time. Many were still living in tents, and a few were in barns. The existing houses had proved uncomfortable. Much more construction was needed. There was insufficient food for many families. Patches decorated everyone's clothes. Farm machinery and tools were broken and rusted. There were almost no pumps for wells. All conversations centered around The People's misery.

And then, for Dilth-cleyhen, Beshád-e, and Arnold Kinzhuma there was added sorrow. Cora died April 3, 1919.

"Aye-yaaa!"

Old Man Arnold grieved, but did not want to stay anywhere near his abandoned camp.

"Do you think it will be all right with my mother-in-law if I come up to White Tail? I could do so many things that need doing and help take care of all of you."

And so it came to be.

In accordance with Apache custom, it was natural for Hosteen Arnold to be near his sister-in-law at this time. He and Beshád-e had been friends for so long; their houses had been close at Fort Sill. Even before they were prisoners of war, his family had often been with hers, for he came from Warm Springs. Now she needed his physical strength in tilling, sowing, and caring for the fields, his ability to mend machinery; now she needed his advice. He was more able to deal with white men's decrees. He could help her make good decisions. On the other hand, he needed a woman's hand with food and clothing. His three children were still young, and during the summer months they needed a mother, though even the youngest could be put in boarding school in the fall—or so he reasoned.

The name, Kinzhuma (or Kinzhuna or Kin-june) was an English appellation. In Indian he was called Tchu-je, the translation of which meant "Pretty Foot" or "Pretty Moccasin."

Beshád-e laughed. "I guess that means I should get busy tanning buckskin. You need some moccasins to go with your name—all beaded and bright with a fancy upright toe!"

Arnold, the brother of Kaahteney, another neighbor at Fort Sill, had attended Carlisle for two years and then in 1889 was sent to Alabama. Here he had met and later married Cora.[92] He became part of Company I, Twelfth Infantry Regiment. When the Chiricahua were transferred to Fort Sill, he joined Troop L of the Cavalry Regiment. His service entitled him to a pension.

Within the year Beshád-e and Arnold Kinzhuma were wed. She was fifty years of age, and he was fifty-four.

The children of the extended family continued to address him with respect, calling him Hosteen Arnold, "Old Man Arnold."

There were many decisions for the new couple to make.

Even before the marriage, Arnold had been asked his opinion as to whether Christine's Feast should be given. He felt it should be held as planned, and he contributed effort and money.

It was a glorious Feast. How proud Beshád-e was of Christine's running.

How stately was White-Painted-Woman!

After it was over there were mundane tasks and plans for the future. Beshád-e's household would be somewhat more prosperous now, though the newlyweds never had lots of cash. Nonetheless, there was money from the sale of their cattle, from Arnold's pension, and from the sale of timber, part of the tribal lumber enterprise.

Beshád-e's house had finally been completed, and Arnold did the odd jobs to make it more comfortable. They bought a table and a couple of chairs.

"I still prefer to sit on the floor for eating," Beshád-e said. "But the children coming home from school demand a table." Arnold agreed with her, but the two of them continued to follow the pattern learned in their own childhoods. Their chief concession was a white-man's bed and cots for visiting children and grandchildren.

By 1922 Christine had graduated from high school and returned to the reservation. She looked for work and obtained a good job at the Mescalero Hospital. Oftentimes Beshád-e and Arnold camped at the Feast Ground to make life easier for the young woman and to visit friends and do business at Agency. By now, they had an automobile, so transportation was less of a problem.

As for money, as time went on there was even a little surplus. Arnold was a medicine man, a respected shaman, whose powers had taught him to chase ghosts at times of death. He fumigated the houses in which deaths had occurred; he blessed the bereaved. Beshád-e knew herbal cures and treated patients—mostly within her family. Also, she had power to dispel "doll sickness," an ailment afflicting children who played with white man's dolls. The gifts given to the couple for their healings added fairly substantially to the family belongings. Dilth-cleyhen continued to serve as a midwife for many of the women of White Tail, and this, too, was a help, relieving Arnold of some of the burden of support expected from a son-in-law.

Christine was employed and was paying her own way. It was not long before she became enamoured of a fine man, a hospital worker

who had been educated at both Carlisle and Chilocco. His name was
Tom Duffy. They married. For a time, they lived in White Tail in a
tent near the house of Beshád-e, but within some months the couple
found this too draining in terms of time. They purchased a small
house on the Feast Ground.

"Come camp near us as often as you can," Christine suggested to
her parents.

And so they often did. Arnold and Beshád-e raised their tent close
to the Duffy house, just a little higher on the knoll, with just enough
room for a car to pass between. Dilth-cleyhen often accompanied
them. En route to Mescalero, Arnold made sure he and she could
not see each other while traveling in either car or wagon. Her tent,
a cooking arbor, and sometimes those of Lillian, were set up nearby,
making the the family cluster complete.

Beshád-e and Arnold made other excursions. They shopped at the
trader's store in Mescalero almost weekly, and sometimes down in
Tularosa or Alamogordo. Storekeepers in Ruidoso were less friendly,
but it was closer to White Tail. They drove to their homeland, Warm
Springs, reminiscing about life there. They traveled past Tres Hermanas, the home of the Crown Dancers.

Beshád-e closed her eyes. "I can hear them singing. I can hear the
drums."

They went past the lake in which Apache life began.

When the Kinzhumas were not gallivanting, their house and yard
were increasingly filled with the laughter of playing children: Lillian's brood; Susie's children. There was lots of visiting between
grandmother, mother, and daughter. This provided the core of
everyday interaction.

Arnold kept busy in the fields. He had to attend to all the business
matters that involved Anglos. He took Beshád-e, and any children she
was caring for, to the cow camps to see how the cattle fared. He
once again purchased sheep, half the herd owned by Tom Duffy, half
by Arnold, but kept in the White Tail corral beside Beshád-e's house.
The fences, the stable, or something always needed mending. The
mule and horses required feed when fields did not provide enough.
Every time he turned around, it seemed to cost money. If he took
the family on a trip, expenses for gasoline and food always proved
greater than anticipated. More and more frequently money ran
short.

In 1924 Christine gave birth to a baby girl, Narcissus.

"How sweet she is, how dear in her cradleboard," Beshád-e thought as the infant fingers grasped hers. "I must make sure she learns the old ways. Christine has abandoned them. She even went to the hospital instead of calling on Dilth-cleyhen. I guess it will be up to me. Narcissus must not forget her heritage. She must not be ashamed of the way her forebears lived, no matter what the Dutch Reformed people say, no matter what they teach in white man's schools."

Christine and Tom were devout members of the Reformed Church congregation, attending meetings every Sunday and taking the baby Narcissus with them. Beshád-e and Arnold were cajoled at times to going with them, and into attending services at White Tail, but their attendance was far from regular.

"I don't get anything out of it."

Nor did Dilth-cleyhen, who refused steadfastly to go. She and Beshád-e had more faith in the powers of old that had kept them from danger in the days of the warpath. Arnold, a sincere shaman, a successful ghost chaser, felt there was something to the Jesus way, but the preachings he heard were less than satisfying. Nonetheless, hadn't the God of the white man overcome Apache supernaturals in the days of the wars?

When he broached the subject to Beshád-e, she sighed. "I don't know. I don't have the happiness I should. All these Anglo regulations and deceits keep me confused. I feel worthless, unable to understand anything. I don't even feel like fixing up my place, or planting flowers like Lillian does. All I can do is keep busy and not think. I'm not energetic like I used to be. I feel tired—sometimes I can't even see clearly. Guess I'm getting old. I don't know who to turn to, or who to pray to, either."

Arnold understood. For a time he let the matter be.

In 1927, Christine bore another child, this time a boy. He had an English name, Wendell.

Once again, Beshád-e resolved that her grandchildren must know Apache values.

Some time before the birth of Wendell, Beshád-e and Arnold made a trip to Bylas to visit his relatives. He and Parker West talked long one night, long after Beshád-e had retired to her cot in the arbor beside the house. When Arnold finally came to bed, he touched her shoulder.

"Are you awake?"

When she made a gentle grunt, he continued speaking.

"Remember, I once told you that my brother told me about a preacher, an Indian by the name of Silas John. I came over here several times but didn't learn much. Well, he's here now. My brother says he really has the answers and that we should listen to him. Maybe we can go to the meeting where he speaks?"

"All right."

They went to the scheduled meeting, but Silas John did not appear.

This was not the end of the Kinzhumas's interest. For the next decade or so they were to become more and more involved in "the prophet's" teachings.

Within that period of time, tragedy again touched Beshád-e.

One late afternoon, after she and her mother had been visiting—and soon Old Man Arnold would be coming from the fields—Dilth-cleyhen sighed.

"I feel very tired."

This was unlike her, although in last year or two she had grown increasingly feeble, holding on to the backs of chairs, touching the cot as she passed, as if to steady herself. She was seldom hungry.

"Well, after all, my mother must be over eighty years old," thought Beshád-e. She watched the old lady walk slowly down the slight slope to the road, cross it, and move to her wickiup. She was bent now, no longer the erect, proud woman of wartimes.

"Her hair is so white now. She couldn't walk from the Feast Ground to Windmill now. How Old Lady had loved the intestines, the liver, all the inner parts of the newly butchered beef that were rationed each Saturday in years past!" Dilth-cleyhen had trekked the entire way by foot, just a few years ago, it seemed. Rarely had she accepted offers of rides in auto or wagon. "She would never make it now."

The next morning Beshád-e made coffee for Old Man Arnold. She looked over toward her mother's place. No smoke—nor could she see the shadow of movement within the shelter.

"I think I must get over there. I feel something."

"Shi-ma," she called softly, as she approached the doorway. And then she entered.

Dilth-cleyhen lay, at peace, upon her cot. She was gone.

"Aye-yaaa! Aye-yaaa! Aye-yaaa!"

The old woman was buried, not in a crevice of the mountains as once she would have been, but according to the requirements of Anglos, in the cemetery. She was wrapped tightly in her favorite blanket. A few treasures, for use in the afterlife, were interred with her. Included was her drawstring pouch made of buckskin, which held Bull Durham. Another was filled with pollen.

"Aye-yaaa!" Besháad-e cut short her hair, giving her a disheveled look. What does it matter! I have lost my mother! Lillian grieved with her. She unbound her chignon, and wore her raven locks long, about her shoulders streaming over the black fringed shawl.

The wickiup was burned. Old Man Arnold took over, fumigating the house—although it rarely been used except for storage—and he blessed all members of the family. Black scarf about his neck, he chased away the ghost with reverence, respect.

Within the year Christine grew ill. Very ill.

"Those white doctors say she has tuberculosis," Tom informed Arnold, asking him to relay the information to his mother-in-law.

"I thought that might stop when we left Fort Sill," Besháad-e worried.

Tom Duffy let it be known that he would appreciate Besháad-e's camping near his home to help look after Narcissus and little Wendell, who had been barred from going near their mother. Narcissus was grieving, and they had taken her from school. Tom was beside himself with worry, yet he had to continue with his job at the hospital. They needed the income. Besháad-e complied, of course. She consoled her grandchildren, who were too young to understand.

In 1931 Christine died.

"Aye-yaaa! Aye-yaaa!"

Old Man Arnold again chased the ghost. He fumigated the little Feast Ground house, and once again he prayed. He wanted no one to come down with ghost sickness.

Besháad-e cut Narcissus's hair until it was very short. She trimmed the ends to make them neat. This time her own tresses were left hanging around her shoulders, the hair having grown little since her mother's death.

"Aye-yaaa!"

"Tell Tom I'll stay here on the Feast Ground. I'll care for the children while he works."

The task was a great one, for the seven-year old Narcissus so longed for her mother that she could not eat and she heard Christine's voice in the night. It was ghost sickness. Arnold blessed the child, but it proved insufficient, and they sought the services of a medicine man near the Old Man's relatives in San Carlos.

Tom Duffy set up a tent about thirty feet from that of Besháad-e, and for a while, he was solicitous of his children's needs. But as time passed, he began to grow away from fatherly concerns, leaving the youngsters' care more and more to his mother-in-law and her kin.

How Beshád-e worried over the responsibilities she had taken on. When Tom wanted to put his youngsters in boarding schools away from her, she refused to let them go.

"They need me now. You can't do that to these young ones. I don't care if other people send their children away. I won't let them go. They are too young. I'll make them mine. I'll see that they go to church like you want, but I want them to know my ways."

For some months Old Man Arnold and his wife and the children remained on the Feast Ground. Narcissus and Wendell played, learning from Beshád-e, listening to bedtime stories, tasting traditional foods that had been rare in their mother's kitchen.

Then one day, Arnold spoke his mind, softly.

"Sah-un, Elderly Lady, I think we should move back to White Tail. It is convenient here to go to the Silas John meetings, but we need to get back and work our fields. Let's go up to the mountains."

And so they did. Nonetheless, they came down to the Feast Ground frequently, camping so as to attend the prophet's church.

Silas John and the Four Cross Cult

Some years ago the new religious cult of Silas John had piqued the interest of Old Man Arnold and, to a somewhat lesser degree, that of Beshád-e. They first heard of the prophet during that trip to Bylas, when Arnold had talked to his brother and heard of Silas John. For a time, although other concerns took priority, Arnold felt conflict. Which was right? The Apache powers or the Dutch Reformed's God and Jesus? Yusen sounded much like Jesus. Arnold resolved to seek a solution to his dilemma, but for a time, he delayed the investigation. Finally, his burden of thoughts became too great.

It had been a Sunday morning in the summer of 1922. Beshád-e and Old Man Arnold were camped on the Feast Ground near Agency.

Christine, as yet a novice worker at the hospital, slept and kept her belongings in an adjacent tent. Other structures stood near by for Dilth-cleyhen and for Lillian and her family.

When the sun first beamed over East Mountain, Beshád-e arose, started the fire, and put on the coffee. Arnold stretched, then sat on the edge of his cot.

"Sah-un, I'm not going to the Dutch Reformed services," he muttered. "I'm sick of listening to that preacher ramble on. I never feel satisfied when the meeting is over. They keep telling us we must not listen to our medicine men. Well, I am a medicine man. I know our ways are good. They work, particularly for us old folks. I miss the sacredness and sureness of the old religious ways, the powers of our Crown Dancers." He paused. "What does that white man's word 'pagan' mean, anyway?" There was a long silence. Then he continued.

"Sometimes I feel completely torn apart. I know the minister tries to be good to us. He's a well-meaning man, but he doesn't understand. We need an Indian to tell us what is right for us, to protect us through his powers and give us guidance."

Beshád-e sat on the wooden box. She looked at the old man. "I agree, *Hosteen*." She spoke further. "Nothing feels right in those translated sermons. I, too, come away feeling lonely, depressed, and angry all at once. Since we've come to live here on this reservation with the Mescaleros, all we seem to have is problems. Nobody knows how we feel. Nobody really cares."

For a while Beshád-e watched the flames licking the coffee pot. Then she poured cups of brew on which they sipped. The hot liquid warmed and comforted them. It was a nippy morning. Arnold began to speak once again.

"I'm going away for a few days. I'm going over to San Carlos, over to Bylas. I'll stay with Parker, Parker West.

"You remember the time I went over there before—I think it was in just three or four years after the Fort Sills came to Mescalero. Well, nothing was going on then. Then I went again, about three or four years later, and I heard rumors about a new religion. I didn't like the sound of it, so I decided to stay clear of it. But I went back that winter, you remember. I told you about it. I was with Horace Torres and Charles Belin and his wife.

"Parker said to me, 'We have been doing wrong things. We have been gambling. But there is a man called Silas John who has come into our country, and he is a good man. He speaks the word of Jesus and Yusen, God, to us. He is a very interesting talker, and you should listen to him. I am glad to have him here.' You remember, I told you what Parker said. And Jake Cojo talks about him, too. Well, we looked for Silas, but we did not find him. I'm going over there again, this fourth time. Maybe I'll have better luck."

Within the hour Arnold had contacted Lip Neda (Nata) and made arrangements for the trip. Lip was a San Carlos Apache, a nephew of Old Lady Chatto with whom he stayed frequently. She reared his children.

Old Man Arnold was gone for more than a few days. It was late September before he returned to Mescalero, but when he did, his eyes were bright, and his step somewhat brisker.

"I have a lot to tell you," he said to Beshád-e.

When evening came, the man and his wife sat in the wickiup, warming their hands before the coals of the fire. Beshád-e looked at her husband with anticipation. Slowly he began his narration.[93]

"The prophet is Silas John, just like we heard—Silas John Edwards. He started to preach about three years ago on the Fort Apache–White River Reservation. Lots of those folks listen to him now. He is a great orator. He has power, just like the medicine men of old times. And he tells the Indians to lead good lives, to stop their drinking—no tulapai, nothing intoxicating. He tells the Apaches to stop their gambling and their fighting. He tells them they must not lie, that they must not fool around with other men's wives. He knows all about Christianity and says we should listen to what it says in the Bible. He says our medicine men are no longer enough. We should turn to Jesus, and we should say 'Jesus' instead of 'Yusen' when we pray.

"When I saw him, I said to Silas John, 'I have come a long ways from Mescalero to see you. I have found you at last. I have heard wonderful stories of you, and I heard that you have the word of Christ and of God, all their prayers and songs. I would like to know the message that they gave you. Let me have some of their teachings. I am willing to give up my life to God.' "[94]

Arnold quit talking for a while, then resumed, "There's a reverend over at Rice, Arizona, a Lutheran minister by the name of Uplegger—A. M. Uplegger—who translated a lot of the Bible into Indian. That is what Silas John uses, only he has figured out a whole system so that the Indians can remember the proper prayers and rituals—so they won't make any mistakes. It's just like Lip and Horace have been telling us for several years. That Silas John is a wonderful preacher.

"Well, I went to one of his meetings. It was a four-day session, actually called by Uplegger; but Silas John had arranged everything, and all the Indians knew it was important. About three hundred or more Apaches were at that meeting. So before Uplegger arrived, Silas talked to us. He told us he was the *real* preacher. He was Indian. He had been sent on a cloud by God to lead us Apaches.

"Later, Silas gave me a prayer on a piece of buckskin. He told me his God was my only means of salvation."

Arnold talked for a long time, and much of the information that follows was transmitted to Beshád-e.

The Reverend Gunther, a Lutheran missionary stationed at White River, had met Silas for the first time in the fall of 1911. Silas was an intelligent young man with a good command of English. His early education had been at the Indian school in White River. Then he transferred to an institution in Phoenix, from which he had run away. On his return to the reservation he served as a "translator" for the reverend. Records show, however, that Silas had not always proved trustworthy. Once when Gunther was away on business and had left him in charge of the church and minister's home, the young man had brought in women. This resulted in his being discharged of further duties.

Silas took up other pursuits. For many years he made a living trapping beavers; then he began selling the skins of rattlesnakes to soldiers. But it was his success as a budding medicine man–preacher that led to his greatest fame.

In about 1920 Silas John Edwards again took an interest in Christianity. One of the Lutheran missionaries baptized him, his wife, and his four children in May of that year. Gradually he began to relate Bible stories to the Indians, and when he felt his own charismatic charms to be sufficiently strong, he formed his own cult. He displayed his powers openly. Reverend Gunther was told that Silas introduced rattlesnakes into the cult.

Old Man Arnold was impressed, but did not feel he was strong enough to handle snakes, although he saw three rattlers in a box.

"Silas said pollen is their only food. They live on it.

"That prophet can cure the sick, and he takes no payment for it.[95] What you must do, according to Silas John, is lead a good life, quit drinking and fighting and lying, and be sexually moral.[96] We should help the poor.

"We must stop going to other medicine men. They are no good. Silas even exposed some witches while I was there. He took away all the magical things they use. They are afraid of him. They know he is more powerful than they are. The snakes rattle when they come near a witch.

"And look what else he gave me."

Arnold pulled out a small wooden cross with an eagle feather and a bit of turquoise. "He blessed this and gave it to me. It will protect me against disease and lightning.

"When he cures, he uses sand paintings as well as those snakes. What he did while I watched was get a bunch of boys and girls to go with him up into the hills. Then a snake appeared,[97] and he told one of the kids to pick it up. Afterward, he cured the bitten youngster through his magic. He controls those snakes by putting pollen in their mouths.[98]

"We must all learn his prayers. Because he knows most of us cannot read English, he worked out a system so we can remember them. And he taught us songs. Silas says we should go to *his* church every Sunday. When he preaches, he takes a sweat bath; all the people who go to church can take a sweat bath if they want to. Everything in God's church should be clean."[99]

All that Beshád-e heard appealed to her.

"Let's talk to the other people who believe in that Prophet. Let's hear what Horace Torres thinks," was all she said.

Within the next six years Hosteen Torres went several times to San Carlos because he felt ill, once staying with Silas John for a month and a half. He learned songs and a prayer. Finally he returned to Mescalero with a large cross and considerable paraphernalia. He formed a church and worked among the Apaches, trying to convert them. Usually fifteen to twenty people attended his services, Arnold and Beshád-e among them.

In 1928 Jake Cojo brought back convincing testimony from San Carlos.

"That man is a man of God," he said on his return.

"I took my wife Catherine and our daughter there. My wife has heart trouble. Our girl had whooping cough. He blessed them, that Prophet blessed them. And now they are well.

"I'm supposed to preach to all the people here in Mescalero and to go to Silas's Church every Sunday. He gave me a little cross with turquoise to remind me."

Jake and Catherine became two of the most staunch of Silas's disciples, keeping the church accoutrements on the walls of their home long after the cult had seemingly disappeared from the reservation.

Others of the early converts were Charles Belin, Dan Morgan, and the medicine man, Elmer Wilson, and his son Woodrow. Charles and Dan were the ones who brought the Prophet from Arizona to the

Mescalero Reservation, where Silas stayed with Elmer at his camp behind the south hill, out Elk Silver way, on the road to Cloudcroft. The year of his visit is somewhat uncertain, but it was probably either 1928 or 1929.[100] The month was February.[101]

Silas John attracted considerable attention. Indians and Mexicans came to shake his hand. But when time came to conduct the meeting, the leader stopped.

"There are too many witches here!" That night there was nothing doing. Beshád-e and Old Man Arnold returned to their home.

The talk of witches had frightened Beshád-e.

"Who was he talking about?" she wondered. After a while she questioned Arnold.

"I wonder if this is the *true* prophet—the one we've been told to expect. Over and over again in my life I've heard about prophets. They teach strong for awhile, then something happens, and they disappear.

"Remember that medicine man Nakai-doklini?[102] Long long ago, before the Chiricahuas were shipped to Florida, all the White Mountain Apaches, just lots of people at San Carlos, were impressed by him. Many slipped away to hear him. Were you there too, Sah-un? I remember that man. He looked so frail until he began to speak. But then, the power of his words shook us. He told us that some of the dead Indian leaders would be resurrected. All the Anglos would die. All whites must be dead before we could have our former world. And yet he talked of peace. My mother said his peace talk sounded like Victorio. But the soldiers killed that prophet on Cibecue Creek, up there, a long ride northwest of Fort Apache.[103] There was a fierce battle between the military and Indians. Our family and that of Chatto and Naiche fled the fort and escaped to the Sierra Madre in Old Mexico.

"Then much, much later, when I was a grown woman—it was a few years before we were stationed in Fort Sill—the Kiowas told my mother about a man called Sitting Bull, an Arapaho, who talked to them of Jesus. Jesus, I guess the same Jesus the Dutch Reformed people talk about, would bring a new earth to the Indians, one with buffalo, elk, antelope, and wild horses. On that earth would be all the resurrected spirits of our dead. There would be no death, no disease, no misery. The Kiowas really liked that Sitting Bull. But nothing came of it. The movement had been started by a Paiute who was a fraud.[104] Even Sitting Bull had been fooled.

"I think it was about that same time that another Paiute prophet appeared. He meant well. His name was Wovoka, as I remember it.

He too said there would be a resurrection of our people. The earth would be renewed and better. There would be peace everywhere. The Sioux liked Wovoka's religion. When it began, I remember somebody said that six Apaches went to the first big dance at Walker Lake Reservation in Nevada. It was just after all of us Chiricahuas were shipped to Fort Marion. We had no chance to learn about it, and the Mescaleros did not get involved."

Beshád-e was quiet for a long time. In a soft voice, she then resumed her thoughts.

"With all the terrible things that have happened to us since I was a young girl,—even here in Mescalero, the Anglos have done nothing but betray us, tll us one thing and do another—well, I just know there must be something more. I don't know what. I do know my grandchildren must learn to cope with white ways, but it is just too much to ask of me. Somehow my mother, Dilth-cleyhen, seems resigned—more than I am. She clings to our old customs and ignores everything new. But I am tired. I can't learn English at my age. I can't read or write. I don't know when they are cheating me. Maybe this Silas man has the answers."

Indeed, many of the Chiricahua and Mescalero Apaches had endured as much as they could bear. The anomie that settled upon them was dispelled for a time by hopes offered by messianic religions such as the Silas John cult.[105] Beshád-e and Old Man Arnold grasped the new faith, ever more eagerly. So did some of their friends. Among them were Joe Caje, Peter Bigrope, Horace Yahnaki, Christian Naiche, and Jewett Tissnolthis. Their families listened and became converts.

One time the men were shown a quart bottle of water that Silas had brought from White River. He told them, "This holy water is rain water. It is alive. I have had it six years, and it never goes out. It always fills up. I am going to give you this water and make you learn the song."

Silas filled a cup with the liquid that represented the water of life. He had a blue stone, a bit of turquoise about half an inch square. He said, "I am going to put this blue stone in the holy water, and it is going to turn into yellow powder. It will become pollen. It will be dry. You people will learn the songs."

The prophet prayed, holding his hand over his heart. The men raised their hands. Silas made a cross over the cup and then made a clockwise circle four times before he inserted the stone. "If this does not turn into yellow powder, you will not hear the songs," he stated. When he poured out the water, indeed there was totally dry pollen

the bottom of the cup. With great solemnity Silas pronounced, "Why
didn't the yellow powder get wet like flour? Because God and Jesus
stand beside me. They are the ones that did it."

The preaching that night was impressive.

Silas called on the witches.

"You witches out there. Just try to witch any of these men in front
of me. If you try it, you will kill *yourself* with your witch! These men
work for God now."

The meeting lasted until midnight.[106]

The next day Silas set up the Holy Ground. "When other churches
are finished, then you come over here and have services in your own
way," he advised.

Silas made promises.

"In 1932 there will be much sickness.

"Christ will soon come back. The time is close. But before he
comes back, we will see much sickness. I ask you people to be good
and pray. Start today."

"You know those big boulders over there near the top of the hill,
across from this dance ground? There is some writing on them, writing made by witches. Well, when the next thunderstorm comes, the
big boulder over there will be destroyed." This came true. During
the next major rainfall, the boulder crumbled. Lip Neda went to the
spot, examined the pieces, and where the great stone had been, a
metal cross lay in its stead.[107]

Silas preached in Mescalero for three days; then the skies became
cloudy, and it rained. It even snowed. The Prophet went among the
people and visited the home of Arnold and Beshád-e. Most of those
whom he contacted gave money as a contribution.

After a week, Silas said he must leave. He promised to return, but
he never did. When he reached White River, he was put into jail for
having left Arizona after the law had told him he must not do so.
He was sent to prison in Globe.

The religion lasted openly on the Mescalero Reservation for some
months; it lasted much, much longer privately, in the homes and
hearts of the converts. Some of the women, such as Catherine Cojo
and Mrs. Tissnolthis, knew the prayers as well as did the male leaders
of the rituals on the Holy Ground.

Disharmony appeared among some leaders on the reservation,
some interpreting Silas one way, others in different ways. But on the
whole the cult proceeded without the presence of its prophet. It
seemed an appropriate link between the traditional Apache faith and
that of the Christians. For a time it was satisfying.

Occasionally some of the male members went to Arizona and consulted with Silas. Arnold went at least once with Lip Neda.

On his return he spoke to Beshád-e. "Silas says it is all right for me to use my Owl power. He says it is all right because it is on God's side. Curing ghost sickness is good because ghosts come from the devil. Ghost sickness is as bad as the witch. It's the same. It's like the devil witches you. I'll use the Silas John prayer.[108] The Jesus road is safer than my old way. It helps you cure without putting you in danger." [109]

A bit later he continued, "It is all right to hold the girl's ceremony, too. That was from the very beginning of time." Then silence.

"It troubles me that Silas doesn't like the Crown Dancers. He said their dances belong to the devil and do harm. That is hard for me to understand because I know their blessings have helped our people. But I guess we should follow the prophet.

"I have a prayer that Silas gave me. He wrote it down for me. I asked him to explain each term because sometimes the words in his dialect are different from mine. He got through most of the words."

Silas John mailed prayers to Horace Torres in May of 1931. They were in mnemonic symbols that Horace could not understand. "But Silas says God will make the meaning clear to me. I must pray."[110]

Old Man Arnold knew only the Cult Prayer. A part of this follows:[111]

> When the earth was made, When the sky was made
> In the very beginning, They walk around with Jesus.
> It will be In the center of the earth.
> God, his pollen, The cross of pollen
> The pollen that lives.
> Pollen, God who blows four times with it,
> God, that which is his life, four times in Heaven,
> With it he makes us powerful. . . .

The Old Man's prized possession became the cross Silas had given him, as he had given to each loyal member of his sect. It was known as the cult badge. He and Beshád-e compared those given them.

The cross, not more than one and one-half inches over all, had a hole in its center. Through this passed a buckskin lace to which was attached an eagle feather. Arnold's had a bit of turquoise as well; Beshád-e's a small piece of white shell.

"This cross is no good without the feather. That and the stone are the main thing," commented the old man. "We should wear it outside our clothes for everybody to see. The witches will see it and will leave us alone. It will keep the lightning from striking us. And when the end of the world comes, if we are wearing our cross, then God and Jesus will take us to heaven. It is our identification badge."

A bit later he decided, "I think the carving on the cross is to keep off disease. It's the carving that does that." [112]

Beshád-e rubbed her bracelet, which was also a sign of membership. It consisted of four strings of buckskin twisted together to form a thong. To this were attached one piece of turquoise and three beads of white shell, spaced evenly around the whole. The turquoise rested on the left side of Beshád-e's right wrist. "This is sacred, too." She had been told it would cure pain when passed in the four directions over the hurting spot.

"Ella Sampson told me that the turquoise represents the sky, the white shells are clouds, and the thong is lightning." [113]

The bracelet had certain dangerous aspects. If it were to hit anything living, that being would die immediately. Most of the religious followers pinned it underneath their long sleeves, fearing accidental harm to others.

"These things we have been given, we are responsible for using them right."

Beshád-e and her husband took their cult obligations seriously. They talked to Narcissus and Wendell, cautioning them about the cross. Neither child had yet received a bracelet. Arnold looked forward to the time he would know more of Silas's curing ceremonies and be able to use the larger crosses covered with black, white, yellow, and blue symbols. He had heard that some of these spoke to their owners.

"Lip Neda told me one of his crosses talks to him when he dreams. It tells him how to cure. He said to me, 'The cross is like the cross of Christ.'" [114]

Sundays were the most joyous days of the week for Beshád-e and Arnold. In mid-morning they, Narcissus, and Wendell climbed into the car and drove to the Holy Grounds which Silas had established in Head Springs.

The "church" consisted of a rectangle about six feet by four feet. Its sides faced the sacred four directions: the long sides were north and south, the short sides, east and west. A five-foot cross stood at each corner. Juniper was used for this because "lightning will not strike it." [115] Its crosspiece pointed north and south.

When the leader of the service approached the Holy Ground, he removed his hat, placing it to the east side of the plot. Then he walked to the west side of the rectangle and knelt, facing east. He took some religious items from a white silk wrapper and placed them in a row from south to north: first, a large buckskin-covered cross; then, a large buckskin; next, a small buckskin. From a small buckskin bag he took a pinch of pollen in his right hand, holding it to the east while his left hand, palm in, lay across his breast. He touched his right shoulder, the top of his head and his breast with the yellow powder, finishing by making two clockwise circles over his head. Then he touched the paraphernalia with pollen. He blessed each cross with pollen.

Beshád-e, Wendell, and Narcissus stood together on the north side of the Holy Ground, watching with alert eyes. Old Man Arnold stepped forward. Like the leader, he placed a pinch of pollen on the cross and buckskins on the west side of the rectangle. He stood, his fingers holding tight a bit of pollen. He uttered a prayer—very rapidly—and then stepped to the center of the rectangle and prayed once more. He turned clockwise and stepped outside the church, joining the leader and other men on the south side.

All was quiet for about fifteen minutes, and then once again the leader came forth. He walked to the paraphernalia and faced east. His head was bowed, his right arm was bent at the elbow, the palm of his hand facing the sun. He marked the palm with pollen, then touched the yellow to his right shoulder, his head, and his breast. He prayed just as Arnold had. This done, he moved alongside the latter, who continued to pray by the southwest cross.

After he had taken his position, Beshád-e nudged the children. "Come, it is our turn."

They moved to the leader, who offered them pollen. Each one made the markings, imitating those created by the head disciple. Then he in turn blessed them. Each person placed pollen on the paraphernalia, some adding their own crosses to the pile. After the ritual was complete, the girl children stepped from the eastern end of the Grounds to the north, while the boys turned south.

After all members had been blessed, the leader once again prayed and made further markings with pollen on cheek, chest, and head. He circled once again and left the church. Formal services were over for the day.

And so it was each Sabbath, with minor variations, different leaders. Sometimes, but not always, there was preaching. Narcissus and Wendell squirmed slightly when the talking started, but Beshád-e quickly reminded them of their manners, and they stood still. Sometimes there were cures, requiring songs and drums, and that took longer still. Dancing was a part of most services. When Narcissus was reluctant, Beshád-e urged her on, insistent.

Then came social activities. The men took sweat baths; the women prepared food; and everyone shared the news, the gossip of the times. They talked of the powers of Silas, the greatness of his medicine, his handling of snakes on other reservations.

"Silas converses with God."

"He sees angels, angels with wings, dressed all in white."

"Silas has thirty two kinds of medicine. That's all there is in the world now."

"Everything listens to Silas—even the clouds."

"He can bring a dead man back to life."

"They say he has a drum. He just puts that drum on the ground, and it beats by itself when Silas talks to it."[116]

One such Sunday, Old Man Arnold told a story he had been told, the story of a journey to heaven made by the prophet.

"Well, once the prophet became unconscious. He doesn't know how it happened. His life seemed to rise from his body and go way up. He traveled skyward with the Holy Spirit.

"Silas was traveling home. He had left his school. Somehow he reached a creek or something and was cold. He built a fire. He heard some wings flapping, and when he looked up, he saw two owls on a tree.

"One said to him, 'May we come down and visit you?' Those owls came down and sat with him. But then more and more came. Owls came from every direction. Well, Silas had a gun, a .22-caliber gun. He shot at the owls. It did not harm them. They had taken Silas's life. They killed Silas.

"Those owls took Silas about twenty feet. They took his coat off. They moved him a little farther. Then they took his pants. Farther, and they took his shoes. The owls took him to the side of a rocky hill and laid him between two boulders. His nose began to bleed, and the blood covered him. As he lay there, he heard a voice.

"'Get up,' it said. 'Hurry, we must go.' Silas couldn't see anyone; but he knew the voice came from above, and it went on and on. And Silas started up with the voice always before him." Hosteen Arnold paused.

Wendell had squirmed as he heard about the owls. He nudged Narcissus. "Are those owls the ones our grandmother told us about? Are they the Eye Killers—the ones that kill you if you even look at them?"

"Be quiet," his sister said. "You're not supposed to ask questions. It's bad manners." But her eyes looked troubled. How did this fit with the myths Beshád-e related? Her grandmother had emphasized the stories she related were fact. But then *these* owls killed too! "I guess it all fits somehow. Hosteen Arnold believes." She listened intently, slightly afraid, as her grandfather continued.

"During his flight, he came to a place just like this earth. But he went on and came to the next above. This earth was covered with flowers. Then he rose to a third earth, and here he met strange people with wings. He did not know what kind of people they were.

"The voice kept on, calling Silas 'Brother.' It was probably that of the Spirit.

"The Spirit said to Silas, 'It is about time something was done. I want you to save as many people as you can. Get them into this road of ours, have them follow in the footsteps of Jesus Christ.' Jesus did not know when he was coming back. 'Go back home, Silas, and prepare the people for when I come back.'"

Narcissus's mind wandered. "I guess this is the Spirit they tell us about in Dutch Reformed Sunday school. But it sounds different." She listened as Arnold resumed his story.

"And the Spirit said to him, 'You have seen both sides of this life—the bad life and the true life. You have been leading the life that was wrong. I am talking to you about eternal life. By making medicine you have saved many a life. But the life I am giving you is a better life. It rests with you whether you will throw away your old ways and go on this right road. I am going to show you what the devil has in store for the bad people.'

"Silas looked far away and saw a big fire. The Spirit said, 'If you are a thief, murderer, commit adultery, or are a troublemaker, or use bad language, that is the place for people like that. It is from those things that Satan's power is within you. You have your power from that. It is from the evil powers that you have gotten possession of your money and the things of this world. The life I am going to show you is eternal. When the world passes away, you will always have a home.'"

Arnold leaned back. He surveyed his audience. All were still, contemplating.

"So that is why the prophet never takes any money. He changed his ways. I guess that is what we should do. Change our ways." Then he went on with his tale.

"Silas John told me that a snake visited his home in 1913—just the time the Fort Sills arrived here. It wouldn't go away. So Silas decided to put some beads around its neck. He did that, and the fourth time he did it, the snake left for good. Silas told me that by then he had already given up his medicines.

"When Silas was in heaven, the Spirit said, 'You had a visitor. I

am going to show you this visitor.' They went to a green spot where
there were sixty-four snakes. They all stood up. 'Pick out the one
you put the beads on.'

"Silas came back to earth again. Between the two boulders, instead
of his own body, he saw an old man. He was going to step over it,
but then he realized that was his body. He did not know that life
must have come back to his body. He felt himself. He found that he
was covered with blood. He found his shoes, coat, and trousers. He
got back to the owls. The owls were still around the fire. He clubbed
all the owls but one and threw them into the fire. He thought he
would eat that one. Instead of eating it there, he moved a little ways.

"It was just below Camp Verde in Arizona. There he met two girls
riding on a burro. They were white children. They asked him to
come and have something to eat with them. He did not go. They
gave him one box of crackers, a can of tomatoes, and a can of jam.

"Silas went back home and began his preaching. Some people believed in him. He could really perform miracles. But some of the old
medicine men did not like his ways. They did not believe that he was
a stronger man."

For a while there was silence among the disciples at Head Springs.
Everyone was thinking about Old Man Arnold's recital.

Again Wendell nudged his sister. "Snakes, too. They scare me."
Narcissus merely nodded. She looked toward some of the girls with
whom she had danced after services. They were quiet, still wide-eyed.

Other Sabbaths there were more stories about Silas John and the
way he had been tested by the Lord, about the thousands of people
who work for the devil, about the time the witches tried to kill the
prophet, about the way Silas had become poor. When he had practiced medicine, he had owned stock, saddles, and many material
things, but no longer. Things had changed.

There was talk of the way the witches and medicine men made
trouble for Silas. They complained to the agent at White River, saying the prophet had been drinking or bootlegging. "He's been jailed
a thousand times—almost every week."

These aspects of the prophet's life were common knowledge among
the disciples. What they did not know, or chose not to talk about,
was the fact that he was a philanderer who caused considerable domestic strife.

However, when Arnold was alone with Beshád-e, he confided,
"The prophet had lots of trouble with his wife. She scolded and
nagged and at meal time threw dishes at him. Silas took good care
of her, but she thought he went with other women. So, he had to

leave her. And then he married the wife of his dead brother. They had troubles, too."

In fact, those early loyal disciples in Mescalero knew few facts about Silas John. He had a long history of immorality, and at one time he was convinced he would die from gonorrheal rheumatism.[117]

Gradually, without the personal guidance of the prophet, the church in Mescalero became less popular. The many nonbelievers scoffed at those with cult talismans. "That man Silas was an imposter—even more, what he preached is dangerous. He mixes our old beliefs and Christianity in a way that is just not right. You people are crazy to believe in him."

Fewer and fewer individuals made the trip to Head Springs. For a time members guarded their crosses and bracelets, but now they seemed less protective. The armor of security had dents.

Arnold continued to use the prayers to a certain degree, but more and more he found himself referring to Yusen, as did Beshád-e.

With passing years they reverted more appreciably to traditional patterns of prayer. Their lives were emptier, filled once again with disillusionment.

Interim

Even while they were fully involved in the church, Beshád-e and Arnold often sought diversion. Their nomadic spirits often found them riding in the car, enjoying the countryside. Even a trip to Ruidoso relieved the monotony of everyday chores.

One day, as they drove through Dark Canyon on the now widened and paved highway that stretched from Tularosa through the reservation and on to the busy summer resort town, Beshád-e recalled that area as it had been in 1913 when they had first arrived from Fort Sill. "When we first got here, this place was just dark, dark with the towering pines covering the steep canyon sides. Lots of places, only one wagon could go through at a time. And they told us that before then, lots of the trail was filled with grama grass, clear up to the horses' bellies!"

Another time, perhaps as early as 1930 or so, the Kinzhumas longed for their homeland. Beshád-e was caring for Marcelline, Susie's daughter, who was then about two years old. "It'll be all right. We'll just take her with us."

"I don't feel like driving all that way," Arnold had said.

"Well, we can hire Glenn Sundayman. He likes to drive."

Glenn had agreed to go. Old Lady Sundayman expressed a desire to accompany them. The five got in the car and made the long distance to Monticello, New Mexico, in the vicinity of Warm Springs.

On arrival they looked around the plaza and then headed to the adobe home of Mexican friends. How happy was their greeting! Tears and laughter intermingled. They chatted half the night. The old Mexican man brought out a bottle of whiskey to celebrate. Tongues were loosened; conviviality reigned.

Soon, more Mexican friends arrived. More whiskey came with them. Bottles continued to make the circle.

Old Lady Sundayman was at her best, speaking halting Spanish mixed with broken English.

"All this—" her arms swung wide, encompassing Monticello and far beyond. "*All* this, *my* place, down here. This people—" she gestured toward her hosts, "This people, all *my* friends."

Marcelline began to fret. Beshád-e took an empty whiskey bottle and walked outside, down to the river bank. She washed the bottle and filled it with fresh water. Going back into the house, she gave the toddler a sip. Then she tucked the bottle under the pillow of the bed where she had been invited to sleep. With that, she again began drinking and visiting.

Exhausted finally, the guests went home. Beshád-e and Arnold retired. Suddenly the old man sat up. "There's something hard under here." He felt beneath the pillow and pulled out the bottle. "Ahhh," he opened it and began slugging down the liquid.

Beshád-e became excited.

"Stop, Old Man, stop!" The room was pitch black. All she knew was that her husband was drinking. She thought it was more whiskey. She grabbed the bottle.

"You can't drink all by yourself," she cried, "I have to drink with you!"

She took a deep swallow.

Water! Marcelline's water! She began to laugh, and Arnold laughed with her. For years, they teased each other.

How their heads ached the next morning.

"I guess we should stick to tulapai. Silas told us not to drink, didn't he?"

Beshád-e and Arnold enjoyed drinking Apache brew, but in those days their imbibing was usually in moderation. They enjoyed the lift it gave them, the sociability it inspired. But they did not like drunkenness.

It was only in later years, after the Silas John services stopped, when they were increasingly disheartened with their lives, that they became addicted to white man's liquor. It was then that they spent whatever money they had—and some they did not have—for its purchase.

Life went on quietly in White Tail. The sheep were sold and more cattle purchased based on advice of officials at Agency. There was no longer any income from the sale of wool.

Farming was started some years, but not during others.

Often there was not enough money. The car was sold. The couple began to rely in part on the bimonthly checks that were the inheritance of Narcissus and Wendell. It was money available to the youngsters because of Christine's investments in cattle. Usually the grandchildren simply handed their checks over to their grandparents, who doled out what was needed by any kin member. The four payments came to about two hundred extra dollars per month. This was a great help in buying clothes, food, and school supplies, as well as small luxuries such as candies and Bull Durham.

When youngsters wanted to try smoking, Beshád-e cautioned, "Tobacco is not for youths! It is sacred. It should be used only by those with power, and then with great respect."

Days for Beshád-e were busy with household chores and washing. There was buckskin to tan; sometimes robes were needed for girls' Feasts.

"I think it is time to think of a da-i-dá for Narcissus. I want all the girls of the family to have Feasts. I want them to remember White-Painted-Woman, to feel her power."

She measured Narcissus for her buckskin robe and moccasins. She worried about getting hides enough to make it ample, to have fringe long enough to sway dramatically during the run. She must begin cutting triangles from tin cans and rolling them around a pointed twig to create the jingles—at least two hundred would be required. Her mind wandered to the Feasts she had given—for Christine, for Evelyn and Marilyn Martine, and for Gwendolyn Magooshboy. And there were others yet to give. So much work, so much expense. Nonetheless, feasts must be given for the welfare of the family—and the tribe.

Sometimes, of a morning, Old Man Arnold donned his black kerchief, pulling it around his neck and holding it in place with a big turquoise ring slipped up over the two ends that dangled over his chest.

"I've been asked to chase the ghost," he would say, and then he would leave.

Beshád-e as well was sometimes hired to commune with her powers on behalf of someone who was ill. She knew the ghost-chasing ceremony but was reluctant to use it, being content to cure doll sickness or to gather and prescribe herbal medicines and often to administer them.

During the years that Narcissus attended grammar school in White Tail, Beshád-e found it harder and harder to do mending, to sew patches on clothing. She simply could no longer see the eye of the needle.

"Will you help me, Narcissus? Thread some needles for me before you go to school." Narcissus complied.

Many of the women at White Tail attended Ladies' Aid meetings, sponsored by the Dutch Reformed Church.

"I just don't want to go," Beshád-e told Old Man Arnold. "They are quilting over there. I can't see. I don't go on Sunday because I don't care for the preaching, even though those Van Es people who are now in charge are honest and good. I guess I should go. I insist the children attend. They have to go to Bible school.

"The Dutch Reformed missionaries helped us so much in Fort Sill. I remember they taught us how to till, how to harrow, and how to plant the seed. They taught the young ones how to cope with Anglos. Their intentions were right."

Sometimes, but only when she felt a need for companionship, she walked to the church. She stayed at the Ladies' Aid meeting long enough to greet her friends and to pretend she could see their fine stitching. Then, with a toss of her proud head, she always managed, very quietly, to leave.

From time to time, Beshád-e suggested that she and Arnold pitch a tent at Feast Ground for awhile. Sometimes she grew lonely up at White Tail, her nomadic youth calling to her. The house was too quiet. Narcissus had gone to school in Santa Fe. Beshád-e did not feel well.

"Maybe they'll give you a job, Hosteen. You can ask up at Agency." Even though by now Arnold was becoming thin and more frail, he never turned down an odd job or two, when such were offered him.

Once he was hired to help build a stone wall on the side of the hill below the hospital, across from the tribal store. It was a very, very hot day.

Old Man Arnold had no proper handkerchief. He couldn't afford that kind of luxury. But Beshád-e had done her best. She sometimes bought flour in white sacks rather than in the small flowered ones that she preferred. Once, after the contents were used up, Beshád-e tore the bag so that she had a small square. She hemmed the raw edges as best she could.

"Here. Use this for a handkerchief," she said.

So, that day, sweat oozing from every pore, Old Man Arnold pulled out the white square. He mopped his brow, then his entire face.

After working all afternoon, he came back to the tent to have his dinner. He was tired, dirty. He walked to the gray enamel basin, filled it with water, and washed his hands. When he had completed the ablutions, he pulled out the handkerchief to dry himself. He burst into peals of laughter.

"Sah-un," he said, "look at this *ba-i-yo*." He was referring to his handkerchief. "All those men at work started laughing at me. I was wiping the sweat off my face. When I was through, all the men started laughing. Then they told me. I had flour all over my face!"

One night in the autumn of 1935 there was a frantic knocking on Beshád-e's door. She was apprehensive. What could it be? Arnold was away for a few days. Had something happened?

Lillian's sons, Philip and Ringlin, began pulling at their aunt. "Come, come, come quick! Our mother! She is hurting!"

Beshád-e knew immediately what was wrong. Her sister's baby was due. She grabbed a shawl and awakened Narcissus and Wendell.

"Get your sweaters and shoes—and your blankets. I don't want you here alone. It may be a long time before I am back." She and the children strode, often running, the six long miles to the Martine home. Indeed, Lillian, who had refused to go to the hospital, was in labor.

The children were bedded down in one bedroom while Beshád-e set to work in the other. "Oh, Lillian, I am going to need some help. I must pray. I don't know about delivering babies!"

In the next hours, she prayed many times, calling on all her powers. She lamented the absence of Dilth-cleyhen, who would have known just what to do. "Oh, how I wish she were here!" And when the labor was ever more prolonged, "I've got to get you to Agency. You need a doctor and the hospital."

"Help me, my sister. Help me. I won't go down there. That place is just for those who are going to die!"

After several hours, the baby came. It was a girl-child, a perfect child whose cries were lusty.

Beshád-e made Lillian as comfortable as she could, telling her to rest. "I'll be back in the morning." She and her grandchildren trudged back home.

She awakened early the next morning, getting breakfast for Narcissus and Wendell and seeing that they were at the bus stop. Again, she walked to the next canyon to check on her sister. Lillian looked tired, but she was busy cooking for her youngsters and making sure they were clean for school. The baby was asleep. The women conversed about her cradleboard.

"I'm naming her 'Imogene.'"

Later that day, when she was back home, Beshád-e confessed. "There was something wrong about the way that baby was born. There should have been some blood. But there wasn't even a drop."

During the next few weeks, all seemed well, although Lillian lacked vitality. Arnold and Beshád-e had business at Agency and were camping at the Feast Ground when George Martine came to them, very disturbed. "Lillian is very sick. She won't see a doctor. What do you think I should do?"

Beshád-e insisted that he bring his wife to the Feast Ground and set up a tent for her there. "I'll get a doctor to see her."

But Beshád-e's efforts were unsuccessful, although Lillian came to Mescalero. The doctors at the hospital refused to make a visit to the camp.

"That woman would not come for prenatal care. We can't just go to everybody's camp when they don't do as they know they should! Our work load here at the hospital is more than we can handle. She's just stubborn—stupid!"

Beshád-e did not give up. She had Arnold drive her to Alamogordo, where she went to see a Dr. Simms. He arrived on the Feast Ground within a few hours and examined Lillian. "It's infection. Your sister is in a bad way. She did not deliver all the afterbirth."

Dr. Simms prescribed medication, but within three or four months Lillian died.

"Aye-yaaa. Aye-yaaa." Once again keening resounded over the Feast Ground, coming from the bordering treeline, both in early morning and evening.

Old Man Arnold took charge of the burning of the tent wherein Lillian had passed away. George Martine and Evelyn, now twenty-three years of age, were distraught, the children crying and bewildered. Hosteen Arnold blessed them. He conducted the ghost-chasing ceremony at the house in White Tail, but George and his family remained at Feast Ground or with friends or kin for the winter and much of the coming year.

Beshád-e cared for the infant Imogene for several months. Evelyn often stayed with her in White Tail, bringing her wards along. Others of the Martine youngsters were put in boarding school.

Oh, how Beshád-e missed her sister.

"I guess it's like Silas told us. He said there would be a lot of sickness and—." Her voice trailed off as she spoke to Arnold. "My mother, my daughter, and now my sister, too."

The next year, 1936, the elderly people of White Tail were told they must leave their remote district, that four-room houses would be provided for them four miles from Agency. This was nearer social services and hospital care. The new location came to be known as Old People's Village, or, because there were so many widows, Squaw Town.

Squaw Town

Soon after the move to Squaw Town, Beshád-e and Old Man Arnold conferred as to where Narcissus should go to school.

"Maybe she would get a better education up in Santa Fe," thought Beshád-e, and her husband agreed. He spoke to Tom Duffy about it, and soon the matter was settled.

"After all," said Tom, "it would be good for her to have a broader perspective of life than she can get on the reservation. I'm all for it."

Thus it was when the new semester began, Narcissus left the household to attend the Indian Boarding School. Beshád-e missed her. "She was such a help to me," she realized.

Living in Squaw Town was indeed a change for the Kinzhumas. The altitude was over one thousand feet lower than in White Tail. The summers were hot and dusty; the winters were less severe than those the couple had experienced in recent years.

Here it was almost like city life, with four-room dwellings and backyards just large enough for a few fruit trees and some vegetables to be grown. Each was adjacent to those of neighbors. If voices were raised in one house, every word could be heard next door. Arnold looked at his yard.

"These days, this plot is just about as much as I care to handle," Arnold commented as he began to work with shovel and hoe.

He planted corn, corn of many colors, placing the seeds in mounds. Beshád-e was pleased. "I'll make you a fine meal when that is ripe." Arnold smiled. He envisioned the preparation. The ripe kernels, cut from the cob, were first dried. Then, when the family was hungry for corn, the varicolored morsels were dropped in boiling water. Sometimes the water held strips of dried beef. Sometimes Beshád-e added pinto beans. The very thought made his mouth water, and spurred on his greater effort.

Old Man Arnold planted radishes, onions, beets, turnips, carrots, and potatoes. It was a sight to behold! Until the rains came. They came in torrents, and most of the season's work was washed away, down the furrowed road.

Arnold Kinzhuma was such a proud old man. He and Beshád-e made a stately couple even yet—he with his black neckerchief, she with her black shawl.

Old Man fretted when he was not busy. Now he began making walking canes. He created bows and arrows, decorating them with designs depicting the desert life of the Southwest. These he took to local stores, which bought them and in turn sold them to tourists. Thus he realized a little extra cash.

Sometimes, too, when he was able, and he could find a companion, he went hunting—mostly for deer, but occasionally for turkeys. The pelts of the animals kept Beshád-e busy tanning.

Unfortunately the old lady was no longer strong. She was unable to wield the axe and chop wood as she had done throughout her life, from early childhood. She tried, but Arnold stopped her. "I can do that for you now."

Beshád-e had constant pain in her right side, under her ribs. Often now, she lay on her bed. It was Arnold who cooked, and cleaned, and straightened the house.

"I think you should go to the hospital," she was advised.

"No," was ever her reply.

The months passed. Sometimes she felt better. "I'll be glad when the school year is up," Beshád-e said. "I miss Narcissus." Almost every month she sent her granddaughter treats— piñons, fry bread, sweet potatoes.

Finally, it was indeed summer, and Narcissus got off the bus and was transported to Squaw Town. What a celebration! She and her grandmother hugged and laughed and cried. For long hours Beshád-e held the gangly child in her arms. They talked and talked and talked.

Narcissus was a typical Apache teenager. She soon found her old girl friends to pal around with. They walked the roads day and night, finding groups of boys and other girls. Sometimes she stayed out very late. This began to worry Beshád-e.

"That child is too young to know what she's doing. She doesn't know the trouble she can get into just loitering around."

She talked to the girl, saying that no proper young woman behaved that way. Narcissus shrugged, "I'm not doing anything wrong. Everybody does it." Beshád-e's advice was ignored.

It was particularly troublesome at Feast time. Narcissus stayed out almost all the night—participating in the various kinds of dancing, some ceremonial, some purely social. But then she did not come home.

Beshád-e fretted. "I'm going after her. There's lots of drinking on that Feast Ground. That child has no idea the temptations that may come her way. I don't want her drinking. She is too young. I wish her father would take some responsibility—but he doesn't. Now he's married to somebody else, it's like he has forgotten his own."

Beshád-e was relentless in her search, looking in wickiups and tents, calling—until she found her granddaughter. There was a great confrontation.

"How can you embarrass me like this!" was Narcissus's outcry.

The relationship between Beshád-e and her granddaughter became even more strained, this time over money.

Narcissus decided she no longer was going to hand over the checks she received each month from the sale of her mother's cattle. She began telling fibs, hiding the reimbursement.

Beshád-e needed the cash. There were lots of expenses. She and Arnold no longer had any funds for simple pleasures. They could not afford beer or any kind of wine to serve when their friends came over in the evening to be sociable. "How can I be generous, as an

Apache should be when guests arrive? I always am in debt to others."
She searched through all Narcissus's belongings, to no avail.

"Where *is* that check?" she asked angrily.

Narcissus simply left the house and went to be with her friends, strolling the streets, going up to Agency and over to the Feast Ground.

This went on for months. Narcissus refused to go back to Santa Fe. "I like it here!" she stated bluntly.

Beshád-e was beside herself with anger. She spoke to Arnold, "It's a good thing we didn't put out a lot of time and money on that rebellious girl, that we didn't work so hard to give her a Feast." She told Narcissus as much.

And later, to her husband, she said, "I guess I'm getting too old to care for a teenager. I'm glad Wendell does not take after her."

Perhaps it was this hard fact of having no da-i-dá, along with other of Beshád-e's brutal comments, that brought Narcissus to a sense of greater maturity. What she was doing was indeed childish, stubborn, and unproductive. She was growing up, abruptly.

"I think I'll return to Santa Fe to school," she told Beshád-e. And so she did, eventually.

For the remainder of the summer evenings, peace reigned in the household. Narcissus was with her friends by day, but at nightfall she began to enjoy staying at home. When the friends of her grandparents came to visit, often about 8 or 9 P.M., she and Wendell had usually retired. When she heard them come in, she propped the door open so she could listen to the reminiscences.

The most usual topics were concerned with the warpath days— the days of glorious youth and acts of bravery in the homeland. They talked of General Crook, of Anglo atrocities, and those of their own. Occasionally they whispered, "Remember that white boy Charley McComas? The one taken from the wagon train?" Sometimes they talked of the time of incarceration.

"Do you remember how they lined us all up when we were in Alabama? That was when Tom was given the name of 'Duffy' and his brother James was called 'James Russell.' Those Anglos couldn't pronounce Apache names, so they just made up anything that came to their minds—regardless of kinship. But those names don't mean anything, though they have stuck in the records."

Most of the time the group talked for hours, drinking coffee. Sometimes one of the Kinzhumas' friends held a tulapai party in another home. That was wonderful, although the making and consuming of the mild corn beer was illegal.

In the first months in Squaw Town, the couple rarely drank liquor with much alcoholic content. Their grandchildren did not see them drunk, or loud, or hateful—only sentimental and talkative. At such parties and even at home, when tulapai was brought, the adults poured the liquor into a bucket which was passed around. There was a common dipper from which everybody drank in turn until the pail was dry. Someone always found a drum. An Apache beat commenced, and songs of the past were sung. By that time, conversation deteriorated, the tales brought hurtful memories, and many of the old people began to weep.

Last Days

It was only in later months and years that drinking began to be a problem for Beshád-e and Arnold. Squaw Town was constricting. "We can leave here whenever we want, I know, but somehow, I feel imprisoned."

More frequently than ever before they asked someone to bring them a bottle, or they hired someone to take them to a bar just off the reservation. When they were completely without money, they went to Tularosa. There was a pawnbroker there who would buy things, never paying enough—but then he was willing to sell them illegal liquor at outlandish prices.

The Kinzhumas realized vaguely that they were being cheated, but the hot liquid relaxed them, made them briefly happy, and made them forget that Silas John could not have been a true prophet and that their own powers seemed less effective. It even eased their aches and pains.

It was April 15, 1941.

Beshád-e said to Arnold. "I'd like to go down to Tularosa. Let's see if Roy Sundayman will take us. I need some groceries, and maybe we can stop in at the bar for just one drink."

Roy was willing.

They made the trip, did their buying, went to the pawnbroker, and then decided to sample the wares that he sold. The bottle was passed round and round.

On the way home, the car spun out of Roy's control. It crashed into the side of the concrete bridge just outside the reservation boundary. Careening wildly, it skidded off the road, turning over and over, groceries flying.

In the morning the bodies were found. All three were dead.

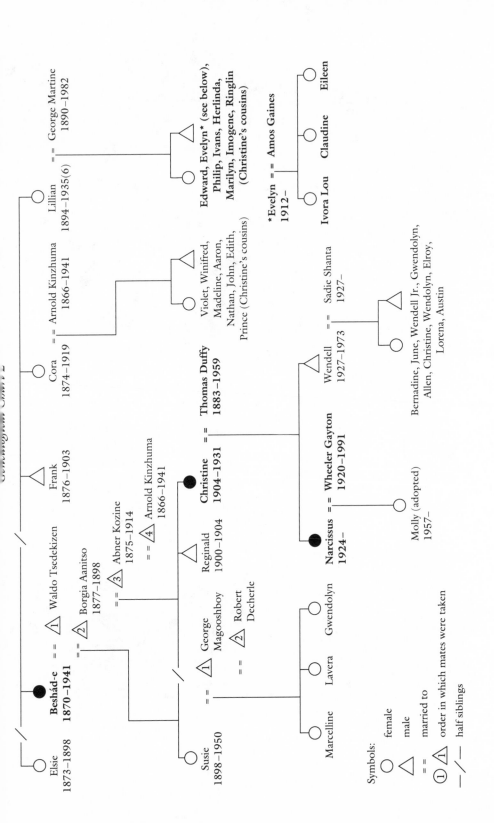

Genealogical Chart 2

Elsie 1873–1898

Frank 1876–1903

Cora 1874–1919

Lillian 1894–1935(6)

Beshád-e 1870–1941

Waldo Tsedekizen

Borgia Aanitso 1877–1898

Arnold Kinzhuma 1866–1941

George Martine 1890–1982

Violet, Winifred, Madeline, Aaron, Nathan, John, Edith, Prince (Christine's cousins)

Edward, Evelyn* (see below), Philip, Ivans, Herlinda, Marilyn, Imogene, Ringlin (Christine's cousins)

*Evelyn 1912– == Amos Gaines

Ivora Lou   Claudine   Eileen

Susie 1898–1950

George Magooshboy

Robert Decherle

Abner Kozine 1875–1914

Arnold Kinzhuma 1866–1941

Reginald 1900–1904

Christine 1904–1931 == Thomas Duffy 1883–1959

Marcelline   Lavera   Gwendolyn

Narcissus 1924– == Wheeler Gayton 1920–1991

Wendell 1927–1973 == Sadie Shanta 1927–

Molly (adopted) 1957–

Bernadine, June, Wendell Jr., Gwendolyn, Allen, Christine, Wendolyn, Elroy, Lorena, Austin

Symbols:

◯ female

△ male

== married to

①△ order in which mates were taken

—/— half siblings

Capture of Apache women and children, 1885. Cradleboard can be seen at far right. *(Courtesy of the Arizona Pioneers' Historical Society, Tucson)*

Fort Pickens, Florida: the cell block where Chiricahua men were imprisoned. *(Photo 44288, courtesy of the Arizona Pioneers' Historical Society, Tucson)*

Left. Chatto and his medal, 1927. *(Courtesy of the Arizona Pioneers' Historical Society, Tucson)*
Below. Evelyn Martine (Gaines) in cradleboard, Fort Sill, 1912. *(Courtesy of Narcissus Duffy Gayton)*

Left to right, Jason Betzinez, Abner Kozine, and Johnny Loco, Fort Sill. *(Courtesy of Nar. Duffy Gayton)*

Cross, cult badge of the Silas John Cult; shown actual size. *(Drawing by Ruth Boyer, from Henry n.d., 102)*

Apache camp with tipis, Mescalero. *(Courtesy of the Arizona Pioneers' Historical Society, Tucson)*

Anice Kozine, sister of Abner Kozine, Carlisle Indian School, Pennsylvania. Anice married Sam Kenoi. Standing figure is unidentified. *(Courtesy of Narcissus Duffy Gayton)*

Part Three

Days of Adjustment and Acculturation

The Life of Christine Louise Kozine

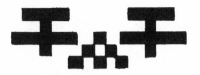

Early Life

Christine Louise, born March 16, 1904, according to the census of Fort Sill,[1] was the second child of Beshád-e and Abner Kozine. She was christened in the Dutch Reformed Church and given her English name. That same year her brother Reginald died of tuberculosis. He was only four years old. There were so many interments at the fort that the wail of women's keening was an ever-present sound. Pulmonary disorders accounted for much of the high rate of death.

To the Apaches the Oklahoma countryside was far more attractive than that of Florida and Alabama.[2] In Oklahoma they found trees, streams, and open meadows. Bluejays pestered and squirrels scolded. The women laughed in sheer delight when first they heard coyotes howling. How long it had been! "You'd think we were back home— free!" they said. It seemed a good sound, despite the fact that hearing a coyote howl meant someone was about to die.

Now, once again, women gathered their families' foodstuffs, and adminstrators allowed the men to hunt. Further, the Apaches owned herds of horses and cattle, so that an occasional animal could be slaughtered when protein was difficult to come by. Deer and a few antelope roamed the Rainy Mountain area, so their hides were available for ceremonial clothing. Women made no complaint when backs ached from the tedious task of flensing and softening the skins. Times of want had taught them to be grateful. Turkeys and prairie chickens were abundant. Rabbits tended to be scarce; too often they fell prey to wolves and coyotes. Ducks filled the heavens with migrating patterns; geese soared in V-formation, honking all the while. The handiwork of beavers was seen in the dams along Medicine Creek. Because fish were so plentiful, the Chiricahuas began once again to enjoy their flavor. Even young children learned to bait a hook and sit by the stream waiting patiently for the bass to bite.

Beshád-e, Abner, Christine, and Susie Aanitso, Christine's half-sister, lived in one of the houses in Carl Mangas's Village. Carl had died in 1901, but the village retained his name. When special leadership or some bit of crucial advice was needed, the group turned to Naiche, whom they knew to be trustworthy. He and his kin lived in

Naiche's Village, immediately adjacent to that of Chatto, directly south of Christine's home, on the other side of Medicine Bluff Creek at Four Mile Crossing.[3] Naiche's parents were the great chief Cochise and his principal wife Dos-teh-seh, whose name, according to the Fort Sill census, means "Something-at-the-campfire-already-cooked." She was a daughter of Mangas Coloradas and the sister of Carl Mangas, but the records are incomplete as to their mother or mothers. Carl and Dilth-cleyhen had trusted Naiche in the days of the warpath in Old Mexico, and the family group continued to appreciate him. Chatto, too, gave worthy counsel.

Dilth-cleyhen, Lillian, Cora, and her husband Arnold Kinzhuma with their youngsters provided the remaining core of Mangas's Village. In 1910 the latter couple's brood consisted of Edith and Madeline (both of whom died in 1911), Nathan, and Winifred. Aaron, John, and Violet had succumbed to chest disorders; Prince was yet to be born. Elsie Vance Chestuan, Beshád-e's younger sister by some three years, had been sent to Carlisle. All attempts to avoid the transfer had proved futile. She had died at the age of twenty-five, four years after the village was established.

Sometimes Sam Kenoi resided with or near Dilth-cleyhen.[4] He had been reared by her and Mangas after Sam's parents had died in Alabama. At Christine's birth, this young man was twenty-three years of age and was supposed to be attending Carlisle Indian School, but he hated it. So he ran away. Sometimes, too, there was Charles Istee and his wife, the widow Dora Chaendee.

Slightly to the west of this cluster of farm houses and the adjoining fields was To-clanny's Village. Here Rogers To-clanny lived with his third wife, Tsa-kan-e (Sy-e-konne).[5] The stepdaughter of Chief Loco, she was a particularly close friend of Dilth-cleyhen and of Beshád-e. *To-clanny* means "lots of water." Rogers was a man of peace and wisdom. He had served in the days of the warpath as a Scout commissioned to round up Apache renegades. That proved to be worth nothing: he had been sent to Florida with the very men he had helped to capture.

When the Chiricahua were finally moved to Fort Sill, Rogers transferred from the United States Army Company I, of the Twelfth Infantry, in which he had served while in Alabama, and enlisted in Troop L of the Seventh Cavalry. According to the Fort Sill census, his was the longest record held by any Apache as a Scout and soldier in the regular army; never had he borne arms against the United States. By the time Christine was born he had been in the Indian Scout Detachment of the fort for seven years and was in charge of one of the villages. Actually, all the head men within the villages were active as Scouts.

Rogers and his wife had eight children, but three of them had died before Christine's birth. Those left were Emma, Edith (Lola), Peter, Oliver, and the sickly Lawton, who was overcome by tuberculosis in 1911. Emma was a teenager and friend of Lillian; Peter, named after a military officer with whom his father had served, and Oliver were closer to Christine in age but wanted nothing to do with her. "She's just a girl!" It was Edith who became her loyal playmate. Edith, Christine, and Winifred Kinzhuma were fast friends.

One might have thought Susie Aanitso would have joined Lillian and Christine in their various outings, but she rarely did so. When Christine was born, Susie was six years old. She had never known her father, for he had died the year of her birth. Later, she showed clearly her resentment of the affection between her stepfather, Abner, and Beshád-e. Susie chafed even more under the preferential treatment accorded baby Christine. Whenever Beshád-e left her daughters together, Susie made her emotions clear. Throughout their lives she and Christine disliked one another and avoided close contact. It was sad that they had none of the love for each other that was shared by the half-sisters Beshád-e and Lillian.[6]

Lillian adored the baby Christine. Even though there were ten years between their ages, they became the most frequent of companions. Lillian was a baby-sitter and surrogate mother. First, she watched over the toddler; later, she kept the preschooler from getting into mischief, from wandering too far afield. She educated her in the ways of the white people of the fort. She showed her all twelve villages and taught her their names. She shared the gossip about the inhabitants of each one.[7]

One day, the two walked eastward through Kaahteney's Village, past his fields of melons and kafir corn—staying south, clear of Chihuahua's place. Just short of Cache Creek, where the leaders Noche, Kayitah, Geronimo, and Perico had farms, the girls crossed Medicine Bluff Creek. Then they gazed into the fort itself.

Fort Sill was quite unlike a fortress, even though it had been built specifically as a protection against attacks by Indians.[8] In its center was a common square, a parade ground on all sides of which were stone buildings surrounded by lawns and gardens. In the middle of the square was a pole bearing a flag.

Lillian pointed to the red, white, and blue banner. "That's the flag of this country, the United States of America. When you go to school, you'll learn how to salute it and how to pledge allegiance to it." Christine watched it wave and flutter. Then, hearing someone talking, she turned her attention to a group of officers' wives holding parasols aloft to shield their whiteness. She noticed soldiers walking toward the barracks. Some were black; some were white. The fort provided much to see.

From the central square a broad graveled path led northward to the commanding officer's quarters. "That's where those ladies live," explained Lillian. A similar walkway to the south ran to post head-quarters. On the west were three barracks consisting of long, single-story buildings of light gray limestone with wide, covered porches. Farther west, back of the barracks, were latrines and washrooms, and still farther away were the stables with covered stalls for the horses used by the cavalry. Christine's father had shown her the animals on other occasions. He was a blacksmith for the Apaches, as were Old Man John Loco and Jason Betzinez.

Lillian continued, "Those ladies live to the north—over there where you see three double and two single sets of buildings, and also to the east where there are six double sets. Look at that great big house. That's for the commanding officer—the house with two sto-ries. The house of the major is only one story high, like ours." Chris-tine saw little resemblance between this elegant stone house and her own little wooden home, with its picket construction and its breeze-way between two cramped rooms.

Each set of quarters was enclosed by a neat, whitewashed fence. Lillian said, "That fence is not there to keep out Apaches. The sol-diers want to make sure our cattle, any that get out of our corrals, don't get in. They'd destroy the flowers."⁹ She paused a moment and then continued, "Let's go in. It's all right." The older girl pulled her somewhat reluctant ward behind her, past the row of red, yellow, and white rosebushes. The fragrance was exquisite.

"The major's wife is nice," she commented.

Lillian pressed her nose flat against the nearest window pane. Soon Christine followed her example.

Peering through the fine mesh of the white curtains, she saw a round table covered with a cloth of lace. There were four chairs. At the center of the table was an elegant silver bowl filled with roses. There were pictures in gold frames on the walls. How neat and clean it was! What a wonder! Suddenly a woman came into the room holding silver knives, forks, and spoons which she placed in a precise way on the table in front of each chair. Christine started when the lady looked up and glanced at the window. She was about to run, but then the woman smiled. The girls remained until they were tired.

Christine asked to go look at the nearby church. Maybe they could go to the general store as well, to pick up some sweets.

On their way home, Lillian chattered on. "When you go to school, you'll learn all about the proper way to use that silver stuff—the knives and the forks and the spoons. Each one is used for a different kind of food." Christine considered the possibilities of the wonders she would learn at school, then looked earnestly at her aunt.

"Why don't you like school?" she inquired.

Lillian was silent for a time and then murmured, "Oh, I prefer the Apache way."

Another silence. Then she spoke again. "Sometimes those white people are just loco, though. You were about three, I guess. It was a little over a year ago. There was this crazy machine! It came to the fort from Lawton.[10]

"I remember it was springtime, and the leaves on the trees were all pale green. But the roads were dry and dusty. Well, we could hear that thing all the way back in our village. What a racket! We all rushed down to headquarters to see what was going on. We just *ran* toward the fort itself. There was that thing tearing round and round the post. It looked like a buggy, but there wasn't even one horse. It banged and banged and banged just like a shotgun. It snorted. There was a man sitting in it. He was wearing a great big coat and had big round things over his eyes—like spectacles only bigger and rounder. He kept squeezing a round thing in front which made a squawk like a goose! You should have seen it. But that Major Taylor put an end to those things coming here. They called it an automobile. They can't bring them into the fort or even onto the reservation now. But they say there are lots of those things in Lawton."

The girls walked toward Mangas's Village, the dust of the wagon-trail swirling behind their heels.

"You should have seen it," mused Lillian. "All the horses tied in front of the barracks stood on their hind legs. A buggy was over-turned. Even some of the hitching posts were pulled up. Cats and dogs ran like crazy until that thing finally stopped."

"I *will* see some of those things. I'm going to Lawton. And I know I will *like* school," Christine made mental note. Tired by now, the girls trudged homeward.

Occasionally Christine told Lillian a secret. Once, late in the afternoon of a fine spring day, the girls decided to go fishing. Winifred had gone somewhere, so the two were left to their own plans. It had been a long time since they had had a fish dinner. The old people preferred eating meat, so they rarely participated in the sport of wielding hook and line. In fact, they usually discouraged their children from doing so. Beshád-e had warned the girls about the steepness of the bluffs overlooking the cascading creek just south of Mangas's Village.

She told Christine, "I don't want you going there with Edith or the To-clanny boys. I don't want you by those bluffs even if Lawton is there. It's dangerous!" But Lillian was considered to be sufficiently mature to look after her niece.

"Let's get Emma and Edith. They like bass," suggested Christine.

"All right. We can try." But Lillian was not sure Emma would go. Emma was infatuated with Morgan Kazhe. It was nearly time for her Feast, and oh, how she hoped Morgan would race for her on the fifth morning.

The girls looked for the long branches they had used as poles last year. When they were found, they were discovered to be brittle, incapable of restraining a desperate fish. Lillian threw them on the woodpile and off the girls set, taking along an axe, a small coal scuttle that might serve to dig up worms, a battered spoon that might prove more functional than the scoop, and a small pail to hold the bait. They made a shortcut to To-clanny's Village, ignoring the swinging picket gate that gave formal entrance to the Mangas's plot. Their route took them directly through the wire lines encircling the dwelling area. Holding close their full cotton print skirts, they managed to avoid the wicked barbs.

"Watch it," cautioned Lillian.

After braving the yapping To-clanny dogs, the girls found no one home. They continued on toward the creek just north of Chiricahua Tom's. "The worms are good there."

Christine broke a period of silence. "You know," she confided, "Edith and I did something we weren't supposed to last year."

"Yes?" encouraged Lillian.

"Well, that old Peter and Oliver. They dared Edith and me to dig our worms down by Four Mile Crossing. The water is shallow there, and it is level along the shore. That's what those boys said. Well, we went. But those boys! You know the way the hills just east of there are all steep and rocky. They made us go up there with them. Then they found a horny toad and a bunch of awful crawly things. They tried to put them on us. We just yelled! It was awful." Christine grinned despite her tale, but Lillian looked stern.

"Christine, I don't want you to ever do that again. I better tell their mother. Those boys know better. Those crawly things are very bad. They can do bad things to you."

"I know it," Christine agreed. "Those boys saw a tarantula, too. Even *they* were scared of it. They wouldn't touch it."

Lillian stopped walking and looked sternly at her niece. "It's worse than you know. There are lots of rattlers there at Four Mile Crossing. Abner, your father Abner, told us about them. There's even a big den of rattlesnakes at the base of a cliff over there, not exactly at the *best* crossing, but near there. In winter time those snakes just roll together in a great big slimy ball so that they can keep warm.[11] Don't you ever go there alone or with those kids." Lillian had whispered as she spoke about the snakes, and now she paused and looked at Christine to make sure her warning was sinking in.

"And don't ever even say their name—that name 'rattler'—because saying their name will call them to you."

"I know."

For a while they walked on, ever slower, each girl submerged in her own thoughts. Finally Christine looked up and said, "Let's go home. I don't feel like fishing."

There were many things to fear in Fort Sill. Christine started learning about them even while a cradle-child. Evil things and beings would encroach on her liberty and consciousness for the remainder of her life. Beshád-e, Dilth-cleyhen, and Lillian apprised her of places, people, and things she must avoid. Until Lillian was married, she and Christine had daily conversation, sharing intimacies and general facts about the world.

One day the two had gone to the trader's store. Beshád-e wanted yardage—dark blue printed cotton for a Sunday dress.

"You know what I like. Come home and tell me what you find." She gave them a few precious dollars, which they were to apply to the family account. "Because you are good girls for doing that for me, you can buy a can of pears and one of peaches, even if it is expensive." Actually, Dilth-cleyhen wanted the tin of the cans in order to make a few more jingles for Lillian's ceremonial dress, soon to be completed and ready for the maiden's Feast.

As was the usual situation, the store was filled with Indians and whites, plus a few black soldiers. Often there were chance travelers or cattlemen whose business was concerned with the Apache herds.[12] Christine liked to listen to their conversations but understood little of what was said. Her English was rudimentary at best. That would be corrected when she started school—very soon! The trader was courteous. After their business was transacted, the girls lingered in a corner, watching to see what each newcomer was buying. Finally tiring of this, they strolled past the shop filled with saddles and other gear. Next to it was the blacksmith shop. Dave Belin, a Lipan Apache, was there.[13] He was related to Ih-Tedda (which means "young girl"), a Mescalero who had been Geronimo's seventh wife when they were in Fort Apache long ago. The renegade had sent her back to her own tribe in New Mexico when the Chiricahua were incarcerated in Mount Vernon Barracks.

Dave stood there, busily hammering out some nails. Abner was working also. Seeing the girls, he put down the bellows and greeted them with a nod and smile. Both men were skilled at their craft, having learned it at Carlisle Indian Industrial School.

It was hot in the shop. Lillian and Christine wandered back to the parade grounds. There they sat on the lawn, eating crackers. It was dusk before they started home. They took the long way round, across the creek and then straight north toward Perico's fields.

They heard the sound of keening. "Don't look that way," cautioned Lillian. "It must be somebody in Geronimo's camp. They just keep *dying.*"

Christine could not resist a small peek. She pursed her lips, designating the villages on their right. "But the Pericos and the Guydelkons, they're nice. And I like Azul, Geronimo's wife." Lillian nodded in agreement. "Yes, they're good people." Sunseto, or Old Lady Yellow[14] as she was called in English, went most frequently by her Spanish name, Azul. Long ago in the days of the warpath, she had been taken captive by Mexicans, but she had escaped and returned to her kin, the Guydelkons. Eventually she became Geronimo's ninth and last wife.

"Yes, she's all right. But that Geronimo is a witch!" noted Lillian.

Christine was silent. She had heard many things about Geronimo. Her grandmother and mother did not like him. He was sly, not to be trusted. He was currently exploiting the white visitors to the fort, selling them the buttons "from his jacket," or so he said. Actually, he just had a lot of buttons. He had no dignity, no pride. He had proven that to the Chiricahuas.

Yet, in the past he had done wondrous things with the powers he possessed. Once he had stopped the sun from rising.

Old Man Chatto and Jasper Kanseah had visited Mangas's Village one evening, and everyone was talking about the warpath days and the exploits of the various warriors, including Geronimo.

"I remember one time Geronimo and his people were nearly where they wanted to be. It was still very dark, but it was near daybreak. The warriors needed the darkness so as to avoid being seen by the enemy. The enemy had lots of spies around.

"Well, that old Geronimo, he began to sing. He sang a long time.

The men kept moving until they reached a mountain spot that had lots of big boulders. The men could hide safely there.

"Well, do you know the sun stayed down until they were safe! It did not come up at its usual time. It was two or three hours later than usual." Chatto had called Geronimo's power *In-dáh keh-ho-ndi*, "Enemies-against" power. It was war power. Geronimo used it when he made and blessed shields and war amulets.[15]

Yes, Geronimo truly possessed great powers. He was a shaman. The trouble was that as he approached old age, his powers were diverted from taking *Geronimo's* life. Instead, they were taking the lives of his relatives, one by one. That renegade was responsible for the deaths. Or so it was said by the old people of many villages. Not just infants were dying in his family, not just the infirm, but strong adults, young people in their prime!

Certainly Dilth-cleyhen blamed Geronimo for this. But he countered by claiming it was someone else in Fort Sill who was guilty. Someone else was "witching" his kin, trying to get back at him. He raged. Who was it? He would find out! To do so, he held a ceremony down near Naiche's camp.

Geronimo asked Lot Eyelash[16] to be in charge of the sacred dancers, to perform the necessary ritual. He could trust Lot, who had been with him and Jasper Kanseah and Jason Betzinez in 1882 and 1883. Geronimo was confident. Lot would find the witch.

All started well. There were three or four songs. Then suddenly the singing and dancing stopped. Lot was ready. After a dramatic pause, he called out, "It was you, Geronimo. *You* did it! You did it to save your own life!"[17]

Christine wondered. Could Shi-ma, my mother, be right? Maybe it was true what they said. Zi-yeh, another of Geronimo's wives, had died just one year after arriving with him at Fort Sill.

"He's bad. He lies all the time. He goes on all those trips to expositions where the white people think he is wonderful, and he can show off. He betrayed all of us. He deceived his own people—even after accepting our hospitality. At Warm Springs he and his family camped with Victorio for over a year. That man has a forked tongue, worse even than whites. And now he is rewarded while the rest of us are in hardship," Dilth-cleyhen had said. Her words reflected the opinion of many others in Oklahoma and became Geronimo's general reputation until his death in 1909. Certainly, in Fort Sill he was never accorded the prestige given Naiche either by whites or Indians. Even as late as the 1960s certain Chiricahuas then living in Mescalero were adamant in their condemnation.[18]

Beshád-e backed up her mother's statements. "If it had not been for that scoundrel, many fewer of our young warriors would have died. He was interested only in his own welfare. He put others in useless danger. We all wanted peace. But he double-talked us. He double-talked the army officers. So finally the army made everyone a prisoner, no matter what their attitude, no matter how much they cooperated with the military demands. If it had not been for that man Geronimo, we would now be in our own homeland, just like the Mescaleros."

Once Christine heard Tsa-kan-e whisper, "He's got Coyote power." Coyote power was especially strong and dangerous if not used correctly. Maybe he is practicing Coyote power now, thought the child.

Power was not a subject to be taken lightly. It was not something for casual conversation, Christine knew. But she had seen the effect of Geronimo's Coyote power. He could cure "coyote sickness," an ailment caused by any contact with a coyote, a wolf, or a fox—or even the tracks or leavings of these animals.[19] Dogs were scary, too. Any canine could cause a person to shake, his lips to twist, and his eyes to cross. Christine remembered the old lady in Fort Sill who had these symptoms. She had gone to Geronimo, and he had sung over her. He cured her. He used his powers for good that time.

"Why can't he always be good?" she questioned. "There are a few good curers right here in Fort Sill. Slim Woman, Ist-sun-isht-us'n, is respected. She's related to Tom Duffy and his brother, James Russell."

Christine remembered the time a cousin of Eugene Chihuahua came back from Carlisle. He could not move. Eugene had requested the services of Slim Woman.

"All you young men and boys just stand back," the old woman said. She waved them back with her hand, motioning them to do her bidding. Her hand was outstretched. Then she looked at Eugene. He had seemed reluctant, as though he did not know what was expected.

"You—you just look on the top of my hand!" Somewhat sheepishly, Eugene had looked at her hand. "He can't move because *you*—you are not *lookin'* in the right way." Christine recalled that Slim Woman had helped the young man. To be sure, he got sick again, and was then diagnosed by the white physicians to have had tuberculosis. But Slim Woman was a good curer.

Christine's thoughts wandered to the graveyards. All elderly Apaches, including Dilth-cleyhen and even Beshád-e and Abner, were reluctant to go near them. The ghosts of the deceased lurked in that vicinity, always eager to lure the souls from living people.

Many of Christine's kin and friends were buried there in the fashion the whites had insisted on. There were markers for most of those who had gone, including one for Nana, that great and valiant warrior. He had died in 1896. Blind by then, he was over ninety years of age.[20] Some of the dead had signposts in the main Apache cemetery near Beef Creek; others were in the Bailtso and Chihuahua cemeteries on the East Range.

So many were gone. Even Carl Mangas had passed away, as had the student, Elsie Vance Chestuan. Cora Kinzhuma had escaped both lung ailments and witchcraft, but, as noted previously, not all her children survived. Even now Madeline, her daughter, was suffering from tuberculosis. That's why the medical people told Beshád-e she must not let Christine play in Cora's house even though it was within the same village. So far Nathan and Winifred had escaped, but the family had had a mighty share of keening. Dilth-cleyhen had lost others: Frank, Faith, and Flora. Beshád-e had buried Borgia Aanitso and Reginald.

"Now there is only Beshád-e and Lillian and me," Christine contemplated. "Well, I guess I should count those boys that Dilth-cleyhen used to care for: Charlie Istee and Sam Kenoi. And that Susie. She's always healthy. She's always around." But were the others, those in the graveyards; had they been the targets of the witches? The thought was troublesome.

On Sundays the preacher said, "No. There's no such thing as witchcraft; that is just superstition."

Christine was a faithful member of the Dutch Reformed Church. Its mission was located in a sheltered hollow known as the Punch Bowl,[21] less than a mile from Mangas's Village and about two miles northwest of the post itself. It was adjacent to Kaahteney's Village. Beshád-e insisted each Sunday that Christine attend church services. It was essential that her daughter learn all the white man's ways, and that included knowing his God and receiving the blessings therefrom. After all, the power of that God had been proven on the days of the warpath. Therefore, Christine grew up recognizing and respecting not only Apache powers but those of Christianity as well.

Springtime moved toward summer. Lillian, who by nature was reticent and shy among all but her kind, was given a Feast announcing her womanhood. Dilth-cleyhen had worked long hours on the ceremonial buckskin dress, rubbed thoroughly with pollen so that it was a beautiful deep yellow. A circle of red paint taken from the earth formed a yoke. Here and there along its edge were tin jingles, metallic ornaments that shone in the bright sunlight and added a faint tinkling sound when the maiden moved. Lillian's manner was modest, in keeping with her natural ways. But she held her head high, tilted slightly, as was her custom. She was a young woman of great worth. Christine looked on her with adoring admiration. The child looked at the toe extensions of Lillian's moccasins. They had been painted red. How beautiful.

"One day I'll look like that—when I am White-Painted-Woman," the youngster dreamed.

On the morning of the fifth day of Lillian's Feast, it was time for the maiden to run. As she ran, the pollen from her head and shoulders blew on the boys who were close behind, thus blessing them. Lillian ran well. It was good. Finally, acorn meal, symbolic of plenty, was poured over her head.

At the completion of the Feast, Lillian's long and flowing hair was arranged to communicate her new status. It was combed back, and a cloth the length of the tresses was placed beneath. One side of the textile was folded over the hair; then the other side was likewise treated. Finally, starting from the bottom the entire length was folded end over end and tied at the nape of Lillian's neck. A hairpiece in an hourglass shape was added over this. Its base was rawhide, covered with beaded buckskin. Then at the center of her forehead was tied a crescent-shaped abalone shell, representing the water of life.[22]

Before the year was out George Martine, the son of Old Man Charles Martine, married Lillian and came to live in Mangas's Village. His former home was just north of Geronimo's, in that cluster of houses belonging jointly to the Kayitahs and Martines. A double name for the group had resulted when Charles became a Scout in 1900 and assumed village leadership.

The year of Lillian's marriage was also the year when Christine first attended school. She joined the thirty to forty day-school pupils of the mission school of the Dutch Reformed Church. There were about two dozen other students who slept and boarded in two dormitories. The church preferred that all the students live in the boarding residences. Here they would surely learn the white man's ways, being less influenced by Apache culture. That was the plan, but parents tended to be unwilling to part with their children. Some of the youngsters walked from six to eight miles each way in order to receive their education. The mission accommodated the younger Chiricahuas; older children were sent off the fort, usually to the Chilocco Indian School.[23]

Christine was eager. On school mornings, she arose early, putting on the dark skirt and light-colored print blouse that were the accepted uniform. The sleeves were long, the neck high. Underneath she wore a pretty petticoat. She pulled on long black stockings and buttoned her dark high-top shoes. After brushing her hair until it shone, she plaited two braids that hung over her shoulders. She was ready, all but her silver bracelet. She admired her outfit, but even more she liked Sunday clothes. Then she wore a dainty print dress, pale in color, with ruffles at her elbows and around the collar yoke.

Christine grabbed a piece of fry bread. The teacher had told her pupils they must always eat breakfast before attending class. The morsel consumed, the child dashed out the door. Usually Winifred, her cousin, was already ambling down the road, scuffing the dust. Christine ran to meet her, and the two walked hand in hand toward the mission.

The Dutch Reformed Church had long been associated with the Chiricahua Apaches. In 1869, when the latter were at odds with the military forces of the United States, and when Gen. George Crook was advocating peace, certain organizations campaigning to halt the needless warfare and bloodshed were talking to President Ulysses S. Grant.[24] He met with many church men, with the executives of missionary societies as well as with Indian sympathizers. Out of these meetings evolved what would later become known as Grant's Peace Policy, sometimes called Grant's Quaker Policy. The main objective of the program was to civilize and Christianize the red "pagans" through religious and educational work. Men closely affiliated with various religions would be appointed as Indian agents, missionaries would be teachers, and reservations would be established whereon Indians would be taught agricultural skills. In 1873 the scheme was activated, and the Chiricahua Apaches were assigned to the Reformed Church in America, the direct descendant of the protestant Dutch Reformed Church. Originally this was in Arizona, an area wherein the sect had few members and Christian effectiveness was minimal. However, when the Chiricahua were removed from their homeland and made prisoners of war, the church kept contact, helped in the adjustments that had to be made in the difficult days of semiacculturation, and frequently acted as go-between for the Indians, many of whom spoke minimal English, and their white captors.

At Fort Sill the work of the ministry began to bear fruit. In 1895 the Reformed Church in America sent its first missionary, Frank Hall Wright, who was a Choctaw, to Oklahoma, but for a time the army banned his being with the newly arrived Apaches. Later, however,

188 : Christine Louise Kozine

the denomination was permitted a mission among the Cheyennes. Wright and Dr. Walter C. Roe, who headed the latter mission, called a council with the Apaches. With the cooperation of Lt. Francis Henry Beach, then in charge of the Chiricahuas, a plan was drawn up which would concentrate first on educating the children of Fort Sill.

The War Department gave its permission for the construction of various mission buildings on the reservation. The first structure was the schoolhouse, built with a room in which the teacher could live. The teacher was expected to be nurse and home visitor as well as instructor of the primary grade children. Religious services were conducted in the same building in those early days, with Wright and Roe as preachers. Sunday School was well attended, and a Christian Endeavor Society was commenced.

Every summer there was a camp meeting on the grounds of the Punch Bowl. The entire congregation met in a large tent. Indians set up their individual family tents near by. Christine anticipated the event with pleasure. It was a diversion equal in excitement to the Fourth of July races held in front of the trader's store, the stables, and the blacksmith shop.

Eventually the Dutch Reformed Church constructed five buildings: a church; an enlarged schoolhouse; a separate teachers' home; and the two structures comprising the boys' and girls' dormitories, whose purposes included housing all orphaned youngsters. The dormitories were rarely if ever filled to capacity, for Apaches expected kin—no matter how distant the relationship—to care for the offspring of the deceased. Ordinarily the echoing buildings contained only two or three children whose parents for some reason neglected them, and perhaps a few very young whose homes were too distant for the daily walk.

The Apaches appreciated the efforts of the church. Noche was the first among the Indian leaders to be converted by the missionaries. Then came Chihuahua, Naiche, and Chatto, and their womenfolk. The Sunday congregation was further enlarged by the attendance of those who had become Christians while at Carlisle. Such was Abner Kozine.

Many of the children thrived under white man's instruction, both religious and secular. They sang the songs; they listened to the sermons, even though the latter were sometimes confusing. The Dutch Reformed ministers taught that Crown Dancers could perform no miracles, could put an end to no epidemics or evil situations, that Indian prayers to Apache creators and other powers of the universe were "pagan," and that there were no beings such as ghosts and witches. Apache beliefs were nothing but superstition and ignorance! But how could that be true, when Beshád-e and Dilth-cleyhen could testify otherwise? Besides, the prayers to God in English seemed identical, if not in actual words, at least in meaning, to those proffered in Indian.

Aside from such contradictions and mysteries, Christine loved being "educated." She was eager to communicate in the language of whites, to learn the names of lovely objects such as parasols. She struggled to speak properly, to use the "he's" and "she's" and the "his's" and "her's" in accordance with her teacher's dictates. She began to learn to read and to write, as well as to do rudimentary arithmetic. The old people had told her that at one time they had used knots in cordage to keep track of time and to help them with simple addition and subtraction, but now she must memorize and keep calculations in her head. Beshád-e encouraged her efforts, telling her repeatedly what a help she would be to a mother who had such difficulty understanding the confusing documents she was faced with from time to time. Were the whites cheating her? What did all the papers mean? Where must she put her X?

The first year or so of Christine's schooling passed all too quickly. Each morning as she dressed in her uniform, so clean, so pretty, she smoothed the skirt down in front. It was just like the clothing of the white children at headquarters. Christine stood tall. She had acquired already a "style" characteristic of Fort Sill Apaches, one that distinguished these women from other Apaches of New Mexico in future years.

At home Christine enjoyed the members of her family and the frequent guests who visited from the nearby households. The older women and men gambled, shouting with glee when they won. They played the boot game, which is explained in Apache mythology. Christine watched them maneuvering the sticks used as playing pieces. One day she asked her mother to tell the story associated with the high-topped moccasins[25] which Beshád-e called "boots."

"Well," her mother began, "it happened a long, long time ago, in the times when things were being created. All the animals were in a small cave. The birds were sitting outside, just at the entrance, looking in. The animals and the birds looked at each other, trying to decide whether there should be *daylight* forever, or whether there should be *darkness* forever on the face of this earth. The birds wanted it to be daylight, but the animals wanted the darkness. They decided to gamble in order to solve the dilemma. The winners would have their choice as the prize.

"Well, they waited until midnight to start. But before that, they built a curtain of brush, thick enough to divide the animals from the birds, thick so that they could not see each other." As Beshád-e told the story, she sang songs in the appropriate places, songs Christine loved to hear.

"Well, at midnight the animals and the birds began to play. They lined up ten boots in a row. One boot was put down. Its toe faced the animals. The next boot was put down. Its toe faced the opposite direction, toward the birds. And so on, all down the row." Again, Beshád-e sang.

When that game got under way, they had to guess in turn, the animals and the birds, into which boot the opposing team had hidden a segment of the vertebra of some animal. Each contestant was blindfolded, one at a time, and took a stick and hit one of the boots. That boot was supposed to hold the bone."

"That sounds fun," mused Christine. "It should have been easy. There were only ten boots."

"Not so easy," countered Beshád-e. "Under the ground, a little gopher ran around. Just as somebody was going to hit the right boot, that gopher changed the positions of the moccasins all around! Everybody got confused." Christine laughed happily.

"Well, the turkey was scorekeeper. He had a lot of little sticks so he could keep tally. Roadrunner helped him keep the record straight. And the animals and the birds played, and they played, and they played. Just at the time it was about to be dawn, the birds began to win. They started a choir of chirping."

"Just like we do at the school," interrupted Christine.

"Well, yes. Those birds began chirping, 'It's morning! It's morning! It's morning!'" Beshád-e sang. "When the animals saw the daylight, they knew they were beaten. They just disappeared. They knew they were beaten."

Beshád-e stopped her narration. Christine waited for a time and then requested, "Finish the story, Shi-ma. What about Gá, the cottontail?"

"Oh, yes. Well, that little cottontail kept running back and forth in front of the opening to the cave where they had gambled. He was all excited. He ran, he jumped, and he hopped around. He kept repeating, 'Which way do you think the sun will come up?' He faced one direction and said, 'Maybe it will come up on this side.' Then he faced the opposite direction and said, 'No, here's the sun. It's going to come up on *this* side.' Finally he made up his mind. He sat down. 'The sun is going to come up from *this* direction. I'll be facing it when it does.' So he sat.

"The sun rose in the East. But Gá, that little cottontail, was facing West.

"The sun came up. It came up *behind* him. As it arose, one ray barely touched the cottontail."

"I know! I know!" shouted Christine. "When you look at a cottontail, right there at the back of his head, right on his neck, that is where the sunlight hit him. You can see that little yellow spot."

Beshád-e smiled and continued, "Well, Shosh, the bear, was one of the very last animals to leave the gambling cave. He was in such a hurry when he finally got underway that he put his right moccasin on his left foot, and his left moccasin on his right foot. Now, I don't want you to go looking for any bear, young lady, but I can tell you that old bear always looks as if he had put his shoes on the wrong foot.

"Well, finally, all the birds left the cave, too, one by one.

"Turkey, Zith-ga-tazh or 'rough feet,' was in a hurry, just like Shosh, and he kept all those scorekeeping sticks in his pocket instead of throwing them away. Did you know, Christine, that every turkey has an extra bone in his body because Turkey forgot and left one stick in his pocket when he was getting under way?

"Roadrunner was frightened when he saw all the birds starting to leave. He grabbed a stick and started off, but that great big stick was just too long. That is why he cannot fly very high even today. He just flies a short distance, and then down he comes, falling to earth and running along on his two feet."

Christine interrupted, "Lillian says it is Roadrunner who has the extra bone."

"Yes, that's what some folks say." Beshád-e paused, then went on. "Quail sat quietly on the ground. Everybody had left. Then, the fire they had built in the cave spurted out some sparks, and the brush partition caught fire and began to fall. Cinders scattered everywhere. Some dropped on Quail's back. Some dropped on Fawn. That is why both Quail and Fawn have spots where those cinders fell on them.

"And so, my daughter, that is the way the boot game ended. The birds flew out, and they continue to soar in the skies during the daytime. All the animals lurked around at night. Birds enjoy hunting in sunlight when they see better. Animals hunt at night when it is dark. Shosh wanders around both day and night. He was the very last animal to leave the cave."

Beshád-e was quiet for a while. Then she reminisced, "We used to play the gambling game connected to that story, long ago, when I was a girl and when we were on the warpath. That game was just the same then as now."

Sometimes when the old folks visited, sitting around the stove of an evening, they enjoyed a little illegal tulapai, not enough to make them drunk or quarrelsome, but sufficient to make memories more vivid. Occasionally, they were nostalgic about the warpath days, about the plentiful game in Arizona—the deer, antelope, and elk, which the men took by means of a "surround."

One such evening the women were telling Abner about Dilth-cleyhen's agility. It seems a group of the Warm Springs were camped near the mountains in antelope country. The men had gone off to the nearby flatter lands below. They had formed a wide circle of hunters and were beginning to move toward the center, enclosing a large number of the animals. Antelope are so stupid, they are usually easy to kill. They panic in such a situation and then, in bewilderment, stand stock-still in a cluster, waiting to be shot with bow and arrow or gun. Beshád-e told the story.

"I remember we were really hungry that time. We hadn't had much meat for a while—just jerky. And those antelope were there, just waiting for us. The men were all in position; the women were busy back at camp. Suddenly, the women heard a noise. Those antelope were trapped by the men, down on the plain, all but one! And that one was really crazy! It broke loose and headed toward the mountain. It dashed right into the camp. Well, we were ready for anything in those days. We had to be. A bunch of us grabbed knives, and we chased that antelope all around the camp, in and around all the wickiups.

"But Shi-ma was always the most fleet of foot, quicker than all the rest. She was really fast! She just grabbed that antelope and held him tight and stuck her knife in his throat. Boy, we really had a feast that night!" From behind the blanket that hung as a partition between Dilth-cleyhen and her son-in-law, to provide privacy and as an indication of respect between the two, the visitors and Abner heard a chuckle. Dilth-cleyhen was still awake.

Another evening when Rogers To-clanny and his wife Tsa-kan-e were at the house, Mrs. To-clanny told a funny story.

It involved her life and happened when she was about fifteen years of age. The year was 1880 or so. Her parents had arranged what they thought would be an advantageous marriage for her. They had given her to a Navaho man whose reputation was good and who was supposed to have a lot of sheep. Tsa-kan-e was dismayed. She did not like the Navaho one bit.

"They just made me get back of that man on a horse, and he took me way over there, way over to the Navaho country." She paused, thought for a while, and then continued, "Well, I wasn't going to have anything to do with that man. As soon as it got dark, I ran away from him. I hid, and I found my way back home, miles and miles back to Monticello. But, you know, that darn man came after me. He took me away a second time. I ran away a second time. That happened three times. He wouldn't give up.

"I remember one of those times, I was running, and I got real thirsty even though I held a pebble in my mouth. I saw a mule train going along. I didn't know who it was. Maybe they would shoot me. But I took a chance. It was some Mexicans hauling groceries back to their homes. I just begged them for some water. I remember they were real nice. They gave me a drink of water. I finally got home, and then that Navaho man came to get me a fourth time.

"I thought I was going to be sick. I just begged and pleaded with my parents. 'Please, please don't send me back with him,' I said. Finally, my parents relented."

Everyone laughed, including Rogers, whom Tsa-kan-e had married some five years after this event. Abner, who was Tsa-kan-e's cousin, nodded affirmation of what had transpired, commenting that the girl's behavior was certainly out of line.

"Well, that Navaho man was tall and just skinny! He had a funny-looking moustache, a real thick one," Tsa-kan-e vindicated herself.

Christine was quiet, thinking about the situation. She drew a mental image of the Navaho, then looked carefully at Rogers. *Rogers* was tall and skinny. *He* had a moustache, a thick one, just like that Mrs. To-clanny had described. Christine suppressed a grin. "I don't understand about those old-time marriages," she thought. "If Mrs. To-clanny had actually married that Navaho, there would have been no one to take care of her parents in their old age. That's the job of a son-in-law. Those newlyweds would have been off in the boondocks somewhere, off in Navaho country, with *his* people, it sounded like. That was not the right way of settling down, the usual way, even with Navahos. Beshád-e had told her about those Indians. They had many customs like those of Apaches. They talked almost like Apaches. Still, in a marriage like that, Tsa-kan-e would have been too far from her home to care for the needs of her mother and father, and her husband could not have paid them their proper respect. "Boy, I'm not going to marry a Navaho, either."

It was good when the old folks sat around, singing songs, and someone began to drum. One could hear the sounds among all the villages from time to time. Lots of nights there was a gentle breeze and the music and laughter carried long distances. On the rare nights when someone needed special supernatural aid and there was ritual, one heard other songs, louder drumming. The Crown Dancers were performing. If there were a Feast, if it were part of a young girl's puberty ceremony, the whole family bundled up and joined the other Fort Sills, as they were beginning to call themselves. Then they could watch the Mountain Gods as they thrust their swords toward the firelight and made things right with the world.

Life seemed good to Christine.

Evenings were special, but there were also numerous daytime diversions throughout the year. Men and boys played baseball with gusto as soon as weather would permit; women and younger children rooted enthusiastically for their team, their kin. Anyone could go to the creek and fish when weather was good. Then, early summer was branding time. The bawling of calves rent the air. If children stayed out of the way, they could watch the strong Apache cowboys with their big black hats and special boots, white men's boots. The cowhands sizzled the letters U.S. on the shoulder of each young animal. Then the individual family number, such as 4 or 11 or 14, or whatever it was, was branded on its hip to make identification of ownership sure. In the fall Apache women were granted permission to travel the short distance outside the Fort where there were sufficient mesquite bushes to provide beans for later feasting. And all summer and autumn long there was some kind of harvesting: hay, pumpkins, rutabagas, kafir corn.

In February of 1910 Lillian gave birth to her first child, a son. Dilthcleyhen attended her as midwife. Lillian named him Edward, sometimes shown in the records as Ealdon. Christine loved to take care of the baby boy. She rushed home in order to hold him, rock him, sing to him. She encouraged his progress, not so much in crawling as in his first few steps.

Then one day there was an announcement at school. Even the youngsters in the first few grades were to be transferred to the Indian

Boarding School in Chilocco. Susie had been sent there a year or so before.

The thought of leaving Beshád-e frightened Christine, but simultaneously, the idea of traveling, of seeing new countryside, meeting children of other tribes, and of joining the "big kids" stirred her sense of adventure.

It was once again the aim of governmental administrators to expedite the acculturation of Apache and other Indian youths by removing them from their parents, who continued to teach and practice traditional ways. In Chilocco the children could be immersed totally in the learning and customs of the white man.

Boarding Schools and Vacation

Chilocco is located in Kay County, far in northern Oklahoma, bordering Kansas. The primary task of the boarding school was teaching the children to read, write, and speak English. Most of the youngsters tried, primarily because they needed companionship. Inasmuch as a number of tribes were represented among them, and therefore many Indian tongues and dialects were spoken, the new language provided a common starting point for communication.

Learning to accomplish simple household tasks and to practice white etiquette were among other required accomplishments. Every child was expected to make his bed; everyone had to use tableware properly. Gradually boys were exposed to some kinds of farmwork and various trades; girls were taught to clean and cook. After the strangeness began to fade, Christine enjoyed the latter. The majority of the children preferred recess to all other class periods. In decent weather they romped outside, playing games such as baseball, engaging in contests and races, much the same as they had done in their many homelands, or, in the case of the Chiricahuas, in Fort Sill.

The first week in Chilocco, Christine had looked for Susie. The actual meeting was disappointing. Old tensions surfaced. Susie greeted her half-sister with less than enthusiasm. And so the two kept their distance—just as they had at home. Christine found friends among the younger children; Susie, always a loner, preferred the company of older students when she sought any company at all.

Christine found that most of her classmates had a level of education equal to her own. Many of them were shy, as she was, but most of them welcomed companionship. The girl Christine liked most of all was a Cherokee. Her name was Narcissus. Years later, Christine called her firstborn daughter Narcissus, in memory of that first Chilocco friend.

In March 1912 a letter arrived from Fort Sill, from Lillian. It announced the birth of her second child on February 1. This was Evelyn, or, as shown in the Fort Sill records, Eveline. This baby was to become a very special person in Christine's life, and later still, in that of her daughter, Narcissus. Always, Evelyn and her slightly older cousin were to be like sisters, sharing love and assistance whenever needed.

Now, Christine could scarcely wait for summer to come, for it meant a special vacation, one in which she could be with Lillian and the new baby. Indeed, the holiday lived up to her expectations, even though it was far too short.

Then it was back to school. The ensuing months, filled with the routine of study, dragged more than previously. When next Christine saw her family, it was December and Christmastime.

As a special treat, in the first few days of the January holiday the women of the family had a professional photographer do a group picture. Their heads high, Lillian and Beshád-e stood behind the others. Christine held baby Evelyn, and Edward sat on the arm of the chair. How handsome they looked in their Sunday best! Edward wore his new striped jumpsuit; the little girls were in sheer white dresses with rows of lace and tucking; both women had stylish high-necked and long-sleeved white blouses above their trim black skirts. This portrait was to become an heirloom.

Back at Chilocco, the days dragged on. What had been so exciting at first had by now become routine. Letters from home were few and far between. Everyone was so busy back there. If her mother wrote, she had to get someone else to do the penmanship and the mailing. Sometimes Beshád-e sought the aid of missionaries at the Dutch Reformed Church. The white man George Wratten, who had been her friend long ago in San Carlos, and then later in Florida and in Alabama, and who had followed and interpreted for the Apaches throughout all their trials and troubles, was very ill that spring of

1912.[26] Wratten, like General Crook, was a truthful, loyal white man. Now, it seemed, he was nearing death, and she could not disturb him for so small a thing as a letter to a daughter. Christine appreciated that it was hard for Beshád-e to write; it was not a task that came to her mother naturally.

Then, early in 1913, long awaited news arrived. The Chiricahua were free at last! The transfer from Oklahoma to New Mexico was to be reality! They would live on a reservation, confined in a sense, but the only other Indians there were Apache—the Mescaleros who had always been friends, friends of Victorio. No more Fort Sill! No more the life of prisoners!

Christine was ready to pack her clothes. But no, she was told, not yet. Information was scanty. Soon the administrators told the Chiricahua youngsters they must remain at Chilocco until reservation housing was ready. The government officials did not want the children to live in the tents that had been set up initially for the Fort Sill Indians on the Feast Ground near the Mescalero Agency. After months passed, there was more delay. The newcomers had been taken by wagon to the district known as White Tail Canyon. Each family was assigned a tract of land; houses and barns were being constructed. But the Chiricahua were still living in tents. Their children must not join them. The winter months were bitterly cold in White Tail; canvas and skin were proving to be inadequate shelter. Many people were ill. The ultimatum was: "Keep the children at the boarding school."

One day Christine's teacher called her to the office to deliver very bad news. There had been a death at home; Abner had become sick, and he had died. My father, the child's heart cried. That man, that good man, my father, he has gone! How she longed to wail and weep away the empty hurting. But no, her mother said, "Don't come home. There is nothing you can do here. Stay in Oklahoma." Susie provided no comfort; after all, Abner was not *her* father.

Springtime passed. Summer vacation approached, and although a few of the houses at White Tail had been started, those of Beshád-e, Dilth-cleyhen, and Lillian were not among them. Nevertheless, Christine and Susie were allowed to go home.

Beshád-e met them. She and Dilth-cleyhen had come to Agency. They had hitched the horses and wagon to a post adjacent to the building that housed the Bureau of Indian Affairs. Beshád-e, now in her forties, was a handsome woman, capable-looking and trim despite the tired sadness of her eyes. Dilth-cleyhen, too, was aging well. She appeared to be spry, just as an Apache woman should. There was joy in their greeting as the women and daughters held each other in close embrace. Then they wept together over the recent sorrow. But not for long, as Beshád-e hurried them into the wagon. It was an all-day trip. White Tail was over twenty miles away, and the sun was already bright, directly overhead.

The countryside was green and lush as soon as they left the dusty roads and open lots surrounding the administrative offices. Sunflowers lined the paths that vehicles had carved into wet earth. Here and there horses grazed in the open meadows.

Heading east, they passed the Feast Ground to their left. Many tents and wickiups were still in use. Beshád-e indicated the space where she and Abner had camped. Christine turned around, looking back toward Agency. She asked about other structures. She was informed there was a trader's store, a hospital, and a school.

"Where is Lillian's house?" she queried.

"Six miles down the canyon from us in White Tail," answered her mother. The wagon lumbered on.

Just to the south, while they were still in the community of Agency, stood several low buildings atop a knoll. The largest, an adobe, had a steeple and was topped with a cross. The other, long and narrow, was fronted by four stout pillars. This was St. Joseph's Mission.[27] Beshád-e spoke, "Most of the Mescaleros are Catholic. The priest comes up here each week from Tularosa to conduct services." After a moment, she added, "They're nice. They can be trusted, those people. They tried to convert a lot of us when we came from Fort Sill and were camped up there on the hill. But I prefer the missionaries of the Dutch Reformed Church. They've been good to us for so long. They still relay our needs to the authorities. They have stuck with us for many, many years—even before Fort Sill. They are planning to build us a church up in White Tail." The word she used for White Tail was *be-ho-yan*, meaning "up in the high mountains."

Farther on, Susie nudged Christine. She lip-pointed to a group of girls huddled together on a rise north of the road. "They must be Mescaleros." The unknown girls made no attempt to disguise their staring. They whispered from behind their hands and did not appear friendly. One of them seemed to giggle. Christine felt as though the very seams of her blouse had been picked apart.

"Do they always glare like that?" Christine asked her mother.

"Yes. They don't much like us Fort Sills. All the women do that. Pay no attention. Hold your head up high," was the response. "How strange," thought Christine. "We are all Apaches, all on the same side; all of us have suffered; all of us have spent some of our lives as prisoners."

Miles passed, and the terrain changed. At the higher altitude pines replaced grasses, rabbitbrush, greasewood, and clumps of salt cedar that Christine and Susie had seen on the way up from Tularosa. The rocking and creaking of the wagon lulled the girls to sleep, until Beshád-e touched their shoulders and awakened them. It was time to eat.

Already their mother had built a small, smokeless fire. Coffee was brewing in a tin can. Beshád-e pulled out cold boiled beef and big homemade biscuits from the recesses of a printed flour sack. A can of apricots completed the repast.

"Enjoy it," she said. "This is a celebration! We can't afford such luxuries often, now that that Old Man is gone. We are just poor. No more pension." Abner had enjoyed a small pension because of his earlier service as an Apache Scout, but this money was not available to his widow. The funds the couple had accumulated at Fort Sill were depleted; the sale of the cattle had been profitable but the proceeds were pigeonholed for the promised housing.

"We're still in tents. A few houses have been started, but most of us have put up shelters for the summer."

With the arrival of warm weather Dilth-cleyhen had set up a couple of wickiups. Within them she could feel the gentleness of the occasional breeze, could see the stars and heavens beyond the rustling leaves of the intertwined branches.

Leaving the main road from Agency, the wagonload of women turned at the White Tail intersection. The trail became rougher. The horses labored en route to Summit and then continued, moving slowly. Finally, Beshád-e pursed her lips to her left. "Those fields are my land," she said. To the right, on the opposite side of the road, there were tents, several wickiups, capped with canvas in case there should be rain, and a cooking arbor. These had been constructed on Dilth-cleyhen's allotment. Lillian and George had been assigned a place within a six-mile walking distance farther down the canyon. Cora and Arnold Kinzhuma were still living at the Feast Ground. Cora was not well and needed to be near medical care.

All the men living in the White Tail district had begun to till their fields. Occasionally they hunted in order to fill family larders. They built fences and did whatever manual tasks were necessary to start life anew. It was hard work and often discouraging. There was no running water. Instead, a pipe extended the length of the canyon. Faucets were available near the various homesites so that water could be drawn and hauled as necessary. Until vegetables could be harvested, most families relied on rations doled out in Agency.

But, oh, if only the houses were ready!

For most youngsters home from boarding schools, it was a wonderful summer. Christine loved being with Beshád-e, with Lillian and her children, with Dilth-cleyhen. She explored the forest near her home, she climbed the nearby foothills. Wildlife was plentiful: white-tail deer and an occasional black-tail; a mountain lion, almost invisible; a bear, to be avoided; wild turkeys scurrying into the underbrush. Sometimes a wild white stallion encroached on the meadows, guiding and guarding his brood of mares. At the approach of Abner or Arnold it reared onto its hind feet, whinnied a challenge, and pawed the air with its forelegs. It was a proud creature, too regal to take. The family laughed when the men retreated, leaving the horse in peace. Christine watched the hawks as they soared overhead, the butterflies; and when she spotted a dread owl, harbinger of death, she averted her eyes.

September approached all too soon. This meant play with cousins would soon terminate. It was again time to think of school.

Beshád-e talked to her daughter.

"Christine, I want you to get a good education. We have decided it is best for you to go to Albuquerque. There is a boarding school there for Indians. Many of the families from here are sending their children, so you won't be alone. I want you to go, too. There is no housing here, and maybe the winter will be too harsh for you. There will be lots of rain and lots of snow." And so Christine left at the designated time on a bus with the other youngsters.

Education was good in Albuquerque, and the young girl attended the Indian School for several years. She became expert at crafts, including complex beading. She enjoyed her classes in home economics; she became sufficiently proficient in basic studies that she was able to apply eventually for a job doing general office work. Until she was nearly eighteen years old, she continued studying from September until June, spending her summer vacations in White Tail.

However, during the first year Christine was gone, Beshád-e's predictions of a hard winter proved true. By mid-October of 1914 the Indian Office at Mescalero stopped the Chiricahuas' food rations. There were six weeks without rain. A fire wiped out most of the oat crop. Nor was this all the devastation. The snow came early and was heavier than normal, making threshing impossible. Spring arrived, and still the crop remained in the fields.

Further, and adding to the Fort Sills' discomfort, the promised housing was still incomplete. Those dwellings that had been constructed were of wretched quality. James O. Arthur, the Reformed Church missionary on the Mescalero Reservation, noted that the drying of the wood left cracks and knotholes, through which the west winds swept. The houses were drafty and next to impossible to heat. Earlier, when carpenters had been working, sap had oozed out whenever a nail was driven into a board.[28] Chiricahua spokesmen protested. So did many forthright whites who recognized the injustices: J. W. Prude, the trader at Mescalero; Richard Henry Harper, who initially established the Reformed Church's mission on the reservation; William A. Light, a new agent who replaced the well-meaning but somewhat ineffectual Clarence R. Jefferis. Unfortunately, there where also white opponents who possessed political power: Senators Albert B. Fall and Thomas B. Catron and their stockmen constituents had fought against the transfer of the Apaches from Fort Sill to New Mexico. In 1916 Fall initiated legislation to make Mescalero a national park.[29]

The year 1917 brought some economic improvement to the people in White Tail. Twelve hundred head of Hereford cattle had been purchased with Chiricahua funds, and individual families added another seven hundred using their own money. By December there were 3,160 head. Some storage sheds, cisterns, root cellars, and fencing had been completed.[30] Prosperity seemed in sight.

That summer when Christine returned for vacation, Dilth-cleyhen talked to her. "It is time we started to prepare for your da-i-dá, your Puberty Feast." Christine was elated. She was measured for her buckskin robe; they started gathering pollen and all the sacred foods; they began buying gifts for the chaperone and all the helpers, the cooks, those who would haul wood—everyone. And they must hire a team of Crown Dancers. It would take well over a year to be ready. Everyone rejoiced. Christine was concerned with every detail.

Optimism was short-lived. Beshád-e's half-sister Cora died April 3, 1919. Her husband, Old Man Arnold, moved from Feast Ground to White Tail, where he camped near his deceased wife's kin. He felt obligated to help them when he could.

The previous spring, that of 1918, had been one of drought, and the oat crop had failed once again. Less than 70 acres were productive out of 608 planted. The Indians' disappointment was bitter. Families needed cash to buy supplies. They had insufficient clothing. Harnesses, other equipment, in fact, utensils of all kinds were lacking, and local stores had cut off Chiricahua credit. Barns were yet to be built; a traction engine was a necessity for threshing the oats. There was no blacksmith at White Tail. The only medical facility to care for the numerous ill was located far away in Agency. Housing was still inadequate.[31] Many families were forced even yet to live in tents. With all these adverse circumstances, and now the death of Cora, should they proceed with plans for a Feast?

Beshád-e and Dilth-cleyhen spent long hours weighing the pros and cons. Could they afford to kill enough beef to feed their many guests? Could they have a four-day ceremony for Christine? Or should they limit it to one or two days? The latter was a possibility and no disgrace. Many Chiricahua were reduced to this, both when on the warpath and when prisoners of war. A four-day Feast with all the dancing could be given a bit later.

"No, let us do it right, just as planned," they decided. "Four days for Christine's da-i-dá, her time of being White-Painted-Woman." They would go ahead with gathering and preparing the sacred foods: baked mescal, yucca fruit, mesquite beans. They would need piñons and, of course, the pollen.

All members of the family helped. Not only did they assist with the food supplies, but they gave their manual skills. The Feast would be held in White Tail in the Chiricahua way, not in the custom of the Mescaleros, who used a Big Tipi. Tables for serving and a cooking arbor would be constructed near Dilth-cleyhen's house site.

Shortly after Christine returned from Albuquerque the next summer, relatives and close friends of the family began settling in camps on the land assigned Beshád-e and Dilth-cleyhen. It was a time to rejoice, to visit, and to help with the last-minute preparations. Dilth-cleyhen and Beshád-e reminisced that it would be a Feast identical to theirs. It would be as taught by White-Painted-Woman.

The Da-i-dá

First, four poles were set up, fir trees, to designate the corners of a square, each side measuring fourteen feet or thereabouts. Branches were woven in and out at the top only, to form a leafy shade or roof. There was no pit for a fire, and there would be no dancing inside by the maiden. These are Mescalero ways. The only time a Chiricahua maiden goes beneath the canopy is immediately before she makes her four runs.

Christine was modest and beautiful in her buckskin. Her soft black hair streamed behind her, unchecked by pins such as she used at school to confine it into a neat bun. She was nervous. What if someone were witching her and would cause her to fall during the runs? But if such a thing should happen, Old Man Arnold had promised to pick her up, straighten her, turn her around four times, and then push her forward once again. It would be all right.

Christine's beautiful white robes had been made by Beshád-e. The fringes around the circular yoke of the blouse were elegant; the hides were wide and almost covered her hands, while the undulating natural body shape of the deer from which the garment was made, created a soft, flowing hemline. The fringed skirt almost touched the ankles of the wide moccasins with their upturned toes. This same outfit would be worn in later years by both Evelyn and her sister Marilyn, and still later by Susie's daughter Gwendolyn when Beshád-e financed their respective da-i-dás.

Christine need not have been apprehensive. As the ritual commenced, the Mountain Gods blessed her. She in turn used her power as White-Painted-Woman, anointing with pollen the women and children who sought her gifts of health and well-being. The sun shone upon the congregated Apaches. During the four runs of the first morning, and also the fifth, Christine's feet were swift, sure. In between, during the evenings when the Mountain Gods, the Crown Dancers, appeared and danced around the great bonfire, she moved in sedate rhythm behind them. When they left, she retired. Truly, she had embodied White-Painted-Woman, created by the power of Yusen.

During her final run children had followed her. Among them were some of her cousins, offspring of Lillian and of Susie. For some years now Susie had been married to George Magooshboy, a Mescalero. They had chosen not to live in White Tail near Beshád-e but in a remote area called Elk Silver. Only rarely did Susie visit her kin, usually only when she wanted to leave her children with them for awhile.

The guests who had come to the Feast complimented their hosts. "It was a fine da-i-dá. For four days you have fed us well—every morning, noon, evening, and again at midnight, you gave us beans, boiled beef, fry bread, coffee, fruit—plenty of everything." Beshád-e and Dilth-cleyhen had fulfilled the meaning of the word da-i-dá: "It is for everybody."

In addition to its religious significance, the Feast is a time for social dancing, and there had been lots of that. There was the Back-and-Forth Dance during the day. The women interlocked their arms with those of men, each person in turn facing an opposing direction. They stepped back and forth in unison following the beat of the drum, the cadence of the singing. The men sang, standing in the center of the clearing in front of the arbor until a woman came up. She tagged the one she wanted as a partner. He must be non-kin, going back to the fourth cousin or further if a relationship were known. Then they joined the group. At certain changes in the music everyone in the line turned and faced the opposite way and then continued dancing. Occasionally one man danced with two women, one on each side. After the music stopped, the man paid his partners. Usually the payment consisted of money, but it might be groceries or dress material or even a blanket.

Dancing at night took a different form. First came the Crown Dancers. When they left, maybe as late as ten or eleven o'clock, the Round Dance commenced. There are two kinds of round dance, one being very slow, the other fast. It all depends on the singing. The participants form a circle around the bonfire. The drumming begins; the dancers follow the beat, moving clockwise.

During Christine's Feast, the guests enjoyed the Round Dance until the morning star arose, and the "morning song" began. Then once more, they danced back and forth, but the formation differed from that of the daytime. Men formed one line, women and girls another. The lines of people faced each other. Back and forth they stepped until it was daylight and exhaustion took over.

Long ago, Beshád-e told Christine, before the prisoner of war and reservation days, all the guests who danced or sang all night long that last night of the Feast were given presents by the hosts. To the women, four yards of cloth was customary; to the men, neckerchiefs or cigarettes or socks.

The elation Christine felt during the Feast lasted all summer long. She felt great pride in her heritage. When she grew up, she would, like Dilth-cleyhen, be a good woman, a respected woman, fit to be a chaperone, an *i-dilth-cleyhen*.

In July 1919 Ernest Stecker became the new agent at Mescalero. He produced a plan of economic development for all the reservation based on the sale of timber. At least half of the money made available from this source would be used to increase the tribal cattle herds to six thousand head.[32] It took almost three years before Stecker's plan could be realized, but there was now hope. Perhaps one day the Chiricahua could again attain something close to the prosperity they had enjoyed at Fort Sill.

Students of the caliber of Christine Kozine were a positive, though small, factor in economic recovery. For several more years the young woman attended the Albuquerque Indian School before returning to Mescalero. By then she had had far more learning than most Apaches of her time. She was qualified to be an excellent home-maker in any culture's terms; furthermore, she could take a job and cope with the majority of problems that her own or white people might present.

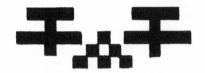

Mescalero and Marriage

Christine returned home in 1922, finding things somewhat changed. Beshád-e and Old Man Arnold had wed. It was Apache custom for an unmarried woman to marry her deceased sister's widower. These newlyweds had much in common: the period of incarceration; the days of living in adjacent houses at Fort Sill and still later on the camping grounds in Mescalero. Arnold, like Abner, had been an Apache Scout and, as such, received a pension. This added income ensured a better livelihood for Beshád-e.

Christine took a job as cook at the hospital in Mescalero. There she met a man whose ideals were close to her own. This man was Tom Duffy. They became good friends.

Tom was older than Christine by more than twenty years. The date of his birth is listed in the tribal census and in that of Fort Sill as 1883, but Tom's descendants are sure that is incorrect. It had to have been later. Dates were a figment of the white man's need for calendars and some kind of documentation! In any event, it is clear that Tom was born at Mount Vernon Barracks in Alabama. The exact day was July 4.

There is no record of Tom's mother who died "long, long ago" and whose name was not spoken afterward. His father was Ah-dis (Artis), one of the Scouts at Fort Apache. He was Net'na, born in

1851. Tom had a brother named James Russell, his elder by some six or so years. Ah-dis died in 1895 at Fort Sill at the age of forty-four. His sons were then reared by a woman named Ni-yeh, the grandmother of Robert Goody, and a distant relative of Tom. In 1897 Tom, along with Sam Kenoi, was sent to the Industrial Indian School at Carlisle Barracks in Pennsylvania. James grew to manhood, was designated a Scout, and married Jeanette Woods (Ba-gust-tet-ahn), but then he contracted tuberculosis. He died in Fort Sill in 1911, leaving no offspring.

Tom liked Carlisle. He mastered the three Rs and spoke English fluently. He enjoyed farming, animal husbandry, and the opportunity to drive large machinery. He was an excellent baseball player, and one of his teammates was Jim Thorpe. Thorpe came from the Algonkian-speaking Sac-Fox tribe of eastern Oklahoma. He was the greatest all-around athlete of the first half of the twentieth century, playing both football and baseball. He participated in the 1912 Olympic Games at Stockholm, where he won the pentathlon and decathlon. In 1913 he played professional baseball with the New York Giants, and later with the Boston Braves. Tom Duffy kept track of the progress of his former teammate with a feeling of genuine pride.

Tom did not graduate from Carlisle "university," as he referred to it. He became ill and was sent back to Fort Sill. For a short while during his recovery period he attended classes at the Dutch Reformed Mission. Then, like Christine, he went to Chilocco. His education had been a good one, and he was qualified for a number of different kinds of jobs.

While at Fort Sill he farmed, raising hay and other crops. He helped with the cattle. He became a Scout and assumed a certain amount of authority within his community. He married Ella Yuzos, and in 1913 they moved to the Mescalero Reservation. However, their union proved incompatible, and they soon divorced. His second wife was Henrietta Keesa (Kisa), the daughter of Tissnolthis and Oskissay. They had two children: Austin and Rosaline. Unfortunately, Henrietta passed away, so that when Christine met Tom, he was a widower.

Tom was a fine man, sober and reliable. The whites liked and trusted him. He worked for the Indian Service at the Mescalero Indian Hospital for over thirty-two years. He drove all kinds of cars, trucks, and ambulances; he was a maintenance man; sometimes he performed janitorial services. Tom labored diligently, thereby earning a good income. He and Christine were attracted to each other, eventually fell in love, and were wed.

For a while they tried living in White Tail near Beshád-e, but the trip into Mescalero each day proved too exhausting even though they had an automobile. Both Tom and his bride continued to work at the hospital. His job started very early in the morning. Consequently, the couple purchased a home situated by the Feast Grounds. It was a small frame house, consisting of two rooms with a low, one-step stoop just outside the front door.

The location of the dwelling was ideal. It was a simple matter to get to work, either by walking or by driving, no matter what the weather. Further, there was considerable space on the slope above the house for the tents and wickiups of Christine's family when anyone wanted to camp.

To purchase a home was unusual among the Indians. Most of them relied on the Bureau of Indian Affairs and the tribe to provide shelter. Christine and Tom were an exception; they were an industrious, proud, and independent pair. They took good care of their many "white man's" possessions, such as their automobile.

Christine proved to be a fine homemaker. She loved to cook. She practiced all the arts she had been taught in Albuquerque and Chilocco. She made sure her meals were nutritious according to the rules she had learned. She put up jams and jellies from elderberries, chokecherries, and prickly pears. Fresh vegetables, eggs, and fruits were purchased at the store or from vendors. Her kitchen was stocked with baked bread, pies, and cakes. Tom brought home fresh milk. In those days there were government boarding schools in Mescalero, and a herd of cattle was kept in order to supply milk to the schoolchildren and to hospital patients. If there were extra milk, it was available to Tom. Neither he nor Christine drank alcohol, so they saved much of their income. The house, always clean and neat, was truly a haven for the couple.

Children

For the first year, the gentle, soft-spoken Christine worked and kept house simultaneously. Then she quit her duties at the hospital. The couple's first child was born on October 18, 1924. They named their daughter Narcissus.

"She is my Na-shí," said Tom proudly.

In accordance with traditional Chiricahua ways, the new parents asked Dilth-cleyhen to make a cradle for the baby. All the rites appropriate to each stage of Narcissus's development were performed. The child gradually learned proper kin terms for immediate relatives, for Beshád-e, Dilth-cleyhen, and Lillian. The latter was to be called "Little Grandmother." Arnold Kinzhuma was "Old Man Arnold," a term which in Indian is not disrespectful, but instead is a translation of Apache *Hosteen* or Mister.

All the adults spoiled the baby, playing with her endlessly, gratifying her every whim. Lillian's daughter, Evelyn, so beloved of Christine, adored the child and spent many hours and days at the Duffy's, lugging the cradled infant about.

When Narcissus was some two-and-a-half years old, there was an addition to the family. The arrival of a baby is always exciting, but the events of July 3, 1927, were indeed dramatic for the Duffy household. For several days Tom and Christine had been setting up camp adjacent to the ceremonial grounds so that they could take active part in all the festivities associated with honoring the maidens who had reached puberty. Tom looked forward to his role as one of those who would sing and dance.

At their camping site he did all the heavy work, even those tasks that were usually done by women, for Christine was heavy with child. After the tent was set up Christine started checking to make sure they had brought everything they might need for a stay of a week or so. They had previously decided to throw a mattress on the ground for sleeping purposes. It was too much work and expense to get cots and separate mattresses. They owned a sufficient number of pots and pans, tin plates, and eating and stirring utensils if they needed them. Most of their food would be provided by the Feastgivers.

In her search, Christine discovered they had no adequate container for keeping water. Tom decided to drive to Alamogordo where there was greater choice in such items and where the price would be better than in Ruidoso and in reservation stores. He called Narcissus and invited Charlie Smith, a resident of White Tail, to go along for the ride.

All went well during the shopping excursion; they found just what they needed. They started back to Mescalero, Tom at the wheel. By this time, darkness had fallen.

It was a routine journey, with the adults visiting and sharing local gossip. Then, at Round Mountain, just outside the reservation, a car approached on the two-lane highway. Its lights were on high. Tom was blinded. His car went off the road. Tom tried desperately to right it, but it had a mind of its own, and over and over it rolled. Narcissus was thrown from the side window, landing on the earth nearby. Stunned, the adults remained within the vehicle until it finally shuddered still.

A bit later passersby began gathering at the site, to see if they could help. This was fortunate. Christine began to feel labor pains. Someone among the crowd took her into Mescalero and up to the hospital.

Back at the wreck there was great confusion. Tom looked around in bewilderment. Where was his daughter? He could not find her in the car! Charlie Smith called out, "She's all right. She's right here with me." He had located her a few feet back. Aside from a deep cut on the right side of her head, the child appeared in satisfactory condition. Charlie cleaned the wound as best he could and then made sure nothing was broken. Tom stared in dismay at the tangled mass of metal.

Then, as suddenly as the mishap had occurred and people had gathered, the bystanders simply disappeared. Tom, Narcissus, and Charlie found themselves alone. No one had offered to drive them the six or seven miles up the road to Mescalero. There was nothing to do but to walk. Charlie lifted Narcissus to his shoulders and carried her piggyback all the way.

Once inside the reservation, the bedraggled trio located the nearest house. By this time, their clothes were soaking wet. What had started as a sprinkle on their homeward trek was now a full-blown storm. Tom was exhausted and wanted only to get to bed. Someone loaned him a pickup. First he drove to the hospital to make sure his wife had arrived safely, and then he and Narcissus went on to the tent.

The storm was violent. There was lightning and thunder. Rain came down in sharp, cutting sheets. It was not long before there was a steady full stream of water running into the tent and under the mattress lying on the ground. In disgust and frustration, and despite his aching muscles, Tom arose, fighting back his feelings of shock and exhaustion. The situation was impossible. They must leave before both he and his daughter caught pneumonia.

"Get up, child. We can't stay here." He bundled Narcissus in a blanket and carried her to the pickup. He threw the soggy mattress in back, along with some of the clothing and food that would be damaged by the flood. He then drove home, and the two fell into their beds.

Narcissus slept late the next morning. She knew nothing until her father stood above her, shaking her, forcing her return from drowziness.

"You have a brother, Na-shí. He was born very early, before the sun came up. He was born on July 4 just to celebrate my birthday. Today is my birthday. Did you remember? Quite a present for me."

The Duffys named their son Wendell. He would be their last child, although they did not know this at the time.

Tom was proud of his family: his wife, his daughter, and now the new baby.

Concerns, Teachings, and Happy Times

Christine was a pretty woman. She was fastidious and well-groomed, continuing to dress and to wear her hair in a bun in the "Fort Sill style." Every day she brushed her long dark tresses. After her hair was soft and neat, without snarls, she removed each strand carefully from the brush. After collecting several lengths, she folded them together, back and forth, finally wrapping still another strand around the middle of the bundle. This tying held all the hairs fast. She saved all brushings until she had accumulated a ball some four inches wide. This she burned carefully, making sure no lengths remained. Then she stirred the ashes. There were some old Chiricahua customs Christine could not ignore despite her acculturated white ways. All her life her mother and grandmother had instilled in her a fear that she could not dispel. A single loose hair might make her ill or cause her death if a witch should find it and use it in evil ways. Thus, every strand of hair must be accounted for—never left in a casual manner.

Christine was concerned about the education of her daughter. She wanted Narcissus to know and have the best of white culture; at the same time she wanted her to be a proper Apache. The girl must know her genealogy. She must know the proper word to use for every relative; how each one was to be treated; how to show respect, what the obligations were. Christine preached daily to the little girl as soon as she felt that the child was old enough to understand.

Christine told Narcissus, "You must not eat anywhere but in your own home. You come home at noon and again at suppertime. If you are away playing, don't go into someone's house and eat. That is not right. You have a good home. You must come back to it. We have plenty of food for you, so don't eat somebody else's food. They might need it. If you stay for a meal, they will think we are not good providers," she said in Indian.

Later this advice backfired. One time when Narcissus was some five years old, she was playing near the house of a Fort Sill Chiricahua, a distant relative by the name of Clara Spitty, or Ga-lot-a. Narcissus had often visited the Spittys with her mother, grandmother, and great grandmother, so she felt quite comfortable going there on her own.

That day happened to be the birthday of Clara's husband Albert, and she had baked him a special cake to celebrate. Albert saw Narcissus and her playmates and invited them into the house to share his treat. The youngsters began to troop in, but Narcissus remembered her mother's words. "No," said the little girl. "We can't eat it. My mother told me not to accept anything from anybody. Some people like to feed you, and then they go around talking about it, just bragging about their own generosity."

Clara was furious. The well-meaning Narcissus had committed a serious Apache breach of etiquette. Her mother's rule did not apply in the case of relatives. One should never insult kin in this way under any circumstance.

Clara said nothing to Narcissus. That, too, would have been improper. She went directly to Christine. She told her of Narcissus's rudeness. Christine apologized profusely, and in turn spoke seriously to her daughter, again emphasizing obligation and polite behavior toward anyone in the family, no matter how distant the relationship. *Family* members were supposed to *share*, especially when it concerned food. For the next few weeks, Christine's daily lessons were even more stern than usual. She harped incessantly on the theme of kinship and reciprocity, proper kinship terminology, the correct manner of addressing any relative, especially anyone older.

An Apache mother is expected to teach her children through example and through talking to them, but not through physical discipline. Fathers should do likewise. No other individual, with the possible exception of mother's mother, or mother's sister, has the right even to scold. Always, one must discuss the matter with the parents of a rude or naughty child. The mother and the father are ultimately responsible.

Generosity was another theme that received attention, and Christine was herself a fine example of one who practiced what she preached. Much of her activity was devoted to helping others. Because she had access to a car, and most of her kin did not, she made sure no one needed transportation if she could provide it. She hauled them to the Feast Ground from White Tail.

With the help of George Martine and Old Man Arnold, the women pitched the tents and built their wickiups above the Duffy's house. Christine was always there to lend her hand. Sometimes there were three or four or more tents. In the wintertime, when it was cold and bitter, Beshád-e set up a special tent in which she did the cooking. In the summer, when it was hot, she built a long arbor, interlacing the leafy branches over a framework of sturdier limbs. All the women joined her there, preparing the food in the coolness of the shade. In this season the tents were for sleeping, resting, and sometimes visiting. Lillian and George and their small children had one tent. The older ones, such as Evelyn, stayed in another. Dilth-cleyhen had her own tent and wickiup; so did Susie and her youngsters when she occasionally visited. Beshád-e and Arnold needed still another one or two. It was a compatible group, with lots of visiting and laughter among them—and lots of sharing of burdensome tasks.

When Evelyn went to the Phoenix Indian School in Arizona, where she obtained her education, Christine made frequent trips to see her. "I don't want you getting homesick," she explained. When there was a vacation interval, such as at Christmas, Christine, with Narcissus and Wendell, drove west to pick up Evelyn and her luggage. She brought her to Mescalero, and then, when it was time for classes to resume, she took her back to the boarding house. Truly, they were more like sisters than cousins.

Christine enjoyed driving. She savored the countryside. But she was not one to tour aimlessly every day, uselessly consuming gas, as so many of the young Apache women do even yet.

An occasional picnic in the mountains, in order to avoid the continual dustiness of the Feast Ground and Agency area, provided a change of pace. If Evelyn were not away at school, she accompanied the family. Narcissus, Wendell, Evelyn, and Christine were a usual foursome. They sang as they rode along, their happiness apparent.

Sometimes the outings served useful as well as recreational ends. The small party gathered piñon nuts, mesquite beans, yucca, and prickly pear fruit, whatever was seasonal. In the springtime, sometimes Tom helped them in such practical pursuits, and they all picked cherries from the trees growing in front of the hospital. They gathered them in pails, took them home, and Christine made cherry pie.

Tom loved to hunt. From time to time he went turkey hunting with an eye specialist who worked for the Indian Service, a man named Smith. Narcissus wondered at her parents' friendship for the old man.

"Why do you like him?" she asked. "He's just a finicky old thing! And why does he always wear the same old gray suit?"

Dr. Smith came to the house very often. "Let's go get us a turkey, Tom," he would say. And they would set a date, and arrangements were made as to who would round up the horses.

When the appointed day arrived, Narcissus watched the preparations with interest. Her father and the Eye-Man dressed in identical garb. They wore knee-length trousers with a baggy section on the outer edge of the leg. Then they pulled on socks that reached to the hemline of the trousers. But it was the leggings that most intrigued the little girl. Both men held two rolls of cloth that looked like a bandage roll.

"What are you going to do with that?" she asked.

"Just watch," responded Tom, and he began to wrap his lower legs, over the socks, round and round and round, until the entire lengths of the rolls had been used. He had created leggings. Dr. Smith did the same. "Boy, they sure go to a lot of trouble dressing up like that just to go hunting, when all they need to do is just jump on a horse and take off!" But she kept such thoughts to herself, knowing her father would not appreciate them.

Both men always got at least one bird. There were many wild turkeys up near White Tail and out by Elk Silver. After one or two birds had been shot, the hunters cleaned and feathered them and rode home. Christine oven-cooked them. When the game was well done, and ready to eat, Old Doctor Smith always said, "Just give me a leg. That's plenty for me." He carved off a choice piece, and off he went to his own home.

Occasionally Dilth-cleyhen was camping nearby. After the men were through eating, she looked at the cooked fowl with some disdain. Gingerly, she took a bite, then set the piece of breast down.

"We never would have eaten such stuff in the old days. When we lived in Warm Springs, any bird that ate snakes was not fit for human consumption!"[33] With dignity she held her head high and sauntered off to her tent to partake of fry bread.

When Tom and Christine camped near Beshád-e, and that happened from time to time, Tom loved to see the fog roll in. "I'm going to find George Martine," he would say, and grabbing a couple of gunnysacks, off he would go. In a few hours the two returned, the sacks about half filled with quail. It took them a while to dress the tiny birds. By that time Lillian and her brood of children had usually arrived. Tom built a fire out in the yard and everyone salivated in anticipation, waiting for the wood to burn down. The birds were skewered on a stick, then roasted. Occasionally, a droplet of fat hissed as it hit the red-hot coals. Cooked out of doors and shared, the meat was delicious.

"Why don't we eat quail more often, Shi-ma?" Narcissus asked her mother. "Why must my father wait for fog?"

"It's easier to fool the birds when they can't see you clearly," was Christine's response, but Narcissus never truly understood. The quail were a special treat, but only when the Duffys camped at White Tail. Tom's visits there were short: he had to get back to the hospital, and Christine preferred being with him. There was a livelihood to make.

To bring in extra income, Christine sold various beaded articles of her own making. She needed buckskin to serve as a base for the design. Sometimes Tom hunted deer or antelope, and Beshád-e or Dilth-cleyhen did the tedious tanning. Christine purchased beads from one of the traders and set to work. She created the beautiful Indian motifs she had learned at school. Sometimes she improvised. Narcissus watched the growing work with fascination. She coaxed to be taught, and her mother obliged when she felt the child was old enough. She taught Narcissus first to string the beads, and then later, as her small fingers became more adept, to do some actual sewing.

With the exception of her contacts with Susie, Christine enjoyed being near the womenfolk comprising her extended family. She and Tom had only the rarest of differences, and when they argued at all, it was more a mild discussion than a quarrel.

Tom always avoided his mother-in-law out of respect for her. This form of politeness was extended to Lillian and Dilth-cleyhen. He was also polite, though on a somewhat different level, to Old Man Arnold. They never teased each other.

One day, however, there was some slight excitement over sheep. By this time, many of the Fort Sills owned not only cattle but sheep as well. They herded the sheep themselves, but the cattle were out on the range or at cow camps where cowboys looked after them. Christine and Tom kept their sheep with those of Beshád-e and Arnold up at White Tail. In order to designate the precise ownership of each animal, Arnold marked the Duffys' with a T for Tom; his and Beshád-e's were painted with an A.

One bright Saturday, just about time for the winter season, Tom had a holiday that freed him from hospital chores. The Duffy family drove to White Tail for a visit. As the adults talked, Narcissus and Wendell wandered to the sheep corral to see the livestock. The circular corral was made of pine trees placed close together. It was a high enclosure so as to discourage marauding coyotes, which were numerous in White Tail. The bleating sheep were jammed together, straining the corral fence nearly to the bursting point. Wendell was in the process of learning to count. One, two, three. . . . and on and on, A's. Then the T's. Behold, there were many more A's than T's. The children dashed to the house. Narcissus informed her father excitedly. The men got up quickly and went to investigate. They, too, counted the animals. Yes, indeed, Wendell and Narcissus were correct.

"How come you have more sheep than I do?" asked Tom. "We started out even." His voice had assumed a higher timber than usual. Old Man Arnold was nonplussed.

"They must have gotten out. It is so crowded in there. Some must have gotten out through a hole *under* the fence somewhere."

And so they had. The space was located and filled in promptly. There was no further rancor, no more raised voices.

The fall of 1930 was the first year of school for Narcissus. She attended the government boarding school in Mescalero along with all the other reservation children. Boys were in one dormitory, girls in another. It was a confusing time for the little girl. The Mescalero children still made fun of the speech of those whose parents had come from Fort Sill.

The children were expected to attend religious services. Narcissus attended the Dutch Reformed, the church of her parents. The children were lined up before entering, boys in one line, girls in another. During the meeting sometimes she sat with her mother, but Christine was going to the chapel less and less. All the men of the congregation sat on the right side of the chapel; the women sat on the left.

Christine did not look well. She was tired much of the time. Then, too, Dilth-cleyhen was no longer active, having reached some eighty-two years. Lillian, her daughter, cared for her, bringing her food, tending to her needs. When Christine felt well enough, she took over on Sunday afternoons.

Before the year was out, Dilth-cleyhen died.[34] The womenfolk keened. The men grieved more quietly. For many, many years the fine old woman's name was rarely, if ever, spoken aloud.

Illness

Christine's illness became ever more apparent. For some time she refused to see a doctor. When finally she did so, he insisted that she be isolated in one part of her home. It would be better, he had said, if she went somewhere else altogether, but Christine resisted stubbornly. She would not leave the house at the Feast Ground. Beshád-e took care of her.

When Narcissus was permitted to come home from the boarding school over the weekends, she could not understand what was happening.

"Shi-choo, my grandmother, why can't I hug my mother? Why must I talk to her from a distance?"

"She is sick," was the only response.

They placed everything Christine needed in the corner by her bed. They were instructed to destroy all the family's dishes. The doctor told Beshád-e to buy new plates, new tableware, everything.

Beshád-e took Narcissus to the trader's store to help choose the patterns. She purchased a special plate for her granddaughter. It was cut glass, light pink in color, with sharp scallops around its edge. The center had ridges which created three compartments to separate different kinds of food. To Narcissus it was a special heirloom, one to be treasured throughout her life.

Narcissus rarely had enthusiasm for play during the period her mother was so ill. During the Christmas holiday she sat in the house, as close to Christine as the doctor would permit. The two talked, mother to daughter.

Christine reiterated her former teachings. She talked of respect for relatives. She listed them one by one, explaining for a final time the exact relationship and what her daughter was expected to do and how kin could be expected to reciprocate. She told Narcissus that she must get a good education, and above all, that she should always be a good and honest girl. She talked of her own school days, the happy times she had had. She told of the Cherokee friend, Narcissus.

Christine had tuberculosis. She died during the night in February 1931. Narcissus was seven; Wendell three. Mourning was immediate.

Beshád-e was grief-stricken. She sat on the ground on a piece of folded canvas at the side of her tent. She wailed aloud. "Aye-yaaa" she cried. Then came the high-pitched, sad sound so characteristic of keening. "Aye" is pronounced like the English "eye," and means "you're hurting" or "when you're hurt." Beshád-e wept and wailed again, then dried her tears, trying to keep busy with her daily chores.

Other women in the camp keened, too. Late each evening, and again fairly early in the morning, the sad sounds rent the air. The wailing lasted for some fifteen or twenty minutes. Then there was silence.

Narcissus, lonely, not quite understanding, stood for a while up on the hill by the trees. She listened. Then, she hid herself in the outhouse where she gave in to convulsive crying.

Old Man Arnold and Beshád-e told Narcissus that her mother was truly gone. She must never again call to her, never say her name.

She was told, "You say 'My mother, she was,' if a referral to her is necessary." "If you say her actual name, you will get ghost sickness, or maybe you will die. That is what her ghost has the power to do to you if you call it."

Beshád-e cut Narcissus's short hair even shorter on the sides and trimmed the bangs. It was customary for a daughter, particularly the eldest, to have her hair cut in this way at the death of her mother, as an outward sign of mourning. Beshád-e's might also have been shorn, since that was a usual mode of communication for an adult woman losing a sister, son, or daughter, but in this case, her hair was so very long and thick that she wore it straight down her back, not confining it to a chignon as was her usual fashion. The cut ends of Narcissus's hair were tied in an old rag, then hung in a tree deep in the forest where no one would be apt to find them. It was an offering, an appeasement, to the ghost.

All Christine's belongings were burned or broken up or thrown away, except for those few items that would be buried with her. Old Man Arnold chopped up her phonograph and the recordings it played. The machine, an Edison Gramophone, had been a joy to the family. The "records"—actually cylinders which were inserted into the mechanism—were of Indian songs, including many rituals such as doll sickness, ghost-chasing ceremonies, and puberty rites of the maidens. All her clothing and bedding were destroyed with a single exception: the family saved her buckskin dress, the one she had worn when she had been White-Painted-Woman.

Christine was buried in the cemetery in Mescalero. The buckskin was laid over her body. As Tom wanted a headstone, he went some seventy-five miles away, to the mountains near Las Cruces, east and almost adjacent to the Organ Mountains. He found a rocky cliff where the stone is white. He dug out a chunk of rock and hauled it to the cemetery. Through time much of it has now crumbled, but for many years it was an impressive marker.

As Tom placed the headstone, all the old folks from Fort Sill attended, as did the immediate relatives. They brushed themselves down from head to toe with a short branch of sagebrush. From time to time one of them spat unobtrusively. This was meant to dispel any evil in the graveyard. Hopefully, the spitting and the sagebrush would be sufficient safeguard. Sage was a traditional defense against unknown dangers, particularly those associated with death. It guarded against being hit by lightning, as well. All the Fort Sills kept a couple of sticks of gray sagebrush hanging on the inside wall above the doors of their houses. Other sprigs were inside their cars, and still others nestled within the headpieces of the babies' cradleboards.

After the burial, Christine's ghost was chased from the Duffy home. It was feared that the deceased might return in spirit form and bother her loved ones, leading to dire circumstances. Her living kin took every precaution not to tempt her back to earth. They dared not display their grief too openly, or for too long a time, lest she should take pity and try to return to them, or worse, to lure them to *her* realm.

The ghost-chasing ceremony was led by Arnold Kinzhuma, who was versed in such things. The English translation of the Indian word for the ghost-chasing ritual is "darkness." They held the ceremony for four nights, each time starting at dusk and ending at midnight. Old Man Arnold said the special prayers and sang the appropriate songs most carefully.

Each night Christine's family arrived just at twilight. Everyone must be blessed. Old Man Arnold reached for a pack of cigarettes and began to smoke. Smoke is sacred. Each member of the family came to him in turn, standing before him. He placed his hands upon the head of each one, drew on the cigarette, then blew a puff of smoke first to the east, then to the south, west, and north. Then he took a pinch of cigarette ashes between his thumb and index finger and motioned toward the cardinal points. In ghost-chasing rites, ashes are substituted for the yellow tule pollen that is used in most Apache rituals. Then the old man marked the person before him with the ash, first on the top of the head, then on the middle of the chest, on both the shoulders and finally on the back.

Holding the person's head between his hands, he prayed again. He made the sound MMMmmmmmm. And then he sang. One of his songs pertained to dreaming, and the beginning of the refrain was thus:

> This dream you are dreaming.
> And dream, and dream, and dream. . . .

Songs of special meaning and beauty continued for hours. All members of the family took their turn standing before Arnold, seeking the protection of his power to communicate in all the proper ways with Yusen, with the Lord of All Men. Most of the ghost-chasing ritual consisted of his songs.

After the rite was completed, Tom Duffy insisted on paying Old Man Arnold, even though the latter was now a member of the family by marriage. Four presents were given to him: Bull Durham tobacco in a cloth bag, a pocket knife with a black handle (the color black was essential, though it could have been a paring or a butcher knife), a buckskin, and a black shawl with fringe. It was generous payment, but to Tom it was important. His wife's ghost was chased away with respect and dignity.

The house itself needed fumigation. Tom gathered greasewood. He burned the leafy parts. He might have used sage, or what the Apaches call "cedar," but whatever it was, its smoke must fill every nook and cranny of every room. When cedar was used, the very greenest branches were burned, so as to create the densest of smoke. While the burning was in progress, the lid of the firebox was removed from the wood and coal stove to permit the fumes to billow out.

One could not live in a house where any person had died. The restriction lasted at least a year. Even then, the dwelling had to have been properly fumigated or to have been purified by the blessings of the Ja-ja-deh, the Mountain Gods, who, wearing their towering crowns, danced around the home while singing their special ritual songs.

Tom deserted his former home at Feast Ground. Never again did he live in it.

He set up a tent about thirty or forty feet away from that of Beshád-e on the slope behind the fumigated house. All the doors to the tents that formed the family cluster faced toward the sacred East. This provided privacy to each unit. Tom kept his two children with him, but they were close to their grandmother who cared for them while her son-in-law was at work.

It was a time of great sadness, of emptiness and loss.

Narcissus could not bear the thought of going back to the dormitory. She was permitted to remain at home in the camp for the remainder of the school year.

In due time Tom Duffy sold his two-room house. More and more he left the care of Narcissus and Wendell to Beshád-e. For these youngsters, the modern ways of their mother was at an end.

Family portrait, Fort Sill, 1913. *Clockwise from upper left,* Lillian Mangas (Little Grandmother), Beshád-e (Grandmother), Christine Kozine, Evelyn Martine (Gaines), and Edward Martine. *(Courtesy of Narcissus Duffy Gayton)*

Above. Fort Sill portrait, 1910. *Clockwise from upper left,* Grace Sunday-man, Irene Guydelkon, Isabel Enjady, Lillian Mangas, Lucy Gonaltsie, Susie Aanitso. *(Courtesy of Narcissus Duffy Gayton)*
Right. Susie Aanitso, Fort Sill, 1912. *(Courtesy of Narcissus Duffy Gayton)*

Daytime scene of Crown Dancers (Mountain Gods) [and] Clown on Feast Ground, Mescalero Reservation. [Blea]chers in background are for spectators; stands behind [blea]chers sell refreshments. *(Courtesy of Barbara* [*Birk*]*hauser)*

[Abov]e Left. Casper Callis, Kent Kayitah, and Tom Duffy, [Fort] Sill. *(Courtesy of Narcissus Duffy Gayton)*

[Righ]t. Christine Kozine at the Fort Sill Mission School, [1]909. *(Courtesy of Narcissus Duffy Gayton)*

Christine Kozine as a schoolgirl, Albuquerque. *(Courtesy of Narcissus Duffy Gayton)*

Christine Kozine and Gwendolyn Mago boy in front of Jasper Kanseah's hous Mescalero. Christine is home from sc during vacation; Gwendolyn is the daug of Christine's half-sister, Susie Aanitso gooshboy. *(Courtesy of Narcissus Duffy Ga)*

Mescalero Apache baseball team, Cloudcroft, New Mexico. *First at left,* Edmond Simmons; *second from right,* Tom Duffy. Other figures are unidentified. *(Courtesy of Narcissus Duffy Gayton)*

Mescalero scenery: *Left,* White Tail. *Right,* lower Mescalero with yucca. *(Courtesy of L. Bryce Boyer)*

Dilth-cleyhen's house in White Tail. *(Courtesy of L. Bryce Boyer)*

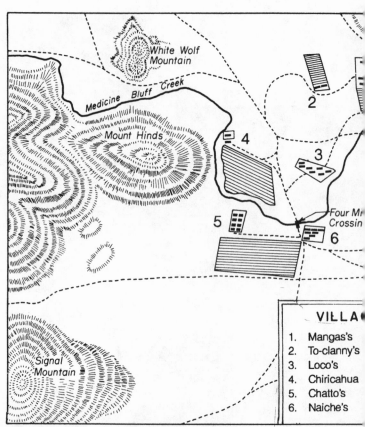

Apache villages and cultivated fields at Fort Sill.

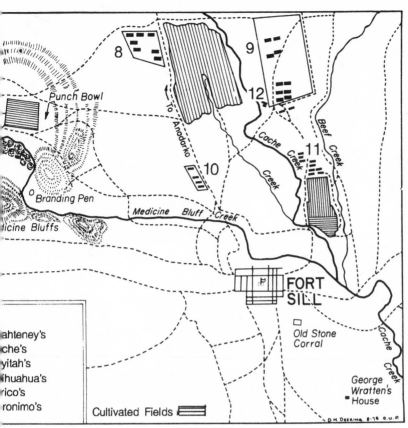

8

9

12

Punch Bowl

To Anadarko

10

Cache Creek

Creek

Beef Creek

11

Branding Pen

Medicine Bluff Creek

icine Bluffs

FORT
SILL

Old Stone
Corral

Cache Creek

ahteney's
che's
yitah's
huahua's
rico's
ronimo's

Cultivated Fields

George
Wratten's
House

D.H. DEERING 8-76 O.U.P.

from Geronimo, *by Angie Debo, copyright © 1976 by the University of Oklahoma Press)

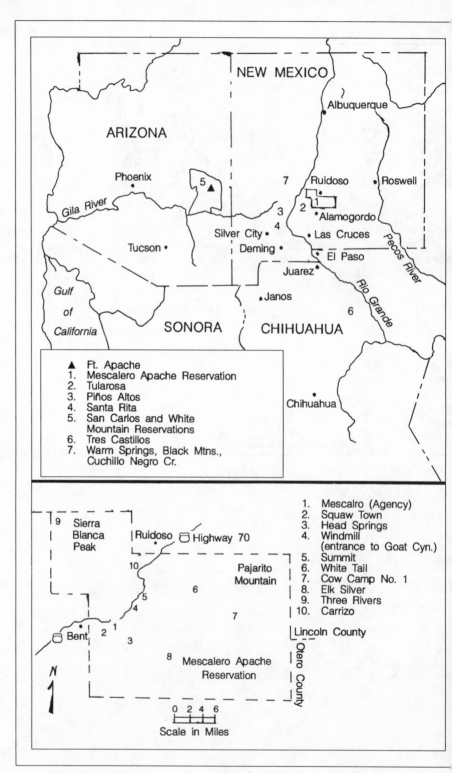

NEW MEXICO
ARIZONA
Albuquerque
Phoenix
Ruidoso
Roswell
Gila River
Alamogordo
Silver City
Las Cruces
Tucson
Deming
El Paso
Pecos River
Juarez
Rio Grande
Gulf of California
Janos
SONORA
CHIHUAHUA
Chihuahua
▲ Ft. Apache
1. Mescalero Apache Reservation
2. Tularosa
3. Piños Altos
4. Santa Rita
5. San Carlos and White Mountain Reservations
6. Tres Castillos
7. Warm Springs, Black Mtns., Cuchillo Negro Cr.
Sierra Blanca Peak
Ruidoso
Highway 70
Pajarito Mountain
Bent
Lincoln County
Otero County
Mescalero Apache Reservation
N
0 2 4 6
Scale in Miles
1. Mescalro (Agency)
2. Squaw Town
3. Head Springs
4. Windmill (entrance to Goat Cyn.)
5. Summit
6. White Tail
7. Cow Camp No. 1
8. Elk Silver
9. Three Rivers
10. Carrizo

Mescalero Apache Reservation and adjacent sites; bottom, Mescalero Apache Reservation, detail.

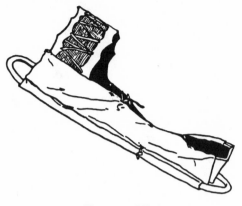

Part Four

Today's Apache Woman

Narcissus Duffy Gayton

A Time of Grief

Days merged without coherence for Narcissus. During the months following her mother's death she felt great loneliness. It mattered not that Beshád-e was near and cared so deeply. Even her father could not ease the memories that bombarded her continually. Everywhere Narcissus looked, she remembered events associated with her mother. Tears welled in her eyes and streamed down her cheeks no matter how hard she tried to stop them.

How she wished she had been a more obedient daughter. She would give anything now just to hear her mother preach. If I had been a better girl, would *Shi-ma* still be with me? Would she have gotten so sick? Such were her anguished thoughts.

There had been the time of the tattooing. Narcissus looked at her wrist. Such a miserable little mark it was now—that scrawny little N.

When Narcissus had been lured into creating it, the whole business had seemed so innocent. Yet the end result had caused great commotion. It all began when Susie's daughter Gwendolyn and Evelyn's sister Marilyn were playing on the mountainside just north of the Duffy's Feast Ground house.

That day Narcissus was at home, alone with her kittens, putting them in doll cradleboards, lacing them in just as she had seen her mother enclose Wendell. From time to time the mother cat sauntered by, rubbing her back against the child's knee. I wonder why the kittens are always *lots* of colors instead of plain black like their mother, mused Narcissus. The cats were a source of annoyance to Christine. Her daughter spent too much time with them, even getting up from the table at dinner time to pour them a saucer of milk. Nonetheless, the pets were tolerated.

After a time Narcissus became aware that the girls were calling her. She went to the door. Marilyn yelled down, coaxing her to join them up on the slope. "Come on with us," she said. "We want to tattoo your hands." It took little persuasion; her Aunt Susie sported markings on her arms and hands, designs beautiful in Narcissus's eyes. And the child had seen tattoos on many an older Apache: initials, hearts, or, more frequently, just a small circle or dot. The latter was located usually in the middle of the forehead between the eyebrows, or above the first joint of a finger. Oh, how grand to get a tattoo!

Narcissus ran up the hill. Gwendolyn took her by the hand and led her to a secluded spot where a fire was blazing. Black charcoal was heaped in the fire pit. Carefully Gwendolyn removed a large coal to let it cool. Then she crushed it to a fine powder. "This is just the way the old people used to do it. My mother told me," she said. She told Narcissus to sit down. The girls examined her left hand and after slight deliberation decided the best spot was at the juncture between index finger and thumb.

Then the procedure began. Marilyn held Narcissus' hand still, while Gwendolyn sprinkled the appropriate area of skin with the pulverized charcoal. All went smoothly until the tattoo artist picked up a long cactus thorn and began to make a series of deep pricks through the black dust. Beads of blood began to appear and Narcissus let out a yell of pain. Up she jumped! She tried running away, but Marilyn grabbed her other arm and held on with great determination. Struggling was of no avail. Narcissus decided to "tough it out" as a good Apache should. The small victim closed her eyes and clenched her teeth. Jab, jab, jab. Gwendolyn was taking forever. When it was finally over, Narcissus noted the original choice of locations had been abandoned. There was now an N of sorts on the inner side of her left arm just above the wrist. It hurt so badly. Narcissus had a vague feeling it wasn't quite as beautiful as she had anticipated. Nonetheless, she hurried home, hoping her mother had returned (as indeed she had) and expecting maternal sympathy and perhaps some relief from the pain.

"*Shi-ma*, look!" She held up her dirty wrist with its streaked and dried rivulets of deep red blood. Instead of the anticipated praise and comfort she had hoped for, her mother looked horrified. "What on earth have you done, Narcissus! Don't you know that no decent Christian person wears a tattoo! What a terrible thing you have done. Don't you have any sense at all!" Roughly she grabbed her daughter and started scrubbing on the N, trying desperately to make it disappear. Perhaps her immediate efforts had some effect: in adult life Narcissus's tattoo is faint and hard to decipher. All while Christine was trying to erase the marks, she kept on with her preaching. And when she had finished with Narcissus, she went straight to Susie, scolding her soundly for the actions of Gwendolyn. She had no jurisdiction over the discipline of the girls, but she seemed to enjoy reprimanding Susie. Christine spoke also to Evelyn, but with less vehemence.

Narcissus felt so ashamed. Why hadn't she asked her mother *first*! But *now*, with no mother at all, she even missed her scolding.

Christine's dislike of Susie had often bewildered Narcissus. There was always such tension when the two half-sisters had any kind of association. It didn't seem to matter to whom Susie was married or where she actually lived. For example, George Magooshboy had died, and Susie married Robert Decherle. They had a house in an isolated part of Elk Silver where they stayed most of the time. But Susie sometimes camped on the Feast Ground when she had business at Agency, and sometimes she stayed with Beshád-e in White Tail.

Occasionally Beshád-e, Dilth-cleyhen, Little Grandmother Lillian, Evelyn, Susie, and all the children would head for Mescalero and the Agency area in order to go to the trader's store for supplies, perhaps to see the doctor at the hospital, or just for the sake of the excursion. It was customary for them to camp alongside the Duffy house. This permitted lots of visiting with Christine and gave the group access to business offices and rarely seen friends. Then, as they were departing, early of a morning, it was not unusual for Beshád-e to invite Narcissus to accompany them back to White Tail. Oh, how the little girl loved to go. It was so nice up there under the pine trees, not hot and dusty like Mescalero. It was fun to ride in a wagon rather than an automobile, and she could play with her cousins, rather than just her brother.

Each time she was invited, Narcissus coaxed her mother, who always said no if Susie were among the group. The child wheedled and begged, tears in her eyes, until finally her mother relented. "Well, it's all right," she would say as she packed a bundle of clean clothing. As quickly as possible, before her mother could reverse the decision, Narcissus climbed into the back of the wagon, and off the group would go. All day they rode. It was not just a matter of half an hour or so as it was when they used the Duffy car or pickup. This was a *real* excursion! The kids jumped off and romped from time to time, playing tag or a kind of blind man's buff; and then, tiring, they clambered back on the bed of the wagon once again. When they were hungry, Beshád-e stopped, made coffee, and handed out biscuits and sometimes meat. Oh, how good it tasted! Finally they reached the turnoff from the main road to Ruidoso, and they bumped along until they finally came to the house. The adults unloaded the supplies, and the children played to their hearts' content, usually until it was about time to go to bed.

Then, inevitably, Narcissus could hear an automobile chugging along the road, nearing Beshád-e's property. It stopped. Sure enough, Christine and Wendell came up to the house. Narcissus had known it was too good to last! Christine talked briefly to Beshád-e, then went to the bedroom and told Narcissus to get up. She took her by the hand and led her to the car, and the trio drove back to the Feast Ground. This was always the sequence of events. Never once was the small girl permitted to stay in White Tail without her mother. Narcissus simply could not understand.

It was not until her mother's fatal illness that the child had enough courage to question her. "*Shi-ma*, why did you always come for me when we went out to White Tail? Why did you always bring me back home?"

"Well, Susie doesn't like me, and I am always afraid that she might take that dislike out on you. She might be mean to you and make you feel bad. I don't want that ever to happen. That's the reason why."

Narcissus had accepted her mother's logic then. And now, in her grief, she was sorry she had ever doubted *anything* her mother did. She concluded that the tattooing had been a matter of her own misjudgment. She had considered tattoos beautiful; she expected her mother to feel the same way. After all, Christine loved pretty things. She loved jewelry, especially earrings, and she owned several pairs. Whenever Pueblo Indian and Navajo craftsmen came to feasts and sold their silver work, Christine examined every piece, and if she liked something, and she could afford it, she made a purchase. Further, there was an Apache woman in Mescalero who was married to a Navaho by the name of Lee Antonio. He was a very fine silversmith, and many of Christine's earrings had been crafted by him. On one visit to his home Christine had taken Narcissus with her. She told her daughter it was time to have her ears pierced, and that she was going to order some earrings for her from Lee.

"Apaches have always worn earrings," she said to Narcissus. "You have seen Beshád-e's, and you know Old Man Arnold has pierced ears—just like your father." Indeed, Tom Duffy had a damaged ear. There was a deep, ugly tear in it just where one of the holes for an earring should have been.

Christine and Lee had talked for a long time about what kind of ring should be made for Narcissus. The girl did not need the dangly kind that her mother preferred, but she should wear something in plain silver. A triangular shape would be best, perhaps with small pieces of silver loosely suspended from the bottom edge. Narcissus was delighted. She remembered now how she had anticipated the way the jewelry would swing when she turned her head. She could barely wait to get them. But that day was not to come. It was just about then that her mother got sick, oh, so sick, and all her father and her grandmother would tell her was, "She is sick. You must stay away."

Mother and daughter had been so devoted, sharing all the simple joys and jokes that occur in everyday life. How they had laughed when Wendell did "dumb" things. Narcissus recalled the time that he and his best friend—his cousin Ivans Martine, Little Grandmother Lillian's son—had been playing together. They were too young to play softball with the other boys, and so they found their own diversions. Ivans was about one year older than Wendell.

It was one day in February or March. Narcissus would never forget it. The wind was terrible. Everything was dry and dusty; she had had nothing to do. No one her age was near. It was so cold up on the Feast Ground, even colder than if it had been snowing. Little Grandmother had come to Agency with Ivans. Narcissus knew the boys were together, and she set out to find them. She looked around, but they were nowhere. She shrugged. Well, she bet she knew where they were. They would be out by that big, old cedar tree. They went there often. It was away from the camping area and gave them lots of privacy. In fact, it seemed to be their favorite hideaway.

Narcissus ran up the slope, and as she neared the old cedar, she could hear the murmur of the boys' voices. She hid so that she could watch. Ivans and Wendell were sitting on one of the low branches that spread parallel to the ground. The limb was bare. Many days of children's playing had worn away its foliage. So there the two boys sat, holding an old gunnysack. They were covered with the dust which swirled around them.

Their hair was a mass of tangles. Narcissus listened, sneaky-like.

Why, those crazy boys were pretending they were an old married couple!

"My wife," Wendell said to Ivans.

"What?" Ivans asked in Indian.

"You be my wife, and I'll be your husband," Wendell continued. The two wriggled around on the branch, and then continued conversing. Narcissus held her hand over her mouth to suppress her giggles.

Soon Ivans said, "Let's get off and go down the road and smoke a cigarette." Down they scrambled and strode off in search of some proper tree bark. Then who knows what they might do! Narcissus could barely wait to get home. Her insides hurt with her silent laughter. Her mother, busy at the kitchen stove, took time to listen to her daughter. The sharing of secrets, the funny things that made life such fun, these things were so precious in the closely bound relationship of Narcissus and Christine.

Later in the day Christine had told Evelyn about these antics of the latter's younger brother, and oh, how they had teased both boys. Even in adulthood Ivans and Wendell could not overcome the embarrassment of playing at being married. Apache boys just don't do that! Their pretend game had been spoken entirely in Indian, which had made the conversations especially humorous.

"Oh, Shi-ma, I wish we could laugh about it now. Such simple things gave us pleasure. Just riding around in the car together—how I miss it!"

Very often the family had driven into the countryside to have picnics. Sometimes Narcissus's father went along, but more frequently the group consisted of Christine, Narcissus, Wendell, and Evelyn, if she were on vacation from school.

One memorable day the latter four drove toward Capitan. There were always lots of animals to be seen: quail, turkey, deer, wild horses sometimes, and even more rarely, a mountain lion or bear. If they drove to the flatlands, an occasional antelope stared back before bounding away. Narcissus watched especially for the tiny cottontails that dashed in and out of the bushes alongside the road. That day there were many of the little creatures. Narcissus was so delighted that she began to sing in Indian:

> Little rabbits, little rabbits,
> Come out! I want to look at you.
> Because you are a little rabbit.

Over and over she sang. Again, this seemingly insignificant verse has persisted as part of the family's tradition. When Evelyn and Narcissus are together, sometimes Evelyn teases her niece by singing the words, and then they laugh, sharing memories of rides and little rabbits. Many Chiricahua songs probably had their origins in this kind of spontaneity, in bursts of joyous inspiration.

But now Narcissus felt little like singing. She really had no interest in anything.

From time to time she continued to go to the outhouse where she could be alone and cry. When she was by herself, she could hear her mother calling to her. At night, lying in the darkness of the tent, the voice sounded stronger yet. The rain came down incessantly. It was dark and gloomy. Everyone went to bed early to avoid the muck and mud of the Feast Ground.

It took hours before Narcissus could fall asleep. She lay restlessly, thinking about her loss, and when slumber finally came, there were nightmares. Her grandmother heard her talking in her sleep, tossing. Sometimes the child's arms or legs jerked uncontrollably.

Beshád-e became concerned. These were obvious signs of ghost sickness. She questioned her granddaughter. "Have you said that lady's name? Maybe she thinks you are calling her." Beshád-e reviewed in her mind the ceremonies and fumigation. Had they left out anything? She was sure they had not. When Narcissus became too disturbed, her grandmother arose, took ashes from the cooking pit, and came to the little girl. She marked a gray cross on the girl's forehead; she sprinkled more ashes around the child's bed. Sometimes she tucked a black-handled knife under her pillow. That seemed to help. It kept the ghost from bothering her sleep, but it was only a temporary measure.

Even after several months Narcissus could not eat. She walked about as though in a daze. Beshád-e turned to Arnold Kinzhuma, the widower, the man whom she would wed in just a few months. "Arnold," Beshád-e said, "You must perform the ghost-chasing ceremony for Narcissus yet another time. She looks too sick. She is getting too thin." And so, once again, Narcissus was blessed.

She stood before Arnold. He sang and drove away the darkness with his his prayers and his sacred smoke. He touched her head, chest, shoulders, and back with ashes. Beshád-e was sure this time it would be effective.

But it was not.

In another few weeks Arnold and Beshád-e took Narcissus to a renowned medicine man who lived on the San Carlos Reservation in Arizona. He, too, chased Christine's ghost. He followed exactly the same procedure. But for some reason, perhaps his powers were stronger than Arnold's, Narcissus recovered. The ghost left.

The Routine of Life

As the days and weeks and months dragged on, Narcissus's life became more tolerable. Everyone settled into routine tasks and behaviors.

Even though the rains continued, there was compensation. Going to bed when it was still dusk could be pleasant, especially when she and Wendell slept in Beshád-e's rather than Tom's tent. Their grandmother entertained them by telling about the days when she was a girl, when the Tchi-héné were fleeing from soldiers. Sometimes it was necessary for The People to cross the Rio Grande in order to reach the homeland of those Mescaleros who were the friends of Victorio. But even when the enemy was very close, the river gave the Indians pause.

"All water is sacred, my grandchildren, but especially that water which is like a great divide. One must pray to it before entering its depths." Beshád-e paused. "That river used to get real high when the rain came down, when it just kept pouring, like it is doing right now. Then the river's flow was swift and dangerous." After a moment Beshád-e continued, "Even if you come to just a small stream and are going to wash in it, you must speak prayerfully to the water. You must not just dip your hand in it and dash the cold water on your face carelessly. You must be respectful. You must walk slowly to the stream. You scoop up a handful of the water and splash it on your face *four* times, and then, with your head down, you must pray. All the water in the old Chiricahua territory is sacred to us. We had our beginnings, our origin, near the water, near that lake. One day I'll take you there so that you can see it for yourselves."

Thus Narcissus began to learn much more than her mother had told her about the old ways. She absorbed the lore almost unconsciously She learned those aspects of life that were most important to her grandmother's and even her great grandmother's generations. Sometimes she heard frightening accounts of battles, raids, and atrocities. Proof of the veracity of the tales was there for her to see. When Beshád-e washed Old Man Arnold's hair in yucca root suds, she one time called the children's attention to the bullet scars he bore from shooting encounters in the days of the warpath. This sobered the wide-eyed youngster. But not all her tales were so grim.

"In those days when we were on the warpath, way down south, I think it was in Mexico or someplace very close to the border, there was a special retreat we went to when the soldiers and General Crook got too close. It was a place high among the jagged peaks. The lookouts could hide behind the rocks. They warned us in plenty of time if our pursuers kept coming. Those white people didn't like to go there. It was too hard on their horses and mules and especially their boots. It was hard on us, too, but Apaches are used to hardship. We were well trained for it. We could get into those precipitous and wild mountains, and nobody could find us—except maybe an Apache tracker. It was really rugged.

"Well, one time we had to go down there. It was getting dark when we reached the retreat, and so we bedded down in exhaustion. When morning came, all was peaceful. One old man began looking around. I guess he hadn't been in that particular place before. When I got up and started to fix the coffee, I could see him. He was standing near the edge of a cliff, looking down, down, down at the pointed crags, surveying all the steep ridges and canyons below as they stretched out into the far distance. He stood there for a long time, just looking. Finally he put his hands on his hips. He turned to the women around the fire.

"'Whoever made this here land must not have had any common sense!' He went back to the edge, staring at the forbidding rocks. 'This land is really bad,' he went on. 'It's inconvenient! What can anyone do with it? The Man who made this canyon must not have had any sense at all. He just didn't have *any* sense to have made this kind of land.'" Beshád-e chuckled as she told the story, and the children giggled. "The one without sense was that old man. Not the Creator. Not Yusen. But that foolish old man was upset, upset over a single canyon—a canyon that was a protection for us. Everybody in that camp laughed behind their hands."

"I wish I'd lived in those days," muttered Wendell to his sister just before both fell asleep. "I'd have been trained like a warrior. I'd have had a special man's language that you couldn't understand."

Mornings always came early. Beshád-e was up long before the children awakened. She started the coffee after building her cooking fire. Then she came to the sleeping tent and told Narcissus to get up. "Take this coffee to your father," she instructed. Respect prevented Beshád-e from taking the cup to Tom, her son-in-law. Always there must be a go-between.

With early morning coffee the day began.

Sometimes Narcissus and Wendell ate with their father—leftovers, usually fry bread or biscuits; sometimes Tom ate in the cooking arbor, but if he did so, Beshád-e had to step inside her tent and close the flaps. After Tom had gone off to work, she came out to eat her meal.

Narcissus felt the whole procedure was just a big nuisance. All she did was take food or messages from one person to another. She would tell her grandmother what her father said, but she had to discuss him using the third person. "*He* said for you to do this," or "*He* wants to know about this or that," Beshád-e would say, "Ask *him* if he wants to do this or that." There was so much message-relaying that there was scarcely any time for play.

Many times it was necessary for the family, including Beshád-e, to go to Alamogordo or Tularosa for supplies or special foods or whatever was deemed best if purchased off the reservation. This took preparation. Beshád-e and Tom must not see each other despite their riding in the same car at the same time.

First, a bedspread was fastened, by means of safety pins, to the ceiling of the car. This made the back seat into a private compartment. Beshád-e was installed therein. Tom walked over, keeping eyes riveted on the front part of the car. He climbed into the driver's seat, the youngsters piled in, and off they drove to their destination.

When they arrived in town, Tom got out and quickly walked away. Narcissus and Wendell reported to Beshád-e the moment that he was out of sight, so that she could open the car door and do her various errands. Tom gave his mother-in-law plenty of time to leave. He then returned and stood by the car while she shopped. When it came time for her to return, his children ran to the car to tell him, and once again, he did his disappearing act, thus giving Beshád-e the privacy she required to reestablish her composure in the back seat. This accomplished, with everyone installed, Tom drove back to Mescalero. Respect had been maintained.

Beshád-e preached about respect so frequently that her interdictions seemed incessant to her grandchildren. Narcissus must respect Wendell; in turn, he must respect her—for they were sister and brother. She must not sit on his bed; she must not touch his belongings; and again, vice versa. Although Apaches love to tease, these two must be circumspect in this regard. Formality and restraint were also expected between father-in-law and daughter-in-law and between brothers-in-law. Sisters-in-law had greater choice in their interactions and might speak directly and openly one to another. The grandchildren shrugged. Most of these things did not pertain to them. After all, thought Wendell, I'm never going to marry anybody! I won't have any in-laws to bother about!

The day came when Narcissus and Wendell moved into Beshád-e's tent permanently, although they still were with their father (when he was around) in the early evenings. More and more he was finding diversions or necessary errands away from camp.

Beshád-e gave the children tasks to do. She acted as if she were their mother. She began to discipline them like a mother. There was always wood to haul in and water to fetch. "I need some kindling,"

"Get me a bucket of water," or "Bring me that bag of potatoes." She always wanted something.

Food was simple. One main dish sufficed for a meal, and it consisted of staples such as potatoes, onions, beans, and rice—rice with canned milk and sugar. If there were meat, it was usually dried—deer or antelope if Arnold had been hunting, or beef. Whichever was used, it was fried, and a gravy was made from the droppings. The beef ordinarily came from the family's herd but the killing required special permission from tribal officials. It was not a matter of arbitrary choice. Fresh beef turned an ordinary meal into a special occasion. Old Man Arnold rigged up a grill from bailing wire and placed it over the fire pit under Beshád-e's cooking arbor. After preparing the coals, his wife then roasted a big slab until it tested well done. Then she cut it into strips about three or four inches long and about one inch wide. Theses were further sliced, not quite through, into bite-sized chunks, and doled out to the entire group who then ate finger-style. Oh, it was good.

The main dish was accompanied by coffee. Even the children drank coffee with sugar. Usually this was taken with canned milk diluted, half and half, with water. The youngsters also liked Apache Indian tea made from the coneflower, or milk supplied by Tom from excess at the hospital. Occasionally Beshád-e fried bread as well, and even more rarely, she baked at the fire pit. For this, she mixed a dough and rolled it into pieces the size and shape of dumplings. She placed these close to the coals, testing them from time to time with a table knife to see if they were cooked. When fully dry, they were eaten plain or, once in a while, with jam. Beshád-e told the children, "This is the way we used to make bread, before the white man taught us to use stoves."

Though very good, the food was less nutritious and varied than it had been when Christine was alive. Narcissus was delighted, therefore, when the weather grew mild, permitting the Mexican food vendors to come periodically to the Feast Ground. The sounds of creaking wheels as they drove in, and then the voices announcing the day's delicacies, filled the child with anticipation. She ran from her grandmother's arbor to see what they might be selling. Different men came on different days.

In later years Narcissus remembered one salesman who came in a black buggy drawn by a single horse. He carried a very thin whip. In order to make the horse climb the steep dirt trail to the camping site, the Mexican had to whip the tired beast over and over, simultaneously yelling, "Chili for sale! Peaches for sale!"

That fresh green chili was indeed wonderful. Later in the year would come corn on the cob and all kinds of fruit, such as apricots, apples, cantaloupes, and watermelons. Whenever it was available, Beshád-e bought the chili, and she got the corn when it was summer-ripe. She ground the kernels on a metate and mixed them with the green peppers, portioning the final concoction to fill three or four corn husks. These were folded, thus forming a container which was tied at the top and then dropped into boiling water. When Beshád-e scooped them from the spot, they resembled a meatless tamale. All the family ate with gusto.

Occasions of special food treats were memorable.

So were the special stories told by Beshád-e to her restless grandchildren during the long winter evenings before they fell asleep. They were not only about the warpath days, but some were concerned with that rascal, that trickster, Coyote, whose name in Apache is M'baye.[1] Night must fall before these tales can be related; if one talks of Coyote's antics in the daylight hours, misfortune is bound to result.

"Shi-choo, my grandmother, tell us the one about the Mexican that had all those sheep," Wendell begged. And so Beshád-e began.

"Well, it seems that Coyote was visiting with a Mexican man." Beshád-e used the Indian word for Mexican, which translates as "an ugly white man," thus reflecting the many years of conflict between the natives of the two countries.

"Those two talked for a while, just visiting.

"Well, finally the Mexican had to go to town to buy himself some groceries. And he had lots of sheep. He kept looking around, as though he had lost something. He needed someone to care for those animals while he was gone. "What am I going to do about my sheep?" he said. At first Coyote pretended that he was concerned, too. Finally he volunteered to act as sheepherder. He smiled, 'Don't worry. I'll look after your sheep for you. You just go ahead to town. I'll take care of all the livestock. I'll be the sheepherder while you are gone.'

"So the Mexican packed a sack with the things he would need for his trip. Coyote was smug and kept watching him. He was just waiting. The Mexican got on his horse, and before long he had disappeared around the bend. Quick as a wink, Coyote sprang into action. He dashed out where the herd was and herded the sheep up into the canyon. There, one by one, he killed the animals. Then he prepared a feast for himself. He ate and ate and ate. He ate every one of the sheep, leaving only their tails. He piled the tails in a heap beside him.

Then he looked around, looking for water and a muddy spot. Ah, there was just the place. A great big muddy area. He put all the tails in a basket and carried them to the mire. Carefully he stuck each one upright in the mud, just about a foot or so apart. Then he went back, to the Mexican's house. He sat outside, basking in the warmth of the summer sun.

"After a while, the Mexican came back. He looked about him and couldn't see a single animal—not even a lamb!

"'Where are my sheep?' His voice was all excited. Coyote pretended to be crestfallen. Sadly he replied, 'Well, I decided to take the sheep up in that canyon behind the house so they could get some water to drink and more food to eat, but there was a great big muddy area up there, and when those sheep came to it, they started walking over it—but what do you know! They began to sink. Each one in turn came along, and each one just sank farther and farther into the mud. All of them did that, just sinking down, and I couldn't stop them. They sank down until all that could be seen of them was their tails.'

"The Mexican was horrified. He could not believe his ears. Surely this was a dream. All his beautiful sheep! 'Coyote, you just take me up there. I have to see for myself,' he said.

"So Coyote and the Mexican went up the canyon. There were the tails, all right, just sticking out of the mud. '*Madre de dios*,' the Mexican cried. He dashed to the mud and began to pull out the sheep tails, one by one, tossing them aside, moaning with each throw. When he had finished, he turned around angrily, brandishing the last tail like a club. 'You good-for-nothing! You bandit! You thief!' He was going to beat that Coyote-Less-Than-Good-Sheepherder.

"But the Mexican was waving to the empty skies. Coyote had long since disappeared."[2]

Narcissus and Wendell laughed with delight. They had heard the tale so many times. "That will teach that old Mexican that M-baye is not a shepherd," observed Wendell. "You sure can't trust him," added his sister.

The next stormy night the request was for a story about the Rabbits and Coyote.

"Well," started Beshád-e, "those Rabbits were playing on a little prairie. Coyote was loping along a nearby trail. He saw them out of the corner of his eye. They seemed to be playing some kind of game. Coyote trotted over, sitting in the shade of a mesquite bush. He watched them. So that's what they were doing—juggling! Those Rabbits were juggling walnuts. Some of the Rabbits were real good.

Their jugglery became fancier and fancier. They threw the walnuts high in the air and then caught and threw them high again. Coyote watched for a long time, moving slightly as the shade from the mesquite changed position. Finally, he could restrain himself no longer. He walked over and asked if he could play, too. The Rabbits hesitated, then looked him over and finally said yes. So he began to throw up a few walnuts.

"After a while, Coyote started to get hungry. He eyed the jugglers. Most of them looked nice and round and juicy. Soon one or two Rabbits noticed the new gleam in Coyote's stare. They warned their mates. Finally a few of them went behind some big rocks, being careful that Coyote did not notice their absence. The Rabbits began to make bowel movements. The pellets are round, dark little things. When they had enough of them, the Rabbits substituted the black pellets for the walnuts. Then they came from behind the rocks and once again began to juggle, around and around and around. But this time it was not walnuts.

"Before long Coyote noticed that they were using something different from what he was juggling, and he asked them what it was that they were now tossing into the air.

"'We're juggling our eyeballs,' the Rabbits said. 'Can't you see? We just throw up our own eyeballs.'

"Coyote stared at them in amazement.

"Their own eyeballs! 'How remarkable,' he murmured. 'How can those little Rabbits see if they are tossing their eyeballs around?' He watched some more.

"'Well, if you can do it, so can I!' he told them finally.

"So Coyote pulled out his own eyeballs. He tossed one up, then the other, and started juggling with them.

"The minute he did so, the Rabbits saw their chance. Off they ran, each one dashing down his own rabbit hole while a blind Coyote threw his eyes toward the sky."[3]

One night Beshád-e told her grandchildren that Coyote was really scared of Hell—maybe he knew where he was going. And he was always curious, as they knew, and just suspicious of everyone. "For example, there was that time he met the Stinkbug." Beshád-e called Stinkbug Goot-lijeh-n-cheh. And so another bedtime story began.

"Well, you know how 'foxy' and competitive that old M-baye is. That old Coyote was always curious, but sometimes he was suspicious, too.

"This one day he was just walking along, walking along a path on a mountainside. He was walking very slowly. His head was down.

His hands were in his pockets. He looked at the ground as he went along, noting all the bugs and the ants that he passed.

"Soon he met Stinkbug. Now Stinkbug always had *his* head looking down at the ground. Coyote stopped. 'What's that bug up to,' he was thinking. 'He's probably up to no good. I will find out.'

"'What are you doing?' he asked. 'How come you always bend down real low? Every time you meet somebody, your head just goes down, and your tail goes up.'

"Stinkbug looked up at him. He was all ready to emit his peculiar perfume. Then finally he said. 'I *want* to lean way down. I want to keep my ear to the ground because I want to know what all the people who are buried under the ground are saying. All those people, they are just talking down there.'

"'What?' asked Coyote. 'What do you mean? Who is talking down there?'

"Stinkbug looked superior and wise. 'Well, all those people in *Hell* are visiting with each other. And I want to know what they are talking about.'

"'In *Hell*!' The fur around Coyote's neck stood up. His knees began to tremble. As soon as he could get his wits about him, he took off—running as fast as he could down the trail. He wanted nothing to do with Hell.

"Stinkbug chuckled. He continued to creep along as he had before, all the while keeping his head down as though he were listening."

After the story, Beshád-e told the children to close their eyes. Finally, they fell asleep, thinking about old Stinkbug, old Goot-lijeh-n-cheh.

Boarding School in Mescalero

It must have been May or June. Narcissus's strength and appetite had returned and she had fewer bad dreams. Tom and Beshád-e decided she was well enough to return to school. For the past two or three months following her mother's illness and death, the girl had been too overwrought to concentrate on anything. Her ghost sickness had been recognized and treated. Now, once again, it was time for education.

But where should she go? The question was urgent. Tom and Beshád-e argued, considered, and argued again.

One day Narcissus entered her grandmother's tent after playing with neighboring children. She asked Beshád-e what was wrong.

"Oh, that man just makes me angry. He wants to send you and Wendell to a Presbyterian boarding school. We are not Presbyterians! Even little Wendell he wants to send, and that boy is just too young to be away from home. And that school is way off in Tucson, Arizona." The words poured in rapid succession from Beshád-e's lips, and her stance was tense. As she listened, Narcissus's face registered equal dismay.

Beshád-e continued, "It's just wrong! I don't know what that man is thinking about! You children are *both* too young to be so far away from anybody that cares about you. You can't take care of yourselves yet. You need to be close by, where I can look after you and where you can see all your folks." She began to stir the fire, but went on, "That man must be up to something. He just acts like he wants to get rid of you!"

Just how Tom and Beshád-e came to terms is not remembered, nor is the name of the go-between in this delicate matter. Nonetheless, a settlement was reached. Wendell would remain with his grandmother; Narcissus would continue her lessons at the Mescalero Agency Boarding School.

Once again the little girl wore the school uniform. It consisted of a relatively plain dress made from heavy blue-and-white-striped denim. It hung straight from the shoulders, was short sleeved, and had a small tie at the neckline. Black cotton stockings and black shoes completed the ensemble. A red sweater was supplied for chilly days.

Narcissus still wore her hair very short. She looked at the long hair of some of the other girls and wished hers would grow faster. A few had very long hair, which the matron braided. "How I wish my hair were like hers," Narcissus thought as she watched one child's shiny tresses being brushed and plaited. Then the end was pulled up and secured with a taffeta ribbon. It looked so stylish.

Narcissus lived in the girls' dormitory, adjacent to that for the boys. The sexes were strictly segregated. In class the boys sat on one side, the girls on the other, just as they did when they were ushered into meetings at the Dutch Reformed Church on Sundays. Here again, men sat on the right side, women on the left.

Whenever the government agencies managed the way things were done, procedures resulted in a kind of military style. Thus, life often resembled that experienced when the Chiricahua were prisoners of war at Fort Sill. For example, if there were a program in the school auditorium, the children were told to line up, boys and girls in separate queues. Younger students stood in front, older ones in back. When the matron gave the signal, the pupils marched in. At mealtime, it was the same. There was a lineup, and when the matron rang the bell, everyone walked into the dining room.

Food was served family-style. Big bowls and platters heaped with food were in the center of the tables. So were pitchers of milk. The children ate from government-issue flatware, tin plates, and cups with handles. They were given a clean bowl when dessert arrived. As soon as they had completed their meal, the youngsters could leave the room and were free, at least for a time, to indulge in their own activities.

Except for the actual classroom hours, there was much undirected time. But Apaches have always been ingenious, and the children found special pastimes. A favorite escapade was stealing food.

There was a cellar behind the dining room. It was cool inside and was used to store apples, carrots, potatoes, and turnips, and other foods that were purchased in quantity. Whenever the school cooks needed a particular fruit or vegetable, a man was sent to the cellar to get it. Sometimes his arms were so full when he went back to the kitchen that he neglected to close the cellar door behind him. All the children kept careful watch. The moment he entered the kitchen, a designated thief ran into the cellar, grabbing carrots or whatever else was most handy. In a moment or two the man appeared once again, but he saw no children for they were by then in hiding. At the next kitchen delivery, out came another stealthy student. This time a different item was grabbed, perhaps some apples. Each and every child had to take a turn at filching.

Narcissus once grabbed some round white-and-purple things. "What are these?" she asked her conspirators. "How do I know?" "How do we eat them?" Thereupon a brave soul bit into one, finding it was quite edible, almost like an apple. "It's pretty good," was the consensus. From then on, turnips were considered one of the better prizes.

Whenever children were ill, or when vaccinations or immunizations were in order, the students were taken immediately to the hospital. There was no nurse at the boarding school. Even those who were underweight and needed cod liver oil were taken to the hospital for their dosages. Narcissus was among them. In the middle of the morning they were bundled up and escorted to the hospital hall, where they stood in line waiting their turn to see the nurse. She gave each one a tablespoon of cod liver oil and an orange. It was customary for the students to take the oil in their mouths but not to swallow it. Instead, as soon as they reached the outside door, they spat it out and then ate the orange.

Soon after Narcissus started back to school, she was taken for her vaccination against smallpox. Her arm became swollen and hurt. It was just a day or two prior to a visit from Beshád-e. When she asked how her granddaughter was getting along, Narcissus commented that her arm was bad. "Let me see it," directed her grandmother. The child pulled off her sweater sleeve to display the redness. "What have you got! Why, you have a skin disease! They've given you impetigo! What is the matter with this place!" Beshád-e had never seen a vaccination before. It took Narcissus some time before she could calm her grandmother by informing her that *all* students had to be protected; that this was good, not bad, and it was not impetigo. Beshád-e remained unconvinced. "This school is doing something wrong if they give you *sores* on your arm!"

The reservation physician gave each child a complete physical examination at the beginning of the school year. Narcissus had missed hers for one or another reason, and the nurse rescheduled it. The school transported her to the hospital. When the doctor listened to her chest, he looked worried. "Narcissus, you are not gaining enough weight. Are you eating well?" "Yes," she replied. He was not satisfied. "I think you should be hospitalized for a time for more observation," he finally decided.

Throughout grammar school Narcissus came to expect a week or two at either the hospital or an infirmary at the beginning of the semester. Each time that her turn came for a doctor's appointment, the physician feared she had tuberculosis. The suspicions were never confirmed, but the problem continued to be worrisome for all of her days.

Narcissus dreaded going to the hospital. Her grandmother's horror of its association with the dead and dying had penetrated her consciousness. For such a small girl, the place was stark, lonely. Furthermore, strange things occurred there. For example, many of the schoolchildren had trachoma that first spring, and what happened to them shouldn't happen to anybody!

Teachers were alerted to the trachoma problem, and they inspected the youngsters every morning. Those with sticky eyelids were sent to the hospital where they were retained for a week or two. When they returned to the dormitories, their eyes were exceedingly red.

Narcissus was curious, "What did they do to you?"

"Oh, the doctors turned my eyelids inside out, and then they scratched the inner surface of the lids. That's why my eyes are red." The youngsters complained that it had been a painful experience.

"I can do without that!" thought Narcissus. "Grandmother would *never* understand what they were doing."

Sometimes Narcissus was homesick while attending the boarding school. Then Beshád-e's visits were particularly welcome. When she came, the weather was usually good enough for the two to sit outside. They sat on the ground and talked. Beshád-e was careful in arranging herself. She stretched her legs out straight in front of her and then crossed them at the ankles. At a very tender age, as soon as they could understand any of the proprieties, she had taught her granddaughters to be modest. "You must always sit properly. You must be modest at all times. Before you become a woman," she would say, "you should always kneel down, then sit back with your knees in front of you and your skirts down around you." But at the boarding school, she herself sat with legs straight in front of her.

Not only Beshád-e came to visit Narcissus. Just as frequently, or perhaps more often, it was Little Grandmother Lillian. The schoolgirl anticipated her comings; intuitively Narcissus knew that someone would be arriving to check on her welfare. Out she would dash into the school yard. The lonely child stood near the Girls' Building, peering down the road until she could see a familiar figure coming over the hill. Always Little Grandmother came at the same time of day.

How welcome was the sight! Lillian wore a long Indian dress of cloth of discrete print. Her shoulders were mantled in a purple plaid wool shawl. Its fringes swung with each purposeful stride. Over cotton stockings were black high-top shoes laced in front. Her beautiful hair was combed straight back, then braided. The wind blew both dress and shawl taut against her body. She clutched a large paper bag containing cookies, candy, and fruit for the child. How wonderful it was to hold each other close. Later, Narcissus savored the treats, sharing at least a few of them with girl friends.

One such visit, occurring very shortly after Narcissus's return to the boarding school, was a traumatic learning experience.

The way it happened was this: Narcissus was waiting. Little Grandmother Lillian was coming. In joyful anticipation, Narcissus ran to alert Gwendolyn and Marilyn. They too were attending the boarding school, but they were older and looked like young ladies. Narcissus bounded up the steps of the building and into the living room where the girls were sitting, visiting with young friends, some of whom belonged to the Mescalero rather than the Chiricahua tribe. Narcissus shouted in Indian, "Gwendolyn, Marilyn, my Little Grandmother is coming!" Their response was unexpected. They were totally embarrassed but could not stop Narcissus from babbling excitedly, unaware that she was doing wrong. The *wrong* was her speech: she had the dialect of the Fort Sills, the despised newcomers. She was identifying her sophisticated young kin with the Chiricahuas.

As quickly as possible they grabbed Narcissus. They hauled her into the restroom. They shook her until her teeth chattered. "Don't *ever* come up here and say that in Indian any more. You talked so loud that everybody in that whole living room could hear you. If you want us, you call us. Call to us quietly! We'll come to *you!*"

Tears came to Narcissus's eyes, but already she had sensed the antagonism in the way the Mescalero girls made fun of the Fort Sills, even after nineteen or twenty years of living together on the same reservation. So she understood. The three went outside. They greeted Little Grandmother Lillian and shared the sweets from her bag. It was a lesson Narcissus was never to forget, even when she became a leader among Apaches. The Chiricahua dialect must *not* be as good as the Mescalero, she thought.

Gwendolyn and Marilyn gave her other instructions. Even her behavior with her grandmother was incorrect. Oftentimes the three girls clustered around Beshád-e when she came. As always, the woman preferred to remain outside, so there they sat, right there by the Girls' Building. Everyone had so much to talk about. Before long, Narcissus could not control her desire to be close to her grandmother and inched ever nearer, ending finally on her lap. After the visit had terminated, her more worldly relatives once again grabbed the child.

"You just embarrass us all the time," they said. "When grandmother comes, *why* do you just want to sit on her lap? Why don't you sit like we do?"

How could Narcissus explain? She was so lonely. There was no mother to visit her. The only ones who had any concern for her were her two grandmothers, and yet she could do nothing right when they came.

But she learned. At least most of the criticism ceased.

The learning inside the classroom was based largely on the white man's idea of discipline, with a little drawing, reading, and writing thrown in. Recess, the interval outside the classroom, became her favorite time, as it was for most of the children. She made friends, among them Martha Geronimo, the granddaughter of the renegade.

Their favorite game was jacks, played not with the metal pieces but with black walnuts. Martha tied a bag of the unshelled nuts in her pocket so that if she and Narcissus were challenged to a game, the twosome was ready. They were the champions of the school.

The nuts needed considerable advance preparation. The girls were selective in their choice of those that had fallen to the ground. They needed five of them. They found just the right ones. Then they washed them, scrubbed them, polished them until they shone. Only then were the walnuts fit for competition. The girls practiced and practiced the game, developing all possible complicated moves, keeping their hands perfectly flat for the "table position." Hours and hours were devoted to jacks.

Sometimes, when no one challenged them, the two watched the boys at play. The boys used walnuts, too, but pretended they were marbles. It looked fun, but it was not nearly as great a contest as jacks.

These games were played out of doors whenever possible. If it were raining, and that seemed so frequently to be the case, the students were confined to their classrooms where they could be monitored. The children peered out the windows. What was the weather? Was the sun out?

Narcissus confided to Martha that she knew a way to ensure sunshine and to ward off a lightning strike. "My grandmother knows how. I have watched her; I have listened to her. She always tells Wendell and me what we should do. Whenever there is a thunder and lightning storm, she says, 'Spit! You're supposed to spit—make a little pssst—and then the lightning won't hit you.'" Narcissus paused for that to sink in, and then she continued, "If that doesn't make the storm go away, and the lightning keeps getting closer, my grandmother, she talks to it. She says, 'Make your noise higher up, so it won't hurt our ears down here.' She always knows what to do, my grandmother."

Martha thought about these precautions. Narcissus had more to say, "You know, when we are up there on the Feast Ground in our tents, and it is storming hard, my grandmother always prays. She talks to the thunder and the lightning, all the elements, in a sacred way. She talks to God and Jesus, but she calls them 'Yusen.' And she talks straight to the Lightning. She tells it, 'Yusen didn't let you become Lightning so you could destroy!' She scolds and the storm just goes away." Again, there was a short silence.

Then Martha made her contribution. "I know a sure-fire way. Come outside and I'll show you." They went outside. Martha got a stick and began to draw on the ground right by the Girls' Building. "First you make a great big circle." After this outline was complete, Narcissus found another stick, and both girls added a series of leglike extensions to the outer parts of the circumference. "Those are the rays. Now the sun will come out!" How marvelous it was when the drawing proved to be effective.

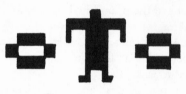

Summertime

The remaining weeks of school dragged, seemingly without end, but finally it was June and time for summer vacation. Narcissus returned to her grandmother's tent at Feast Ground and settled into an Apache routine. At least for a time, she appreciated the peace and quiet of the reservation.

Sometimes the young girl sat in the coolness of the wickiup and watched her stately women-kin, busy at their grooming. Little Grandmother Lillian had long, long black hair; even that of Be-shád-e was rapidly assuming its customary length. Beautiful, shiny tresses were a matter of tribal pride.

One day the child walked into the arbor where Little Grandmother was sitting on a chair. The woman's hair streamed over her shoulders, still damp from a shampoo of yucca root suds. How smooth it looked. How it shone. Her right hand seemed to be stroking it, up and down. As Narcissus drew near, the saw that Lillian held a brush. Its bristles looked like broomstraw. It was the kind the old folks purchased in Juarez, Mexico. The handle was woven so as to create a design. Beshád-e had one that was similar. Narcissus remembered that her great-grandmother, that old lady who was "gone," had had one, too.

Although the youngster tried to dismiss thoughts of the deceased from her mind, as Beshád-e had cautioned her she must, memories kept flooding her consciousness.

She remembered the way in which Dilth-cleyhen moved among the tents and arbors. The old, old woman had been feeble in her last years, but nonetheless, she was impressive. Until the very end she had been active.

Narcissus thought of the way Dilth-cleyhen insisted on walking to Windmill almost every Saturday morning, even when she had grown quite old. From the Feast Ground it is a five-mile trip up and five miles back—a hot way on a summer day, and a mighty cold one when there was frost upon the ground.

The excursions were quite reasonable. Dilth-cleyhen went in order to collect her rations. The government was yet doling them out to some of the more elderly Apaches. Each Saturday cattle were butchered and portions of beef were given to those who were in need. Dilth-cleyhen was particularly fond of the liver, the kidneys, the intestines, and other inner parts. So, when she hungered for such delicacies, off she trekked, as did many other old people. Narcissus always marveled at her great-grandmother's stamina. No wonder she could knife an antelope to death when she was young! The Indians then, as even now, described Dilth-cleyhen as one who could "make distance in a little while."

Narcissus remembered two old ladies who often visited her great-grandmother. They came, burdened with work to do. The three women sat in the arbor, chatting, reminiscing about the days of the warpath. These women were basketmakers. One worked on burden baskets or on water jugs used for tulapai. The other made plaques to be used as trays or hung on the wall for decoration. The soft, low hum of their voices lingered in Narcissus's thoughts.

There were other old ladies to watch—Mescalero ladies. Every afternoon about one o'clock the women trudged past Beshád-e's camp and then continued up the slope, only to disappear among the piñon trees.

"Where do they go every single day? What do they do?" inquired Narcissus. She, her grandmother, and Lillian sat in the arbor and visited, watching the foot parade.

"They are going up there to gamble."

One day Narcissus decided to follow them. She traipsed up the hill, keeping behind trees and bushes so as not to be seen. She stopped from time to time, listening. Finally she saw them. There were a group of six or so women sitting in the shade. They had spread out a tarp, placing a shawl in the center to serve as the playing table, and one woman was dealing cards—the Mexican kind. Narcissus crept back to her own camp and reported her findings. "Sure enough, they are up there gambling." Beshád-e did not approve.

"I wonder who is cleaning their house, doing their housework. Who is taking care of their kids while they are up there gambling away everything they've got!"

One of the women particularly intrigued Narcissus. Always she labored up the hill past the arbor wearing a black shawl over her print dress. Her braided hair hung straight down her back. As she passed, Narcissus noted the blanket under her arm. That would serve as the "table." Her hand clutched a cloth drawstring bag.

"What's in it?" the curious child asked her grandmother.

"That's to hold her gambling money—lots of dimes and quarters with which to bet." Those denominations were the usual wager, but occasionally the old ladies forgot caution when they had a particularly good hand; others prided themselves on their clever bluffing, so sometimes they tossed down as much as fifty cents, but rarely more.

The card players had to be alert. If they heard the slightest crackling of twigs or rustling that might be footsteps, they grabbed the cards and hid them. Gambling was illegal on the reservation. Nonetheless, Apaches have always loved a wager; some Indinas would bet all that they owned of any worth, foolishly, so that the governing forces of the reservation had banned the diversion. As a result, the women kept their voices low, always alert for the sounds of horses. In those days the two policemen, one of whom was Jasper Kanseah, rode horseback. The horses were white, easily spotted between the trees. Well aware of what was occurring up above the Feast Ground, the police patrolled on a regular basis.

More than once Narcissus observed Old Man Jasper as he guided his steed up the hill, ever so quietly. Then, either the horse stepped on a branch, or somehow the old ladies caught a glimpse of him, and oh, how they scrambled! They grabbed cards, blankets, shawls, and tarp, and off they went, running.

Sometimes Narcissus's cousins and other children joined her in spying on the games. They found a good lookout location above the women. It was so nice and cool in the shade, and they could watch and play games of their own, hiding behind the trees, tagging each other, just having fun without being detected. They were not supposed to be there, of course. Their mothers would have disapproved their devious peeping.

One day while they were so engaged, one of the children looked down. He yelled, "Here comes Jasper!" Away the youngsters ran, helter-skelter, as fast as their legs would carry them, most of them moving ever higher. Then Ivans looked back and started to laugh. "Look at those old Mescaleros! They heard us. They are scared, too." And sure enough, just like the young ones, the elderly scurried from sight.

Another time the children scrambled to a spot high up the mountainside, way back in the canyon. They had stumbled upon one of the places where Apaches burned the belongings of those just deceased. The children mistakenly thought they had found an old camp site. They dug into the ashes and the nearby earth. They found thin, old-fashioned frying pans and dented pots of many sizes. They found burned and rusted parts of old stoves which they rearranged to form a make-believe range on which they could "cook." From then on, this remote area became their favorite retreat for playing house.

One day they built a fire in their stove, using piñon cones for kindling. The smell was strong; smoke billowed out. Narcissus was cook. She had some grasses mixed with water in the pot and was totally absorbed in her concoction. Suddenly she was aware of an adult nearby. Startled, she was about to take off, when the woman spoke. It was one of the Mescalero gamblers.

"*What* are you kids doing? Don't you know you shouldn't be here! I could smell this fire all the way down the hill. I thought the whole canyon was on fire."

Apparently the woman kept quiet about the incident, for Beshád-e did not scold, and the police did not stop the youngsters when they returned to their playhouse a few days later. Nonetheless, they kept a more careful lookout.

Once when they were playing there, Gwendolyn yelled out, "There's a *man* up there—a man with a gun!" With that, the hillside became alive with young Chiricahuas dashing every-which-way. They had special cause for terror, for the wild man who roams these wooded mountains is a cultural bogey, used since ancient times as a threat by mothers and grandmothers in order to keep naughty children in line.

Back in the safety of camp, Beshád-e questioned the brood, "What's all this commotion about?" Ringlin, Lillian's son, explained. He got no sympathy. Beshád-e commented calmly, "That's what you get for running around up there in the mountains."

All well and good—but then Ringlin "fixed" his playmates. It seemed he had no sense at all. He said, "We were just playing up there. We were playing with all that stuff." Then he proceeded to go into full detail, describing all the pots and pans and the personal belongings that the children had picked up. Beshád-e grew more and more furious.

"What do you think you kids are doing!" she said. "You are old enough to know you aren't supposed to *bother* those things. In fact, you are not even supposed to *be* in those mountains!" On and on she scolded, finally becoming so irate that she did what a grandmother or even a mother almost never does. She took a stick and gave every one of the nieces, nephews, and grandchildren a thorough spanking.

This is one of the very few times Beshád-e resorted to such measures. The old Apaches did not believe in spanking or even scolding other people's offspring. How often Beshád-e was heard to say, "Don't ever go after someone else's child. You have nothing to say about how that child should be raised. You have no business trying to tell him what to do, or to spank him, or even to get after him at all. You have nothing to do with his feeding, so you don't have the right to scold him." The current matter was of such significance, having to do with the belongings of the dead, that even steadfast rules had to be broken.

Furthermore, Beshád-e was in reality a substitute for her daughter Christine, in the case of Narcissus and Wendell, and because she was so close to Little Grandmother Lillian, her reprimanding Ringlin and the others could be forgiven. Old Man Arnold looked on. He never scolded the youngsters. He was not blood kin.

There was one other time when Beshád-e disciplined Narcissus by physical means. Over and over again she had told her granddaughter never to go down the hill and across the road to the spring in the middle of the day. There, under East Mountain, was where all the campers went daily with their buckets to obtain cool, clear drinking water. There were no strategically placed pipe lines conveying potable liquid on or near the Feast Ground itself.

"Don't you go over to that spring in the middle of the day. The water is too warm then. Go early in the morning, when it is cold and fresh. That water is precious. Water is sacred. Keep it nice and clean for us to drink." The children, especially on the hottest days, did not always heed her words. More than once they sneaked down to the spring in the middle of the afternoon to go wading.

Beshád-e suspected as much. She began to watch precisely where the youngsters went. Were they going back up the canyon? No, they were headed down toward the spring. She followed, catching them in their evil act!

Immediately she cut a thin branch of willow, the willow that grows by the side of the spring. "You kids get out of that water this very minute!" And so they did, scrambling to find socks and shoes. They stood abashed in front of the old woman as she scolded. Nor did they try to run away. Beshád-e whipped the ankles of Ringlin and Ivans, Narcissus and Wendell, all the way back to her arbor. Although she herded the other culprits to the Feast Ground, she did not whip them. Frieda Gallerito and Flora Spitty had to face their own mothers. Their kinship was too distant for punishment by Beshád-e.

Thus, the young ones learned traditional Apache values. There were also practical matters to be learned. In addition to lugging the heavy buckets of water up the hill, Narcissus helped her grandmother collect firewood. Beshád-e described the tumpline that had been used in the days of the warpath. It consisted of a rope about five yards long, cut of rawhide or more often made of strands taken from the yucca plant. Beshád-e demonstrated the way in which the yucca was prepared. She first pulled out the center of the plant and then tore the long green leaves into strips about an inch wide. These lengths were tied together, making strong and practical cordage. Then Beshád-e laid down the pile of wood that she had gathered, keeping it in a bundle. She tied each end, after straightening the crooked twigs as best she could, leaving a loop of the yucca rope in the middle. This loop was about four or five feet long. Then she helped Narcissus hoist the wood to her back, adjusting the rope around the girl's forehead. In this way a small girl could carry a very heavy load.

Narcissus enjoyed going shopping with her grandmother, descending the hill, turning west at the road, and finally entering one of the traders' stores. There was always so much to see.

En route they passed the group of old men who sat every day at the side of Mr. Prude's store, which later became the Tribal Store. It contained a small post office. Everyone congregated there to collect mail and to exchange the latest gossip. News was further expedited by several old men who lingered there for hours, having nothing better to do.

These idlers, inside and out, arrived early in the morning, as soon as the store opened, greeting each other as though they had never gone home, continuing earlier conversations and adding what they had learned the previous night. On warm days, they sat outside in the sun on boxes or cans at the east side of the building. Here they could see everyone who came for mail or groceries. They made spicy comments about each person passing by. On chilly days, all of them stayed inside the store next to the old coal-burning potbellied stove, warming first their hands and then their backsides, taking in whatever the shoppers said, did, or bought.

One memorable summer day Beshád-e took Narcissus to Mr. Prude's store. The girl stood idly beside her grandmother while the latter took her time making momentous decisions as to how she should spend her meagre dollars. The store door opened. In strutted Raymond Chico. He was a lanky cowboy. His spurs jingled as he strode in. Narcissus stared. There was a beautiful star jutting out at the back of the spurs. Raymond looked so handsome in his typical cowboy attire. He looked so fancy in his blue jeans, Levi's jacket, elegant boots, and those silver spurs. After he had bought his tobacco, he left. Narcissus tugged on her grandmother's skirt. "How come those guys wear spurs all the time—even when they are not on a horse?" There was no reply.

The *favorite* store among the family members was that of J. H. McNatt. Although they went to the post office at Prude's, they made most of their purchases at Mr. McNatt's.

McNatt's General Store had a big sign in front and was located on the highway going west from Agency, slightly below Broken Arrow, across from Blazer's Mill. Beshád-e and Old Man McNatt were good friends. He was kind to her. When she was short of cash, she hocked pieces of buckskin or sometimes a shawl in exchange for groceries or even dollars and cents. He understood the problems Indians had in terms of ready money and helped when he could. He visited with The People when they wanted to pass a little time away. He sympathized with their dilemmas and explained situations when they could not understand papers and bills that they received.

Old Man McNatt stood on the raised platform located in the very center of the store. It had a waist-high wall around it. Within the enclosure was a desk that contained all his business papers. Here he cashed checks for the Indians. From here he could peer around his store, checking out every corner in order to keep track of what was going on. He wore old-fashioned round glasses with silver rims. These had a tendency to slip down to the tip of his nose. This never bothered him; he merely looked over them.

There is a story about him and an old lady who regularly removed items from the shelves and stuffed them into the broad sash that she donned when going shopping. She always "forgot" to mention this additional loot when she paid for a few purchases. Old Man McNatt had watched her for some time but had said nothing.

One day he had a number of customers. He saw the habitual filcher near the eggs. Surreptitiously, she slipped one after another into her sash, very carefully, looking nonchalantly around from time to time. After taking a few, she meandered to another part of the store, only to return to the egg area when no one was in the vicinity. This went on for a fair amount of time and her middle was slowly increasing in girth. Then, slowly, Old Man McNatt descended from his central cage. He approached the old lady and put his arm around her, saying in Indian, for he knew the Apache language well, "I'm real glad you came in today. I feel like dancing." With that he put his left arm about her waist, crushed her to him and made several twirls down the aisle. When he released the old lady, the slimy eggs were slithering to the floor, dotted with a few of the eggshells. Women onlookers giggled behind their hands; men guffawed openly. The old lady looked down at the mess. She giggled, too. Never again did she wear a wide sash about her waist while in the McNatt Store.[4] Beshád-e enjoyed the diversion of grocery shopping and her conversations with that old man. She called him "That Left-handed White Man," not meaning to disparage him but to describe his physical attribute. He knew she called him that. He did not mind.

The highlight of that summer was the day Wendell was given his Indian name. It was July, just at the time the boy was turning four years of age. The Feast of the Maidens was taking place. All the tribe was gathered at the Grounds to honor the girls at that stage of their maturity. Beshád-e decided it was a proper time not only to honor her grandson, but also to have a ceremony that would further protect him from his mother's ghost. It had always been the custom of the In-déh to change the name of a child when his close kin died,[5] and although Wendell would retain his English name for the records and when he started school, *she*, Beshád-e, could use the Indian title. It might help. She talked to Jake Cojo, a highly respected Chiricahua singer, who agreed to conduct the ceremony. Wendell would be given a name to fit his personality.

The appointed day arrived. Beshád-e donned her black shawl, and Old Man Arnold wore a black handkerchief around his neck. The color was important, for it served to combat ghost sickness. In the old days many elderly people wore black accessories as a daily protection. For special dress-up occasions, a man wore a brightly colored shirt, but always there was that black kerchief. It was held in place with a large turquoise ring, which was slipped up over the two scarf ends that dangled over his chest, thus creating a tie. The day of the Feast, Beshád-e and Old Man Arnold wore only dark clothing, nothing flashy at all.

The family members gathered in the center of the ceremonial Feast Grounds. It was quiet. It was a sacred occasion, a kind of sing. Wendell stood in front of Jake. Jake prayed in accordance with ritual requirements. The Crown Dancers danced in from the east. The jingles on their skirts rang loud and clear. They moved around the family cluster, gesturing with their swords toward the south, the west, the north, and then the east. At the proper moment, Jake spoke Wendell's new name: So-kus-n, meaning "someone who thinks."

The family remained on the ceremonial grounds most of the day, eating the food supplied by the families of the maidens. They socialized very little, and the small amount of visiting was sober. At night when the Round Dance and Back and Forth Dances began, they retired to their tents. To participate that summer would have been disrespectful.

Just before autumn arrived, news spread that the central boarding school, located near Agency, in Mescalero, was to be replaced by day schools in the outlying districts of Elk, Carrizo, and White Tail. Beshád-e was pleased. "Good. We'll move back to the house in White Tail. You can attend classes in the daytime and live with me and Old Man Arnold. We can be together more. I like that better than a boarding school."

A Few Years in White Tail

The family prepared to move back to the mountains. They packed the gear, dismantled the tents, and loaded everything in a wagon, leaving only the cooking shelter and wickiups as dried and ghostlike reminders of their presence on the Feast Ground.

Once in White Tail Beshád-e insisted her house again be fumigated. It had been vacant for a long time. Further, Christine had lived there when she was a girl, and now she was gone. Old Man Arnold served as singer for the purification.

Narcissus loved White Tail. It was green and beautiful under the trees. Wild game could be seen and hunted by the men folk when they desired. Sheep thrived, and the land was fit for farming. Wild horses grazed in the meadows, stallions keeping watch over their mares. Wild turkeys gobbled and scattered into the bushes. The little girl was content.

Narcissus went to the White Tail Day School that fall and continued her studies there for some four years or so. A total of some one hundred children attended classes. These were held initially in the Dutch Reformed Church building. Although governmental agencies had plans for the construction of permanent school facilities, these took several years to materialize. Beshád-e's house was about four miles from the church; transportation to and from was by bus.

On days when school was in session, Narcissus, Wendell, Ringlin, and Ivans, as well as Susie's daughters, Marcelline and Lavera, waited in a group at their bus stop. They were there promptly at 9 A.M., even though they were the last to be picked up, and it was not unusual for the bus to be late. The driver never had to honk for them. These children were always there, no matter what the weather. Beshád-e and Old Man Arnold were adamant that they get to school on time. "You get there on time! You need all the education you can get!"

There was no clock in Beshád-e's home, but she and Old Man Arnold sensed the hour. They awakened early on school days. First he got up and built a fire in the wood stove. When the house began to get warm, she arose and prepared breakfast. Next, all the children left their beds and dressed for the new day. There was a house full of them: usually Susie's children, and a bit later those of Little Grandmother Lillian, including Evelyn.

At about the time the sun came up, Beshád-e was ready to serve breakfast. She called her brood, instructing them to sit at the table and to eat what she had fixed. Usually this consisted of rice with canned milk and sugar. Sometimes there was gravy made from powdered dried meat—deer or occasionally beef. The gravy was eaten with oven bread or with tortillas made on top of the stove. For a rare treat Beshád-e served fry bread along with canned peaches or apricots. She could not afford fresh eggs and bacon. For a beverage the youngsters occasionally drank coffee, but more often they took canned milk diluted about half and half with water. Evelyn, Beshád-e, and Arnold preferred black coffee.

The children gulped their food rapidly or dawdled, according to their individual inclinations to attend school. While they were so preoccupied, Beshád-e spread a piece of canvas on the floor. This she covered with a tea towel on which she set her plates and dishes and those of Arnold. She laid out two sheepskins, one on each side of the towel. Then the two of them sat on the skins, Beshád-e with her legs stretched in front of her, her ankles crossed. She disliked sitting at a table.

As soon as breakfast was over, the children donned their coats or sweaters and headed for the roadside bus stop. Beshád-e began her chores. She washed the dishes in an enamel dishpan, dried them, and placed them in a cardboard box in which she had brought home groceries. To make it look neat and attractive, she covered it with a large cloth. Then she began housecleaning and straightening whatever mess the youngsters had left. She was never in a hurry.

When necessary, she washed dirty clothing. She used a tin tub, a scrub board, and White King soap, and later she rinsed everything in a big, old-fashioned keg. If the laundry had been done earlier in the week, she ironed. The iron was continually heated on top of the stove. She was always busy at some task or other, sweeping and tidying the house to her satisfaction.

One very cold day in the wintertime, the bus did not come, even though it was at least 9:40. The snow floated down steadily. Six children were waiting: Narcissus, Wendell, Marcelline, Lavera, Ringlin, and Ivans. Oh, how they wished the bus would come and they could get to school where it would be nice and warm. In order to keep warm, they decided to start walking.

After they had ploughed through the heavy snow for about two miles (nearly half of the way to school), Ringlin, Ivans, and Wendell gave up. Lavera and Narcissus did not know what to do. Eventually, they decided the girls would have to carry the boys on their backs. And so they did, everyone putting forth his and her best effort. The small ones became heavier with each step, and the snow kept coming down. From time to time, it was necessary for everyone to walk. The boys were near tears. Finally, hours late, the children arrived. No one had the heart to reprimand them.

There were two teachers in the White Tail Day School: a Mr. and Mrs. Claude Webb, who had come from Wisconsin. She taught the lower grades, and he taught the older children up to the sixth grade. They were a fine, understanding couple who did their best to help the Chiricahuas. They were patient when children did not understand. Mrs. Webb began a Girl Scout troop in order to provide leisure activity of a constructive nature.

One of the major emphases in formal education was that of the importance of cleanliness. The Webbs insisted that the children wash their hands before eating. The couple hauled all the wash water and poured it into two deep oblong tubs situated in front of the church. One tub was filled with cold water, the other with boiling hot water. At the beginning of the school year, each student was issued a large can, the size of those in which fruits and vegetables are packed, as well as a bar of soap and a denim towel. The first assignment was for each student to wash the can thoroughly, dry it, and then paint his or her name on the front.

When washing of hands was in order, before and after lunch especially, the Webbs lined the children in a single queue, boys and girls one behind another. In turn, each child was supposed to dip out half cold water and half hot water from the tubs into his own can. This accomplished, the student was directed to move into the yard and wash up. Ablutions completed, the dirty water was poured out, the soap placed inside the can, the towel hung over the receptacle's edge and the container itself set on the storage shelf.

Narcissus remembers well one day when she was waiting in line to wash. It was right after lunch. She was behind Edmond Sago. Edmond filled his can with hot water. Then somehow, his hands slipped and the boiling water poured over Narcissus's feet. Oh, how it burned! The Webbs were equipped to handle such emergencies, however, and administered first aid.

Lunchtime provided an excellent opportunity to instruct the youngsters concerning good nutrition. Belle Kazhe, who was the school's cook, lectured them about proper diet. She was one of the better-educated Apaches of that day. She also taught the older girls sewing and home economics. She talked to the children in Indian so she was sure they would understand. She was half Chiricahua and could communicate well.

As the children sat in the big room filled with lunch tables, Belle sat in a chair and talked to them. "You children must eat all your food. I prepared a well-balanced lunch for you. You must drink your milk so that your bodies will be strong, strong like an Apache's body should be." Another day she concentrated on vegetables. "Eat all your vegetables, your peas, your carrots, your spinach. They provide you with vitamins and minerals. And eat your meat. That is protein, and you need it to grow tall and straight. These are all healthy foods. You need a well-rounded diet. Eat every bit."

Much of the school day was devoted to practical studies that could be used within the house or in the fields. Nonetheless, the Webbs stressed proper speaking of English and its reading and writing. These were hard tasks for children who spoke only Indian at home.

Narcissus attended school at the church for three years. Then tragedy struck. That night she was at home, and went outside for one or another reason. The sky was red! It looked as though a giant paint-brush had swept across the heavens with ruby pigment. The color seemed to come from the direction of the church, but what could it be?

Indeed, it was the Dutch Reformed Church that had burned. The next day all that was left was the bell from the belfry and the foundation. All the books were destroyed. So were the dresses made in sewing class. That was a special disappointment for the girls, who had expected to display the garments the night of the morning after. The sole consolation for the community was that now the government *must* fulfil its earlier promise of an actual schoolhouse building. However, no classes could be held for the remainder of the spring.

Even when school was in session, there was ample time for playing and doing assigned chores. The bus brought the children home about four o'clock in the afternoon. That left several hours of daylight. During vacations the entire day was devoted to such activities, with the number of chores increasing for Narcissus as Beshád-e and Old Man Arnold grew older.

Beshád-e was clear about her expectations. "You young ones see that the wash tub and those large kegs over there are full of water." Every afternoon Narcissus walked down to the road, crossed it, and went over to the faucet. Here she filled two buckets with water. Then she carried them, splashing as she went, back to the house where she emptied them into the designated receptacles. Over and over again she repeated the trek until the kegs and tub were brimming. Sometimes she was able to induce her brother and cousins to help, but it was her responsibility. After all, Wendell was still quite young.

Another of Narcissus's daily tasks was that of hauling firewood to the house. She must keep the woodbox full of both kindling and logs of appropriate size for the stove. So, she made daily trips to the large wood pile, which, in turn, was replenished from time to time by adults who hauled in wood, either on their backs or in the wagon. Narcissus learned to chop the large tree trunks and limbs into kindling. As she was not yet fully adept at the task, she needed practice—or so Beshád-e said. "Keep that woodbox chuck full for me. We need lots of wood."

The young girl was expected also to help her grandmother prepare the main meal of the day. She did simple things, such as peel potatoes. When there was meat, she cut it into bite-sized portions. Occasionally, when Beshád-e did not feel well or was otherwise occupied, her granddaughter mixed the ingredients for dough and then did the baking. The fragrant bread was stored in a medium-sized empty lard can.

Other chores abounded. Every so often Beshád-e sent the two children to look for red sandstone with which to sharpen the axe and her various favorite knives. A *sharp* knife was necessary in the making of jerky, for the hunks of beef or deer meat must be sliced very, very thin, almost curtainlike, before being hung to dry. Red sandstone was rare at White Tail, so the search was sometimes long. But that was what Beshád-e wanted. "It makes a good whetstone, so you must just keep looking."

Sometimes Narcissus helped in the tanning of hides. In order to make buckskin Beshád-e first soaked and then scraped the hide with a mare's rib covered at the ends with rawhide. Oh, how she scraped! Even on the very edges, she scraped until it was fine and even. Narcissus had difficulty doing it well enough. "You're not finished yet. That's not good enough," her perfectionist grandmother admonished.

Then there was another immersion, this time in a tub of tap water mixed with beef brains that had been squeezed and pulled apart. Soaking in this, plus Beshád-e's extra care in scraping and then some rubbing, made the hide soft. If she wanted to store it at this point, she had Narcissus bring her the can containing bacon grease or lard or bone marrow, and a layer was applied. She made sure there were no bare spots. When it was thoroughly greased, Beshád-e took the hide in her hands and rubbed parts of it together, round and round.

All the youngsters were enlisted in stretching the hide. First Beshád-e took the skin outside, laying it on a sheet of canvas. "Now you kids take off your shoes. I want you to stand barefoot over there on that side of the hide. Be careful. I don't want the buckskin to be dirty." And then the woman began to pull. The children's weight kept it taut. Beshád-e pulled every which way, every direction, stretching the hide to the maximum size. It was then staked out and left to dry thoroughly. Later Beshád-e did a final scraping around the edges with a piece of lava. "Come feel it, Narcissus. Buckskin should be just this soft."

If the family or very good friends did not need the skin for some ceremonial reason, or if Beshád-e were out of cash, she made a trip to Mescalero to sell it. She got good money from Old Man Marce-lino Prelo, who ran the Big Chief Store just west of Agency going toward Bent, so that was her first stop. Or, if she felt like it, she took it to Old Man McNatt who also gave her a good price for good work.

One time a neighbor killed a deer, a doe. When his wife and he butchered the animal, they discovered an unborn fawn, and they gave it to Beshád-e. "This is going to be something special," she informed her granddaughter. Beshád-e soaked the hide, dried it, scraped the inside, and rubbed it with grease. It was so small, no stretching was necessary. Then, in a few days, she made a doll cradle from the prepared skin. "This will bring us more money than just the buckskin. Those tourists that drive through the reservation buy cradles. They like such things for souvenirs."

Another time Wendell and Ivans wandered around with sling-shots. Before long they came back with their quarry, a chipmunk and an innocent little squirrel. They were so proud. Beshád-e re-warded them with ample praise.

Nonetheless, when she was alone, she murmured, "Poor little squirrel. Poor little chipmunk. I'll make you into something beauti-ful." So she skinned the creatures and tanned the hides. With the squirrel skin she lined another doll cradle. She placed a cloth Indian doll inside, covering it with the chipmunk skin, which was as soft as a well-worn rag. This one sold immediately, and Beshád-e received a good commission.

Sometimes there was sheepherding. Many people in White Tail kept sheep. During the winter the animals were kept in corrals near the houses, but in summer, to avoid the expense of feed, they were herded into lush meadows. Each family was responsible for hiring its own herder. Sometimes it was almost impossible to find a good person for this. Beshád-e occasionally had to resort to using grand-children and nephews and nieces in this capacity.

One Saturday as autumn was fast approaching, Gwendolyn and Narcissus were chosen to watch the sheep. Narcissus loved Gwen-dolyn, for she was so jolly.[6] It barely mattered that the rest of the family were going to Mescalero to shop. It was a beautiful day.

The girls herded the sheep across the main highway just above Cherokee Bill, on the reservation border next to Ruidoso. Then they lay on their backs under some trees, looking up at the sky through the leaves, having a glorious visit. Before they knew it, they were asleep. How long they slumbered, they knew not, but when they awakened, there was not a single animal in sight. Even the dogs were gone.

Gwendolyn, being the older of the two, felt responsible. She was all excited. "Where can they be? What shall we do?"

The girls hunted everywhere, but to no avail. They decided to explore a nearby canyon. Fortunately, there they found the missing sheep. With mixed happiness and chagrin at their negligence, they rounded up the bleating creatures and started for home. It grew later and later. The sky was black by the time they arrived. "It's a good thing you found them. You have learned a good lesson." Beshád-e had no need to say more.

Herding sheep often posed a problem. Several years later Beshád-e and Old Man Arnold again needed someone to herd the livestock. They owned a car by then, but Beshád-e never learned to drive, and Old Man Arnold preferred to be a passenger. So they scouted around White Tail and paid one of their neighbors to drive them to Alamogordo, where they then recruited a shepherd. It took several hours to make the round trip. That day, when they returned, there was a tall black man with them. Narcissus looked him over. "I guess he's the new hand," she commented to Wendell.

Beshád-e fed the man his supper. Then she and Old Man Arnold exchanged long looks. What would they do with this stranger? Where could a black man sleep? What on earth can we do with him? Finally, they handed the man some blankets and told him to make a bed for himself in the car.

The next morning the family arose, and Beshád-e prepared break-fast. "Go out and get that man, Narcissus." Her granddaughter went out in the yard. There was no black man. There was no car.

Back she rushed with the news. In consternation, the adults went to the door to check out the situation. Sure enough, no car, no shepherd. "Did you take the keys out of the car when we got home?" asked Old Man Arnold of his wife. "No," she answered. " I thought you would do that!"

A few days later the police way down south in Deming contacted the Mescalero police, who in turn went to White Tail to inform the Kinzhumas. Once again, they hiked around White Tail trying to hire someone to make the long drive to Deming. There the car sat, parked by a filling station.

Another of the occasional chores connected with sheep came in the springtime when shearing took place. This activity went on for at least a week and was one of the busiest times of all the year.

First, every family was responsible for herding its flock to the day school. Eventually, when they were all assembled, a truck arrived dragging a trailer to which twelve sets of shears were attached. Some men were there to help with the initial sheep-dipping, after which the animals were penned in a corral until their pelts had dried some-what. Oh, how they stank! Then the coordinator of the shearing called out the name of a family. That group collected its individual flock and herded the animals close to the truck, twelve at a time. Right next to the trailer a small square wooden structure, a kind of open-topped closet or bin, had been set up. Each family had its own stack of gunnysacks. They were huge, the largest available. Before the men started to shear, a sack was fastened so that it hung inside the bin. The shearers tossed the cut fleece into the gunnysack as they proceeded with their work.

In order to save expenses, Beshád-e wanted as much wool as pos-sible to be packed into a single bag. She set Narcissus, Wendell, and their cousins to work. "I want you to take turns. I want you to get inside that gunnysack that's hanging in that bin, and I want you to stamp on all that wool, just tamp it down as hard as you can. Then it will hold more. And when one of you gets tired, the next one can take a turn."

It looked like fun, but turned out to be hot and tiring work. After stomping on the wool as long as legs and breath held out, each child hoisted himself to the top of the bin and jumped outside so the next one could take over. This went on until all the flock looked sadly naked. Then Arnold hauled the bulging sacks of fleece to the shear-ers' truck and sold the wool to the foreman. This was one of the chief sources of the Kinzhuma's income.

Only rarely did the family butcher an animal for its mutton. But when that occurred, Beshád-e told Arnold to kill two at a time. She cooked the ribs immediately, outside on the coals. They smelled so good. The children danced around in anticipation. Eventually Be-shád-e used every bit of the animal, even saving the stomach so she could make blood sausage.

Later, as soon as she was not too busy, she tanned the pelts, leav-ing the wool on—and Narcissus was expected to help her. These soft skins were used to sit on, for the old lady could never become accus-tomed to chairs. She used her sheep hides when she was in the house or when she was outside on the ground, whenever she was preparing food or when she sewed and always when she ate her meals. Those soft skins were found on the seats of her wagon and under the sad-dles of the horses. They were indispensable.

Beshád-e and Arnold kept sheep for many years, until they were convinced by the governmental officials and those of the tribe that it would be more lucrative to buy cattle. "You won't need to hunt for herders. The cowboys will look after them as a community venture, but you can keep your individual ownership, and you will make a profit," they were told. "Well, all right." The sheep were sold; their corral was empty.

Playing, Preaching, Remembering

There were few white man's toys on the reservation in the 1930s. In general, Indian children "made do" with objects common to their environment, cultivating rich imaginations; or they played with animals.

Narcissus loved small creatures. She liked the lambs, but especially she enjoyed the two pet rabbits brought to White Tail by her father. Her bunny was black; Wendell's was white. "Feel how soft they are," she told Marcelline and Lavera. "You can play with them, too." And so the cousins shared them, at least for a while.

Then one day when Narcissus and Wendell had gone to Agency with their grandmother, Lavera let the rabbits out of their pen, and off they scampered into the woods. At least, all the other children *said* it was Lavera. Perhaps putting the blame on her was justified, for Marcelline and Lavera loved playing jokes on Beshád-e's wards.

Things worked out better with lambs born in early spring. From time to time the ewe died at the time of the births or shortly thereafter. When this happened, Beshád-e might bring as many as two, three, or even four lambs into the house. She prepared a nursery for them in the kitchen behind the woodstove. First she laid down a piece of canvas. This she covered with a pile of gunnysacks on which the baby animals could sleep. Narcissus and Wendell spent hours with the lambs in those cozy quarters, feeding them from baby bottles and spoiling them with cuddling. The animals became so attached to the children that they followed them everywhere, bleating for attention.

And there were horses. Most years Beshád-e owned about four, pasturing them in the yard or keeping them secure within the corral. The children were permitted to ride bareback. As always, there were conditions attached to this fun.

"Horses are valuable. You must not run them too hard."

If the day were particularly warm, Beshád-e tossed a gunnysack over the animals' backs before the youngsters took off.

One year she had only one horse. This did not deter the children. They climbed on, two and three at a time, galloping as fast as they could over the fields and down the road. When they got back to the house, Beshád-e scolded, "You kids are just too hard on that poor old animal. Look at him. He's as thin as a rail! Look at him! He's so tired and sweaty, he can't move. You kids do something else for awhile."

The old lady took the reins and started leading the horse away. But she did not stop talking. "Horses were Apache wealth when I was young. When we rode them this hard, when we were on the warpath, it was because we *had* to. Horses were not just playthings. When I was young, when a man danced with a woman during the Back and Forth Dance, he might present her with a horse as a gift, a thank-you. That was something special. You kids don't appreciate what you have."

There were also mules, but they were less diverting for the children than the horses because their grandmother did not want them to be bothered. Beshád-e had a special fondness for them. She drove her wagon with a team of mules. If she planned a long trip, such as going to Agency, she found mules had more endurance than the horses.

She called her favorite "Pete," one of the few English words she used. A son of Rogers To-clanny was named "Pete." The To-clannys, who had lived near-by when they all lived at Fort Sill, and whose camp had been adjacent to hers in later years at the Feast Ground, continued to be among her closest friends. She liked that boy; she liked the mule, and it seemed quite natural that both be called the same. Beshád-e talked to the mule as she drove along. "Slow, Pete! Slow, Pete!" she cautioned when descending the steep trail that led from the tents to the main road below the Feast Ground.

Then, for some reason, Pete To-clanny died. Immediately Beshád-e began to call the mule Dick, and the grandchildren were told never to use his former name.

Although almost all Apaches owned their own white-faced cattle, the stock was not kept near the houses and barns, but instead, was tended jointly on outlying reservation pastures by groups of cowboys. These men were paid by each family owning animals.[7] The summer range differed from the winter range, and about the middle of August the cowboys rounded up the herds and headed them toward new grazing land. It was glorious to see. No matter how engrossing a game the children might be playing, they immediately abandoned it in favor of watching the cattle.

The first sign of the trek began with an enormous cloud of dust rising into the sky above the pine trees. Then, as this came closer and closer, the youngsters heard the cowboys whistling. "Come on, come on, they are coming! They are coming!" Two hundred cattle, all in one mass, were heading right toward Beshád-e's property on their way to Cow Camp No. 1. What a sight!

One day Beshád-e called, "Come on. Get in the car. We are going to Cow Camp No. 1." Narcissus and Wendell minded with unusual alacrity. En route their grandmother explained that she had just received the required permission to butcher one of her steers. Arnold asked Narcissus, "How will it seem to have some fresh beef for a change?"

As soon as they arrived at their destination, the cowboys shoved a steer into a small enclosure. The poor thing could not move at all. Narcissus began to feel a bit sick in the pit of her stomach. It felt exactly as though she had done something terribly wrong. Then a man with an axe walked up close to the bin. He smashed the steer, right on the forehead. "How could he stand to do that!" thought Narcissus. "He could at least have shot it. That would have been better."

Beshád-e and Arnold set to work immediately. In just a few minutes the animal was completely butchered. Then the family moved a short distance from the bin, built a fire, and prepared to have a barbecue.

First Beshád-e removed the small intestines, washing them off, turning them inside out, washing them, and then turning them to the right side once again, for a final scrub. She cut them into foot-long pieces and threw them on the coals to cook. She added salt only. When they were thoroughly cooked, the family ate them; they were so delicious. After everyone had had his fill, Arnold loaded the cut-up pieces, such as the hind quarter, the front, and the back, into the car and the family headed for home.

On later occasions Narcissus watched her grandmother prepare the stomach of the steer. That was a true delicacy. The brains, too, were retained. They would be dried and used in future days when the women tanned buckskins. The sinew was removed with exceptional care. That from cattle is stronger than that from deer. And finally, even the bones were saved—they added flavor to soup.

The day after the butchering was a busy one. While there was much for children to see, nonetheless, it was exhausting for Beshád-e. The beef must be dried, must be made into jerky, so that it would not spoil. She needed drying racks. She chose a spot in the yard fairly near the house. Here she dug two holes at an appropriate distance apart. Into these she set strong uprights, each one having a Y at its top. She lifted a long pole, similar to those with which she built her tipi, and then lowered it in a horizontal position so that its ends fit securely within the two Ys. She now had a sturdy clothesline.

Beshád-e began to cut the fresh meat, using two very sharp narrow-bladed knives. She cut the beef across the grain into chunks about six inches wide and long enough to fit comfortably within her hands. Then she started peeling the slab, turning it continuously so that she finally had a continuous streamer of very thin meat from that one large piece. She sprinkled it with salt and draped it over the horizontal pole. Then she cut the next ribbon of meat and on and on until the task was completed. Sometimes the strips were very, very long.

"You kids get me some small sticks, about four inches long," she directed. When the children brought them, she inserted the wooden "picks" between the two halves of the dangling meat, thus separating the lengths so air could circulate freely.

One day Narcissus and her grandmother were sitting inside the house after a long morning of cutting jerky. Suddenly they heard a terrible squawking. "Quick, Narcissus. Get out there! Those darn jays are at my meat!" Sure enough. A group of blue jays were flying in fast, like bombers, and picking off a short piece of meat in midflight. Beshád-e was furious. She picked up every rock she could find, even pieces of kindling, and hurled them at the thieves, finally driving them away, at least temporarily.

Narcissus enjoyed dolls, but she had no store-bought doll. Beshád-e would not permit such a toy near her or her grandchildren. Narcissus played with dolls made of rags or even of the husks and silk of corn.

Those of rags were fashioned by Beshád-e and, as soon as her fingers were sufficiently adept, by Narcissus. They used any scrap of cloth that they could forage. Each doll was about four or five inches tall and had a rectangular body. Into the center top of this they stuffed a roll of material which formed the head. Hair consisted of long strands of black thread sewn to the top of the skull. There were no arms or legs, but dresses covered the arm areas and hid the lower part of the doll's body from view. The sleeves were ruffled; the skirts were very long. "Shi-choo, it looks like a *real* Indian, doesn't it?"

Narcissus, her grandmother, and cousins made entire families of dolls. The girls pretended there was a mother, a grandmother, and little girls. Once or twice they had a male doll to represent the father or grandfather. With these toys the children enacted every possible Indian activity. Mother and grandmother doll scolded in Indian, and their play-offspring behaved appropriately, or at least the way Narcissus and her friends wished they themselves might be able to do.

Once Evelyn, the daughter of Little Grandmother Lillian, made a doll for Narcissus. It was special: it was made from goatskin. But someone, one day, took it. It simply disappeared, that treasure.

The dolls needed accessories from time to time in order to enact certain situations. This was no problem even when the exact toy was nonexistent. Narcissus made a wagon from an empty shoe box, tying a string to one end so she could drag it around. She put the dolls inside, making believe they were going for a ride or searching the woods to find firewood. Beshád-e made cradleboards for the smallest dolls so they were just like living babies. Narcissus was soon adept at creating miniature wickiups from grasses and weeds. Inside, she covered the bare earth with tiny reeds, just as she had seen Beshád-e do with those of full-size. The dolls cooked, tanned hides, went to cow camp, and once in a while, they even gave a feast.

Narcissus and her friends decided to make a Big Tipi, as used in the Mescalero ceremony. They searched for a green bushy weed that grows in White Tail and arranged the stalks so the foliage was at the top and the stems spread out—just like the trees used by the Mescaleros in their real-life Tipi at the Feast Ground. The girls were careful to tie the stems together at the top, just below the green, as they knew was proper.

"You take care of all the food and the coffee," Narcissus instructed her playmates. "My doll is the maiden, and I have the grandmother doll who can be her chaperone." The children enacted the entire ceremony as accurately as possible, recreating the dancing, the running, and the blessings. They omitted the sacred songs because only men do that.

One day Marcelline and Lavera were staying at Beshád-e's, and they and Narcissus decided to have a truly wonderful doll Feast. They built the Big Tipi and a row of smaller tipis at the side, one for each maiden doll to be honored. They constructed a long arbor wherein the dolls could cook. All morning the youngsters worked— it had to be just right!

"You girls come in!" called Beshád-e. She had cooked onions and chiles for lunch. "You eat this with some biscuits." Narcissus and the other two bolted their food and ran outside, excited that now they could actually begin the Feast.

They met with disaster. Everything was torn up! Ivans Martine had come up the road. He had kicked all the beautiful handiwork to pieces. In those days, while Narcissus was growing up, Ivans had tended to be an ornery little cuss. He always acted as though everyone were against him.

What a sad sight! It was sickening.

Beshád-e heard the despairing cries and came out. She was always close at hand when grandchildren and nieces were playing. If she thought they were about to quarrel or if they needed guidance of any kind, she was ready to step in. When playing grew wearisome or boring, she was there, showing the youngsters how to make the cradles, or to create a basket from weeds. The best of all were her corn silk dolls.

"This is the way you do it. You get a green husk and fold it in half, like this. Then you get some corn silk. It is the hair." She laid the silk at the open end of the folded husks so part of the silk streamed out. It looked shiny, like hair, even though it was blond. Then she rolled up the husk. About an inch below the top of the section where the hair emerged, she bound the bundle tight. This formed the doll's neck. A little lower still, she made a binding for its waistline. For arms she pulled a couple of narrow strips of husk through the waist tie. "Now, you must put them in the sun and let them dry. They'll be ready to play with in just a little while." And so they were. After that first demonstration, the girls made their own corn dolls, a mother, a daddy, and little girls. They were so nice to touch, especially the hair. It was soft, like real hair.

Narcissus had no need to ask why she could not have a doll from a store. Beshád-e repeatedly told her, warned her. "Those white man's dolls cause doll sickness." Doll sickness is a mental disorder with symptoms much like those of ghost sickness.

When Narcissus was young, many Apache children contracted the ailment, especially little girls who were about three or four years of age. There is no fever, no specific complaint, whereas many victims of ghost sickness often are pale and nauseated. Instead, children who are afflicted with doll sickness begin to *look* like dolls.

"You can tell," said Beshád-e. "They just stare into space. Their eyes are dazed. But most of all, their cheeks get real bright, as though they are painted in red."

The old Apaches warned the young. "Store-bought dolls put a curse on you; if a person dislikes you, she puts a hex on a commercial doll and then she gives that doll to you. Never take a doll like that from anyone. You don't know *who* has had it, or what they might have done to it. If you accept it, you will get sick very shortly afterward." Always, before the old people set up camp anywhere, they searched around in the weeds to make sure no store-bought doll, especially the head, was lying hidden from view. "That sickness makes you look just vacant-minded, like a doll."

Beshád-e had a story. "There was one time at the Feast Ground. An old lady was getting ready to put up her arbor so she could camp. A little bit later, an old faded doll head was found right where she had been working. The folks that found that doll were so upset, they burned the head. But right after the Feast, that old lady died of doll sickness. No one ever told—maybe they didn't know—who had cursed that doll and put it in the old lady's camp."

"You must be careful," she went on. "If you ever see anything like that, you tell me right away. It requires special songs and prayers that pertain to the doll."

Beshád-e was one of the few who had the special power and knowledge to cure doll sickness. Several times during Narcissus's youth, her grandmother was called to cure children of their red cheeks. The ceremony is much like the ghost-chasing rite. But it must be conducted in the early stages of the malady. In the case of the old lady who died, the curse was too strong for Indian medicine. Nothing could have cured it.

All the family enjoyed trips of various length, either in the wagon or in the car. Long rides were best, but even short ones to the Agency or to Ruidoso, Tularosa, or Alamogordo were welcome. Perhaps it was Apache nomadism emerging once again. It was good to roam the countryside, especially to see the former Chiricahua homelands. Sometimes excursions were scheduled at specific times of year when certain foods were ready to harvest—yucca fruit, for example, or the delicious nuts of the piñon tree.

In good years, when the trees were laden heavily with nuts, the family got gunnysacks and took off for a full day of gathering. When they reached a spot on the reservation where the piñons were abundant, they stopped driving. Everyone piled out of the wagon, and Beshád-e began to pray. She prayed that there would be no rain until the nuts were safe within the bags. Only after she had conferred with Yusen could Narcissus and Wendell and whoever else was along begin to pick the ripe, brown nuts from the ground. When the bags were relatively full, Beshád-e drove home. She built a fire in the stove and pulled out her cast iron skillet. The nuts were cooked on top of the range until they got real hot.

Narcissus helped stir. "Let me! Let me!" begged Wendell. "You're too little," his sister replied. It took only a few minutes and the nuts were ready to eat. "You be careful too," cautioned Beshád-e. It is possible to eat uncooked piñon nuts; but they make your mouth pucker, and the taste is less than perfect. Today, Narcissus needs only to bake them for three or four minutes in a 350° or 400° oven and then they are just right. Every Apache child practices the art of putting several nuts in his mouth at one time, biting the shell and ejecting it without further use of fingers and without losing a single bit of the succulent meat.

Trips to Mescalero and Old Man McNatt's store were made every few weeks. If someone needed to see a doctor, if Beshád-e's cures had been inadequate, the ailing one was taken to the hospital. Then, there was always mail to pick up at the post office and business to do at the Tribal Offices at Agency. In summer it was hot and dusty at this lower altitude. "It's so dirty down here. I don't even like it," Narcissus complained. The only compensation came when they could visit friends and drink coffee or have a snack to eat.

Most of Beshád-e's friends were Chiricahuas; they, too, lived in White Tail, a few even within walking distance. But there were exceptions such as Jasper Kanseah, Sr., the policeman who rode a white horse. He and his wife, Lucy Gon-altsis Kanseah, lived near Agency because of his work. She was related to Chatto's people in some way now lost to posterity; her father had died while at Mount Vernon Barracks. She had married Jasper at the turn of the century, and they had begun their family while at Fort Sill. It was cool within her arbor in the summertime, and warm inside the house when there were winter snows.

Sometimes the family drove to Hondo Valley to see George Coe. "He knew Billy the Kid," Narcissus informed her brother. "Billy the Kid was a bad white guy who shot everybody who didn't agree with him." In fact, Billy had shot off one of Mr. Coe's index fingers. Although Beshád-e had told Narcissus she must not stare at it, the little girl had difficulty pulling her eyes away from the dismembered hand. The Kinzhumas and Coes visited. If it were August and the apples were ripe, Beshád-e purchased a box to take home. These were the best apples in all the world.

Other times they traveled to Tularosa which was some thirty-five to forty miles from White Tail. If the family went by wagon, they stopped midway and camped overnight by the ranch at Cottonwood

Springs. They continued the journey into town the next day, going first to the general store owned by R. D. Champion. It contained a butcher shop and hardware supply. There were even clothing items from which to choose. All the Apaches liked Mr. Champion. His trading was fair, above board. He was the one responsible for starting the banking business in Otero County. More recently, a hospital in Alamogordo was named in honor of his son, Gerald.

Each August after Narcissus's mother died, Beshád-e took her granddaughter in her arms and said, "We must get some nice clothes for you. I'm going to take you with me to Tularosa so we can find something. I don't want you to feel ashamed in front of all the Mescalero children."

On arrival at Champion's Store, Beshád-e looked for the Spanish woman who worked there. Beshád-e knew a few Spanish words, but she had Narcissus translate the Indian into English. "My grandmother knows you do beautiful sewing and handwork. She wants you to make me some underclothes, some slips, and waists for me, before I start school again." Beshád-e used the word "waists" for a kind of undershirt, really a camisole. The Spanish woman was delighted. The fitting was done. Narcissus was proud beyond belief. No one else in the family had handsewn undergarments. Only she.

Sometimes Beshád-e and Old Man Arnold made another stop when they went to Tularosa. This stop deeply troubled Narcissus, and as she grew older, it distressed her even more.

There was an Anglo there who ran a secondhand store. Many of the more aged Apaches had difficulty making their dollars stretch far enough to buy necessary clothes or even food. Many went to that pawnshop and hocked their shawls, Indian blankets, buckskins, moccasins, baskets, or whatever they had. Beshád-e and Old Man Arnold sometimes did that. They rarely were given enough cash to make it worth while, but that old Anglo was wily. He kept a goodly store of liquor there.

At that time Indians were not permitted by law to buy alcoholic beverages. So that old man bought it for them. He gave them too little money for their merchandise, and then, because it was illegal, he demanded exorbitant prices for the whiskey. Thus, he was doubly paid, and the Indians suffered.

Narcissus sat in the car, waiting for her grandparents to come out of the pawnshop. How she hated their being there! "Somebody should do something about that old Anglo," she brooded. The situation became worse as she neared her teens. "Maybe I should go to the tribal authorities," she pondered. "Somebody should stop the cheating. Somebody should stop these old people from spending all their money this way, giving away all their treasures." Sometimes she confided to her brother, "Look what's happening. They're just getting cheated again! They won't have a dime to put toward your shoes when that awful old man gets through with them. They work so hard for everything they have. They are always generous. And then they go and get 'taken.'"

Narcissus never informed on the Anglo. Perhaps she was afraid. Certainly, she knew that the secondhand dealer was doing wrong, and that the Apaches were the losers in his fraud.

Sometimes the family's destination was Alamogordo, still another hour by wagon. Here, shopping was cheaper and choices greater than in Tularosa. The family took two and a half days to get there from White Tail. First they stopped and camped in Mescalero. The next day they got as far as Tularosa. Old Man Arnold drove the horses to the Champion's Store and parked the wagon in the service area in the back. He unbridled the team and tied the animals to the wagon. He pulled the bedding from the back part of the vehicle, placing it beneath the wagon. "Come on, you children, bed yourselves down. We can sleep here." After he and Beshád-e had visited for a little while in the store, they joined the youngsters for the night. When morning came, there was ample time to make purchases in Alamogordo and return to Champion's place before dark, again to sleep beneath the wagon.

Longer excursions were sometimes as distant as the state of Arizona, where a few relatives and friends from long ago still lived. Here, far to the west of Mescalero territory, Beshád-e showed her grandchildren the sites sacred to the Chiricahua. She pointed to important landmarks. "You must never forget your roots. You are Chiricahua."

From time to time the Kinzhumas and their grandchildren traveled to some of the areas where The People had once been confined, such as San Carlos and Fort Apache. Arnold had relatives in San Carlos. Every so often he would say to Beshád-e, "Sah-un, it's been a long time since we saw my brother, Parker West.[8] Why don't we go over and see those Bi-in-et-ina?" Beshád-e rarely said no. Packing was done in short order. As she put her things into a box, Narcissus was pensive. Finally she spoke.

"I don't understand why we call those Apaches over on the San Carlos and White River Reservations *Bi-in-et-ina*. They have faces. That word means 'without a face.'" Her grandparents laughed, "It really has a different meaning when we talk about those Indians. It means they are kind of crazy, that they have erratic minds." Still, it was puzzling. Parker West did not seem at all crazy. He and his family spoke almost the same dialect as the Fort Sill Chiricahuas.

One time when they headed for San Carlos, Wendell had a sore ear. The entire area was irritated. By the time they reached Bylas, where Parker West lived, it was clear the redness was caused by poison ivy. Wendell grew sicker and sicker. His face and ears, even the sides of his neck, were so swollen that Beshád-e insisted he be taken to the San Carlos Indian Hospital. Narcissus was disgusted. "Well, this sure puts a damper on having fun. Here we are, just sitting around in hospital halls!"

Life was more difficult in Bylas than it was in Mescalero. The water was bad. It tasted salty—nasty. The children were told, "You kids go get us some fresh drinking water." The youngsters took a bucket and set out for the railroad's water car. It was a long dusty walk. There were almost no trees at Bylas; only a few mesquite bushes provided shade. One time the car had run out; there was no water at all. Back the young ones trudged, bearing the sad news. "Well, we'll have to drive to Geronimo and get some. It's about fifteen miles there and back, so we can't walk," Parker informed his guests. Narcissus groaned to herself, "I'm so thirsty, I'll *die* before we get way over there!"

So often the trips the family took were less enjoyable than anticipated. Sometimes Narcissus blamed the philosophy of her grandparents. They tended to live day by day without looking to the future, without making any provisions for emergencies. Both those old people liked to travel so much that they forgot they had no money on hand. One time they ran totally out of cash by the time they reached San Carlos. Parker could not help them. "What shall we do?" Beshád-e asked. They asked everyone they knew. There was no available money. "Well," said Arnold, "All we can do is to go over to the Agency here and get them to write a letter to Mescalero for us. We have to get somebody to write a check and send it here."

The letter was sent. When Beshád-e asked Arnold what he had said about repaying the debt, he replied, "Oh, I told them we would pay it back with Narcissus's and Wendell's cattle money." Narcissus jerked to attention. Should she complain about his presumption? It mattered little. The check never arrived.

After a week or so went by, someone in Bylas was able to collect enough money to get the Kinzhumas back to White Tail. For a time Arnold was furious that his request had been ignored, but eventually the whole business was forgotten—but not by Narcissus. What a mess!

San Carlos was an excellent location for collecting acorns. These are unavailable in Mescalero but abundant in the vicinity of Bylas. "I just want to taste them again," Beshád-e commented. When she and Narcissus returned from gathering, the old lady poured the acorns from the gunny sack and ran her hands through the brown nuts. Later she would pound them and mix them with dried meat for a special treat.

Beshád-e, Arnold, Narcissus, and Wendell slept outside in the arbor when visiting Parker West. The structure differed from arbors in Mescalero in that it was square rather than round, and it was constructed of willows. One morning Narcissus was awakened very early, before the sun came up. There was the strangest sound—scrape, scrape, scrape. She stirred and looked toward her grandmother's bed, but Beshád-e was already building a fire in the center of the shelter in preparation for brewing coffee and fixing breakfast. Clickety scrape. Clickety scrape. Over and over again.

"What is making that noise, Shi-choo?"

"It's the neighbor woman. She's the one that's making that sound," Beshád-e explained. "Every night she makes dough for tortillas in a big tin dishpan. But she doesn't wash the pan out at night. The leftover bits of dough dry on her pan and in the morning she has to scrape them out." Every morning for the remainder of the visit, Narcissus heard the rasping, the clickety scrape, clickety scrape.

A year or so later, down by Deming, New Mexico, on the way to San Carlos, Beshád-e pursed her lips toward the south. "Narcissus, I want you to remember this. Down there." Again she made the pointing gesture. She was designating the three mountains known as Tres Hermanas.

"Those are sacred mountains. This is Chiricahua homeland. Those mountains are the home of the Crown Dancers. Right there is where they kept all their ceremonial things, the mask and crown, the rods, the skirts and boots with the upturned toes, everything they use in the blessing rites."

Narcissus looked hard at the mountains and began to daydream of all the sacred paraphernalia. She began to worry about something she had done the summer before, something for which she would have received a harsh whipping had Beshád-e known. She had peeked into the tipi where the Crown Dancers were being dressed. It happened like this.

In those days the tribe held a rodeo every August in the district of Carrizo on the reservation. All afternoon the cowboys roped cattle and rode bucking broncos. The kids in the audience had a foot race. Then, in the evening, a big bonfire was built, and all the Apaches gathered round while the Crown Dancers and the sacred Clowns emerged from the darkness to dance. Their presence made the event a special occasion. They blessed The People. Their prayers and intervention with Yusen kept the In-déh in good health, free from trouble for the coming months.

A Singer supervised the dressing of the Dancers in privacy. He wore a black handkerchief for protection from any evil force. Such a medicine man knows the proper prayers and songs required for readying his group of "Mountain Gods." He owns a special set of symbols or markings with which he paints his dancers before they perform. Through his communion with The Greatest Power, through his ritual, the mortal men who make up his chosen team are in essence transformed into sacred beings. No womenfolk or children are permitted around the dressing area. They must not listen to the songs; they must not watch the proceedings.

That rodeo time, Narcissus and a couple of her friends heard some drumming and singing coming from a secluded place in the forest. The girls sneaked over. There was that man and his Dancers. The spying youngsters hid on the mountainside, looking down with wide eyes, taking everything in, suppressing their nervous giggles.

As they watched, the Singer and team finished eating their dinner. Then the Singer blessed each member of the dance troupe. He painted their chests, their arms, and their backs. As each article of ceremonial clothing was donned, the men sang. There was even a special song for moccasins. They danced and held up the boots before putting them on their feet. They sang and danced holding their skirts before they were worn. The Singer prayed. Then there was sacred music and dance for the masks that completely hide the faces of the performers and are topped by the high-spiked crowns.

It took a long time before the dancers were disguised beyond human recognition, but the girls remained until the very end, knowing full well they were being very bad. They just *had* to watch. No one could see them, anyway. Narcissus remembered the misdeed for the remainder of her life. Always, the feeling of guilt prickled.

When darkness fell, the girls crept from their hiding spot and joined the spectators around the great bonfire. That night the dancing of the Mountain Gods seemed especially impressive. In the glow of the firelight the Crown Dancers entered the arena with their high and haunting hooting sounds, gesturing to the four directions. A Clown followed each of the four teams, only one of which had been spied on. The Clown poked his sacred stick repeatedly among the members of the audience, making the smallest youngsters cry and the toddlers scream. When he pointed at an adult, that grownup had to enter the central arena and dance with stately mien.

The observers knew how to behave. They took care not to touch the sacred scabbards. "Don't you touch those sticks, those rods the dancers and Clown carry! Don't you touch a dancer! If you do, you'll go crazy." Every time Narcissus watched, the warning was repeated. "Don't touch their feathers, or skirts or jingles or anything!" If any part of the Crown Dancers' costumes fell to the ground in the course of the dancing, a special ceremony was required before they could pick it up. "Even if you think you know who one of those dancers is in real life, don't you say his name. It's dangerous. Something bad will happen to you."

As they drove along by Deming, Narcissus remembered all those sacred things. She was silent.

Beshád-e interrupted her granddaughter's thoughts. Her lips pointed even further southward. "Down there is 'The Town with Many Burros.' In the days of the warpath our people often went down there. We didn't always fight the Mexicans. Sometimes we were at peace. Some of those people became close friends. Lots of places we went, even as far as that Chihuahua City."

Not all excursions were by wagon or car. Sometimes there were simply walks in the vicinity of the house in White Tail. Narcissus loved meandering under the trees and in the meadows. Sometimes Beshád-e and Wendell went along, occasionally for some distance.

Once the three climbed high on a mountainside where there were crags and scrub oak. "Shi-choo, look!" Narcissus had found a bird egg. Beshád-e was delighted. "It's the kind we used to eat when I was on the run in the warpath days."

Another time Narcissus and her cousins were alone, walking in the canyon behind the site of Dilth-cleyhen's house. They came to a tall pine, and looking up, they saw, half hanging, the U-shaped framework of a dismantled cradleboard. It was old and blackened, looking eerie, looking sad.

They asked Beshád-e about it when they returned home. "After a baby dies or has outgrown its cradle, the mother dismantles it, removing the buckskin. Then she tries to find a tree, usually a cedar tree. There she hangs the buckskin as high as she can reach. She searches for another tree. She fastens the headpiece to it. Finally, she locates one for the framework. That is what you saw." She waited a while, then continued, "That one might have been put there by Susie. She had a son by Robert Decherle, but the child died at about one and a half years of age. I know Susie went behind my mother's place. She really liked it there. Even though she usually stayed out in Elk, she liked to come here and pitch a tent, usually by that old-woman-who-has-gone's place. I think she must have hung that baby's cradle back there. I remember making his cradle."

Beshád-e insisted that any child in her charge be home at supper-time. Before eating could begin, there was a headcount. "Narcissus, Wendell, Lavera, Marcelline, Ivans. Where is Ivans?" The children at the table shrugged. "Narcissus, you go call him. Hunt for him if you have to. No one eats until he comes." Waiting, the other children sat idly at the table, either on chairs or on round paint cans that served as stools. When the tardy one arrived, food was placed on the table, and Beshád-e and Old Man Arnold took their own full plates and arranged themselves on the floor.

Always at mealtime Beshád-e began to preach. "You children should start living your lives properly *right now*. If you don't, you will never accomplish anything." The do's and don'ts were not con-fined to eating times. It seemed Beshád-e preached all the time and on all topics.

For the girls she had special counsel. "You must be a good wife. You must learn to take care of a family. You should stay home when you marry. You should take care of your children, and you should prepare your daughters to be good mothers." Another time: "Be modest. Be chaste. That is very important to an Apache. It is no laughing matter," she warned when the girls started to snicker. "You must give the right impression. You must sit properly. You must behave modestly even when you are real young. After you get mar-ried, you must always be faithful to that man, your husband. When we were on the warpath, a husband had the right to beat an unfaith-ful wife, or he could slit or mutilate her nose if he wanted to. We were always proud of our Apache women. Even the white soldiers respected us."

"You older girls, you must never talk about sex, or menstruation, or pregnancy. It is not proper." In fact, these were subjects that Beshád-e never commented on at the supper table. That would have been bad manners. But when the time was appropriate, she made sure the maturing females in her charge were doing what was right. For example, she never permitted a menstruating girl to ride bare-back when the other children were cavorting with the horses. She always put a gunnysack over the mount's back. "If you don't sit on something when you are in this condition, the horse will get a bad sore." Later, she elaborated, "Do not walk in front of a man when you are menstruating. If you even touch a man when you are having your period, *he* will get sores. Don't sit down on a chair at that time, either. Kneel and tuck your legs under. That is the proper way. If you don't sit like a lady, you will have flat buttocks." Another time, she noted, "You girls are getting too old to sit on the beds of your brothers and male cousins. And you boys, too, must keep away from the beds of your sisters. That is not proper for either of you now."

For the boys, specifically, she also advised, "Be a good husband. You must provide for your family. Work hard in the fields. But above all, be sure to get a good education. Go to school. And always speak English. When you are an Indian, it is hard. You must now learn to do things differently."

Then there was the general preaching:

"Don't let yourself get dirty. Wash your hair and bathe frequently."

"Don't eat at other peoples' houses. Your family has enough to provide for you."

"Don't talk about other people. Don't treat them badly. Don't be a gossip."

"Don't step over a person's legs because that causes the person to have aching limbs."

"Never step over a man's gun, or he will miss the game he is hunting. If you make a mistake and step over a person's legs, or a man's gun, you must turn around right away, and step back over again. Then walk the long way around. That will reverse the bad luck."

When barefoot children were told to put on their shoes, there were precautions: "Don't wear your shoes on the wrong feet. You don't want to look like Shosh." Shosh, the bear, was a beast to be avoided, especially the prevalent black bear. Even to see one in the daytime meant death. Parents immediately changed the shoes of a small tot who mixed up his shoes, putting the right one on the left foot and vice versa.

When the children were about to go outside near a stream, they heard, "Don't play with snakes. Don't touch them. If you do, you will get sores on your skin. You'll look like you have snake's skin. And don't play with frogs or tadpoles, or you will wet the bed."

When the sermons began at mealtime, Narcissus groaned inside. She thought, "Oh, here goes supper again. We can't even go outside to the toilet because we are going to get a good preaching!" Her sentiments reflected the feelings of all the others. How they dreaded the everlasting lectures!

Once Ringlin and Philip were eating at Beshád-e's and she began her "do's" and "don't's." Ringlin was about to slip quietly off his seat, and out the door, but Philip, anticipating the move, kicked Ringlin's ankle. Poor Ringlin was crippled for a moment or two and was unable to escape. Narcissus chafed under the lecturing. She was often bored, but she disapproved of her cousins' total lack of respect. Sometimes they got up and left, or they coughed and whispered loudly even while Beshád-e was talking. On such occasions Narcissus thought, "My grandmother is old. Nobody will even listen to her. She works so hard for us, cooking for us, doing whatever she can to give us the very best. It is sad."

Narcissus was compassionate, and most of the time she tried to be helpful. When school was in session, before she went to the bus stop, she did what she could. Many were the times Beshád-e did not feel well. Old Man Arnold assisted when he was able, but he was not good with domestic chores. Beshád-e was having trouble with her eyesight. When clothes needed patching, Narcissus threaded four needles for her before she went out—two with white thread and two with black—so that her grandmother could do the mending. She could not see the needle's eye.

White Tail was an isolated district, far from Agency. The houses, except for those of kin, were relatively distant from each other. Nonetheless, Narcissus never felt lonely. It was but a short walk to Little Grandmother Lillian's, where there were cousins to play with. Relatives, including Susie and her youngsters, came visiting, as did many friends and neighbors.

One of Narcissus's favorite pastimes as a child was to sit in a secluded place and watch the various White Tail residents as they passed along the road.

There was Fanny Shosh. "I wonder why her name is Shosh! I guess her husband must have fought a bear and got the best of it," contemplated Narcissus. Fanny walked slowly by the house. On occasion she stopped to share gossip. Her sons Samson and Keith sometimes accompanied her, and the children had time for games.

There was the old woman Oot-oo-di.[9] Her house was beyond the day school, about four or five miles down the road. Every two weeks, as regular as clockwork, she came by on horseback, headed for Mescalero. Although most of the families in White Tail had a car of some kind, she did without, perhaps by preference. She started one day; the next she spent near Agency; the third day Narcissus began to watch for her. The child kept a vigilant eye on the road about the time the sun started going down and the shadows from the pine trees grew long and covered the house. By the time there was one big black patch of darkness extending from behind the mountain, she heard the sound of horse hooves on the gravel. Before long, Oot-oo-di appeared around the curve.

The horse trotted along. The white-haired Old Lady held the bridle reins in her left hand. Her long dress was draped behind her, covering the back of the saddle and revealing her moccasins. She carried a whip, sometimes of leather, sometimes a twig from a willow, and from time to time she hit her mount in order to keep it trotting.

Most times a blanket covered Oot-oo-di's lap. Behind her were slung two gunnysacks, full of her purchases. "Wendell, Wendell, come on. The Old Lady's coming!" Narcissus shouted. The two of them ran to the road, sat on one of the logs there, and grinning, awaited the arrival. Oot-oo-di stopped, talked a while, and then, dipping into one of the sacks, pulled out a box of animal cookies, a couple of suckers, or perhaps some Cracker Jack. She never forgot the youngsters whom she knew expected her.

Oot-oo-di was clothed in traditional Chiricahua style. Many of the older Apache women resisted the adornment and customs of whites. They continued to ride horseback, preferring this mode of travel even to riding in a wagon. They looked stately in their long cotton dresses and buckskin moccasins. Younger women who had come from Fort Sill, such as Little Grandmother Lillian, wore button shoes—Anglo shoes—but otherwise retained Indian costume. Both young and elderly women wrapped their shoulders in light-weight black shawls with long fringes. To add color, they tied red and yellow, or sometimes just red, ribbons in between the strands of fringe. On hot days, they shaded themselves with black parasols.

Men, too, dressed much like one another. They wore wide-brimmed hats, black or dark brown, with beautiful beaded headbands. Sometimes they stuck an eagle feather, a white plume, in the band.

Narcissus was less interested in men's fashion than in ladies'. She admired the dark-hued, small-print cotton percale or broadcloth that Beshád-e and most other women used. The material should not be of conspicuous pattern. Further, she loved watching her grandmother sew. Indian styles could not be purchased at Champion's or other stores; they must be made at home. The Chiricahua–Fort Sill blouse was fitted, not full like those used by San Carlos women. Sometimes there were flanges over the shoulders; there were buttons down the front. Whenever Beshád-e pulled out a long length of cloth and got ready to create a dress, Narcissus was at her elbow, watching every step.

First, Beshád-e held the yardage in front of her. For the skirt she measured herself from waist to mid-calf and then tore a strip of cloth of that width. She did not use scissors. Then, she calculated the distance between midcalf and ankle. She tore that. The strips were seamed, and gathers were made at the top of each—all by hand-sewing. For the blouse, measurements were taken of the length of her arm from shoulder to a little above her wrist, and two such pieces were torn. The front and back of the blouse were based on the space from shoulder to a little below the waistline. A narrow band composed the collar.

It took a long time to join all the pieces and make buttonholes. Finally, it was ready to be worn and belted. Just a plain leather strap was customary, but it looked decorative because many items dangled from it. Really *old* women, such as Dilth-cleyhen when she was alive, wore the belt *over* their blouses. Younger women let the top hang loose with the belt beneath.

"Shi-choo, what are you going to fasten to your new belt?" Narcissus inquired.

"Well, my knife in its rawhide case, of course. And my new beaded bag made with tanned deerhide and metal jingles." Narcissus knew this was needed in order to carry sacred pollen. Sometimes Beshád-e kept a root in there too—a root to help cure colds—and an awl.

There was another bag to be hung, a drawstring bag made of scrap cloth. It was about four inches wide and six inches long. Its purpose was to hold matches and Bull Durham. So often Narcissus had seen Beshád-e grab a handful of wooden household matches and throw them into that small bag.

"How come they don't rub together and catch fire?" she once had asked.

"They don't," was the reply. Still another hanging bag consisted of a white man's coin purse, one that snapped. This, of course, contained coins of the white man—a necessary commodity at their stores.

When Narcissus was growing up, one of the most important parts of a young mother's everyday dress was the cradleboard, slung so that it hung down her back. Brightly colored scarves were tied over the headpiece. They fluttered when the wind blew. A few matrons, perhaps less wealthy than those with cradles, carried their infants directly against their backs, securing them there by means of a single blanket.

Necklaces were a part of all female "dress-up" clothing. Some of the oldest women wore protective red bean beads such as Dilth-cleyhen had used when crossing the Rio Grande. Younger ladies flaunted large, clear beads that resembled crystal. Sometimes they donned long strands of black and white or red and blue beads, but more popular when Narcissus was growing up were short-length "chokers." Those women who could afford silver and turquoise made purchases from Navaho silversmiths. Conspicuous rings with large turquoise stones were real prizes. Those are what Beshád-e and Oot-oo-di had.

Those old ladies, all of them, smelled so nice. They used mint for perfume, the mint that grows wild in moist areas such as creek banks. Narcissus and Beshád-e gathered it, dried it, and tied it in little bundles. Then, when Beshád-e was going out, she attached some to her belt.

In addition to Oot-oo-di, there was Old Lady Coonie, whose Indian name was Dah-das-te.[2] She whizzed along the road in her automobile, occasionally stopping to visit. Almost the only time she rode a horse was when she herded her animals. She was a progressive old woman, about ten years older than Beshád-e. Dah-das-te was small in stature but sturdy. Her long Indian dress gave her added height; her black high-top shoes were laced neatly. The two old friends reminisced about warpath and imprisonment days. Dah-das-te had been married then to Ahnandia, a warrior with Geronimo, and had accompanied him on all the forays. Like so many other Chiricahua, he died while at Mount Vernon, Alabama. She then married Old Man Coonie, a former Scout, whose deceased wife had left him with three children. Although they had no offspring, they took in two of Coonie's orphaned nephews, Richard and Samuel Jolsanny. Because of the Old Man's pension, they were always well off financially. They had *lots* of sheep, so considerable time was spent in herding.

When Narcissus and her grandmother went to visit Dah-das-te, as they neared the Coonie house the dogs set up a howl. "Shi-choo, why do they have so many dogs? They scare me. They might bite me."

"It's all right, Narcissus. Stay close to me. They need the dogs. There are so many coyotes around this part of White Tail that they need them. See that chicken wire around the sheep corral? The Old Lady put it up for the same purpose—to keep coyotes away."

There were many other women Beshád-e visited. Of them all, there was really only one whom she disliked, and she lived a long way off, down the road toward Cow Camp No. 1. She was kin to Victorio in some forgotten way, so the Kinzhumas tried to stay on good terms. But no one enjoyed being with her. "Here comes *that* one," they would say when they spotted her coming. Even while in her presence, Beshád-e and Evelyn seemed anxious to avoid her.

There was a nice white couple by the name of Wilson who resided in White Tail. He was a government employee, overseeing agricultural affairs and some of the tribe's cattle business. "Shi-choo, let's go see Mrs. Wilson," Wendell and Narcissus coaxed. "Maybe she made ice cream today." Mrs. Wilsom frequently made up a batch in the summertime. Then she invited Beshád-e and her young charges over. Oh, such a creamy treat!

Most casual visiting done was among the family members, Susie, Little Grandmother Lillian, and all their children, some of whom were getting along in years.

Lots of times in the evening, about when Beshád-e started cooking supper, relatives trooped in. There was almost always an extra child or two in the house. Sometimes it was annoying, for whoever was there "borrowed" whatever they fancied from among Beshád-e's belongings. Later, when she needed something, such as an iron or a special knife for cutting jerky, it had disappeared.

Lillian and her family came, and Susie and Lavera and Marcelline. Beshád-e never asked them if they wanted something. That would have been impolite. Instead, she cooked up more of everything— gravy and dried meat, fried potatoes, and canned fruit. For a special treat, she baked sweet potatoes.

After they had eaten, all the visitors pitched in and washed dishes. Then they stayed for the evening. They never hurried. They left whenever they felt like doing so. "Well, I'm going home," they said, and then set off down the road or to their tent if they were camped across the road. Their nonchalance and seeming lack of courtesy bothered Narcissus, but one should realize there is no Apache equivalent for the English word "goodbye."

Narcissus was ten years old and still attending the White Tail School when Little Grandmother Lillian died, following the birth of her daughter Imogene. For a time the aching within Narcissus seemed unbearable. Lillian had done so many things that Beshád-e never thought of or even cared about. She had seemed so much more modern. Even her house was more beautiful.

One year the Mescalero Tribe set up contests with prizes for the nicest gardens, the prettiest yards. Little Grandmother Lillian had won a set of blue dishes painted with apple blossoms. Her yard was filled with flower beds, with purple iris, flags, next to the house.

"Why don't *we* ever win anything! Why don't *we* ever enter a contest?" Narcissus wondered. "I guess my grandmother is just getting too old."

For the time being, however, Narcissus was largely content with her life in White Tail. Only later would true seeds of discontent begin to sprout.

In the late winter she watched for fresh green signs of oats peeking through the dark soil. When they pried the earth apart, they saw that spring was just around the corner. In summer Narcissus was content to slide down haystacks. With the autumn came harvesting. When the oats were ready, all the neighbor men came to help Old Man Arnold in the fields. The crop was cut, bagged, and then sold to the tribe or the Cattle Growers' Association (CGA). At noon and at completion of the day's work, Beshád-e fed all who came to help. It was hard work, but it was a social event as well.

Of all the yearly activities Narcissus preferred evenings at home in the summertime. Sometimes just Beshád-e, Arnold, Narcissus, Wendell, Evelyn, and Imogene were there. Other times they were joined by kin or friends. The family sat outside on the porch. They listened to the neighboring old men who sang in Indian and beat steady haunting rhythms on their drums.

Sometimes the singing started late in the afternoon. The old men sat in the shade of the trees or waited until after sunset. Then it began, softly at first. Hour after hour, they sang, more and more lustily, and White Tail families all around listened.

When Old Man Jasper Kanseah retired as policeman in Mescalero, he and Lucy moved to White Tail. Evening after evening, he sat on his porch, singing. He knew all the old songs, those for the Back-and-Forth Dance, the Round Dance, even Apache love songs.

When the air is damp, and it is evening at White Tail, the lovely sounds carry from house to house. Nothing compares to it.

Religion

To say that Beshád-e was a religious woman is an understatement. Her faith in Power was the core of her existence. Every breath she took, every action she made, revealed her faith and her fears.

"You go to Church. Every Sunday I want you at the meetings of the Dutch Reformed Church," insisted Beshád-e in her daily instructions to her wards.

The Reverend and Mrs. Peter Van Es came up from Mescalero to conduct the services in White Tail. During the school year, after regular secular classes, the children were taught Christian doctrines. Even during vacations youngsters were expected to attend weekly sessions of Bible school. Beshád-e made sure Narcissus and Wendell were present. Adult women of the district did not go to a Bible school, but Ladies' Aid activities were available for them.

Every student who completed the full course received a plain black Bible. Narcissus received hers. Wendell finished the class somewhat later. By that time the Bibles were nicer, in Narcissus's eyes: the imitation leather binding was elegant; the pages were of onionskin; the printing was fine. Narcissus was jealous.

"Why don't we trade Bibles?" she tempted her brother, knowing that he was too young to know the value of things. Wendell agreed, and the exchange was made. Many years later, after Wendell had gone to live with his Aunt Susie and after Susie passed away, the house had to be cleaned out and fumigated. While cleaning the attic Narcissus found the Bible originally given to her. She dusted it off and took it home, keeping both books.

Beshád-e herself almost never attended the Sunday meetings of the Dutch Reformed Church in White Tail, nor did she take part in the church's social activities. However, most of her friends gathered one day per week for Ladies' Aid. They met in the church building that served as school and community center before it burned down. On occasions Beshád-e showed up, staying just a half hour or so, visiting, but then she left for home. She was getting old, and her eyes were bad. She was unable by now to do any sewing or quilting because she could not see to make the small stitches, or to thread the needles.

Transportation was a prime problem in White Tail. The government's school bus carted the residents everywhere, even to church programs.

One night there was a social affair at the Day School. In the middle of the entertainment, someone came in. "That wind is blowing a gale outside," he mentioned. No one paid attention. After the program was over, everyone got into the bus and started toward home. Sudden gusts of wind made the big bus sway. Outside, huge pine trees had been uprooted and had crashed to the ground. Three or four times en route, all the men had to get off the bus and drag a tree off the road before the driver could continue. Beshád-e's was the last stop, and it had taken a very long time to reach it. The children were frightened as they ran into the house.

There was a tall, dried-up pine about thirty or forty feet from the house. As Narcissus and Wendell prepared for bed, Beshád-e sat by the window watching that tree. It was moonlight. Narcissus looked out. The tree creaked and swayed back and forth, back and forth.

Soon Beshád-e got to her feet. She began to pray, "Yusen, Yusen, keep that tree from falling on our house. Protect this house. Protect those within it. Please, Yusen, don't let that tree fall on us." She prayed for a long time. When Narcissus fell asleep, her grandmother continued to stand before the window.

When the children awakened the next morning, the wind had stopped. They looked out the window. The tree *had* fallen—but *away* from the house.

"Somebody must have heard us," Narcissus thought. "Somebody must have heard my grandmother."

Beshád-e was indeed convincing.

Narcissus learned through what seemed absolute experience that the elements possessed power. She heard her grandmother address the water, lightning, thunder, snow, and wind in a sacred way. She heeded the cautions not to touch lizards, snakes, moths, or the big black and yellow butterflies. Beshád-e said, "If you get powder from the wings of that yellow one in your eyes, you will go blind." She feared the eagle and even the little nightbird—the whippoorwill, or Ja-jo—which would tuck an unwary child into a basket and carry it to a dire demise. Whenever she saw such a bird, Narcissus went quickly into the house and shut the door.

She especially feared the owl, another harbinger of death. When she and Beshád-e went up into the mountains behind their home, sometimes they saw shell-like droppings on the ground. They must be avoided. They were discharge from the owl's nose.

Coyotes, ever so prevalent in White Tail, were evil, as were the black bears. Not only was Narcissus careful not to put her foot in the wrong shoe, but she took care to store the footgear properly under the bed at night. Shoes must be at the foot of the bed, with their toes pointing east. If they were anywhere else, and especially directly under the head of the sleeper, she would have bad dreams.

Narcissus feared going to the outhouse at night. There were strange noises in the woods. There were things you could not see. "Don't be scared," her grandmother comforted her. "You need not go out. I'll leave this can for you."

One moonlit night Narcissus and her cousins were sliding on a haystack. Suddenly a coyote cried. Then came a chorus of howls, answering him. All the children ran for safety to the house, scrambling in a single heap of knees and elbows through the back door.

There sat the old folks, calm as could be. The kerosene lamp burned brightly. It was cozy and warm. No need at all to crash inside. But who could ever be sure?

Even the dogs were frightening when they wailed at night. Like coyotes, they were dangerous. They might serve as good guards, but even so, they had dual personalities. Beshád-e said, "Don't watch dogs when they defecate. If you do, maggots will feed on your eyeballs." Narcissus was particularly terrified when she heard the dogs start a constant howl, a pitiful cry that went on and on. "It means illness, death, perhaps of someone dear to you." Beshád-e's information was far from comforting.

Beshád-e had her own way of dealing with the outside world. She communicated with many powers and with Yusen. Her sacred pollen and talismans had proven to her their effectiveness. The Crown Dancers had long been considered sufficiently sacred to help The People—at least she had thought so until very recently. Why should she go to the Christian church? Beshád-e knew that many Apaches were verbalizing allegiance to both traditional and Christian faiths. They said that having *both* religions on one's side was ultimate insurance. Certainly, she wanted spiritual security for her grandchildren, just as she herself wanted it. But at the Dutch Reformed Church the clergy spoke in English, and the translations into Indian too often made little sense. Beshád-e came to prefer the ceremonies and preaching of Silas John Edwards, the founder of the Four Cross Cult. Nonetheless, she insisted that Narcissus know all three. When the girl was in boarding school, she should go to the Dutch Reformed Sunday School; when at home, she would learn Apache safeguards and attend the Four Cross Church.

For as long as Narcissus could remember, Old Man Arnold had talked about the man he called a prophet, the man known as Silas John. She soon learned that the cult instigated by that preacher was the reason Arnold took the family so often to San Carlos. "Let's go see Parker West" really meant that her grandfather desired deeper indoctrination into the messianic beliefs. Parker, an ardent member of the group, always had news to share. Further, Arnold yearned to speak to the prophet in person, so whenever the Kinzhumas went to Bylas, he began a search. If this were successful, and he found his man, the disciple had high hopes of receiving more blessings and prayers to use at Sunday services in Mescalero.

Silas John came to Mescalero about 1929[11] in order to establish his church more fully and set up the Holy Grounds. Although she was only five years old at the time, Narcissus always remembered his visiting in the home of Old Man Arnold and Beshád-e. The prophet told the family members, "You folks need to accept *Jesus*." He and Arnold acted like friends although it was clear that Old Man was merely a pupil.

The Holy Ground was set up, the four crosses defining its location. This was the church. No building need contain it. When Narcissus asked about this, she was told: "It's not the same as the Dutch Reformed or the Catholic religion. They need an assembly hall. That is not Jesus's way." On week days the open area seemed a desolate, lonely place, but each Sunday it became the scene of great activity.

On the Sabbath, at about 10 A.M., Beshád-e, Old Man Arnold, Narcissus, and Wendell set out, driving over the rough wagon trail to Head Springs. When they reached the sacred ground, they greeted other Apaches in the process of assembling. There were both Mescalero and Chiricahua, mostly elderly, Catholic and Protestant, all worshipping according to Silas John's instructions.

The procedure during services was always the same. Two columns, one for men and one for women and children, stretched from the eastern side of the Holy Ground. Narcissus and Wendell stood with Beshád-e. "Oh, these long, long lines!" whispered the girl to her brother. Mostly, the little girl was patient, occasionally shifting her weight from one foot to the other. The members of the church stood in silence, listening to the initial prayer. They watched the gestures to the four directions as the leader, holding a pinch of pollen from the tule, stood before the eastern cross.

Finally it was time for the people to approach the man conducting the ceremony. A male was supposed to alternate with a female as the lines moved gradually toward the south and into the center of "the church." One individual after another stepped forward and was blessed.

Sometimes Hosteen Arnold stood within the boundaries of the sacred rectangle, officiating. Other times he joined the cluster of singers and drummers who remained just outside it.

There were two drums: one male, one female. These consisted of round containers, usually gallon-size house paint cans, emptied of pigment, their open end covered with taut buckskin. Inside each drum were ashes and charcoal mixed with water. When someone shook the can, that mixture soaked through the buckskin. It emitted a special sound when the drummer began beating with his stick.

Narcissus's thoughts wandered. She had watched Old Man Arnold and other members of the religion prepare such a drum. In the female drum they placed a piece of white shell representing White-Painted-Woman; in the male drum they put turquoise for Yusen, the Life Giver,[12] whom members now called "Jesus." There were special prayers and blessings with pollen before the drum was completed. Arnold did not beat out rhythms during church services. He had special responsibilities then. He was one of Silas's faithful "leaders." Narcissus was proud to see her grandfather in such a light.

It was Easter, the day on which Jesus was resurrected. There was to be a special service at the Holy Grounds. Just before they left home, Beshád-e repeated instructions to the children. "When you pray, you should call Him 'Jesus.' Silas says we should say, 'Jesus' not 'Yusen.' " Narcissus nodded. But she thought to herself, "But you don't do that! I've heard you praying when it really matters, and you say 'Yusen.' "

Easter day was glorious. Narcissus wore a new red crepe dress. The beltline was low and fashionable. Beshád-e had purchased white shoes and socks to complete the stylish effect.

"Will they use the hoops today?" Narcissus asked.

"Probably." And they did.

The hoop, similar to those used by Plains Indians in their dances, was about the size of a Hula-Hoop. At each quarter point around its circumference were tied sacred objects: tail feathers of the eagle, pieces of turquoise, and white shell or wampum in the form of beads.

When it came time for Narcissus to leave the long queue of those waiting to be blessed, she approached the center of the Holy Grounds. Jake Cojo was officiating. He lifted the hoop high over the small girl's head, then slowly lowered it to her feet, praying and blessing her as he did so, keeping her free from illness and safe from the power of witches. Narcissus stepped from the hoop, feeling secure and happy. She swished her red skirt.

Later, when there was dancing, she stood with the women. She remained in one place, her feet treading the dance steps lightly, her dress brilliant in the midday sun.

When they returned home, she asked Old Man Arnold, "Why do we all go to the Four Cross now instead of the Dutch Reformed service?"

"It is better for Apaches. Since the Jews crucified Jesus, the Apaches have become God's favored people. That is what Silas has said.

"I still have my power against the ghosts, against witches, but it is better now. The medicine men in the old time taught anyone who wanted to learn that all power was dangerous. If you slipped in any way in your observances, you might lose your life. That is why Silas's way, the Jesus road, is better."

"If it is so good, why do you always tell me I must not talk about Silas's Church? Why must it be hush-hush?"

Beshád-e broke in, "Because there are lots of enemies to the church right here in Mescalero, and they will make trouble with the tribe and government. They will try to stop us. There are people like Dan Nicholas, Asa Daklugie, Shantaboy, and a lot of others. The Christian ministers and priests don't like what Silas John teaches. You must never talk about the Four Cross to anyone but us. If anyone questions you, you tell them you belong to the Dutch Reformed."

Narcissus was obedient. She did not reveal the family association with this religion until very recently.

The child loved the outings in Head Springs. Many people came from time to time: Jake and Catherine Cojo, Lip Nata—or Neda—who was a San Carlos Apache, Old Lady Chatto and her kin, Charlie Istee and his family, Charles Belin, Elmer Wilson, with whom Silas had stayed, and Elmer's son Woodrow, and their womenfolk. Sometimes there were James and Frank Lapaz, Jewett Tissnolthis, Philemon Venego, Ernest Bigmouth, Joseph Caje, Rufus Lester, Christian Naiche and their wives and children. Attendance depended in large measure on who and how many members were camping near Agency.

Each Sunday by the time the Kinzhumas arrived at the meeting place in Head Springs Canyon, preparations were well under way. Certain individuals had been designated to go early. They built a fire next to the sweat bath wickiups. They piled smooth rocks on top of the fire and kept adding fuel as needed. The sweat bath structures were smaller than dwelling wickiups and differed further in that they had no smoke hole. The framework was made of oak brush covered with canvas. A long flap of canvas served as a door.

As each family drove into the designated site, one and all scrambling out of their various vehicles, the men stripped to their breechcloths. The hot rocks were carried into the wickiup and dropped into a shallow pit, which had been dug into the ground at its center. Then came the tricky job. Narcissus and Wendell were warned, "Don't get in the way! Don't bother those men!"

The steam-makers manipulated the red-hot stones very carefully, using two straight and sturdy oak limbs as though they were giant chopsticks. The branches were tied together close to their "handle" ends. The other extremity of each pole consisted of forklike prongs. Narcissus counted, "One—two—three—four—five—six." Six stones were deemed sufficient. The sweat bath was ready for occupancy.

Several men entered the cleansing wickiup together. Only older men, such as Old Man Arnold, went in. A bucket of water and a drum were all they needed. The canvas door was closed. The men threw water on the rocks, and a dense cloud of purifying steam enveloped them.

Outside the wickiup Wendell and Narcissus awaited the sound of the drums. It was not long before the powerful beat began, as did the songs.

The steam bathing took a long time. One group of men followed another, and as the hours progressed, the musical repertoire was varied. The canyon rang with songs of missing loved ones, songs of love and romance. The womenfolk and children sat around, sharing the latest gossip. The youngest among them played in the meadow and among the trees. They listened to the melodies. They were beautiful, nostalgic.

Each family had brought food. The women built several cooking fires. When the male disciples were suitably cleansed, their wives began to make fry bread or tortillas. There was fresh beef, sometimes soup, and coffee. All afternoon the members of the Four Cross Church enjoyed being with one another. Each person proudly wore a special badge, a cross, designating his or her membership in the cult.

Narcissus cherished her cross. It kept her safe from evil. "Don't put it in your pocket," Beshád-e instructed. She had attached a strap to the cross for her granddaughter. "Just pin that strap and the cross on your underclothes, on the left side, right over your heart."

It was a small cross fashioned from the yellow inner wood of a bush that looked much like holly. It was about one and one-half by one and one-half inches in size. Each arm of the talisman bore a similar motif. The outer edge was scalloped with four indentations. Just above these, a horizontal line was carved. Perpendicular to this were four lines, bent in their center in a counterclockwise manner so as to suggest "bent knees." The carving stopped at the inner end of the arm, leaving a square without decoration. In the center of this square was a hole through which passed a narrow lace of buckskin, a small, fluffy eagle feather, and a bit of white shell, all held securely in place with sinew. Wendell's cross had turquoise rather than shell, for he was male.

Adult Apaches attached to the cross a tiny buckskin bag containing four items that were "good medicines," such as tule pollen, lightning-riven twigs ground to powder, or even a bit of a sandpainting made at San Carlos by Silas John himself.

The day that Narcissus received her cross had been a special ritual occasion. First the leader had taken a pinch of pollen. With this he marked a cross, the yellow coursing along the arms of the wooden badge. Then the leader held the cross above Narcissus's head, making four sunwise circles in the air. Before fastening it to her dress, he held it to her, once, twice, three times, and finally on the fourth gesture, he completed the ceremony, saying, "Wear it proudly. If witches know you have it, they will be afraid."[13]

Later Old Man Arnold explained, "This is like a membership button. You wear it all the time. Jesus put His power in the cross. When you wear it, lightning will not bother you because God makes the rain and the lightning. It has *most* power against witches. They are scared because its power is greater than theirs. If someone tries to witch you now that you are the owner of this cross, that white bead will crack! That bead will crack, and as it cracks, the witch will be killed! So you wear it always, Narcissus."

After a long silence, Hosteen Arnold spoke again, "When the end of the world comes, the men and women who have that cross will belong to God and Jesus. He will take them to heaven. But all the people who have no cross, who try to stop us on the Holy Ground, they will go in the fire."[14]

A year or so later Narcissus had to stay in the hospital for some minor ailment. The nurse said, "Get undressed and put this gown on. I'll come back and help you get into bed." The patient did partly as she was told, but she did not take off the strap and cross. The nurse was annoyed and tried to remove it. Narcissus set up a howl. She was supposed to keep it on at all times. Beshád-e and Old Man Arnold had told her not to take it off. She yelled for her grandmother, and Beshád-e, waiting just down the hall, heard. She came to the child's rescue. Although the nurses succeeded in preventing Narcissus from wearing her cross during the hospital stay, they acquiesced to Beshád-e who took it home where its sacred, protective qualities remained uncontaminated by disbelief.

For many years Narcissus thought about the Four Cross cult which disintegrated gradually as an actual church. Only a few of the most faithful members kept their sacred paraphernalia. "But the prayers are so beautiful," Narcissus mused. They were almost exactly the same as the prayers said by the Christians at the Catholic and

Dutch Reformed Church. They addressed the Supreme Beings, God and Jesus. They were against the evil things on earth.

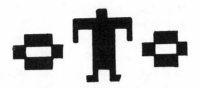

Teenage Trials

In 1936 Beshád-e and Hosteen Arnold were informed that they must move from White Tail to a new community about four miles below Agency, where all elderly Apaches were to be assigned housing. Here tribal and governmental officials could keep a closer eye on them, ostensibly to see that they had food and sufficient medical care. Narcissus was nearing twelve years of age when her family made the transfer to what was called, variously, Old People's Village, Squaw Town, Old Folks' or even Old Ladies' Town. The new four-room frame house was much like the one they had left.

Squaw Town is over 3,000 feet lower in altitude than White Tail. Although it was hot and dusty in the summer, winters were mild, with little snow. Stores, the post office, tribal business centers, and the hospital were readily available. Even so, Narcissus's grandparents often camped up on the Feast Ground where friends convened and business could be transacted even more conveniently. Sometimes the family had a car, sometimes not.

In Narcissus's world the important change was Beshád-e's decision to send her to the Indian Boarding School in Santa Fe.

How wonderful it would be! She could now experience the schooling her mother had painted so deliciously. Life would be modern, not this old-fashioned way of her grandmother! Many youngsters from the reservation, mostly those belonging to the Mescalero Tribe, attended the school in Santa Fe. Narcissus did not know the names of the majority of them. Her best friends were Henrietta Kazhe, who had lived in White Tail, and Aunt Marilyn, Little Grandmother Lillian's daughter.

The morning of departure finally arrived. The family arose early. Beshád-e had packed Narcissus's belongings the day before. At the last minute she gave her granddaughter some money, securing it in a handkerchief.

"Now don't lose this. It is all we can spare," she cautioned as she tied the kerchief tightly to the strap of the youngster's underslip. Then they went to the bus, just a regular school bus. In a few minutes the children were on their way.

The bus seemed to go so slowly. It took a whole day to get to Santa Fe. At noontime they were only at Socorro. Everyone left the vehicle, stretched, and walked over to a cafe for lunch. After the meal, Narcissus realized she needed money to pay for her food. She went to the restroom to untie her handkerchief.

Narcissus tried unknotting it. The intricate hitch remained firm. Again and again she tried to pry the knot apart, but without success. The only thing to do was to get help from Marilyn. Out she went. The two girls returned to the restroom, where they again wrestled in vain with Beshád-e's handiwork. The result of their efforts was a broken slipstrap, but the money was retrieved at last. How could my grandmother have done this to me! It is just so embarrassing! Narcissus felt that everyone in the cafe was staring at the strap dangling beneath her dress.

After what seemed endless hours, the bus arrived in Santa Fe and drove directly to the school. The campus was inviting, with spacious lawns and many trees. There were many students walking around, greeting each other after vacation. Some four hundred youngsters made up the student body. There were impressive buildings: dormitories, business offices, dining and classroom areas. It was cool and clean.

Narcissus was installed in the Junior Girls' Building. Soon she was informed of which courses she must take and which she could choose. In addition to class attendance and study, all students had to work to pay half their room and board.

Narcissus's assigned work was sometimes in the kitchen, other times in the dining room. A kitchen worker must check in every morning by 6 A.M. and then serve breakfast. That was not too bad. On the other hand, a dining room worker waited on the tables at both noon and dinnertime. Because meals were always "family style," food was arranged on large platters or piled into bowls placed centrally on the tables. This completed, the waitresses stood in a row where they could watch to see if everything were satisfactory. If a diner wanted a second serving of meat, or if a dish were empty of something desired, he raised his hand. One of the waitresses removed the empty receptacle, took it to the kitchen to be refilled, and then returned it to the table. Narcissus hated being a waitress. "All you do is just *wait* in order to serve everybody. You just run back and forth," she thought.

Saturday was the worst day of the week. The boys who were dining room workers piled all the chairs on the top of the tables. Then the girls mopped and waxed the floor. The job took forever and cancelled the joy of school.

Despite her initial delight in being sent to Santa Fe, Narcissus managed somehow to start on the wrong foot. After she had been in attendance for three or four weeks, there was a fire drill. She had been forewarned. The teacher had said, "Grab a blanket from your bed and slide down the fire escape as quickly as you can."

Narcissus's bed was on a large sleeping porch along with several other girls. The fire gong sounded. The youngsters rushed into action. The moment they hit the ground outside, they formed a line as they had been instructed. The teachers started counting heads. Four girls were missing. All were from the Mescalero Reservation.

The matron looked indignant. She marched over to Narcissus.

"I want you to give me the names of the missing girls," she said. The child was bewildered. What was the matron talking about? What girls? She had no idea who they were.

"I don't know their names," she said timidly.

But that was not the end of the matter.

Narcissus and her classmates returned to bed. No sooner had she become comfortable, than the matron was standing beside her cot. Narcissus was frightened. She did not know what to think of the domineering white woman.

"You get up, Narcissus. I want you to come down to my office. I need to question you some more."

On the way to the office the girl's mind raced. What should she do? Then she remembered some advice that Beshád-e had given her before she left the reservation. She had told her granddaughter that no matter how unhappy she was, she must not run away from the school. Beshád-e had said, "This was your idea to go to school at Santa Fe. So when you get over there, you stay there." She had warned, "If you run away, you don't know where you are going to sleep and where you are going to eat."

So *that* is what had happened! It suddenly dawned on her. The missing girls must have been unhappy at school. Indians from many tribes found the confinement and regime intolerable. These girls had run away! They had taken off during the confusion of the fire drill.

"Now, I want you to give me the names of those missing girls.

They are from your reservation. I need to know who they are."
She assumed, incorrectly of course, that Narcissus knew everyone
from Mescalero. She was unaware of the general isolation of the
Chiricahuas.

"But I really *don't* know!" The interrogation went on and on. As
the matron's insistence continued, Narcissus feared she would break
down in tears. Finally she thought of a solution, a way to make the
woman stop.

"Why don't you call Henrietta Kazhe? Henrietta will tell you I
really don't know the names of those girls. Please call her."

Henrietta had been attending Santa Fe for several years. When she
entered the matron's office, Narcissus's relief was plainly visible. The
white woman finally understood and permitted the girls to leave and
go to bed.

That incident was not usual, fortunately. Most of the time Narcissus was happy. She was placed in seventh grade and enjoyed all her
studying, even the required and recommended subjects such as English, algebra, history, and science. But it was the electives that gave
her most pleasure. She had a choice of music, photography, sewing,
many kinds of physical education—even tennis. Her greatest interest
proved to be in the arts and crafts.

Narcissus learned to make pottery the way the Pueblos do, shap-
ing the clay and using dried cow manure in the firing. She wove on
wide looms that made cloth forty-five inches across. She created narrow belts on small table looms. She embroidered in cross stitch to
embellish pillow tops, the edges of drapes, table runners, and lun-
cheon sets. She made a billfold with a Crown Dancer on it and gave
it to her Uncle Edmond Simmons, who proudly displayed it when
he visited the reservation. When it came time to do beadwork, it was
really a review, for her mother Christine had shown her how, many
long years ago. The school children were permitted to sell their
handiwork, reciving a small percentage of the profits. Narcissus
earned two dollars one year when she made Christmas cards.

Miss Morgan was her English teacher one year. She was strict, but
Narcissus truly liked her. Whenever Miss Morgan caught someone
chewing gum in her classroom, she made him sign the blackboard,
remove the gum, and stick it by the name. There was one boy who
loved gum and chewed it constantly. It was a simple matter to locate
him, any time at all. You could hear the "Pop! Pop! Pop!" of that
gum. It sounded like a *huge* wad. Then, to everyone's surprise, when
he stuck it to the blackboard, it was just a skinny, miserable, *little* piece.

Realizing that English was not spoken in most of her pupils' homes, Miss Morgan stressed speech. She tried to make them talk precisely, to say *exactly* what they meant. For instance, when a student needed to write something down, he might go to her desk and say, "Please give me a piece of paper." She handed him a newspaper. The student, disgusted, once again said, "I don't want a newspaper. I just want a *piece* of paper." Miss Morgan continued to give him the newspaper until he asked for "writing paper." Then, and only then, was his request granted.

In Santa Fe there was considerable homework. Study periods were scheduled in the evening from 7 to 8:30. Lights were out by 9 P.M. Unfortunately, Narcissus could rarely complete her assignments in that limited time. So, she and some of the other girls worked by flashlight, piling pillows and blankets in front of their doors in order to mask the light. Thus they continued to study long after curfew.

Although Sunday afternoon was set aside for recreation, that, too, was often spent in "cramming" for examinations or in doing the endless laundry. More enjoyable activities consisted of the 4-H Club, the Boy Scouts, and the Girl Scouts. Narcissus participated in the latter just as she had while attending boarding school at Mescalero and day school at White Tail. Scout leaders arranged for many leisure activities and outings. Sometimes they scheduled hikes. Once the students went to Dallas, Texas, to visit the zoo and perform some Indian dances.

Narcissus was not happy about the dancing. She was among those in the Eagle Dance. The costume provided her consisted in part of very short shorts. "No Apache girl should have to dress like that," she thought. "We are supposed to be modest." She felt undressed and self-conscious. A trip to Denver, Colorado, was more to her liking. There were visits to a big library and the capitol building.

Other diversions consisted of Saturday night dances with music provided by the school orchestra. Narcissus dreaded these affairs, but some of the girls from other tribes could hardly wait to go. Narcissus preferred to watch basketball, football, and baseball games where there was keen competition with the athletes of other schools in the vicinity. Physical activity on her own part, aside from the classes in physical education, consisted primarily of tennis and roller-skating.

Narcissus developed considerable skill in tennis, playing with her three best friends, Berdian Sombrero and Alvina Spear, from Mescalero, and Elsie Beyal, a Navajo. Berdian was Narcissus's roommate at one time. They became fast friends, remaining close even during vacations in Squaw Town. When school was in session the four girls challenged everyone who came by the tennis courts.

The roller-skating took place in the "family room" located in the basement of the school. A piano provided an opportunity to hear and play music. All kinds of games were permitted in that large room, but it was the freedom she felt in skating that Narcissus relished most. Sometimes this exercise was allowed in the gymnasium—but only on Sunday afternoons.

One year there was a big homecoming celebration. A queen was chosen, and the entire town turned out to watch the parade along the downtown streets. Then there were the movies. Narcissus saw her first film in Santa Fe. This was a good place to be. Nonetheless, the young girl sometimes suffered. She was homesick. Visitors and packages from home were *so* welcome.

Sometimes Beshád-e sent piñons, dried meat, fry bread, or an occasional baked sweet potato. Oh, how Narcissus had missed those flavors. More than once she and Berdian shared the feast.

The moment the package from home arrived, Narcissus and Berdian grabbed it and dashed down the stairs and into a shower stall. Once inside they sat on stools in the corner of the cubicle, their feet planted firmly, high on the opposite wall. That was a necessary precaution. If a teacher or other checker came to inspect the stalls, to see if any students were avoiding supper in the dining room, she could not see the girls' feet by looking under the compartment dividers. The school was strict about eating meals, on being sure no one had run away, that no one was ill. When Narcissus and Berdian were comfortably installed, they tore into the food Beshád-e had sent, devouring every crumb, feeling great.

Once in a while Narcissus examined her clothing. It did not seem as new, as fashionable, as the skirts, blouses, and dresses that most of the students wore. Further, she had only a few garments in the dresser drawers and in the closets. Those of most girls were full. She deplored the fact that she had no money, that she could not go into town and buy things for herself. Henrietta Kazhe had a solution.

"Why don't you shop from a catalog? You don't have to send any money. Just write down the things that you want and send the list to your grandmother. She can do the actual ordering, and you'll get what you want. That's what I do."

Narcissus found the idea promising and began scanning the catalog pages at once. When Beshád-e received the list, she asked the woman at the post office to make out a money order and she sent the payment with the list of clothes to the mail-order store. Often it took months for the items to arrive at Santa Fe, and sometimes the store mailed things to Mescalero because the payment was postmarked there. It seemed such foolish confusion. But eventually Narcissus received what she wanted. She matched the student stereotype.

One day she received a letter from Besháde. It was written by Aunt Evelyn because Narcissus's grandmother never learned to read or write.

The letter said, "Please, Narcissus, do not request too many things for me to order for you. We are having a hard time making our money stretch." The poignant letter must have been difficult for the generous grandmother to send. She hated depriving the children. She should have communicated with Narcissus earlier, but it was hard to find anyone to serve as scribe.

As Narcissus read, her heart grew heavy. Her insides ached. She understood the problems. "My poor old grandmother is way over there by herself and has nobody to write a letter for her or to help her the way I used to," she thought. "I'll bet the ones who write for her don't tell me all the news. I'll bet they leave out things my grandmother tells them to include."

In the next letter Besháde sent Narcissus some money. The girl ran downstairs to the shower stall and burst into tears. "When I grow up, if my grandmother is still living, I will do all those things for her—the things she can't do by herself," she thought.

This was the beginning of Narcissus's more mature sense of responsibility. She realized how tough it was for old people on reservations, people who were too feeble to have jobs and increase their incomes. She began to understand the true value of education.

Just before the summer recess Narcissus wrote to Besháde, telling her the date of arrival in Mescalero. The old woman cleaned her house so everything would be spotless for her granddaughter. Then, when Narcissus finally came, when she opened the door, there was Besháde sitting on a chair, waiting. As lanky as she was, the girl ran to her grandmother, hugged her, draped herself in the old woman's lap. They talked and talked and talked.

Unfortunately, Narcissus's cooperation and loving attitude lasted only a few weeks.

Besháde was so strict. Other girls had freedom to do what they wanted. "My grandmother is just so old-fashioned, it makes me sick!" Narcissus stewed. "Golly, some of these young people have their mother and their father. They seem so modern. Here we are, Wendell and me, with our grandmother. It seems like we are not up-to-date. We're just *old Indians*," she thought. It was embarrassing.

For example, at the time of the Puberty Feast in July all the young people stay up late at night, remaining on the Feast Ground or in tents of camping friends almost the entire night. Everyone can do it. It's expected. But Beshád-e! Oh, no. When Narcissus stayed out late so as to take part in the social dancing—the slow and fast Round Dance, and the Back-and-Forth Dance—which began between about II P.M. and midnight, right after the Crown Dancers retired for the night, then grandmother tracked her down. "You get to bed! It's time for you to be in bed!" That old lady spoiled everything.

One of Narcissus's favorite parts of the Feast occurred on the last night of the celebration. Friends danced together all night long, then lingered to listen to the "morning song." As soon as the morning star came out, the men lined up in one column, the women in another. Everyone, even the singers, continued to dance back and forth until it was daybreak. It was so wonderful.

It was then that the families whose daughters were honored maidens came forth. They gave every woman dancer four yards of dress material; every male received a neckerchief, cigarettes, or socks. Then, exhausted, all participants retired.

If Narcissus chose to remain with a girl friend, she could count on Beshád-e's snooping and searching. The Old Lady brought her lantern and pried into every tent and wickiup and arbor on the Feast Ground. She even looked under blankets to see if Narcissus might be there. "She just doesn't trust me! She expects to find me with a boy!" fumed Narcissus. "I can't do anything like the other girls do."

The summer was a quiet one. Berdian Sombrero, Narcissus, and sometimes Alvina Spear spent as much time as possible together, just strolling around, talking, watching for other groups of girls—or boys. Sometimes they went into the hills, searching for big knots of red pitch on piñon trees. This same kind of pitch had long ago been gathered in a bucket by Dilth-cleyhen. She had heated it until it became liquid. Thereupon, she coated her closely twined water jug baskets with it, thus rendering them completely waterproof. Narcissus and her friends never gathered very much. All they wanted was enough to serve as chewing gum, a tasteless gum to be sure, but it was the reddish color of Dentyne, and provided something to do.

On Sunday the three girls attended the II A.M. service at the Dutch Reformed Church. After Silas John's death no one used the Four Cross Holy Grounds, and only a few old people continued to practice the cult's rituals in private. But Beshád-e insisted still on Narcissus's going to church. Each one of the trio took a sandwich, an orange, or an apple so that she could have a picnic lunch. As soon as the meeting was over, they walked behind the Catholic Church, over to East Mountain, and then began hiking up its slopes. They could see the entire valley. It was so peaceful. They enjoyed lunch, then just sat, talked, and looked over the vistas. By one or two o'clock they started down, ambling along, sharing confidences. Even Beshád-e did not disapprove.

When vacation was nearing its end, Narcissus looked at her wardrobe. "I just don't have anything decent to wear," she thought.

"Shi-choo, when can we go shopping? I need a sweater, a skirt, and some blouses for school," she commented to Beshád-e.

She did not expect her grandmother's reaction.

"Narcissus, you want too much! All the time you are asking for something. You are never satisfied!" Then began a tirade of preaching.

"You are using up all the money, and you are *just a woman!* All you will be good for is to be a housewife and have children. We are more interested in your *brother.* We want to do whatever we can for him! He will be a *man!* He will be a provider. He is the one who needs an education. He is the one who must be taught a lot of things. You, Narcissus, you just want to be dominating!"

Narcissus was shocked. What did her grandmother mean? What was she implying? Apache women had always been as important as the men!

Narcissus rebelled; she refused to return to school in Santa Fe.

Beshád-e was disappointed. Always she had preached in favor of good education. She had felt that the schooling received in Santa Fe was superior to that on the reservation. However, there was little she could do to change her granddaughter's mind: Narcissus was set on remaining in Mescalero during her eighth grade. "I want you to study hard, go to every class. Don't be tardy. You must learn everything about the white man's ways." Narcissus shrugged. She was sick of the scolding, the preaching.

Much of the dissension between Beshád-e and Narcissus had to do with family finances. They were very poor. They had no car, just as they had had none in the last months at White Tail. When they wanted to go somewhere, they had to hitchhike. They spent many a long hour at the roadside before someone picked them up.

The Kinzhumas' sole income was derived from Old Man Arnold's pensions and checks issued to Narcissus and Wendell. This was the youngsters' "cattle money."

Christine, their mother, had owned cattle. After she died, state law decreed that their father Tom should inherit ownership and the profits from all sales. However, he had decided to marry once again. He gave half the cattle to Narcissus and half to Wendell. As a result, each of them received bimonthly payments amounting to forty or fifty dollars per month for a long period of time. The total family income was sufficient for necessities but nothing more.

Problems emerged because of emergencies—not within the four-member household, but because the extended kin group kept making demands. Whoever had need turned to Beshád-e, the eldest matriarch. She never refused if she had a cent to her name.

Narcissus brooded. "If I didn't have to help buy so many things for all those other kids, maybe I could have something for myself. I'm just poor because I live here with my grandmother," she complained.

When the children's cattle checks arrived on the first and fifteenth of each month, Wendell signed his promptly and gave it to Beshád-e. Narcissus had always done the same, but now she reconsidered. Why should she just give it all away?

She recalled the time her grandmother had used the check made out to Narcissus to buy shoes for some of her cousins. As soon as the money was gone, the sole of one of Narcissus's shoes became torn. A hole developed. Resourcefully, the child found a piece of cardboard and stuffed it between her foot and the sole. For a while the mend helped, but then the whole thing deteriorated and the sole flapped back and forth.

All week Narcissus was embarrassed to attend classes that way, just like trash. She eyed her cousins' new footwear. It's not fair. They spent *my* check! It was small consolation that the next payment was used to buy her a shiny pair. It was still unfair.

Beshád-e tried to explain, "We must always help our relatives when they need something. We never know when we will be the ones who need assistance."

That philosophy was understandable; Narcissus had heard it since she was baby, but now she found it totally unacceptable. She began to guard her funds, being "cagey," almost stingy.

"They are not going to get my whole check at once," she decided.

A payment arrived. Wendell signed his and handed it to Beshád-e, who said, "Narcissus, you better bring me your check, too." Narcissus had hers, but she refused to turn it over. Her grandmother and Old Man Arnold began to hunt. They looked everywhere. They ransacked all Narcissus's belongings, looking in every pocket, under her pillow, every spot they could think of. No success. The girl had found a safe hiding place.

At that time there was no dresser in the children's room. All they had was a table on which Narcissus kept her school books and Bible. There was also a dictionary. That was the one. It held the money. Beshád-e had no thought of looking in books. The strategy had worked and Narcissus continued to use it. Sometimes the poor old people hunted for over a week. It was only when truly they did not have a dime that Narcissus relented, retrieving the check secretly and handing it over. Beshád-e looked half angry, but she took it every time.

Another time dissension arose because of Narcissus's leisure time activities. Beshád-e considered them improper.

"You are not very old. I don't want you getting into any trouble. You are thirteen, and you could get in *serious* trouble. I want you home at night where I can keep my eye on you."

When the weather was good, many teenage girls in Mescalero sauntered about the reservation at night, not having any particular destination or planned recreation in mind. They "fooled around," talked with boys, giggled, and gossiped. Mostly they walked in groups along the roads, arm in arm, enjoying themselves.

"That is just not right! An Apache girl should be modest, virtuous, and give nobody the wrong impression. You have no business running around." This was the scolding Narcissus received almost every night. It did little to detain her from her favorite walk from Squaw Town to Agency and back.

In her own room, her anger mounted as she thought about it. "Those old-fashioned folks! They think it's practically a sin even to speak to a boy." In fact, Narcissus's teenage years were innocent of wrongdoing. But how could Beshád-e know?

As Narcissus's involvement with her peer group increased—and her interest in boys—her pleasure in classroom learning declined rapidly. She began to play hooky. Beshád-e had specifically directed her against this.

When her grandmother learned of the truancy, she was more than upset, she was *furious*. She berated Narcissus about her midnight escapades and running around, about her avoiding classes and general disregard of everything she had been taught.

"It's a good thing I didn't have a Feast for *you!*" she said to Narcissus.

Those words truly bothered her granddaughter. It sounded as though the girl was not fit for a Feast.

The matter of the Puberty Feast had already caused a wound deep within Narcissus. Beshád-e had had her measured for the buckskin, but for some reason—undoubtedly money—nothing further had transpired.

The omission now brought tears to the young girl's eyes. Beshád-e had given a Feast for Lavera, Susie's daughter. To be sure, her grandmother had by then so little money that she could not afford to buy enough food and gifts for a big four-day Feast, so Lavera had had to get along with just the upper part of the dress. The Feast had lasted only one day. But it was a Feast.

Further, Beshád-e was already beginning to store some of the ceremonial foods and sacred items that would be required for a Feast for Imogene, Little Grandmother Lillian's daughter. They were up in the attic of the house.

When Beshád-e mentioned Imogene's celebration, she emphasized certain qualities: "Imogene is so timid and shy. She needs someone to honor her. She will be a beautiful White-Painted-Woman. This Feast is partly for her, and partly for her mother. We'll have it next summer."

Narcissus did not deny Imogene's obedience and propriety. Nonetheless, what seemed obvious favoritism on her grandmother's part was a stab within her heart. How could Narcissus guess that Imogene's Feast would never come about?

Then, too, her grandparents' drinking rankled. If they had a cent of money after groceries were purchased, they spent it on liquor— not just brewing up some tulapai and sharing it with friends, all becoming happy-drunk, but on hard alcohol. They kept coaxing someone to drive them to Tularosa or a bar. Then the whole carload got drunk. It disgusted Narcissus; it worried her. Then came the climax.

The family was camping at the Feast Ground for a day or so. They chose a site directly below Tom Duffy's house, next to the highway that goes toward the Mescalero Community Center. Beshád-e and Old Man Arnold drank and scolded every minute of their waking hours. It was too much!

Narcissus walked over to the Bureau of Indian Affairs. She talked to the superintendent, telling him her guardians were always drunk. Apparently, he talked to Tom.

In just a few hours Narcissus's father came for her and Wendell, taking them into his own household. By then, he and his new wife had had a couple of children. The crowded home was not very pleasant for Narcissus, who felt that only her father welcomed her presence. She was told she had no choice. She must live with her stepmother for at least a short time.

She sat in Tom's arbor, peeping toward Beshád-e's camp. She saw

Old Man Arnold walking on the path. "Oh, how I wish I were down there!" The abiding love she had for her grandmother surfaced—and remained.

Actually, many pleasant memories lingered from that year in Mescalero. Especially poignant were the stories of the warpath and imprisonment days. During the winter months Narcissus and Wendell went to bed very early. About 8 or 9 P.M., one or two friends arrived to chat with Beshád-e and Old Man Arnold. They drank coffee and sometimes pulled out a drum and sang. Very rarely they poured some tulapai into a bucket and drank the mild brew from a common dipper.

On such occasions Narcissus tiptoed to the door, making sure it was slightly ajar. Soft snores came from Wendell. The youngsters slept in the same room, Narcissus's bed being catty-corner from the doorway. For hours she lay there, listening.

"That old General Crook was really a good man. We should have listened to him. He never lied to us."

"That Geronimo killed all our young men. He caused us to be imprisoned."

Among the most frequent visitors were Rogers To-clanny and his wife, now Squaw Town neighbors. He came in gentlemanly style, wearing his dark suit jacket and the medal he had earned as an Apache Scout. Old Lady Chatto, another neighbor and a distant aunt of Tom Duffy, brought her deceased husband's medal, the one awarded by the president of the United States. Occasionally she brought one of her exquisite baskets, for she was one of the finest workers in this craft. She loved to sing, and when she was present, everyone sang war songs.

The tall, white-haired Dash-den-zhoes, Lena Morgan's mother, brought her drawstring "smoking bag" with its Bull Durham tobacco. At that time it was proper for old folks—but not young ones—to use tobacco. All the guests and Narcissus's grandparents rolled their own, lit up, and held their cigarettes beneath their cupped fingers while they visited.

Then there was the short, fat Duncan Balatche who was paralyzed on the left side. His wife Hannah had died. He cared for their sons, Walter and Orlin, and they came along, too. When it grew very late, Beshád-e made a bed for the boys under the table.

Grandpa Charlie Istee and his wife, Dora, usually arrived early. Dora addressed Narcissus and Wendell. "You go over there and speak to your grandfather." It was always like that whenever she met

Beshád-e's wards. Even when her own children were almost grown, she called them, "Baby."

The stories those old people told were an education. After one evening, when a tale had been told of flight before a troop of army soldiers, Narcissus asked Old Man Arnold, "Did they shoot at you?"

"Indeed they did." Beshád-e was shampooing his hair for him. He grabbed a towel and rubbed it over his head.

"You come over here, Narcissus. Look right there on my scalp. See the scars? Those are the result of that battle." Nothing could have been more impressive.

New Year's Eve was perhaps the most exciting night of that entire year. Old Man Arnold sat waiting for 12 A.M. He and Beshád-e drank a little, but not too much. He held his rifle, anticipating. Suddenly bells rang from the church steeples. People in their cars honked horns madly. Yells sounded from every house. It was midnight.

Arnold went outside. He lifted his rifle to the stars and shot three times. In those years houses were not wired for electricity, and the Kinzhumas burned only kerosene lamps, so the house was fairly dark. Narcissus peered out the window. She saw the Old Man's silhouette as he stood in the dark, aiming straight up. Fire sparked at each gunshot. The new year was born.

1940—1942

The fall of 1940 Narcissus returned to Santa Fe Boarding School. Her stay at home had given her time to think about her life. She settled down, studied, and took part in many social and political activities.

She changed dormitories, moving to the Senior Girls' Building, which housed juniors and seniors. Three girls shared one room. Berdian was one of Narcissus's roommates, and Alvina was nearby. Again the trio enjoyed close companionship.

Narcissus kept busy. At one time she was in charge of the athletic program for the student body, having the title "Athletic Commissioner." Later she was "Representative for the Mescalero Apaches" and attended all Student Council meetings, at which many school policies were established. The position entitled her to special privileges. She was assigned a room for two, with a private bath, and shared that good fortune with Alvina.

Narcissus was determined to make Beshád-e proud of her, to be the kind of daughter Christine would have loved.

The years 1940 to 1942 were war years—World War II. Many young men from Mescalero had enlisted, joining the ranks of the United States Army or Navy to serve their country. Often they were "backward" and somewhat bashful. Nonetheless, not knowing whether they would return from battle, they made a point of visiting the pupils at Santa Fe, even when they had no kin in attendance. They sought the company of anyone from the reservation.

The military men were classified by the matron as "special visitors." The students were permitted to entertain them in the spacious living room, with its couches and comfortable chairs. The men were handsome warriors, proud of their uniforms. Their presence in the school was sobering.

Narcissus was sixteen years old when Beshád-e and Old Man Arnold were killed in the automobile accident.

The accident occurred on April 15, 1941; Narcissus learned of it on the seventeenth. School had just started. A messenger came to the classroom and spoke to the teacher. "Narcissus, you are wanted in the principal's office."

There was a sick feeling in Narcissus's stomach.

The principal greeted her, and as soon as they were alone, the woman began, "One of your relatives was hurt badly. They want you to come home."

The principal continued, "The daily milk truck leaves at ten, and you must be on it. You run to your room and get a few things together. I've told your cousin—Ringlin Martine—and the two of you get on that truck. The driver will drop you off in Albuquerque, and someone will come for you there."

Narcissus rushed to her room and put a few things in a little bag. She and Ringlin, who had been at the Santa Fe school for a year or so, boarded the milk truck and eventually reached their destination. There they were joined by Marcelline and Lavera, who attended Albuquerque Indian School.

"What is wrong, Narcissus? Who was hurt?"

No one knew anything.

The four young people sat on the lawn, apprehensive, talking softly.

About two in the afternoon the matron of the school came out.

"Narcissus, your father will arrive for all of you about five o'clock."

It was later than that when Tom Duffy and George Martine came. The men ignored the children's inquiries. All four youngsters sat in the back seat. Tom Duffy drove, and George sat beside him.

It is a long drive to Mescalero. Tom got sleepy. Twice Narcissus yelled at him when it seemed he was about to run off the road.

Finally they reached the reservation. First Tom deposited Marcelline and Lavera at their mother's. When he took Narcissus to her Aunt Evelyn's, it was after midnight. He and Ringlin stayed as well. Tom did not go home to his wife. Everyone was exhausted and went to bed. As yet, no one had told Narcissus the news.[15]

Early the next morning, before breakfast, Evelyn called Narcissus into the kitchen. Tom was there, but he uttered no word.

Evelyn said, "Narcissus, you have to know. There was an accident in the car. Those old folks that took care of you, they are dead."

Narcissus felt the world had come to an end.

Her father left the house, going home to talk to his wife. Soon he returned, remaining with his daughter until she had to return to Santa Fe. There was much to do in the interim.

Beshád-e's house was cleaned and fumigated. Some of her belongings were tied in a blanket, and other things were wrapped in a shawl, both to be buried with her. Tribal records say that Beshád-e was seventy years old. She was older than that, but of course she had no birth certificate. She was placed in the same grave as her husband, Arnold, in the Mescalero cemetery.

Narcissus felt an incredible loneliness. She ached. She felt that nothing in the world was left to her. Beshád-e had been her mainstay.

Nonetheless, in a week or so the young lady returned to school, finished the term.

The summer immediately following Beshád-e's funeral had started as disaster for Narcissus. Without Aunt Evelyn, her life would have been intolerable.

In May 1941 a bus brought all the children who had gone to school in Santa Fe back to Mescalero, so that they could spend the summer with their families. The youngsters came on the first trip; the bus had to make a second journey in order to accommodate the bulky luggage. The driver was anxious to be on his way. He simply dumped the children.

Most of the young students laughed happily and ran to the sides of parents or relatives who were awaiting them. Narcissus looked around. Nobody was there for her.

She stood at the stop for a long time. The bus was gone. She and her little suitcase waited, waited for just *anyone* to come by. She knew not what to do, nor where to go. Finally a police car drove by.

"What are you still doing here?" the driver asked.

"Nobody came to meet me. Can you drive me to White Tail? I want to go to my Aunt Evelyn's, and she's moved up there."

"You're not supposed to go to Evelyn's. You're supposed to go to Elk and stay with your Aunt Susie. The court decided that's the place for you," the policeman said. "Get in. We'll take you."

There was nothing to do but follow his instructions.

It was another long drive to Elk Silver where Susie lived, far from other habitation. Narcissus felt depressed, almost paralyzed with dread. She and Susie had never been close. There had been such antagonism between Christine and Susie. It had always made Narcissus uncomfortable. And now!

For two long weeks she tolerated being there. Her brother Wendell lived now with Susie, but he did not seem to mind. In fact, he remained contentedly in Elk Silver until he went to Indian schools, first in Albuquerque and later in Phoenix. But Narcissus suffered.

One lonesome night she sat, looking out the window at the road. She could not sleep.

"This place is way out in the boondocks. I hate it."

Something deep inside told her she should pack her clothes. She rolled up her mattress, folded her bed, and put all her possessions in the suitcase. She returned to the window, watching. She knew not what she expected.

How long she waited, Narcissus no longer remembers. But, sure enough, eventually she saw car lights coming down the road. The vehicle turned into Susie's gateway. It was Evelyn. After a short talk with Susie, she loaded the young girl's belongings into the car and took her niece back to White Tail. Narcissus never returned to Elk Silver.

From then on, things were happier. Narcissus welcomed her aunt's preaching, which reminded her of her mother and Beshád-e.

Evelyn lectured to her and to Imogene, Evelyn's younger sister, saying, "You must get an education. I don't want you running around. I don't want you to drink. You just keep on going to school. I don't want you around here washing dishes and cleaning house for whites! You need to stay in school, finish school, so you learn to talk good English."

Evelyn warned the young girls about men, especially men who drink. "Just don't hang around where they are. Don't get involved."

Mostly, Narcissus and Imogene were discreet, and when the family camped at the Feast Ground for a few days, the girls were back in the tent at a reasonable hour. But sometimes they were later than Evelyn felt they should be. Just like Beshád-e, she went looking for them.

Evelyn worked as cook at the White Tail Grammar School, yet she did not hesitate when called upon to care for both Imogene and Narcissus. Further, she had her own small child, Ivora Lou, born in 1938. Narcissus had always loved the baby, pampering it, looking after its needs. Now there was ample opportunity for her to do so, thus relieving Evelyn, who often had a difficult time finding a good baby-sitter. Just anyone would not do. Evelyn would have preferred being at home, but she needed the job and had taken it shortly after Ivora Lou was born. Working for the school system permitted her to have vacation time with the girls.

Before Evelyn left for work, she gave detailed instructions about the young child's care.

"Give her a bottle. Bathe her. Then after you bathe her, put her right in her cradleboard. Just let her sleep there. Don't wake her up. She will awaken all by herself when she's ready."

Narcissus relished the task. As she had seen many mothers do, she placed the cradleboard across her legs, keeping her knees together. Then she swayed back and forth, right to left, left to right, rocking the little one. "*Ai-lo, ai-lo, ai-lo,*" she sang. It was a lullaby. There were no other words. It was a soft, restful tune. Now, of course, the child was older, but it was joy to be with her.

On Evelyn's day off, the woman and her charges climbed into the old Chevy. They drove to Mescalero to buy food. On the way back, Evelyn permitted Narcissus to take the wheel. These were her first driving lessons.

One time Narcissus was at home with Imogene and Ivora Lou. Evelyn and Abby Gaines, one of her cousins, left in the Chevy.

"We won't be too long. We're going to get some piñons." There are many such trees in the woods around White Tail. The nuts are delicious.

The women were not gone long before Narcissus heard the car chugging back toward the house. In walked Abby and Evelyn. They were carrying a twenty-five-pound flour sack, three-quarters full of pinenuts. It was tied at the top.

"We found a squirrel's nest right away. It was stocked real full with these piñons. We just robbed that poor old squirrel," Abby laughed.

Evelyn handed the bag to Narcissus, instructing, "Clean these nuts good because they are dirty. We'll go back and look for some more. Wash them good and then spread them on top of a canvas so they can dry." With that, Abby and Evelyn drove off once again.

A bewildered Narcissus stared at the nuts. She had no idea how to clean them. Beshád-e had always taken care of dirty piñons. Finally, the youngster filled a big pan with water. She added soap, stirring to make full, foaming suds. Then, batch by batch, she dumped in the kernels. She deposited the pan in a secluded corner of the bedroom, out of the way. She let the piñons soak, and soak, and soak.

A few days later Evelyn asked for the nuts. When she saw the soggy mess, she gasped, "What did you do! They are ruined. You put them in soap and just left them to rot! You were supposed to rinse them carefully, but not *soak* them!"

Evelyn put all the piñons in the oven to roast, hoping to salvage a few, but it was too late. The entire lot was garbage.

Evelyn was a kind, loving woman. She was the only person to whom Narcissus felt close. Sometimes the girl missed her father, Tom Duffy, but their relationship had changed since his remarriage in the mid 1930s.

When he first started seeing Josephine Ramirez, he had come to his daughter.

"Na-shi," he said, "I'm going to marry her. You will always be welcome in our home." Unfortunately, this was not the case. Josephine had had other children before Tom's, and she resented Narcissus and Wendell. She told Tom she did not like his children by Christine, that she did not want them in her house. Even when Tom merely talked to them, she chastised him. "They are a part of your past. We are the future. You shouldn't even write to those kids."

Tom continued to work at the Mescalero Hospital for a total of thirty-two years. That proved to be the only place where Narcissus and Wendell could visit and get needed advice from him. Tom took his daughter down into the basement where she confided in him. This occurred during the early years, shortly after her mother's death. Although Narcissus loved and admired her father, their chats became less frequent and less satisfying.

Much later, when Tom retired from the Indian Service, he took various jobs, one of which was to serve as cook at various cow camps. By this time Narcissus was an adult and married. She and her husband, Wheeler, visited Tom once in a while in the summertime. They phoned the Cattle Growers' Association office to locate his whereabouts, and then in the cool of the late afternoon or early evening, they drove to see him. Those were pleasant times. They watched him cook.

That summer of 1941, however, there was only Evelyn.

When Narcissus returned to Mescalero for short vacations from the boarding school at Santa Fe, Evelyn was there at the bus stop, waiting to welcome her niece. Every single time she was there, even when she had to walk. Narcissus adored her and came to rely on her.

Even so, Narcissus had problems.

Narcissus had to have money. She had to become independent. She feared asking her father. She knew his wife would deny any requests. Sometimes the young woman felt desperate, not knowing what to do.

During her senior year Narcissus had come to a major decision. After she graduated from Santa Fe, she would become a registered nurse.

Finding a Professional Niche

Narcissus's first thoughts about a career in nursing had been triggered by her Uncle Edmond Simmons, who had visited Beshád-e before and after Abner Kozine died. Edmond was the son of Anice, Abner's sister. Anice had had four children: Morton and Edmond Simmons, and Constance and Catherine, whose last names were Kenoi. Beshád-e had cared for the boys when they were small. Their father, Simmons, was a white man who had worked as a hospital corpsman when the Kozines had been imprisoned at Fort Sill. To Narcissus, Edmond and Morton were a bit awesome; they were so sophisticated! They had attended Chilocco and both had become successful in the Anglo world, never living long on any reservation. Edmond had joined the navy and was a worldwide traveler; Morton set up residence near Los Angeles. Here Narcissus pays him visits even yet.

These two men were responsible for Narcissus's thoughts about nursing. When she was very young, her Uncle Edmond talked to her about her future.

"You ought to be a nurse," he said. "Those navy nurses are really pretty. They are all lieutenants, junior grade." His words made a lasting impression. Narcissus watched the practical nurses working at the hospital in Santa Fe.

Evelyn contributed to Narcissus's decision in a less direct way. She, Beshád-e, and Christine had always urged the girl to do something constructive with her life. The church people, the Dutch Reformed missionaries, encouraged all the young Apaches to prepare themselves for useful occupations. Very few of the Indians graduated from high school at that time. Only a handful started professional schools or college training. They seemed to fear leaving the reservation and starting on their own. But Narcissus was not afraid.

She was further challenged when she remembered Beshád-e's hurting words: "You are just a woman. We need our money for your brother. All you will be is just a housewife!"

From then on, Narcissus was aware of this chauvinist attitude among her people. Previously, even when she was shocked by Beshád-e's words, she knew that women were the mainstay of the In-déh. Indeed, Virginia Klinekole was elected some years later as president of the Mescalero tribe and served one four-year term.

On many a night during her senior year in Santa Fe, Narcissus lay awake, thinking. She prayed to God, "Help me to be a nurse."

She talked to Alvina and Berdian. All three decided to apply for training at the Practical Nurses' School of the Kiowa Indian Hospital in Lawton, Oklahoma. It was run by the Bureau of Indian Affairs.

All three applications were accepted. "You are to report in Lawton one week after your graduation ceremony in Santa Fe," the letter read. That would be June 1, 1942.

Narcissus informed her family of the good news. Everyone approved. Her father signed the necessary papers. She packed her belongings and went to Oklahoma.

Studies went well. Just before she was to receive her diploma, after the nine-month course had been completed successfully, Narcissus ran into a problem. One of the requirements for acceptance at Lawton was that the applicant be eighteen years of age. Narcissus was seventeen—so she lied.

She did not dream they would check, but they did. They sent for each student's birth certificate and these had now been received. The director of the school sent for Narcissus.

"Miss Duffy, how old are you?" she asked.

"Eighteen."

"Did you know that you are only seventeen years old? You won't

be eighteen until October. This school does not accept students under eighteen."

"I know that."

The director immediately showed her anger. "I guess that you
know you are creating a lot of disturbance!"

"What kind of disturbance?" Narcissus asked.

"You can't be employed in a hospital when you are only seventeen
years old. To be a regular employee, somebody has to be responsible
for you. Somebody has to sign for you." Narcissus did not know
what to think or how to respond.

Finally, the director said, "Well, you will just have to stay here at
Lawton until you are eighteen."

Narcissus left the room. She did not feel bad. She liked being at
the Kiowa Indian Hospital. In fact, she obtained employment elsewhere immediately after graduation. They needed a practical nurse
at Crown Point, New Mexico, on the Navaho Reservation. The director of nurses at Crown Point signed for her. Narcissus's career
was launched.

Her two friends completed the course also. Berdian signed up for
the Women's Auxiliary Corps. She was the first woman to join after
it was renamed Women's Army Corps. When the war was over, she
returned to a practical nursing career in the Indian Hospital in Santa
Fe. Alvina took advanced training in the University Hospital in
Oklahoma City but did not complete the work or continue in the
field.

But oh, Crown Point! Narcissus's enthusiasm waned when she saw
the place. It was way out in the middle of nowhere! There were only
a few buildings: the hospital, a small Bureau of Indian Affairs Boarding School, the little BIA office itself, and the Dutch Reformed
Church.

It was just a sad place. It was sandy, and when the wind blew, the
sand was so thick that no one could get to a town. The only transportation was by the mail truck from the Trading Post itself to the
railroad track. Then the train to Gallup had to be flagged down.

Narcissus learned very soon that it was even worse on the return
trip. The best solution, the young nurse found, was to phone one of
the girls who lived at Fort Defiance and with whom she had trained
in Lawton. "Can you find somebody to take me to Crown Point?"

Usually that worked. But once it did not. She could not find a
single person to take her back. She was very late in reporting for
work and she was almost fired. When those in charge reprimanded
her, she put on a bold front.

"Well, it's all right if you discharge me. I've decided to go back to school and get registered nurses' training."

"That is a very good idea. You would be best off to get that training right away and not stay any longer in Crown Point!"

Narcissus resigned and returned to the Mescalero Reservation.

Narcissus was at home for just one week when the principal of the Mescalero School, who also worked at Agency, came to Aunt Evelyn's house in search of Narcissus. His name was Carson Ryan.

"We just received a telegram at Agency. It's from your school—the Santa Fe Indian School. They need an assistant librarian. I think you could do the work. Would you like the job?" Narcissus said yes. She worked in the library at Santa Fe until the summer break.

As she sorted and classified books and checked students' identification cards, she became even more determined to continue her nursing career on a higher level. Becoming a registered nurse would require money. *How* to get enough!

Had it not been for the small sum she received from her mother's cattle, she could not have attended Lawton. She had been unable to save a penny of her salary as a librarian because her rent and board were so expensive. She needed three hundred dollars to enter training to be a registered nurse. Narcissus was determined to obtain it some way.

By May 1944 she had applied to several nursing schools. She wrote to Charity Hospital, in New Orleans, Hillcrest Memorial Hospital in Tulsa, and to the Muskogee General Hospital, also in Oklahoma. All three institutions accepted her applications. Narcissus decided she would like to go to New Orleans. She spoke of this choice to Miss Rae Seibert, who was in charge of the Santa Fe Library.

"You shouldn't even *think* of going there! You won't be happy there," the librarian advised.

Narcissus did not understand. Miss Seibert continued, "I don't want you to go there. People won't treat you right. You will get discouraged and come home. I want you to go to a hospital where they will accept you, where you will be happy, so that you can finish what you start. After all, it will take a lot of money. I don't want you to be miserable and fail to accomplish your goal."

Narcissus had no idea what the librarian was talking about—Narcissus had not experienced racial prejudice. In Mescalero and in Santa Fe everyone with whom she had contact was Indian. The whites she knew had been in charge and tended to "baby" and "shelter" the Apaches. It was not until years later when she saw news reports of troubles between whites and blacks that she understood what her fate might have been in the South. How grateful she was to Miss Seibert.

"If I can get the money together, I will go to the Muskogee General Hospital School of Nursing. My training will take three years." This was her final decision.

It seemed best to return to Mescalero and try to borrow cash. "Perhaps they'll give me some money for my cattle."

But when she contacted the proper officials, they denied her request. "You're not yet twenty-one. Someone will have to sign for you." It was the same old story.

Narcissus went to the first male relative she could think of. He did not want to sign.

Then she went to her father, but he refused!

She asked other kin. No one was willing to help. All it would have taken was their name on a slip of paper.

The refusals hurt. Several times Narcissus returned to the house to cry in solitude. It did not seem possible that relatives would not stand behind her. It opposed what Beshád-e had taught her to expect. The young woman felt alone and thwarted.

Eventually the pain abated somewhat and changed to determination. "I'm going to get that money! I'm going to Muskogee! I'll do what I planned *because* they refused to help!"

Narcissus headed for the red brick administration building just east of the hospital. She went directly to the Tribal Council office. They said, "There is nothing we can do for you."

Once again, her spirits sagged. She left and walked down the hall, her head held low, so that no one would see her tears.

Just then a man came from an office doorway and began talking to her. She was so choked up, she could hardly speak. She kept her head averted to hide her swollen eyes. As he kept talking, she realized it was Carson Ryan.

"Tell me, what is wrong, Narcissus?" he asked. She poured out her predicament.

"You bring that paper into my office," he said. "I'll sign for you." And so he did.

Narcissus explained she would need a second signature. A Mrs. Black was working there at Agency, doing home extension work. Mr. Ryan took Narcissus into Mrs. Black's office and explained the situation.

"Give me the paper, Narcissus. I'll sign it, too."

Thus, two Anglos started Narcissus on her way to becoming a registered nurse. Her relatives had failed her. A sum of money was issued to her, and she started preparations for her trip to Oklahoma.

All was not yet rosy, however. Finances continued to plague Narcissus. Through her years at Lawton and Muskogee, she needed every cent she could put her hands on. She waited eagerly for the checks from Mescalero, and they were meager. She received only ten dollars a month from her mother's cattle. These were still the war years. Many items were scarce and expensive. Coupons were necessary for meat and for shoes. She learned the nursing school needed some of her quota in order to purchase sugar. Things were tight everywhere.

Narcissus arrived at the bus station in Muskogee in July of 1944, just at noon. A cab took her to the hospital where a "greeter" ushered her to the basement cafeteria, and she ate her first meal. The room assigned her was shared with Caroline June Odell, a white girl from Oklahoma. Aside from Caroline, Narcissus knew no one. She had no idea what to expect in her training; yet she remained calm, collected, and determined to do well.

Hers was the class of 1947. When instruction began, the group had an enrollment of thirty-two. Narcissus was the only Indian. Actually, there were few Indians in all three classes of students. Before long, however, Narcissus was drawn to those there were. A favorite was a Creek Indian named Ida Mae Bearhead, whose home was Oklahoma City. The two spent their recreation hours together. Ida Mae liked spectator sports. She had attended Bacone College, so she and Narcissus went to all the Bacone football games. Mostly, the training itself consumed their waking hours.

The probation period for all entrants was three months. At the end of that time, each one was interviewed by staff members of both the nursing school and the hospital. Narcissus was terrified.

"What if I get sent home! What am I going to *be* if they send me home!" she thought.

The interrogation was held in a small room.

An instructor began, "Where did you go to high school?" Narcissus told her.

The teacher continued, "You mean they teach you how to study at an *Indian* school?"

Narcissus replied, "Yes, they did." She went on to describe the subjects she had taken, the study periods, and general routine.

"Why did you choose to become a nurse?" was the next question. Narcissus was hard pressed to respond. She feared that if she told them all the incidents that had led to her ultimate decision, they would laugh at her. Finally, she spoke of the encouragement of her uncles, Morton and Edmond.

When the interview ended, Narcissus was told she had passed. She was now eligible to be in the candlelight ceremony where she would receive a nurse's cap.

Within herself, Narcissus rejoiced. Probation was over.

It had been a terrible strain. Many young hopefuls had been rejected and they were heartbroken. Narcissus empathized.

Training began during the war years—World War II. The army needed qualified nursing recruits and contacted the school at Muskogee. Narcissus was interested. "You will be a cadet and receive a monthly stipend of thirty-six dollars," she was told. This sounded most attractive. Narcissus signed the papers. She proudly wore the cadet uniform throughout her three years. She would have been quite willing to serve her country overseas, but by the time her schooling was completed, the war had ended.

Odell remained her roommate for all three years. She taught Narcissus what it meant to *really* study, to concentrate, and to take examinations. On days off, they went together, visiting with friends, fishing, and going to movies.

One of the highlights of those years was a dinner given annually by the Dakota Indian Club, which belonged to the Federated Indian Women's Club located in Muskogee. Narcissus attended. They served Indian food. Oh, how good it tasted after all the Anglo fare. It made her lonely for home.

Part of the nurses' training included going to the University Hospital in Oklahoma City, which offered courses other than those available at Muskogee. Five students attended at a time, until the entire class had had the opportunity. This additional instruction is part of Oklahoma law, and all nurses training in that state must participate before they can receive diplomas.

Twice during her training at Muskogee the Mescalero Tribal Council wrote to the director of nurses asking how Narcissus was getting along. This infuriated Narcissus because of the tribe's attitude toward her when she had needed assistance.

She told the director, "Don't even answer that letter!" The administrator tore up the first that came and perhaps the second as well.

Graduation came at last. Narcissus stood with the other members of the class of 1947. By now its number had dwindled to fourteen. Eighteen had been dropped. It was a proud moment for this strong-hearted Apache.

Now, Narcissus was ready for a *real* job. She took employment at the Indian Hospital in Pawnee, Oklahoma.

Early Years of Marriage

While working in Pawnee, Narcissus met a handsome Ponca Indian by the name of Wheeler Gayton. Their introduction was through his cousin, a young woman who was attending Bacone College.

At the time, Wheeler was in the military service. During World War II he had been a technical sergeant, a radio operator, and a tail gunner in the Army Air Force. When peace was declared, he enlisted for a second time. He was a tall, broad-shouldered, slim-hipped, athletic-looking man who wore his uniform well.

He had been reared by his parents and was especially close to his mother. When Wheeler was young, his father had difficulty with a drinking problem and squandered much of the family income. Frequently, the youngster and his brother Everett were cared for by a great-aunt whom they called "grandmother," a loving woman for whom Wheeler had great affection. Both mother and great aunt advocated good education. When "grandmother" died, the boys started studying at the Pawnee Indian School.

Already Wheeler's ability as an athlete was recognized; many high schools tried to recruit him to play football and basketball. He decided on Hominy, a small town northeast of Pawnee. He became a football star. After his graduation, he attended Tulsa University on a football scholarship. He studied there two years; but then the war broke out, and he enlisted in the Army Air Force.

Narcissus and Wheeler were attracted to each other from their first meeting. They dated for about six months. Then, in November of 1948 they married. The wedding was a simple civil ceremony, taking place in Omaha, Nebraska, where Wheeler was stationed.

When Narcissus was contemplative, she smiled to herself, "I guess

I shouldn't have worried when I was a teenager. I always lived in mortal dread that my grandmother might marry me off for a horse! She might not even ask me if I liked the man. She was so old-fashioned. It was part of the tradition she never escaped. But I myself selected the man I married."

A good choice it proved to be. The couple's closeness was always exemplary.

Narcissus quit working at the hospital, and the newlyweds remained in Omaha for about five months. During this time they made many trips to Ponca City, Oklahoma. This was pleasant. Wheeler's father was by now a teetotaler. Because of the Ponca tribe's practice of "respect," not unlike that of Apaches, Narcissus and her father-in-law had no conversations together. She and her mother-in-law liked each other immediately.

The moment the couple arrived in Ponca City, Wheeler, Everett, and their mother huddled together. For many hours they talked. Narcissus understood almost nothing except the word for "daughter-in-law," for they spoke the Ponca language, but she felt their affection and acceptance. The old lady gave Narcissus a pair of blue beaded moccasins that she herself had worn as a young womand when she danced at Indian celebrations. Later she gave many beautiful hand-sewn quilts to her son and his new wife.

Sometime late that winter Evelyn wrote, "I am planning a Feast for Ivora Lou this next summer."

Narcissus wanted to attend. She could then help her aunt honor Ivora Lou, for whom she had been a babysitter, and have Wheeler meet her relatives. Wheeler resigned from the service in April 1949, and within a month or so he and Narcissus were in Mescalero, residing in an apartment at the Employees' Club next to the Mescalero Hospital.

Then, by September the Gaytons returned to Ponca City, to be near Wheeler's people. Narcissus found employment at the hospital there.

Before many months had passed, there were momentous decisions to make.

"Let's *move* to Mescalero," Narcissus said to her husband. "I know I can get a job at the hospital or do something involved with nursing. And I am pretty sure you can find employment too." She paused.

"Or do you prefer to finish college? You could study at the university and I could continue working in Ponca City."

"No. I don't need to go back to college. I don't want you to have a hard time. It would take several years. I'll take care of you," Wheeler answered.

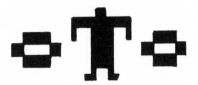

Work in Mescalero

In 1950 the couple became permanent residents of Mescalero, New Mexico.

Almost immediately Narcissus began to work at the Mescalero Hospital. Wheeler had a more difficult time. Apaches were not interested in hiring a Ponca or anyone else who did not belong to their own tribe. He applied in nearby towns, willing to take any decent employment. He "contented" himself with odd jobs, all of short duration. For several months he worked at Three Rivers for the Bureau of Indian Affairs which was supervising the building of a dam there.

Three Rivers is about seventy five miles from Agency by automobile. One travels west, leaving the reservation and driving through Bent and Tularosa. Then one turns to the north and reenters the northwestern part of Apache territory. All the workers on the dam were taken to the site by truck on Sunday evening. They stayed there during the week and were brought back on Friday night in order to spend the weekend with their families.

One week while Wheeler was on the job, a letter came for him. Her husband had given Narcissus permission to open all mail in his absence. It came from Holloman Air Force Base, south of Alamogordo, one of the locations Wheeler had applied for work.

Wheeler had a job! Narcissus tried to phone Virginia Klinekole who lives in Three Rivers, but could not make connection. She dashed for her car and, despite the heat of the day, drove the long distance, almost bursting with the happy news. Wheeler quit working on the dam, and they returned home, jubilant. The next day Wheeler began his new employment. For fifteen years he worked at Holloman. He cleaned, repaired, and packed parachutes.

With both members of the household holding steady jobs, the couple decided to invest in a home of their own.

"Let's not rely on anyone—not the tribe or the government or anybody!" they agreed. "Let's do what my folks did," Wheeler said, "and buy our own place."

Narcissus and Wheeler thus revealed their pride and independence. They didn't want or need the kind of land or dwelling assignment accepted by most Apaches who paid very low monthly rents. They wanted a home that was strictly their own.

The Gaytons' purchase was just off the highway at the entrance to Goat Canyon, below the Windmill tract. The home was in a beautiful setting with many trees. It proved to be fine for Narcissus, but inconvenient for Wheeler. The drive to Holloman was at least sixty miles each way, and so he arose at five o'clock in the morning and returned after six o'clock in the evening. Wheeler never complained. He worked every day until his reliability paid off. In ten years he was named foreman of the parachute shop. The Gaytons were comfortable, secure in residence and employment.

Narcissus found her position in the hospital especially challenging. Because the administrative staff, the doctors, and the other nurses were unaccustomed to Apache ways, there was misunderstanding between patients and staff. Few of the Indians knew what the Anglos and nurses from other tribes were talking about. They could not understand the medical terminology. Even the names of diseases meant nothing. Narcissus recognized the problem, studied the situation, and tried to alleviate it.

One example involved the custom of respect.

One time Solon Sombrero and Lucius Peso were in the same ward. Lucius was half-brother to Katarina, Solon's wife, so the two men were brothers-in-law. Apache ways dictated that they not look at each other. So Solon lay on his side facing the door and Lucius looked in the opposite direction. Hours and hours went by, each man growing more and more uncomfortable. But they had to be polite.

Eventually Lucius needed care, and Narcissus attended his call. The patient requested that a screen be placed at the bottom of his bed so as to prevent his seeing Solon.

"Put a sheet over it too, just to make sure no one can see through it," he said. Narcissus complied, understanding completely. Just then a Pueblo Indian nurse came in.

"What are you doing with that screen?" she asked. She refused to listen to Narcissus's explanation, but, instead, folded the divider and put it aside.

As soon as the Pueblo woman left, Narcissus noted Lucius's unhappiness. Once again she set up the screen. The other nurse was insistent, coming back and putting away the partition. This happened several times. Finally Narcissus demanded that her co-worker listen and learn about the custom of respect. Reluctantly, even then, she permitted the screen to be at the foot of Lucius's bed.

Oftentimes Narcissus spent hours explaining ailments to patients. Some Anglo doctors tried earnestly, but there was a special difficulty in that the Apache language has no words for many parts of human anatomy. For instance, there is no word for "gall bladder," and many Indians have ailments associated with it. Other Apaches are diabetic, but no words exist to explain the cause of the trouble. The same holds true for pancreatitis. After the medical doctor made rounds, the patients who knew Narcissus asked to see her, hoping for greater understanding.

Elderly people, in particular, associated the hospital with death. Consequently, they did not seek medical attention until ailments had progressed so far that they were incurable.

The situation has improved greatly since 1950. Today all young people speak English; the doctors are more sophisticated concerning the linguistic problem, and many sympathize and cooperate. Further, the Mescalero Community Health Representative Program was set up. Narcissus was later to be its director. One of its functions was to make sure that patients in hospitals, and outpatients who remain at home, were fully aware of their conditions. Bilingual representatives discussed health problems with those who were puzzled. Also, some doctors in more recent years have understood about respect and about the need, particularly among elderly patients, to have the blessings of a medicine man or woman in addition to Anglo care. This practice was not permitted in those early days of Narcissus's career.

White and Pueblo nurses would not allow Indian healers to administer to anyone during, or even after, visiting hours. Narcissus was aware that there was a psychological need if the patient were to get well. Three old medicine ladies, in particular, waited until Nurse Gayton was on duty. Then they arrived, in the evening, with their herbs, with certain plants they had prepared and blessed, to further the cure. Narcissus never watched. She preferred to be "ignorant" of ministrations that were contrary to hospital procedures. Sometimes, however, she recalled the medications used by her grandmother.

Beshád-e had used the crystal-clear pitch, not the red of the piñon. It cured and cleaned wounds. The same material got rid of impetigo. Roots were pounded, boiled, and strained, and their brew was dripped into the ear for earache and swallowed to alleviate coughs and to open nasal passages. Another remedy for ear trouble was wild buckwheat, *dilth-pa-ze*, or "blood medicine." Its reddish-brown root, dried, then ground and mixed with water and applied into the ear, stopped the aching, cleared up sores, and irrigated a draining middle ear. A drop of this was dabbed on the buckskin suit of the maiden at her Puberty Feast. Bad headaches called for a rag to be tightly bound about the head. The cheeks of a child with mumps were covered with the raw side of a split leaf of the prickly pear cactus from which the stickers had been brushed. For nosebleed Beshád-e, who never considered herself a "medicine woman," stuffed youngsters' nostrils with tiny crushed black ants. The formic acid contained in the minute bodies tightened the capillary walls and stopped the bleeding. For toothache or decay old medicine women heated a steel awl in the fire, then pressed the hot tip into the hole of the tooth. Another home remedy recalled by Narcissus involved babies and very small children. So often they had suffered from de-hydration, diarrhea, and high fever. The medicine women advised the mother to mix up a sticky dough of flour and water and to plaster it on top of the small ones' heads, covering the concoction with a piece of cloth to hold it in place. When this dried, a new dough was applied to the sunken fontanel.

In those early days of Narcissus's career, many a young woman having her first baby preferred to talk about prenatal care to a mid-wife rather than the Anglo doctor at the hospital. Pregnant women were modest, shy about their condition. Sometimes at the time of actual delivery, the mother-to-be brought her midwife with her to bless her, and ease the pain and tension. Not all nurses looked upon this favorably. Narcissus understood. She had seen her Little Grand-mother Lillian's insistence on being with Beshád-e only. A woman giving birth wanted special prayers.

In the traditional Apache way, after the birth, the umbilicus was tied, and the infant was bathed in water in which the green part of the greasewood shrub had been boiled and then strained. For many weeks following, the child was bathed in such prepared water, espe-cially where the cord had been cut. When the latter dried up and fell off, it was wrapped carefully in beaded buckskin. Narcissus remem-bered one such within her family. It represented a turtle. Turtle's power was strong in deflecting lightning.

In addition to consulting with her people concerning their health, the young nurse proved to be an advisor among those who learned to trust her. They brought their legal documents, wanting to know what they were, what they should do with them. "Does this need a signature?" "Is this a receipt or a bill?" "I still can't read. Please read this letter for me." "What do I do with this check?" All kinds of information was needed. Narcissus understood. Over and over again, she had seen Beshád-e in similar dilemmas. If the nurse felt inadequate to help the inquirers, she sent them to the proper authorities on the reservation. A few did not realize, for example, that they were eligible for welfare and that there were bureaus close by with personnel to assist them in their applications.

In 1955 Narcissus took a position as school nurse. The day schools in Mescalero had become "public," under the jurisdiction of the Department of Education of the State of New Mexico. Law required a nurse to supervise the health of attending children, to administer first aid, and to advise hospitalization as necessary. This interested Narcissus and she transferred her attention to the young.

The school was located in Agency. It was an old, old building that long since has been torn down. There was no room adequate for inspecting the children or for dealing with their emergencies, so Narcissus was crammed into a small closet that served as an office. Here she held consultations and stored her supplies.

When children appeared to need attention, their teacher sent them to Narcissus. Often the interviews were in the hall, for the office was overcrowded. Or, when more privacy was needed, a child was taken to the lavatory. The school had only one such facility and it was used by both boys and girls. The most usual maladies were eye infections, sores of the scalp, an occasional case of head lice, and lots of impetigo, particularly at the beginning of the school term. If the diagnosis were something more serious, Narcissus took the child to the hospital and informed his or her parents.

Other school nurse duties consisted of immunizing, of vaccinating against disease. Many parents were skeptical, believing that these new-fangled Anglo practices would *cause* the illness rather than prevent it. In the 1950s they had no choice; all the schoolchildren were immunized. Narcissus was responsible for doling out health information, and each year she arranged for talks about the care of the body by a qualified individual such as the hospital physician. He spoke to the boys, and then later to the girls, especially those in the upper grades.

Occasionally unusual services were required—assistance outside the realm of Narcissus's actual duties. A mother might send a note with an older child stating that her baby was ill and that she had no means of transportation to the hospital. Narcissus relayed the information to the latter institution as a courtesy. Sometimes house visits were necessary in order to give a mother important information about the health of her child and to dole out any prescribed medicines and explain their proper use. Sometimes finding a specific parent proved interesting.

On one instance Narcissus knocked on Old Lady Chatto's door to make an inquiry. She was invited inside, where she found a group of men and women gambling. This pastime was still illegal. However, the group did not scatter as they usually did when anyone associated with "authority" came by. They trusted Narcissus. They continued dealing out the Mexican cards as the nurse watched and visited before continuing her search.

After five years of duty as school nurse, the challenge of the work had paled. Narcissus returned to hospital nursing. It was 1960.

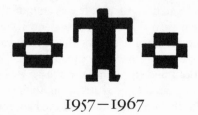

1957—1967

Early in 1957 several people came to Narcissus, suggesting she run for office on the Mescalero Apache Tribal Council. Four individuals had to sign for her. Then the name "Narcissus Gayton" was printed on the ballot. She was elected, becoming the first woman to hold such office as the result of a popular vote. The only other woman who had served had been appointed.

At the beginning of her term of office, she made the following statement: "Women members of the tribe need a new status. I hope my place on the Council will contribute to this end."

Positions on the Council are of two years' duration. An officer may run again in the next election. Narcissus was repeatedly chosen by the members of the tribes in Mescalero. She resigned only when she accepted the directorship of the Representative Health Program in 1970. Legally, she could not serve in both capacities simultaneously.

While she was on the Council she had various duties, such as secretary and then treasurer. For several years she was chair of the Com-

munity Services Committee. This group supervises all education, including high school and college dropouts, and investigates anything
pertaining to the health and welfare of the Apaches. Council members oversee the girls' Puberty Feast held each July. This celebration
was always more time-consuming than expected. The Tribal Consti-
tution and Bylaws were revised while Narcissus held office, and she
was active in her contributions to those activities.

Meetings, meetings, endless meetings! Special problems cropped
up, such as the land claims for the Mescalero and Chiricahua. Each
Council member was obliged to travel to all conferences and listen
to long reports. Narcissus had been involved in this investigation
while she was serving as school nurse, and she was now assigned the
task of researching all aspects of the Chiricahua homelands so that
the Tribe could negotiate for the betterment of Indians.

Early in these land claims studies certain Council members were
designated to travel to the Warm Springs area to learn what resources the Apaches had relinquished when they were driven from
there. Narcissus was among those who went. The trip touched her
emotionally, for this was Victorio's favorite camp. It was where both
Dilth-cleyhen and Beshád-e had spent many early years.

The group drove to Monticello, New Mexico—in Indian called
keto-tuye, meaning "old, ugly, dilapidated house." The town is situated in a small valley adjacent to the Alamosa River. Following the
river beyond the town, steep rocky cliffs rise from both sides of the
canyon.

Narcissus walked within the town, looking at the adobe houses
and the roads, scanning the surrounding countryside. A Mexican
man came up to her as she stood by a small house, a bit higher than
a chicken coop, right in the middle of the central plaza. Two posts
stood on either side of the structure. High in the air, adjoining the
uprights, was a crossbar. An old rope dangled from the horizontal
pole. The old man pointed to the adobe "coop." "That's where they
used to put the Indians in jail," he said. "And that's where they used
to hang the bad ones," he continued, pointing to the rope and crossbar. Suddenly Narcissus's insides felt weak. She could not bear to
listen further. She could envision a relative hanging there. She turned
and walked away. The jest was far from amusing. Tales of atrocities
in this vicinity had been etched deep into her memory.

Later she learned the small adobe building sheltered a pump used
by the townspeople. Kids had been playing with the rope, trying to
make a swing. It was partial relief to know.

Narcissus and Wheeler had planned to add to their family from the very beginning of their marriage. As the years rolled on, they remained childless. Narcissus went to the doctor. She came home, disconsolate.

"Wheeler," she said, "You remember I told you about my early school days, when each time school started, they sent me to the infirmary. And you remember the physicians always feared I had TB, and they gave me all that cod liver oil and the orange? Well, that diagnosis was right. The disease has affected me. I never can have children of my own." This was a time of sadness, but it was not insurmountable.

"Well, if that's the way it's going to be, why get all upset about it?" Narcissus philosophized. There were many Indian children without good homes, without parents to love them. The Gaytons decided adoption would be a good idea.

First, they adopted a six-year-old boy from another Indian tribe. This was on a trial basis. It proved to be a disaster. From the very beginning, he seemed to hate Wheeler and Narcissus no matter what they did to be kind and understanding. All he would say is, "I want to go back to my own people!" There was complete incompatibility.

They decided to sell their home in Goat Canyon. There were too many difficulties. The dwelling was cold and damp. It was too far for Wheeler to drive to Holloman. The couple took a house in the town of Tularosa. Perhaps the boy would be happier in town. The move did not help the situation, however, and finally the youngster was returned to his original home. The adoption had failed.

Narcissus never enjoyed living in Tularosa. The summer heat was stifling. Now *she*, as well as Wheeler, was commuting long distances. Further, her father, Tom Duffy, became ill and was hospitalized in Roswell, New Mexico. He was now in his seventies. Narcissus wanted to visit him as often as possible. She found she could not work in Mescalero, live in Tularosa, and drive to Roswell, too. The Gaytons moved back to the reservation, taking an apartment close to the hospital on the upper floor of the pink house next to the old Tribal Store on the main highway, the road that leads to Agency.

On September 23, 1957, just days after the baby's birth, Narcissus and Wheeler adopted Molly Ann, who became the focus and joy of the next years of their life.

The baby was named Molly after Wheeler's aunt, his father's sister. The child inherited the aunt's Ponca name as well. The Poncas call her Mi-hind-a-beh. When Molly was two weeks old, she was placed in a cradle, a plain one, painted yellow, but without talismans or other trimming.

Narcissus continued working at the hospital, but she arranged her schedule so that she could be with the baby during many of her waking hours. When she was on duty, she found reliable baby-sitting.

The years were pleasant; work worries were minimal. Narcissus and Wheeler watched their daughter develop from "cradleboarder" to toddler, to walking child, and finally to schoolgirl. For them, as for most parents worldwide, *their* child was exceptional!

There were varied diversions on days free from work. The three drove leisurely to White Tail, strolling over Beshád-e's and Dilth-cleyhen's formerly assigned land, peeping into whatever barns and other structures remained. All were empty now, seemingly resigned to loneliness. They visited Aunt Evelyn and her children, and Narcissus's brother, Wendell, his wife Sadie, and their young ones.

Evelyn had moved to Old Road and lived in a neat, fresh-looking home with her husband Amos Gaines. They had two daughters of their own whom they encouraged to go to school, to get advanced training that would equip them to live in an Anglo world. Narcissus and Evelyn visited each other frequently, the difference in their ages diminishing as they grew older. Nonetheless, the younger woman respected her aunt, listened with open ears to her advice, and asked questions concerning certain unfamiliar but traditional ways.

Wendell had not entirely lived up to Beshád-e's expectations of male superiority in education, though he had more schooling than most Apaches of his day. After his grandmother died, he stayed first with Aunt Susie and then went to schools in Albuquerque and in Phoenix. During World War II he joined the navy, where he acquired status among Apaches as a "modern-day warrior."

When Wendell returned to Mescalero, he married Sadie Shanta. They lived in a house in the Carrizo District near Sadie's parents and other kin. The couple had difficulty making ends meet. It was hard for Wendell to get steady work, and he had a number of mouths to feed, eventually fathering ten children. However, no matter how desperate he was for money, he refused to ask Narcissus for help. The Gaytons knew of his financial straits only when Sadie came in confidence and asked for minor assistance. As soon as she could, Sadie paid the debt. For example, when Narcissus returned from either a business or pleasure trip, she often found her home cleaned and straightened from top to bottom. Either Sadie or Aunt Evelyn had done the work.

About the time their oldest children were of grammar school age, Wendell and Sadie moved to Oakland, California. They remained several years. The youngsters "forgot" how to speak Apache; when the family returned to Mescalero, they had difficulty with their native tongue. Even now they pronounce the words as a white man does. Wendell and Sadie never really liked Oakland. It had no forests, no good clean countryside in which to hunt and fish. There was no outdoor life for Wendell such as he had known as a little boy.

The relationship between Wendell and Narcissus was often strained while he was struggling economically. His sister seemed so prosperous, so politically strong. The two agreed on almost nothing.

The situation was otherwise between Wendell and Wheeler. Apache custom required that brothers-in-law show restraint and respect toward each other. Even so, these men developed a close friendship. Their mutual liking began when Wheeler had first arrived in Mescalero.

As a boy, Wheeler did not learn to hunt or fish. These activities were not part of traditional Ponca culture. He had no knowledge of the way game should be butchered after being killed, nor did he know how to clean fish. Narcissus and her brother had often eaten fish as children, partly because their father liked the flavor so much. So, when Wheeler expressed interest, Wendell took it upon himself to teach his brother-in-law the artistry of wielding both gun and rod. The men's excursions in search of animals or fish provided recreation for the two wives and the children, as well.

The event that most marred Narcissus's general state of happiness during this entire decade was the death of her father, Tom Duffy. On September 4, 1959, he passed away. The funeral services were held in his wife's church. He was buried in the Mescalero cemetery, which is reached by driving farther along the road in front of the Gayton home.

Tom had been a good man.

He had tried to be a good father as well.

After a few years of living in the apartment, Wheeler said, "I think we need to plan for Molly's future. This place is too small for the three of us. Let's build us a house that we can *live* in and that will be Molly's when we pass on."

Plans were begun; a search was made for a suitable location. Eventually they built on a rise overlooking a narrow valley. From some of their house windows the roof of the hospital at Agency was visible. Half a block away, and down the hill, the new Mescalero community center and Tribal Headquarters would be established. Both Narcissus and Wheeler would have offices there in years to come.

The grammar school was just across the road from the Gaytons': it was the school in which Molly would learn the three Rs. The child grew up speaking English. That was the language used by her family. An Indian tongue was not possible: Wheeler spoke Ponca and Narcissus spoke Chiricahua, so they used words they had learned in school.

The home was constructed primarily of wood and had a large brick fireplace. Initially, it included a living room, dining room, three bedrooms, two baths, and a kitchen equipped with the latest electrical conveniences. The family room had specific space for a television set. There was a library stocked with good books, many of them telling about Indians. Adequate property surrounded the house to allow for future expansion. Some years later, a studio was added in which to store and display Apache and Ponca treasures, and still later, an even more spacious room that was used briefly as a shop from which to sell Indian-made items.

The Gaytons moved into the home in 1967. That same year Wheeler left his job at Holloman Air Force Base and came to work in Mescalero for the tribe as supervisor of the Youth Social Development Program. Apaches had come to respect him. He was well liked in this position, wherein he planned and coordinated the recreation and extracurricular education of the young people.

When Molly was very small, Wheeler talked seriously to her, and for many years thereafter, he told her how much happiness she had brought him and Narcissus.

He said, "I built this house for you, so you will have something over your head after I am dead and gone." When she was older, he teased, "Now don't you bring home a *lazy* young man, or I will send him over the hill!"

Work Continues

Narcissus's work continued to satisfy her. Old people whom she had known as a child sometimes came to the hospital for care.

She enjoyed seeing them, but her presence as a nurse often came as a surprise.

One time—actually earlier in her career—Grandpa Charlie Istee and Old Man Kanseah, both of whom were distant kin to Narcissus, came to the hospital to visit Lorraine Enjady's mother, who was Grandpa's stepdaughter. Her name was Minnie Wilson and she was crippled with arthritis. Narcissus was wearing cap and uniform and was cleaning the drug room just off the front lobby. The door to the room was open.

The men did not recognize Narcissus and continued to talk together in Indian, "It looks like we have another new nurse. They always give us a Mexican." Narcissus did not enlighten them, but later she told Minnie, who in turn passed on the news.

Grandpa Charlie was embarrassed. The next day he came down the hospital hall, this time speaking English.

He called, "Narcissus!" She sat at the nurse's desk and said nothing. He shook his finger at her. "Why didn't you tell me that was *you*!" The two rejoiced in seeing one another.

Minnie was very ill. There was no cure for her ailment and soon she died. Once again, Narcissus experienced ghost sickness. At night she heard Minnie calling her; she could see the old woman in her dreams. Three times she awakened to find herself outside in the darkness, standing on the steps in her nightgown. She saw Minnie vividly, lying on her hospital bed, calling, "Narcissus!" The sickness lasted a week. Narcissus underwent no ceremony to chase away the ghost.

Other individuals were gratified and startled to find a nurse who could communicate in Apache. There was the time Old Lady Toclanny, Rogers's wife, did not recognize Narcissus. The Old Lady was the only patient in the hospital. She lay in the women's ward, staring at the ceiling. Narcissus sat on the edge of the bed. The woman smiled but showed no recognition.

"Do you remember me?" Narcissus said. "I'm not a strange person."

The Old Lady laughed, then whispered, as if to herself, "Oh, the nurse talks Indian." She brightened as she listened to further words and then said "Oh, I know. You're Fort Sill! Who's your folks?"

When Narcissus told her, she grabbed the nurse's hand. She cried, saying "Ooooo, Ooooo," again and again. "Well, I didn't know it was you." She held Narcissus's arm and rubbed it. She touched the uniform and the cap.

This incident, as well as similar episodes, made Narcissus both happy and sad. How unfortunate there were so many old people like this. Just Narcissus's being in Mescalero meant so much to these patients.

The feeble woman told everyone who came to visit, "Narcissus is *here*. Narcissus went away and studied. Now she is home, and she will help us." But Old Lady To-clanny never left the hospital. In five days she was dead.

Others showed gratitude and a wish to be remembered—not always in the hospital setting. Once Narcissus drove past Old Lady Chatto's place in Squaw Town. She completed her errand, and on her way back down the road, there was the old lady standing at the corner. A relative had led her there. She could not make the short walk by herself for she was partially blind. Such a pity—in earlier years she had been one of the finest of Apache craftswomen.

Old Lady Chatto waved a basket in the air as soon as she heard the noise of the motor. Narcissus stopped the car, got out and walked briskly toward her, thinking the woman needed money and was trying to sell the container. But no. Gently Old Lady Chatto handed Narcissus the basket.

"I want to give it to you. I am going blind. I am blind in one eye now, and I am almost blind in my good eye. I want you to have it—so you can remember."

The incident itself, as well as the gift, touched Narcissus. She choked up then as she does now, just thinking of it. When Old Lady Chatto died, the nurse felt that most of the history of Apache womenfolk went with her. Certainly, most of Narcissus's blood relatives were gone.

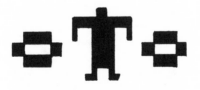

Molly's Feast

As a little girl, Molly liked school and was proficient in her studies, first at the Bent-Mescalero Elementary School across the street from her home and later in high school in Tularosa, where there were many Anglo students and others of Spanish American descent. These latter form two separate cliques, and both make it difficult for the Apache pupils by laughing at the way the Indians talk, dress, and behave. For Molly it was easier than for most reservation girls, not only because she had good command of the English language and her parents had the means to provide her with styles of clothing close to the peer stereotype, but also because she was not afraid to hold her own.

Most youngsters from Mescalero spoke mixed Apache and Anglo. For instance, if they wanted to say, "I am going to eat an apple," they put it as follows: "*Apple, ish, sha-uhn.*" Every sentence uttered in the classroom required them to stop, think hard, and then translate. Often they were reluctant to speak, and then were accused of "stupidity." Only a few teachers understood and recognized those with special talents and intelligence.

Late in 1968, Narcissus spoke to Wheeler. "Molly is getting old enough now. I want her to have a Feast. I had none, and I want one for her. What do you think?" Her husband thought it a good idea. They spoke to Molly, asking if she wanted to be honored, if she wanted to be White-Painted-Woman, to undergo the lessons of the ceremony, to run in order to ensure longevity and well-being, to bless her people. Molly consented.

Her parents began collecting the required items for the Feast as early as the spring of 1969. Molly would be twelve years old that September. Perhaps they could have a private Feast around Labor Day. Narcissus informed her relatives of the plans. Kin who so desired brought her whatever they could afford. Time was short; ordinarily it takes two or three years to accumulate pollen, foods, deerskin, and gifts such as yardage and black shawls.

Molly was fitted for her buckskin suit and moccasins. Neva Guitar created the top, Mary Bottella, the bottom. It was beautiful.

Then one of Narcissus's close cousins, Velma Scott, died. She was the daughter of Jasper and Lucy Kanseah, neighbors in White Tail. The tragedy changed the Gaytons' plans. Narcissus could not celebrate—not just now. The Feast was postponed, to be held with the other maidens the following July.

Certain older ladies in Mescalero were waiting for invitations. They had heard of Narcissus's plans. She told them it was just a postponement. They smiled, saying, "Well, we know that when you have *your* Feast, all the animals and even the trees will get to eat." This was a compliment. It meant that Narcissus was not stingy, that everyone would eat well when Molly was honored.

When finally Narcissus was more or less reconciled to Velma's death, she sought Aunt Evelyn. The two worked together, making all the preparations. Evelyn was the "director" for Molly's part of the ceremony.

In July of 1970 Molly's Feast took place at the Grounds in Mescalero. It was a Chiricahua Feast, precisely like the one that Beshád-e had given Christine.

Many visitors camped in the foothills. Molly's tent and an arbor were set up on the south side of the open space prepared for the ceremonial, alongside those of the other maidens to be honored. Each girl had her own tipi as well. The structures created an impressive row, commanding the attention of tourists driving along the nearby highway.

Nona Blake, a highly respected woman, had taken charge of setting up Molly's tipi. Narcissus wanted to be sure it was done correctly. Nona showed her how to place the twenty-one poles, cover them, and anchor everything securely.

In front of the tipi was the long arbor wherein cooking was done for all the guests. Evelyn had chosen reliable women to do this work, or they had volunteered. These ladies built fires, cooked stew and beans, made the fry bread, and brewed coffee. They made sure that all was ready at mealtimes.

Molly's sponsor was Alberta Begay, a good woman, one skilled in the use of ancient medicines.

On the first day of the Feast, at dawn, Molly was bathed in privacy, and her beautiful long hair was washed in the suds of the yucca root. She faced east, and Alberta assisted her in donning the buckskin robes. As each individual part of the costume was put on, the sponsor said a prayer and gave a blessing. She fed the maiden ceremonial foods that had been blessed and marked with a cross of pollen. Before putting them into Molly's mouth, Alberta held them to the four directions.

The sponsor instructed her ward concerning proper behavior. Throughout the four days and the morning of the fifth, she must be demure, modest, obedient, and dignified. She must under no circumstances lose her temper. Any communication should be brief, quiet, and in good taste.

"If you laugh too much, your face will wrinkle prematurely," Alberta warned. "Do not look up at the sky. That will cause rain." Molly remembered the origin myth of White-Painted-Woman, the rain, and the waterfall. "You must not touch water. You must drink only through this reed that is attached right here to your blouse."

The dressing, feeding and instruction took many hours. Only Molly, Alberta, and Narcissus were present.

Most girls in the Feast, certainly the Mescalero Apache girls, enlist the aid of a medicine man who is present during the dancing and the praying at night in the Big Tipi. That is not the Chiricahua way. Molly had no medicine man, nor had Christine, Beshád-e, or Dilth-cleyhen. According to Chiricahua custom, the sponsor is the important person—such a one as Narcissus's great-grandmother had been.

Today, at the annual Fourth of July Puberty Feast, one of the most impressive sights is the raising of the Big Tipi at the western end of the Grounds. This feat is supervised by a head shaman or medicine man, but other such men of power, who have been hired by the families of Mescalero maidens, are present. All of them pray. They take care that supplications and songs are correctly recited and intoned. The Big Tipi dominates the entire ceremonial arena.

At Molly's Feast, as soon as the Tipi was ready, she and Alberta left the Gayton tent. Alberta laid flat on the ground a buckskin on which the maiden knelt. The sponsor marked her face, shoulders, back, and nose with yellow tule pollen. She paid homage to the four directions. Molly heard the singing of the medicine men. She paid little attention; she was conscious only of her own reactions. When she had received the sacred pollen, she became Istún-e-glesh.

When marked in yellow, Molly had healing power, a blessing power within her. She turned to Alberta, touching her with the powder. Then, long lines of spectators formed, each in turn seeking the maiden's beneficent touch. After further prayers, she lay face down upon the buckskin. Her attendant massaged her from head to foot, right side to left, whispering the reason for every motion.

This completed, Alberta said, "Arise," and when the maiden had done so, her sponsor traced four footprints in pollen upon the buckskin. Then she guided the maiden, saying, "You must start with the *right* foot, not the left." Molly was ready for "the runs," which symbolize fitness and when done well, ensure a fruitful life for the maiden.

At some distance to the east of the Big Tipi, a shallow basket is filled with ritual articles: pollen, red clay, white clay, blue-gray clay, grama grass, and eagle feathers, as well as sacred sticks for the girls who desire to dance in the Tipi on the final night of the Feast. The maidens are expected to run around this basket. The basket contained no sacred sticks for Molly, as dancing within the Tipi was part of only the Mescalero rite.

The maidens stood in a row, their feet steady in the pollen prints. At the prescribed signal, all ran forward, circling the basket in a clockwise direction before returning to their sponsors. In chorus, these ladies uttered high, shrill cries throughout the run, a cry denoting reverence.

Molly and the others ran four times, each succeeding run involving a slightly greater distance. This completed, the maiden picked up her buckskin and, holding it to each of the four directions, shook it.

The running has great significance, and Narcissus feared for her daughter. "Oh, what if she falls!" It had rained hard during the night, and when the sun arose, the entire Feast Ground was a mire of slippery mud. Narcissus knew Wheeler was watching, too, ready to rescue the girl should she stumble. If that happened, he would return with her to her buckskin and she would start out once again. But it would be failure in the eyes of the watching crowd, a sign that the powers were not with Molly. Narcissus's pounding heart returned to normal beat only when her stately child completed all four runs in beauty.

The remainder of the first day of the Feast was busy, preparing and doling out food, throwing gifts to the crowd to distract them while sacred blessings continued for Molly. In the afternoon the dignified maiden mingled with the spectators and guests. Wherever she went, she symbolized goodwill. Her exemplary behavior affected the remainder of her life and provided a benefit to the tribe.

That night, when darkness cast its mantle, the Crown Dancers—the Mountain Gods—emerged in all their splendor. They were followed by the sacred, sometimes comical, Clown, the messenger between man and the supernatural. All were masked; each team had been painted with a different symbol, the meaning of which was secret. The family of each maiden had hired its own set of men representing the Powers.

The Mountain Gods emerged from the blackness, moving into the flickering shadows of the firelight of the great bonfire in the center of the ceremonial ground. There were singers and drummers at one side. The dancers repeated a high-pitched "Hu-hu-hu-huu" as they thrust forward their swords. There was a set sequence to their moves, but each one had individuality.

At the proper moment, Molly and the other maidens joined them, dancing in line and in stately manner. Molly danced all four nights with the Mountain Gods, from just after dusk until almost midnight. The others remained in public for only a short time and then retired to the Big Tipi with their sponsors and medicine men. From outside the Tipi, one could hear the murmur of prayers, the sound of deer hoof rattles, and from time to time the shuffle of moccasined feet. The girls must dance and dance and dance.

The ceremony on the fifth morning resembled that of the first. The medicine men painted outlines of the sun on the palms of their left hands, holding them aloft, toward the rising light over East Mountain. They rubbed the picture over the heads and faces of the maidens for whom they were responsible. Then, using a brush of grama grass and a single eagle feather, they decorated the face, arms, and legs of the girl with white clay instead of pollen. Dots or lines of red and white were put on the right side of her face to represent the rainbow.

Once again, the spectators surged forth, forming a line of people to be blessed. Again, four runs were completed by the maidens. This time the earth was dry. Narcissus felt more confident.

The ritual completed, the Big Tipi was dismantled. A truckload of fruit, tobacco, and sweets arrived at one side of the Feast Ground. The goodies were cast into the air, and in one last wild scramble, the guests retrieved as much as they could carry away. The Feast for Molly was at an end, a Chiricahua Feast like that of Dilth-cleyhen, Beshád-e, and Christine.

Since 1970

Narcissus worked at the hospital until 1970, when a new health program was established on the reservation. She had long been interested in the Community Health Representative Program (CHR), styled after the Office of Economic Opportunity's Program for Health Aides. When Narcissus was asked to become its director, she resigned from both the hospital and the Tribal Council. She spent four weeks at the Desert Willow Training Center in Tucson, Arizona.

The program in Mescalero is better defined than similar ones on other Indian reservations. Here, there is no guesswork, and each representative has a specific duty. The health plan fills the communication gap between Apaches and health and social administrators at every level. The people know who to contact for help, for information. When necessary, bilingual representatives go directly to their homes. Further, the plan involves the schools—the Head Start classes and the day care centers. Whatever pertains to health is part of its dominion.

As its director, Narcissus supervised and coordinated the duties of fourteen or so community health representatives, each of whom spent three weeks at a training center. Because none had other medical training or social work experience, this was not really enough preparation; much of their training came while on the job. At this point Narcissus and the medical doctors assigned to Mescalero began to function. They lectured the representatives concerning the most urgent health needs of the community.

In addition to home visits, the representatives provided transportation between the hospital and the medical and dental clinics. They talked in simple terms about nutrition and the necessity to conform to specially prescribed diets. They explained the dangerous aspects of many communicable diseases such as tuberculosis, and last, but not least, they counseled the problem drinkers and alcoholics.

Narcissus found the program a challenge. She had many conferences with the doctors to help them understand the specific cultural ways of the In-déh. She coordinated the work of the representatives with that of the physicians, arranging for follow-up visits in the homes to check that the physicians' instructions had been fully understood.

About the same time as the inception of the CHR, Narcissus began to participate in the Albuquerque Area Health Board. Its membership represented several Indian tribes of the Southwest. It served in an advisory capacity. Later, Nurse Gayton came to represent this body on a National Indian Board, travelling extensively to various meetings.

Because medicine was an integral part of her life and philosophy, Narcissus was happy to see the beginning of a pap smear clinic, the first of its kind on any Indian reservation. The Apaches received an award from the New Mexico Cancer Society, and in 1972 still another came from the Otero County Cancer Society. Narcissus was proud to be a part of health innovations; she appreciated recognition of the tribe's efforts.

There were many other activities in which she was involved. One was the International Save the Children Federation, one part of which benefitted the American Indian. Perhaps as long as twenty years ago, about 1969 or 1970, a medical social worker by the name of Larry Moss was located in Mescalero. He and Narcissus started the federation program on the reservation. Well over one hundred children received aid as a result of their efforts. Sometimes only one child in a family needed help, other times as many as four siblings obtained funds. Usually the schools suggested the names of students who were obviously deprived, and the federation then located sponsors who sent $180 or so to each of the children. Part of that money went into a community fund to buy equipment needed by all the Apache youngsters. The designated child received twenty-five dollars every three months to help with personal needs such as shoes and everyday clothing. In return for the money, the youngsters corresponded with their sponsors. Sometimes a friendship resulted. One sponsor sent his Apache child through college.

Narcissus served the tribe by trying to alleviate the vexing, and all too prevalent, problem of Apache drunkenness. In this connection she was a member of an Advisory Committee of the New Mexico State Commission on Alcoholism. This group met once per month in Albuquerque. Many individuals in Mescalero were (and are) unable to drink socially. They not only harmed themselves but neglected their children and spouses.

The difficulties encountered by aged Apaches also received Narcissus's attention. As the health situation improved in general, more and more Indians lived well into their seventies, eighties, and even nineties. The nurse served on the National Indian Commission on Aging.

In January 1973 the American Indian Nurses' Association was formed. Narcissus was a charter member. The organization is backed by the American Nurses' Association, and once again, its primary function is to oversee and improve Indian health.

In June of the same year, Narcissus began a year's term as a member of Tularosa School Board, a body that governs the policies at the Bent-Mescalero School as well as those of the town. Most of the Apache students of junior high and high school level attended classes in Tularosa; fewer spent their upper-grade years in Ruidoso.

Another project under Narcissus's supervision was the Traditional Counselors Program. It was started in an effort to preserve the ancient ways of the Chiricahua and Mescalero people. It was composed of older Apaches who started recording everything they could remember of early customs and beliefs. They create beadwork, dolls, cradles, drums, whatever they might have done in the past or had seen their parents do.

On a less formal basis Narcissus gave numerous talks to local civic and social organizations outside the reservation, informing the Anglos and Spanish Americans who lived in Ruidoso, Alamogordo, and Las Cruces about Apache ways. Such groups, particularly the women's clubs, were interested in Indian crafts. Narcissus enjoyed the contact. She felt it promoted better public relations.

In August 1973 Wendell was buried. He had just passed his forty-sixth birthday.

The life of Narcissus's brother was a sad one in many ways. Opportunities for him never seemed to materialize.

He and his wife Sadie, after leaving California, enjoyed a few years in the area known as Carrizo, back on the reservation. Jobs for Wendell continued to be scarce.

In the 1970s the tribe ousted everyone in the district in order to make way for a huge dam. The Duffys moved to Lower Mescalero, below Agency, where they rented a house. The Carrizo dam was finished and on its banks was built an elegant hotel, the Inn of the Mountain Gods. This opened in July of 1975, attracting wealthy tourists who enjoyed the site, the boating, fishing and swimming in the lake, as well as the tennis, skeet shooting, horseback riding and golf.

Wendell did not live to see its completion. One night he was robbed and ultimately beaten to death by a drunken member of the Mescalero community. His murder shook the extended family to its very depths.

Violence on the reservation is all too frequent. The problem is recognized by The People, but no one can prepare emotionally for atrocities against loved ones. Aye-yaaa.

When Molly was given her Feast, Narcissus spoke to her in emphatic terms. "I want you to be more than just a run-of-the-mill Indian!"

The same words were said to Aunt Evelyn's daughters. Several of them went to Haskell Institute in Lawrence, Kansas, to prepare themselves for positions as office clerks. Narcissus said, "That's just fine for you to go there. But you must go beyond being just an ordinary stenographer. That is not enough. You must study further and become specialized. Then you will be respected. Your services will be in demand."

Molly attended high school in Tularosa and earned very good grades. She became interested, too, in her mother's stories of Chiricahua history. She enjoyed going to White Tail, where Narcissus's ancestors had lived. There she saw her biological mother's house, for Molly had learned through the words of unkind peers that she had been adopted shortly after birth. She had come to terms with the fact, recognizing how much Narcissus and Wheeler loved her. She was truly their own.

"You must study hard. You must go to college," her mother preached. "A college education is something no one can take from you. I want you to be independent enough that you can stand up and look the next person right in the eye. You need not be abusive about it, but you are an Apache and you should be proud."

Molly had been given a background in several arts. From the age of five until the late 1960s she took classical ballet lessons and then jazz dancing, which she enjoyed until about 1971. Thereafter, she preferred to perform Indian dances, competing at powwows throughout the Southwest. She took piano lessons, but that was short-lived; although she sometimes played at the Dutch Reformed Church, she was always reluctant.

Molly listened to her mother and attended college, where she pursued several different majors. She showed excellence in them all, but as yet she has not met sufficient requirements to obtain her advanced degree. She has gone to New Mexico State, in Las Cruces, where she received a scholarship for her first year's tuition in civil engineering studies from International Business Machines. She transferred to Brigham Young University in Provo, Utah, but she preferred being nearer home and has since taken courses at New Mexico State Community College in Alamogordo. During one of her classes in geography, she had an opportunity to travel to China. She encountered some difficulties there because officials believed she was Chinese.

While she was yet going to college, Molly married James Peralto. They had two children. Leclair May was born in 1977, Desirée in 1980. As the marriage did not work out, Molly returned to school. Wheeler and Narcissus adopted their grandchildren in 1989.

As years passed Narcissus became increasingly interested in the history of her ancestors. This concern was augmented by her involvement with the Chiricahua land claims, which required precise knowledge of prereservation territories. Further, Beshád-e had raised her in traditional ways and had told her many stories of being "on the run" and of imprisonment. She wanted to see with her own eyes.

Narcissus had heard tales that the descendants of Apaches were still residing in Old Mexico. She listened carefully to the dark-skinned, "Indian-looking" women she saw when she visited Juarez. Some of the words they spoke sounded familiar. Could they bear Chiricahua ancestry? Perhaps.

In curiosity, Narcissus took a tour that led across the border to Mexico. Ostensibly, its purpose was to visit the Tarahumara Indians who dwell in remote retreats. Secretly, she hoped to uncover something about her own tribe.

In July of 1982 Narcissus planned a bus trip for thirty-two Chiricahuas. Together, they traced the path of the Chiricahuas throughout their twenty-seven years of imprisonment, from 1886 to 1913. Wheeler and her granddaughter Leclair accompanied her. In visits to St. Augustine and Fort Pickens, Florida, they saw firsthand the discomfort her ancestors had endured. They saw Mount Vernon Barracks, north of Mobile, Alabama, and then ended their journey in Fort Sill, Oklahoma, where for nineteen years the Apaches—in a state of confinement—raised cattle and farmed.

How different was the environment in all those places from the land that Victorio and his daughter Dilth-cleyhen had loved, how different from Warm Springs, with which Narcissus was familiar already.

In 1986 Narcissus arranged for a centennial celebration in Mescalero to mark the date the In-déh had been betrayed into submission and hauled by force to the sites she had visited four years before. The program was impressive, its meaning heartfelt. A medal was struck as commemoration—one bearing the likeness of an Apache mother with her cradleboard, a warrior, a yucca plant, and the powerful sun.

Memories

Narcissus retired from her professional career in 1989, planning to travel and learn more, if possible, about her people. Sadly, she became ill and was confined to the hospital in Ruidoso. The cause of the illness was at first unknown. Was it her diabetes? Was it a flare-up of the old tuberculosis?

The doctors' final diagnosis after weeks of hospitalization was congestive heart failure. Narcissus suffers still, has lost much weight, and, from time to time, needs intensive care.

The ever-concerned and faithful Wheeler, who recently retired from his position overseeing the rehabilitation of old reservation houses under the auspices of the Housing Urban Development (HUD), remains constantly and attentively by her side.

In the past year or so Narcissus has had considerable time to think back upon her life and the individuals who shaped it.

There was the handsome leader Victorio, whose strength and far-seeing wisdom was advanced beyond his time. His intelligence, courage, and determination inspired his progeny, male and female alike.

There was Dilth-cleyhen. She had seemed so old and feeble when Narcissus was a little girl. Dilth-cleyhen had had long white hair. When she walked, she was a bit hunched over. When she moved toward the door of her tent, or even in her preferred wickiup, she had to lean on the cot for support.

One precious moment remains in Narcissus's memory. She and her great-grandmother were in the wickiup. The child was quiet, just watching. It was hot outside; the sun shone, red and glinting. Within the shady, almost dark shelter, it was cool, inviting. There was but one source of light: a bright ray of the sun came beaming through the smoke hole, right into the wickiup, shining straight down. It created a bright pool on the very spot where Dilth-cleyhen lay sleeping on her bed. Narcissus felt awe and tender respect.

There was Christine, her mother, who had given Narcissus a sense of pride in what a Fort Sill could accomplish, and who had instilled in her the importance of education. This had been furthered by Aunt Evelyn.

Never would Narcissus forget the time when she had been discouraged while in the middle of her training to be a nurse. Three years seemed far too long to endure such a tedious, difficult routine. "Why did I ever get myself into this?" she had asked herself. It was so dreary. She sat down and wrote to Aunt Evelyn, saying she was quitting.

Right away she had a response: a five-page letter by return mail. It was the fastest answer the would-be nurse had ever received.

It read: "You stay up there and finish your training. I don't want you to be a mere meal ticket for a lazy man. I want you to be something special!"

"Dear Aunt Evelyn, without her support, how *ever* could I have endured the hardships after my mother died and during all the years of my schooling. She had such confidence in my ability," Narcissus reminisced.

Then there was Beshád-e. Of all the women kin in Narcissus's life, it was she who had the greatest influence. She was the teacher, the confidante, the one who truly instilled in her granddaughter the love of Chiricahua culture, the one who helped preserve its heritage—the "steadfast pole" in the lives of her kin.

Girls' Building, Santa Fe Indian School. *(Courtesy of L. Bryce Boyer)*

artine Gaines (Aunt Evelyn) in her home in Mescalero, 1970. *of L. Bryce Boyer)*

Narcissus and Wendell, ca. 1929, in front of their home at the Feast Ground. *(Courtesy of Narcissus Duffy Gayton)*

Wendell Duffy in navy uniform, World War II. *(Courtesy of Narcissus Duffy Gayton)*

Narcissus, registered nurse. *(Courtesy of Narcissus Duffy Gayton)*

Wedding portrait of Narcissus Duffy Gayton and Wheeler Gayton, 1948. *(Courtesy of Narcissus Duffy Gayton)*

Mescalero Apache Tribal Council, 1959. *Standing in rear, from left,* John Allard, Andrew Little, Narcissus Gayton, Rufus Sago, Alton Peso, Eric Tortilla; *seated at table, from left,* Trinidad Balatchu, Virginia Klinekole, Samson Miller. *(Courtesy of Narcissus Duffy Gayton)*

Wheeler, Molly, and Narcissus in White Tail, 1969. *(Courtesy of L. Bryce Boyer)*

The Gaytons' home in Mescalero. *(Courtesy of L. Bryce Boyer)*

Raising of the Big Tipi, July 1963. Brush arbor behind line of spectators shelters the cooking fires. Canvas-covered tipi belongs to one of the maidens. *(Courtesy of Barbara Funkhauser)*

Three views of Molly Gayton in her buckskin robes for the Puberty Feast. *Front view:* note the metal jingles at yoke, bottom of upper garment, and on the skirt. *Side view:* the Chiricahua toe on the boots is visible, as is the feather in her hair. *Back view:* this shows the scarf worn at the back of the robes. The scarf in this case is semi-transparent, showing the fringe and jingles underneath. *(Courtesy of L. Bryce Boyer)*

Above. Molly, in her last year of high school, 1974. *(Courtesy of Narcissus Duffy Gayton)*
Right. Molly, later in life. *(Courtesy of Narcissus Duffy Gayton)*

Narcissus, with Old Lady Chatto's basket, 1969. *(Courtesy of L. Bryce Boyer)*

Community center, Mescalero Apache Reservation, 1970. *(Courtesy of L. Bryce Boyer)*

Narcissus and Wheeler in traditional clothing, 1981. Narcissus wears Apache dress with tribal beadwork on her bag and a shawl over her arm. Wheeler is in Plains Indian dance clothing; an otter hide hangs from the back of his neck, and the beadwork he wears is by his uncle. The fan is made of eagle feathers and he holds a flute. The roach is constructed of individual deer tail hairs attached one at a time. *(Courtesy of Narcissus Duffy Gayton)*

Notes

Preface

1. Haley 1981, 14; Hoijer 1938, 5.
2. Opler 1941, 197–98.
3. Hoijer 1938, 48.
4. Bourke 1891, 180.
5. Cremony 1968, 216–17.
6. In speaking of herself and her relatives, Narcissus Gayton says: "We are Tchi-héné." The spelling of the band name varies: Chihenne, Cíhéné, Tci-hene, etc.
7. Other spellings are: Dieth-cley-hen, Dilth-cley-ih, etc.
8. Thrapp 1974, 3–9.

PART ONE: Warfare and Flight
The Early Life of Dilth-cleyhen

1. The Vital Statistics record of the Fort Sill Apaches (Griswold 1958–62, 30) lists 1846 as the date of Dilth-cleyhen's birth.
2. The Athapaskan word *Indéh* (*In-deh*) was translated as "The People" by all Apaches whom the author questioned. Narcissus gives "The People" as the proper meaning. Among the Navaho, also Athapaskan-speakers and the northern neighbors of the Tchi-héné, the equivalent word is *Di-néh*, as they call themselves. Eve Ball and her coauthors (1980) state that *Indéh* means "death," and this is quoted in Bourke ([1886], 1987, foreword by Joseph C. Porter, vii). However, Ball is not using anthropological references; instead, she relies solely on the words of elderly informants despairing at their defeat by the *Indáh*, white men or enemies who continued to "live." It should be recognized that Ball's is an atypical interpretation of *Indéh*—a very special use of the word.
3. Spellings vary. See Cole 1988, 10. Variations include Tchok'anen, Tock-Anen, Tcok?anen, Chokanen, Tookanene, Tsoka-ne-nde, etc.
4. Also seen as Ned-nai, Ne-nai, Nde-nda-i, etc. Opler (1941, 2) calls them *dé'indà-í*, "Enemy People." Narcissus claims that the literal translation is "Indian White Man" which has fit with "enemy." This band is also referred to occasionally as "Pinery Apaches."
5. Also known as "Hot Springs."
6. Narcissus Gayton is positive that Victorio had no Mexican ancestry whatsoever, despite the fact that some writers of history have suggested as much.

7. Sometimes called the "Coppermines" (Debo 1976, 12).
8. Ibid., Map, 10–11; Thrapp 1974, 328 n.8; Moorhead 1968, 172–73.
9. Thrapp 1974, 181.
10. Debo 1976, 123; Terrell 1974, 340.
11. Thrapp 1974, 364–65 n.28.
12. Griswold 1958–62, 63.
13. Obviously, the authors do not know whether these were the actual words spoken. The conversations here, and those of Cradlemaker, are based on observations of child-rearing and cradlemaking practices and were confirmed by Narcissus as being "probable."
14. Some of the information on the cradleboard and the ceremony, including prayers and songs, was obtained by Ruth Boyer, who observed and questioned elderly cradlemakers on the Mescalero Apache Reservation between the years 1959 and 1985. These women told of traditional practices as well as innovations. Narcissus Gayton added those aspects that are peculiar to the Chiricahuas and unlike those of the Mescalero tribe. For example, the latter use oak rather than "heavy wood." Such distinctions are fast becoming forgotten as intermarriage between the tribes and with outsiders increases. To the authors' knowledge no other complete description of the Chiricahua cradle has been published. Much of the reason for this book is the preservation of such information on Tchi-hénè heritage.
15. Again, these are probable conversations, based on events related by Narcissus and the way in which she has often expressed herself.
16. Opler 1941, 354–64. For a more complete list of plants used by the Chiricahua see Castetter and Opler 1936.
17. Opler 1941, 364–65.
18. Ball et al., 1980, 153; Haley 1981, 166.
19. Cruse 1941, 45.
20. Opler 1941, 37–38, 227–29, 306–10.
21. Santee (1947) 1971, 13.
22. Narcissus asserts her family always ate some fish.
23. Opler 1941, 221, 316. Opler identifies *osha* as *Ligusticum porteri*.
24. Boyer and Boyer 1983, 51.
25. There are a number of versions of this event in the literature. Narcissus knows of them. The conversations of Mangas Coloradas and Victorio and all the family members are probable, and reflect the way in which youngsters learned and adults spread news and opinions by verbal communication.
26. Sinclair 1985, 24.
27. Haley 1981, 52
28. Clum 1936, 12; Cremony 1868, 31, 48; Cruse 1941, 59; Haley 1981, 193; Sinclair 1985, 24–29; Wellman 1935, 6–12.
29. Related by Narcissus.
30. Griswold 1958–62, 87; Thrapp 1974, 182.
31. Ball et al. 1980, 53; Terrell 1974, 351.
32. Schroeder 1962, 115.

33. The following events concerning Loco's temper were described by Narcissus.

34. Geronimo is listed as Bedonkohe Apache in the Fort Sill census (Griswold 1958–62, 41–43) although in the literature he is designated most often as Net'na. Both his parents were Bedonkohe, but his father died during his youth. and his mother left the band of her birth to join Chief Juh and the Net'na in northern Sonora. It was here that Geronimo married his first wife. By the time he was captured and made a prisoner of war, he had wed at least six wives, several of whom were Bedonkohe.

35. Debo 1976, 13.

36. Ibid., 7.

37. Ibid., 34–36.

38. Griswold 1958–62, 24–25.

39. Thrapp 1978, 38.

40. Terrell 1974, 220.

41. Haley 1981, 280.

42. Terrell 1974, 180–83.

43. As early as 1837, the Mexican State of Chihuahua announced a "war project" offering bounty for Apache scalps: one hundred dollars for a man's, fifty dollars for a woman's and twenty-five dollars each for those of children. The Mexican State of Sonora already had such a law.

44. Terrell 1974, 189.

45. Ibid., 197.

46. Ibid., 200.

47. Smith 1983, 2–6; Terrell 1974, 203.

48. Opler 1941, 336–49.

49. Ibid., 352–54.

50. The site pointed out is now covered by an artificial body of water, Roberts Lake. We must assume that its waters include that of the lake mentioned by Dilth-cleyhen's grandmother, and later by Beshád-e to Narcissus.

51. Hoijer 1938, 5–6; 13–14.

52. Opler 1941, 370.

53. The red bean referred to was identified by Mrs. Norah van Kleeck, seed analyst of the California Department of Agriculture, Sacramento, in August 1969, as being from a species of *Erythrina*. According to Richard Evans Schultes ("Hallucinogens of Plant Origin" in *Science*, 1969, 163 [No. 3864]: 245–54), the seeds of some species of *Erythrina* resemble the "mescal bean" or "red bean" of *Sophora secundiflora*, a shrub of dry areas of the Southwest and adjacent Mexico. These were used by various Indians as an oracular or divinatory medium, with emetic and stimulant properties. Seeds of *Erythrina* are often sold in markets in Mexico mixed with the "mescal beans," which they resemble.

The white "seed" or bean was identified by Mr. John L. Strother of the Herbarium, Department of Botany, University of California, Berkeley, in July 1969, as being from *Coix lacryma-jobi L.*, a grass.

54. Cremony 1868, 52. Several versions exist telling of this costume and its fate, but all seem to agree that the parts were lost through gambling.
55. The following event is part of Narcissus's family lore.
56. Griswold 1958–62, 24.
57. Terrell 1974, 218–22; Thrapp 1974, 72–74.
58. Narcissus recalls hearing the old folks tell this story as related here.
59. Opler 1941, 84.
60. Hoijer 1938, 49.
61. Clark 1966, 3–8.
62. Ibid., 138; Opler 1941, 396.
63. Opler 1941, 298.
64. Terrell 1974, 210–11.
65. Worcester 1979, 8.
66. Bigelow (1958) 1968, xii.
67. Thrapp 1974, 82–83.
68. Fort McLane was located twenty miles south of Piños Altos and fifteen miles south of Santa Rita. It was established and named in 1860. (Thrapp 1974, 68.)
69. Wellman 1935, 89.
70. Terrell 1974, 254–55.
71. Santee (1947) 1971, 138.
72. Buchanan 1986, 31.
73. In a flyer for New Publications, Spring/Summer 1991, University of Nevada Press, advertising *Women of the Apache Nation: Voices of Truth* by H. Henrietta Stockel, there is a statement that "Lozen, a warrior and medicine woman, threatened to cannibalize her own brother, Chief Victorio of the Warm Springs Apache band, rather than turn him over to government scouts." In a personal communication from Stockel concerning this, reference was made to Thrapp 1967, 201. On that page it states: "Scouts reported having struck Victorio in the leg early in the fight; later a woman, screaming imprecations at them, cried that if Victorio died 'they would eat him, so that no white man should see his body.'" I could find no reference to Lozen. Narcissus stated that she most assuredly does not believe Lozen made such a cannibalistic statement.
74. Ball 1970, 14–15; Buchanan 1986, 28–29; Thrapp 1974, 374 n. 21.
75. Buchanan 1986, 36–37.
76. Wellman 1935, 131–34.
77. Terrell 1974, 254–55.
78. According to Wellman (p. 134) this speech was recorded by Dr. A. N. Ellis who was present. It appears in its entirety in the Kansas Historical Society Collections 13 : 387–92.
79. Ibid.
80. Thrapp 1974, 141.
81. Ibid., 147.
82. Thrapp 1974, 150, 350 n. 26, quotes Oliver Otis Howard's book, *Famous Indian Chiefs I Have Known*, pp. 112–36, as saying of Victorio: "The very

first Indian I saw" at Tularosa, was "a good man who was troubled for his people," and realized that "they were discontented and wanted to go on the warpath, and that it was better for them to keep the peace." Thrapp also points out that Howard says Victorio was Apache. No mention is made of his having any Mexican ancestors; if that story had been current in 1872, Howard most likely would have known and mentioned the fact.

83. Thrapp 1974, 157.
84. Ibid., 159–60.
85. Porter 1986, 167, 170, 193, 246.
86. Griswold 1958–62, 92–93.
87. Thrapp 1974, 161–64.
88. Debo 1976, 91; Thrapp 1974, 166–68.
89. This ambush has been dated as March 1883 (Thrapp 1967, 270). The version given here is the one remembered by Narcissus, who heard it as a youngster from Old Man Chatto and Rogers To-clanny, who were visiting with Dilth-cleyhen and Beshád-e. This is indeed confusing, inasmuch as these men spoke of "Red Beard" as a young man ready for marriage. We must remember that the Chiricahua were imprisoned in 1886. According to Daklugie (Ball et al. 1980, 50–51), the raid in which Judge and Mrs. McComas were killed was led by Chihuahua; Little Charlie was about six or seven years old and was brought back to the other raiders by Chatto. Thus, the boy would have been about nine or ten at the time of Chiricahua imprisonment. Daklugie and Ruey Darrow state that the boy was later killed in a Mexican raid. The latter woman was reluctant to speak of the incident, as were the friends of Dilth-cleyhen. There were several men called "Red Beard" in early Apache history, and as often happens in oral history, individuals may have fused several incidents. The story is retained because Narcissus believes the version she heard.
90. Debo 1976, 81.
91. Terrell 1974, 281.
92. Nantan Lupan is usually translated as Gray Wolf. Eugene Chihuahua states (Ball 1980, 125) that "Gray" is incorrect and should be translated "Tan."
93. Thrapp 1974, 175.
94. Ibid., 182–83.
95. Ibid., 193.
96. Terrell 1974, 327–28.
97. Thrapp 1974, 193.
98. Terrell 1974, 330.
99. Ibid., 334.
100. Ibid., 336–40.
101. Debo 1976, 124–25, 231–32; Thrapp 1974, 342–43.
102. This song was heard in Sonora some fifteen years or so ago by Beverly Munson, who came to know Narcissus and who recognized that the words applied to the latter's famous ancestor.

103. Griswold 1958–62, 110–11.

104. It should be remembered that Apaches reserve the right to judge individuals on their own. Children's opinions need not match those of their parents. Obviously, descendants of Geronimo would not agree with the opinions of Dilth-cleyhen, nor does her opinion of the "renegade" reflect in any way on his kin.

105. Coe 1989, 19; Couchman 1989, 7.

106. Terrell 1974, 381–83.

PART TWO: Beshád-e: Turmoil and Imprisonment

1. Stout 1974, 39–40.

2. Ibid., 41. Thrapp 1974, 141–45, 157–58; 348n. 29, 349n. 10. Fort Tularosa was of short duration. Even whiskey sellers found it too remote. It was created the end of April 1872 and abandoned in November 1874.

3. Stout 1974, 39–40.

4. Basehart 1959, 9.

5. Ball et al. 1980, 91–97.

6. Ibid., 86–87.

7. Ball 1970, 148.

8. Buchanan 1986, 14–15.

9. Ball et al. 1980, 91–97.

10. Terrell 1974, 297–98.

11. Thrapp 1974, 150.

12. Griswold 1958–62, 93.

13. The site that Dilth-cleyhen designated is now that of an artificial lake, Lake Roberts. Undoubtedly there was a body of water there previously, one associated with the creation story of the Tchi-hénè.

14. L. B. Boyer 1965, Sam Kenoi's version.

15. See part 1, note 53.

16. Terrell 1974, 314–29.

17. Ball 1970, 50–51; Haley 1981, 316–17.

18. Terrell 1974, 330.

19. Ibid., 336–37.

20. Haley 1981, 335; Terrell 1974, 346–47.

21. Ball et al. 1980, 53.

22. Griswold, p. 140, translates Tsedekizen's name as Crooked Neck. Narcissus states that it should be Crooked Head. Crooked Neck (Carrizo Gallerito) was Mescalero.

23. B. Davis (1929) 1976, 199.

24. Ball et al. 1980, 118–19.

25. Debo 1976, 310–11.

26. Ibid. 309–12.

27. Ibid. 315–16; "Self-Guided Tour of the Castillo de San Marcos National Monument," National Park Service n.d.; "Apaches Returning to Old City to Honor Memory of Ancestors." *The St. Augustine Record* 17 July 1982, p. 1-A.
28. There is no Apache word that can be translated as "hello." *Yada-chindi* or "What's the news?" is the nearest equivalent.
29. Griswold 1958–62, 7, 15.
30. Ball et al. 1980, 138.
31. Ball 1970, 195; Debo 1976, 318–19.
32. Ball 1970, 141–42.
33. Ibid., 145.
34. The Fort Sill census states that Elsie entered Carlisle on November 4, 1886. (Griswold, 18.)
35. Ball 1970, 197.
36. Ball et al. 1980, 140.
37. Debo 1976, 329.
38. Bourke 1892, 582–84.
39. Griswold 1958–62, 152. Ramon, Zamon, Jamon were his alternate names.
40. Taken from D. Dervin's poem "Not the Dance" (1990) first published in *Hellas*, 1990 1(1) : 115.
41. Utley 1973, 389.
42. Narcissus Gayton is positive she has seen Indians in Juarez who speak Apache rather than any other Indian tongue or Spanish. She has made repeated trips to that city and into the mountainous regions of Chihuahua. She has questioned Tarahumara Indians in hope of learning more. Ruth Boyer has spoken with various residents of Mexico City who likewise claim that Apaches live in some mountain recesses where Narcissus's forebears once took refuge. Specifically, Tati Aldrete, of Mexico City and London, in a personal communication to Boyer, stated that in Cananea, a small coppermining town in Sonora, the people speak of seeing Apaches along the hills. They are reputed to be masters at smuggling.
43. Debo 1976, 324.
44. These were seen and reported by Narcissus Gayton in 1982. See also videotape by Descendants of Apache Prisoners (1982).
45. Debo 1976, 326–28.
46. Kunstadter 1960, 70.
47. Ibid., 335.
48. Ball et al. 1980, 152–54; Debo 1976, 334–35.
49. Kunstadter 1960, 81. Other spellings for Fun's Apache name were Yiyjoll or Yiy-zholl (Griswold 1958–62, 40).
50. Ball et al. 1980, 155.
51. Griswold 1958–62, 90. For many years Narcissus Gayton believed that Lozen did not die in Alabama, but that as an old woman she had lived far out in White Tail on the Mescalero Reservation and that Beshád-e had

visited her occasionally. Narcissus knows that some individuals are listed incorrectly as deceased in Alabama. In fact, they escaped detention there, only to show up in New Mexico at a later date. However, after much investigation she has come to agree with Griswold's records.

52. Debo 1976, 336–57.
53. Ball et al. 1980, 154.
54. Griswold 1958–62, 1.
55. Debo 1976, 365.
56. Skinner 1987, 401.
57. Debo 1976, 365.
58. Ball et al. 1980, 160.
59. Debo 1976, 365–66.
60. Ball et al. 1980, 161; Debo 1976, 365.
61. Ball et al. 1980, 159. The author cites U.S. House Report No. 724, Vol. 6132, 62nd Cong. 2nd Sess., 7.
62. Debo 1976, 372.
63. Ball et al. 1980, 153–54.
64. Ibid., 161.
65. Ibid.
66. Skinner 1987, 398.
67. Debo 1976, 368–69.
68. Kunstadter 1960, 71.
69. Ibid.
70. Ibid. Nye (1937) 1969, 298.
71. Kunstadter 1960, 72. Kunstadter quotes Records of the Commission of Indian Affairs (U.S. Department of the Interior, Report of the Commissioner of Indian Affairs to the Secretary of the Interior) 1898 : 327, 328.
72. Debo 1976, 374.
73. Skinner 1987, 452.
74. Debo 1976, 377.
75. Opler 1941, 6–10.
76. Debo 1976, 428.
77. Debo 1976, 431–32.
78. Griswold 1958–62, 124–25.
79. Cole 1988, 167.
80. Debo 1976, 447–48.
81. Turcheneske 1978. His article is used as a reference for much of what is presented in this book concerning the first ten years (1913–23) the Chiricahua were in Mescalero.
82. Skinner 1987, 479–81; Turcheneske 1978, 111–13.
82. R. Boyer 1962, 16–28.
83. Turcheneske 1978, 109–12.
84. Ibid., 112.
85. Kunstadter 1960, 73, cites U.S. Congress Survey, Part 25 1932 : 13626–37; Part 19 1932 : 10440, 10499.

86. Ball et al. 1980, 275.
87. Turcheneske 1978, 121.
88. Kunstadter 1960, 104, cites U.S. Department of the Interior, *Annual Report of the Indian Commissioner to the Secretary of the Interior* (1918): 53.
89. Ball et al. 1980, 278–79.
90. Kunstadter 1960, 104.
91. Griswold 1958–62, 83.
92. Griswold 1958–62, 83.
93. Information about Silas John and his cult comes from the unpublished documents of Jules Henry, Ph.D., who prior to his death gave permission to Ruth and L. Bryce Boyer to use his fieldwork. Part 4 of this volume contains memories of Narcissus Gayton concerning the ceremonies and meetings which she attended as a child. These conform to Henry's notes, based on information from former cult members and on his observation of paraphernalia.
94. Henry n.d., 176–77.
95. Ibid., 3. Silas John lived on contributions which were so arranged that he was able to avow he had never collected any money.
96. Ibid. Silas John was exceedingly promiscuous, "Like a rooster."
97. Jules Henry (2n. 4, 3) points out that Gunther felt the snakes (which had been detoxified by forcing them to bite raw beef) had been cached in the hills, inasmuch as rattlers are very scarce in the region.
98. Ibid., 18.
99. Ibid., 20.
100. Ibid., 22.
101. Ibid., 26.
102. Sometimes spelled Noch-ay-del-klinne and named The Dreamer by Anglos. Debo 1976, 127–28; Terrell 1974, 347–51.
103. Utley (1973) 1984, 371–73.
104. Nye (1937) 1969, 270–74.
105. Utley 1973, 401–402. This author states: "A decade of intensive and unrelieved civilization programs threw the Indians into a state of shock. The old ways had been purged, or corrupted, or rendered meaningless by the new environment. No satisfactory new ways had been substituted. Anger, bitterness, frustration, resentment, and, above all, a pervasive sense of helplessness and futility settled over the reservations. The people were no longer Indians but not yet whites; indeed, they did not know who they were.

"Throughout history, people subjected to cultural disaster of this magnitude have sought solutions in religion. Often a messiah has come forth to guide the afflicted to the promised land."
106. Henry n.d., 24.
107. Ibid., 25.
108. Ibid., 178.
109. Ibid., 179.

110. Ibid., 35.
111. This prayer was given by Horace Torres and was translated with the help of Dr. Harry Hoijer. Henry n.d., 44–49.
112. Ibid., 115.
113. Ibid.
114. Ibid., 108–109.
115. Ibid., 117–20.
116. Ibid., 152–54.
117. Ibid., 194.

PART THREE: Days of Adjustment and Acculturation
The Life of Christine Louise Kozine

1. Griswold 1958–62, 85.
2. Debo 1976, 377.
3. Ibid., 368–69. Also "Map Showing the Location of the Houses and Farms of the Apache Prisoners of War," n.d., compiled by Capt. Hugh Lenox Scott shortly after the Apaches arrived, Fort Sill Archives.
4. The anthropologist Morris E. Opler talked extensively with Sam Kenoi before publishing *An Apache Life-Way*. Ruth and L. Bryce Boyer knew Sam some years later. Mr. Kenoi acknowledged contributing much to Opler's book. It is highly probable that many of the customs Sam relates were described to him by Dilth-cleyhen.
5. Griswold 1958–62, 135.
6. As noted previously the bond between Chiricahua sisters is one of the strongest dyads in the culture. However, among half-sisters, even those sharing the same mother and growing up together, the tie may be strained, as it was between Susie and Christine. Several factors contribute to disharmony: 1) sibling rivalry, which emerges almost immediately after a lap child or toddler is displaced from "ruler of the household" status by a new baby and henceforth must give in to every whim of the rival; 2) the replacement of the older child's biological father by a new husband, especially if he is the new baby's biological father or favors the new baby; 3) tensions inherent in the prisoner-of-war situation. But the problem is even more complex, as individual personalities must be taken into consideration. Some half-sisters, such as Beshád-e and Lillian, overcome the above obstacles. Susie obviously had more difficulty adjusting. She was an aloof person, preferring solitude at times when most Apaches enjoy company.
7. Narcissus knows that Christine learned much about white culture in her early childhood from conversations with Lillian. The following episodes *may* well have occurred although we have no way of knowing if they happened precisely as recounted. Certainly, the sentiments and prejudices imparted to Christine are part of family lore.

8. Nye (1937) 1969, 280 ff.
9. Ibid., 282–83.
10. Ibid., 316.
11. Ibid., 88.
12. Ibid., 292–95.
13. Emerson 1973, 146.
14. Debo 1976, 397; Griswold 1958–62, 5.
15. Haley 1981, 66; Opler 1941, 216.
16. Griswold 1958–62, 36.
17. Debo 1976, 437.
18. Sam Kenoi, personal communication.
19. Debo 1976, 434–35; Opler 1941, 40–41, 224–31, 256, 260.
20. Griswold 1958–62, 110; Lekson 1987.
21. Debo 1976, 428 ff.
22. This is the description found on a label attached to a Fort Sill doll representing the maiden after her puberty feast. The doll is owned by Mrs. Corinne McNatt, former postmaster at Mescalero.
23. Debo 1976, 428–30.
24. Ball et al. 1980, 161; Terrell 1974, 263–64, 305.
25. A version of "Determination of Night and Day," A1172. See Thompson, 1955–58.
26. Wratten died June 23, 1912. Debo 1976, 448.
27. Emerson 1973, 13–15.
28. Turcheneske 1978, 121.
29. Ibid., 112, 123.
30. Ibid., 124–25.
31. Ibid.
32. Ibid., 126.
33. Opler 1941, 238.
34. Some official records give 1937 as the year of Dilth-cleyhen's death. Narcissus Gayton feels that her death was earlier, during Narcissus's first year at boarding school. However, because of her distressed state during the period of her mother's illness, we suggest that the date be considered tentative.

PART FOUR: Today's Apache Woman
Narcissus Duffy Gayton

1. For a discussion of the importance of Coyote among the Apaches in Mescalero, see L. B. Boyer and R. Boyer 1983.
2. This is a version of the Aarne-Thompson tale type 1004, "Hog in the Mud: Sheep in the Air." See Thompson, 1961.
3. This is a version of "Eye-Juggler," J2423. See Thompson, 1955–58.
4. Personal communication from Stanley McNatt, the son of J. H. McNatt, to Ruth M. Boyer.

5. Opler 1941, 476.

6. Gwendolyn Magooshboy died when she was in her early teens, sometime after Beshád-e had financed a Puberty Feast for her. The cause of death is unknown.

7. In later years, and until recently, the herding of the cattle as well as all associated administrative duties (including hiring cowboys) were under the auspices of a tribal enterprise known as the Cattle Growers' Association (CGA).

8. Arnold Kinzhuma called Parker West "brother" and referred to him as such. According to Jules Henry's study of the Silas John cult, this was a fictive designation. Narcissus Gayton states the two men looked much alike, and she believes they were blood kin. In part, this opinion is based on evidence produced at probate after Parker West's death.

9. *Oot-oo-di* is listed in the Fort Sill census as *O-tó-tie* and *Ihtoty*. Her mother, Nah-kash-ahn, and brother, Mah-gado, died at Fort Sill. Oot-oo-di came to Mescalero with her husband Nah-nall-zhuggi, known also as Leon (a first name) and "Giant Cactus."

10. The Fort Sill census lists alternate names: Tah-das-te; Dah-des-ti; Dah-das-ih. The birth date given is 1860.

11. According to the foreword to Jules Henry's unpublished manuscript (n.d) "The Cult of Silas John," the date of Edwards's visit varies from 1926 to 1929, depending on the memories of different informants. However, Narcissus remembers him; he was in her grandmother's house. In 1929 she was five years old. This suggests 1929 to be the probable year. It is the one given by Horace Torres, the first convert among the Apaches in Mescalero.

12. Henry n.d., III, 115.

13. Ibid., 102–103.

14. Ibid., 103n. Henry reports finding an illustration in the Ninth Annual Report of the Bureau of American Ethnology, 592, that is a near-duplicate of the Four Cross Cult Cross. It was labeled as a trait of traditional Apache religion.

15. The reluctance to discuss the deaths of Beshád-e and Old Man Arnold, or to pronounce their names, should be understood not as willful cruelty to Narcissus, but rather as part of traditional Apache culture. Both these old people were credited with considerable power, especially Arnold. Thus, their ghosts were particularly dangerous and might well lure the living to a similar fate. Their violent demise intensified the threat.

Bibliography

Baldwin, Gordon C. 1965. *The Warrior Apaches: A Story of the Chiricahua and Western Apache*. Tucson, Ariz.: Dale Stuart King.

Ball, Eve. 1970. *In the Days of Victorio*. Tucson: University of Arizona Press.

Ball, Eve, Nora Henn, and Lynda Sanchez. 1980. *Indeh: An Apache Odyssey*. Provo, Utah: Brigham Young University Press.

Barrett, Stephen M., ed. 1906. *Geronimo's Story of His Life*. New York: Duffield.

Bartlett, John Russell. 1854. *Personal Narrative of Explorations and Incidents in Texas, New Mexico, California, Sonora and Chihuahua*. vol. 1. New York: D. Appleton and Co.

Basehart, Harry W. 1959. *Chiricahua Apache Subsistence and Socio-Political Organization*. 2 sections. Albuquerque: The University of New Mexico Mescalero-Chiricahua Land Claims Project Contract Research #290–154.

Basso, Keith. 1977. In Pursuit of the Apaches. *Arizona Highways* 53(7): 2–9, 39–48.

Beck, Colleen. 1983. *Chiricahua Apache Apache Pilgrimage*. Production of KENW3. Videotape.

Bell, Willis H., and Edward F. Castetter. 1937. *The Utilization of Mesquite and Screwbean by the Aborigines in the American Southwest*. Ethnobiological Studies in the American Southwest 5, vol. 5, no. 2. Albuquerque: University of New Mexico Press.

————. 1941. *The Utilization of Yucca, Sotol, and Beargrass*. Ethnobiological Studies in the American Southwest 7, vol. 5, no. 5. Albuquerque: University of New Mexico Press.

Betzinez, Jason, and Wilbur S. Nye. 1959. *I Fought with Geronimo*. Harrisburg, Pa.: Stackpole Co.

Bigelow, John, Lt. [1958] 1968. *On the Bloody Trail of Geronimo*. Los Angeles, Calif.: Westernlore Press.

Billington, Monroe. 1987. Black Soldiers at Fort Selden, New Mexico, 1866–1891. *New Mexico Historical Review* 62:65–80.

Bourke, John Gregory. [1886] 1987. *An Apache Campaign in the Sierra Madre: An Account of the Expedition in Pursuit of the Hostile Chiricahua Apaches in the Spring of 1883*. Lincoln: University of Nebraska Press.

————. 1891. *On the Border with Crook*. New York: Charles Scribner's Sons.

————. 1892. *The Medicine Men of the Apache. Ninth Annual Report of the Bureau of American Ethnology, 1887–1888*.

Bowman, Eldon. 1982. General Crook's Trail: A Rough Road Out of Arizona's Past. *Arizona Highways* 58(7): 2–32.

Boyer, L. Bryce. 1965. Stone as a Symbol in Apache Mythology. *American Imago* 22:14–49.

————. 1979. *Childhood and Folklore: A Psychoanalytic Study of Apache Personality*. New York: Library of Psychological Anthropology.

Boyer, L. Bryce, and Ruth M. Boyer. 1983. The Sacred Clown of the Chiricahua and Mescalero Apaches: Additional Data. *Western Folklore* 42:46–54.

Boyer, Ruth M. 1962. *Social Structure and Socialization among the Apaches of the Mescalero Reservation*. Ph.D. diss., University of California, Berkeley.

Buchanan, Kimberly Moore. 1986 *Apache Women Warriors*. Southwestern Studies Series, no. 79. El Paso: Texas Western Press.

Carroll, John M., ed. 1973. *The Black Military Experience in the American West*. New York: Liveright.

Castetter, Edward F., and Morris E. Opler. 1936. *The Ethnobiology of the Chiricahua and Mescalero Apache. A. The Use of Plants for Foods, Beverages and Narcotics*. Ethnobiological Studies in the American Southwest 3, vol. 4, no. 5. Albuquerque: University of New Mexico Press.

Clark, Laverne Harrell. 1966. *They Sang for Horses: The Impact of the Horse on Navajo and Apache Folklore*. Tucson: University of Arizona Press.

Clum, Woodworth. 1936. *Apache Agent: The Story of John P. Clum*. Boston: Houghton Mifflin.

Coe, Lewis. 1989. Así Es Nuevo México: Heliographs: A Flash from the Past. *New Mexico Magazine* 67(1): 19.

Cole, Donald C. 1988. *The Chiricahua Apache 1846–1876: From War to Reservation*. Albuquerque: University of New Mexico Press.

Couchman, Donald H. 1989. Mailbag: Glaring Error "Heliographs: A Flash from the Past." *New Mexico Magazine* 67(5): 7.

Cremony, John C. 1868. *Life Among the Apaches*. San Francisco: A. Roman. 1970 Edition, Glorieta, N.Mex.: Rio Grande Press.

Cruse, Thomas. 1941. *Apache Days and After*. Caldwell, Idaho: Caxton Printers, Ltd.

Culin, Stewart. 1907. *Games of the North American Indian. Twenty-fourth Annual Report of the Bureau of American Ethnology*. Washington, D.C.: GPO.

Davis, Anne Pence. 1937. Apache Debs. *New Mexico Magazine* 15:10–11, 40.

Davis, Britton. [1929] 1976. *The Truth About Geronimo*. New Haven, Conn.: Yale University Press, Bison Books.

Debo, Angie. 1976. *Geronimo: The Man, His Time, His Place*. Norman: University of Oklahoma Press.

Dervin, Dan. 1990. Not the Dance. *Hellas*. 1(1): 115.

Descendants of Apache Prisoners. July 1982. *A Historical Trip Covering the Journey of Chiricahua Apache Imprisonment, 1886–1913*. Mescalero, New Mexico, Mescalero Apache Tribe. Videotape.

Dinges, Bruce. 1987. The Victorio Campaign of 1880: Cooperation and Conflict on the United States–Mexico Border. *New Mexico Historical Review* 62:81–94.

Dobyns, Harry F. 1976. *Colonial Tucson: A Demographic History*. Tucson: University of Arizona Press.

Emerson, Dorothy. 1973. *Among the Mescalero Apaches: The Story of Father Albert Braun, OFM.* Tucson: University of Arizona Press.

Fatty, Eustace. 1956. Chiricahua Legends. *Western Folklore.* 15(2): 110–12.

French, David. 1942. Comparative Notes on Chiricahua Apache Mythology. *Memoirs of the American Folklore Society* 37:103–11.

Gibson, A. M. 1965. *The Life and Death of Colonel Albert Jennings Fountain.* Norman: University of Oklahoma Press.

Griffen, William B. 1988. *Apaches at War and Peace: The Janos Presidio, 1750–1858.* Albuquerque: University of New Mexico Press.

Griswold, Gillett. 1958–62. *The Fort Sill Apaches: Their Vital Statistics, Tribal Origins, Antecedents.* U.S. Army Field Artillery and Fort Sill Museum, Fort Sill, Oklahoma. Mimeographed Record.

Haley, James L. 1981. *Apaches: A History and Culture Portrait.* Garden City, N.Y.: Doubleday.

Henry, Jules. n.d. The Cult of Silas John. Unpublished manuscript.

Hoffman, Detlef. 1973. *The Playing Card: An Illustrated History.* Greenwich, Conn.: New York Graphic Society.

Hoijer, Harry. 1938. *Chiricahua and Mescalero Apache Texts.* Chicago: University of Chicago Press.

Jacka, Jerry. 1977. The Land of the Free. *Arizona Highways Magazine* 53(7): 20–48.

Kunstadter, Peter. 1960. *Culture Change, Social Structure, and Health Behavior: A Quantitative Study of Clinic Use Among the Apaches of the Mescalero Reservation.* Ph.D. diss., University of Michigan.

Lekson, Stephen H. 1987. *Nana's Raid: Apache Warfare in Southern New Mexico 1881.* Southwestern Studies Series No. 81. El Paso: Texas Western Press.

Lockwood, Frank C. [1938] 1987. *The Apache Indians.* Lincoln: University of Nebraska Press, Bison Books.

Lummis, Charles F. 1952. *The Land of Poco Tiempo.* Albuquerque: University of New Mexico Press.

———. 1966. *General Crook and the Apache Wars.* Flagstaff, Ariz.: Northland Press.

Mails, Thomas E. 1974. *The People Called Apache.* Englewood Cliffs, N.J.: Prentice-Hall.

Mazzanovich, A. 1926. *Trailing Geronimo.* Los Angeles, Calif.: Gem Publishing.

Moorhead, Max L. 1968. *The Apache Frontier.* Norman: University of Oklahoma Press.

Nye, Wilbur S. [1937] 1969. *Carbine and Lance: The Story of Old Fort Sill.* Norman: University of Oklahoma Press.

Opler, Morris Edward. 1937. An Outline of Chiricahua Apache Social Organization. In Fred Eggan, ed., *Social Anthropology of North American Tribes.* Chicago: University of Chicago Press.

———. [1941] 1965. *An Apache Life-Way.* New York: Cooper Square Publishers, Inc.

Pellman, Evelyn. 1950. *The Mescalero Apache Tribe Presents the Debut of Its Most Honored Maidens*. El Paso,Tex.: McMath Co.

Porter, Joseph C. 1986. *Paper Medicine Man: John Gregory Bourke and His American West*. Norman: University of Oklahoma Press.

Quintero, Nita. 1980. Coming of Age the Apache Way. In Lyn Reese, Jean Wilkinson, and Phyllis Sheon Koppelman, eds. *I'm On My Way Running: Women Speak on Coming of Age*. New York: Avon Books.

Reagan, Albert B. 1930. *Notes of the Indians of the Fort Apache Region*. Anthropological Papers of the American Museum of Natural History, vol. 31, part 5. New York: American Museum of Natural History.

Remington, Frederic. [1971] 1973. A Scout with the Buffalo Soldiers. In John M. Carroll, ed., *The Black Military Experience in the American West*. New York: Liveright Publishing Co.

Sánchez, Lynda A. 1986. The Lost Apaches of the Sierra Madre. *Arizona Highways* 62(9): 24–27.

Santee, Ross. [1947] 1971. *Apache Land*. Lincoln: University of Nebraska Press, Bison Books.

Schmitt, Martin F., ed. 1946. *General George Crook, His Autobiography*. Norman: University of Oklahoma Press.

Schroeder, Albert H. 1962. A Study of the Apache Indians: Part IV. The Mogollon, Copper Mine, Mimbres, Warm Spring, and Chiricahua Apaches. Santa Fe, New Mexico. Unpublished manuscript.

Simmons, Marc. 1983. The Captivity of Jimmy McKinn. *New Mexico Magazine* 61(5): 49–50.

Sinclair, John L. 1985. Santa Rita del Cobre. *New Mexico Magazine* 63(3): 24–29.

Skinner, Woodward B. 1987. *The Apache Rock Crumbles: The Captivity of Geronimo's People*. Pensacola, Fla.: Skinner Publications.

Smith, Dean. 1983. General Gadsden's Purchase. *Arizona Highways* 59(4): 2–7.

Smith, Sherry L. 1989. A Window on Themselves: Perceptions of Indians by Military Officers and Their Wives. *New Mexico Historical Review* 64(4): 447–61.

Sonnichsen, C. L. 1986. The Remodeling of Geronimo. *Arizona Highways* 62(9): 2–11.

Stockel, H. Henrietta. In press. *Women of the Apache Nation: Voices of Truth*. Reno: University of Nevada Press.

Stout, Joseph A., Jr. 1974. *Apache Lightning: The Last Great Battles of the Ojo Calientes*. New York: Oxford University Press.

Sweeney, Edwin R. 1989. Cochise and the Prelude to the Bascom Affair. *New Mexico Historical Review* 64(4): 427–46.

Terrell, John Upton. 1974. *Apache Chronicle*. New York: Thomas Y. Crowell, Apollo.

Thomas, Alfred B. 1959. *The Chiricahua Apache 1695–1876*. The University of New Mexico Mescalero-Chiricahua Land Claims Project Contract Research #290–154.

Thompson, Stith. 1955–58. *Motif-Index of Folk Literature*. Bloomington: Indiana University Press.

———. 1961. *The Types of the Folktale*. Helsinki: Suomelainen Tiedeakatemia Academia Scientiarum Fennica.

Thrapp, Dan L. 1967. *The Conquest of Apacheria*. Norman: University of Oklahoma Press.

———. 1974. *Victorio and the Mimbres Apaches*. Norman: University of Oklahoma Press.

———. 1976. A Man Called Geronimo. *Arizona Highways* 52(5): 2–11.

———. 1978. Cochise. *Arizona Highways* 54(10): 38–46.

Trennert, Robert A. 1987. Fairs, Expositions, and the Changing Image of Southwestern Indians, 1876–1904. *New Mexico Historical Review* 62: 127–50.

Turcheneske, John A. 1978. Disaster at White Tail: The Fort Sill Apaches' First Ten Years at Mescalero. *New Mexico Historical Review* 53: 109–32.

U.S. Army Artillery and Missile Center Museum. 1961. Apache Indian Cemeteries, Fort Sill, Oklahoma 1894–1914. Fort Sill, Oklahoma. Unpublished manuscript.

Utley, Robert M. [1973] 1984. *Frontier Regulars: The United States Army and the Indian 1866–1891*. Lincoln: University of Nebraska Press.

———. 1984. The Buffalo Soldiers and Victorio. *New Mexico Magazine* 62(3): 47–54.

Wagoner, Jay J. 1986. Geronimo! *Arizona Highways* 62(9): 12–23.

Wayland, Virginia. 1961. Apache Playing Cards. *The Masterkey* 32(3): 84–98.

———. 1972. The Indian Looks at the White Man: Playing Card Portraits of the Old West. *Expedition* 14(3): 15–24.

Wellman, Paul I. 1935. *Death in the Desert: The Fifty Years War for the Great Southwest*. New York: Macmillan.

Wharfield, Colonel H. B. [1971] 1973. The Tenth Cavalry in the Early Days. In John M. Carroll, ed. *The Black Military Experience in the American West*. New York: Liveright.

Whitaker, Bob. 1986. Return of the Bandit Quail. *Arizona Highways* 62(6): 32–37.

Woodbury, Nathalie F. S. (Dec.) 1986. Past Is Present: Geronimo. *Anthropology Newsletter*, 3.

Worcester, Donald E. 1979 *The Apaches: Eagles of the Southwest*. Norman: University of Oklahoma Press.

Index